Implicit and Explicit Knowledge in Second
Language Learning, Testing and Teaching

SECOND LANGUAGE ACQUISITION
Series Editor: David Singleton, *Trinity College, Dublin, Ireland*

This series brings together titles dealing with a variety of aspects of language acquisition and processing in situations where a language or languages other than the native language is involved. Second language is thus interpreted in its broadest possible sense. The volumes included in the series all offer in their different ways, on the one hand, exposition and discussion of empirical findings and, on the other, some degree of theoretical reflection. In this latter connection, no particular theoretical stance is privileged in the series; nor is any relevant perspective – sociolinguistic, psycholinguistic, neurolinguistic, etc. – deemed out of place. The intended readership of the series includes final-year undergraduates working on second language acquisition projects, postgraduate students involved in second language acquisition research and researchers and teachers in general whose interests include a second language acquisition component.

Full details of all the books in this series and of all our other publications can be found on http://www.multilingual-matters.com, or by writing to Multilingual Matters, St Nicholas House, 31–34 High Street, Bristol, BS1 2AW, UK.

SECOND LANGUAGE ACQUISITION
Series Editor: David Singleton

Implicit and Explicit Knowledge in Second Language Learning, Testing and Teaching

Rod Ellis, Shawn Loewen, Catherine Elder, Rosemary Erlam, Jenefer Philp and Hayo Reinders

MULTILINGUAL MATTERS
Bristol • Buffalo • Toronto

Library of Congress Cataloging in Publication Data
A catalog record for this book is available from the Library of Congress.
Ellis, Rod.
Implicit and Explicit Knowledge in Second Language Learning, Testing and Teaching
Rod Ellis et al.
Second Language Acquisition: 42
Includes bibliographical references and index.
1. Second language acquisition. 2. Language and languages–Study and teaching.
I. Title.
P118.2.E375 2009
418.0071–dc22 2009017375

British Library Cataloguing in Publication Data
A catalogue entry for this book is available from the British Library.

ISBN-13: 978-1-84769-175-0 (hbk)
ISBN-13: 978-1-84769-174-3 (pbk)

Multilingual Matters
UK: St Nicholas House, 31–34 High Street, Bristol BS1 2AW.
USA: UTP, 2250 Military Road, Tonawanda, NY 14150, USA.
Canada: UTP, 5201 Dufferin Street, North York, Ontario M3H 5T8, Canada.

The policy of Multilingual Matters/Channel View Publications is to use papers that are natural,
renewable and recyclable products, made from wood grown in sustainable forests. In the
manufacturing process of our books, and to further support our policy, preference is given to
printers that have FSC and PEFC Chain of Custody certification. The FSC and/or PEFC logos
will appear on those books where full certification has been granted to the printer concerned.

Typeset by Datapage International Ltd.
Printed and bound in Great Britain by Short Run Press Ltd.

15153416

mA

Contents

Authors

Catherine Elder is Associate Professor in the School of Languages and Linguistics and Director of the Language Testing Research Centre at the University of Melbourne. She is co-editor (with Glenn Fulcher) of the journal *Language Testing*. She is author with Alan Davies *et al.* of the *Dictionary of Language Testing* (Cambridge University Press, 1999) and co-editor of *Experimenting with Uncertainty* (Cambridge University Press, 2001) and *Handbook of Applied Linguistics* (Blackwell, 2004).

Rod Ellis is Professor of Applied Language Studies at the University of Auckland and a visiting Professor at Shanghai International Studies University. His publications includes articles and books on second language acquisition, language teaching and teacher education. His most recent is *The Study of Second Language Acquisition 2nd Edition* (Oxford University Press, 2008). He is also editor of the journal *Language Teaching Research*.

Rosemary Erlam is a Senior Lecturer in the Department of Applied Language Studies and Linguistics at the University of Auckland. She comes to Applied Linguistics from backgrounds in Speech-Language Therapy and French teaching. Her research interests include teacher education, form-focused instruction and issues pertinent to the New Zealand educational context.

Shawn Loewen is an Assistant Professor in the Second Language Studies program at Michigan State University. He specializes in second language acquisition and L2 classroom interaction. His recent research has investigated the occurrence and effectiveness of incidental focus on form in a variety of L2 contexts.

Jenefer Philp is a Senior Lecturer at the University of Auckland. Her experimental and classroom-based research centers on the role of interaction in second language development by adults and children She has recently co-edited a book titled *Second Language Acquisition and the Younger Learner: Child's Play?* (John Benjamins, 2008).

Hayo Reinders (www.hayo.nl) is Editor of *Innovation in Language Learning and Teaching*. He was previously Director of the English Language Self-Access Centre and Visiting Professor at Meiji University in Tokyo. His research interests are in the areas of computer-assisted language learning and learner autonomy.

Preface

This book originated in a project funded by the Marsden Fund, a fund administered by the Royal Society of New Zealand to support ideas-driven research. The initial principal investigators were Rod Ellis and Catherine Elder. When Catherine Elder left the project in 2004, her place was taken by Shawn Loewen. Two other researchers at the University of Auckland were also closely involved in the project – Rosemary Erlam and Jenefer Philp – and also, at various times, there were a number of research assistants – in particular, Satomi Mizutani, Keiko Sakui and Thomas Delaney. The successful completion of the project owed much to the combined efforts of all these researchers. The project took place over three years (2002–2005).

There were three major goals:

(1) To develop tests to measure second language (L2) implicit and explicit grammatical knowledge.
(2) To identify the relative contributions of these two types of L2 knowledge to general language proficiency.
(3) To investigate what effect form-focused instruction has on the acquisition of L2 explicit and implicit grammatical knowledge.

These three goals are reflected in the structure of this book. Thus, Part 2 reports the results of the research designed to develop tests of implicit and explicit knowledge, Part 3 contains a number of studies that examined the application of the tests in various applied ways, including the role played by implicit and explicit L2 knowledge in language proficiency and Part 4 addresses the effects of instruction on the acquisition of L2 explicit and implicit grammatical knowledge. This book, therefore, is an attempt to bring together the results of the Marsden Fund Project.

The distinction between implicit and explicit L2 knowledge is fundamental to understanding the nature of L2 acquisition, the role of these two types of knowledge in L2 proficiency and the contribution that various types of instruction can make to L2 acquisition. It is also a distinction that appears to be supported by current neurobiological research, which has shown that the two types of knowledge are neurologically distinct. Because this distinction is central to the whole book, Part 1 (Chapter 1: Introduction) is devoted to its definition and explication.

The distinction has been incorporated into very different theories of L2 acquisition, including those based on an information-processing model and those derived from sociocultural theory. The research reported in this book was informed by an information-processing model, the model most familiar to the researchers involved. This model views knowledge as related to but independent of language use. It is acquired as a result of learners engaging in active processing of the L2 input they are exposed to and is reflected in the gradual and dynamic way in which learners build their interlanguages. Key processes are those relating to attention to form (i.e. noticing and noticing-the-gap), rehearsal in short-term memory, integration into long-term memory and monitoring (see Ellis, 2008). These are terms that will be used throughout the book. In Part 4 (Chapter 14: Conclusion), an attempt will be made to retro-spectively examine the main findings from a different perspective – that afforded by sociocultural theory.

The contents of the book are, in part, based on a number of previously published papers:

Elder, C., Erlam, R. and Philp, J. (2007) Explicit language knowledge and focus on form: Options and obstacles for TESOL teacher trainees. In S. Fotos and H. Nassaji (eds) *Form Focused Instruction and Teacher Education: Studies in Honour of Rod Ellis.* (p. 225–240) Oxford: Oxford University Press (Oxford Applied Linguistics Series).

Ellis, R. (2004) The definition and measurement of L2 explicit knowledge. *Language Learning* 54, 227–275.

Ellis, R. (2004) Measuring implicit and explicit knowledge of a second language: A psychometric study. *Studies in Second Language Acquisition* 27, 141–172.

Ellis, R. (2006) Modelling learning difficulty and second language proficiency: The differential contributions of implicit and explicit knowledge. *Applied Linguistics* 27, 431–63

Ellis, R., Loewen S. and R. Erlam. (2006) Implicit and explicit corrective feedback and the acquisition of L2 grammar. *Studies in Second Language Acquisition* 28, 339–68.

Erlam, R. (2006) Elicited imitation as a measure of L2 implicit knowledge: An empirical validation study. *Applied Linguistics* 27, 464–491.

However, none of these papers has been reproduced verbatim. Rather the contents have been modified to avoid repetition and to ensure continuity from one chapter to the next. The book also contains reports of a number of previously unpublished studies that were part of or were closely related to the Marsden Project (see Chapters 4, 7, 8, 10–12). In addition, Chapter 1 (Introduction) and Chapter 14 (Conclusion) have also been specifically written for this book.

It remains for us to thank the New Zealand Royal Society of Arts for funding the research that led to this book and the University of Auckland's Research Office for its logistic support. I would also like to thank Katherine Cao for her work on the bibliography of the book and the Center for Applied Linguistics in Washington DC for appointing me as Ferguson Fellow for 2008, which made possible the assembling of the final manuscript.

Rod Ellis
University of Auckland

Part 1
Introduction

The chapter in Part 1 introduces the key terms used in this book – implicit/explicit learning, knowledge and instruction. The distinctions between implicit and explicit knowledge and implicit and explicit learning are of central significance in both cognitive psychology and in second language acquisition (SLA) research. The closely related distinction between implicit and explicit instruction is also important for language pedagogy. These distinctions address how we come to know what we know about a second language (L2), how we store that knowledge and the use we make of it. No SLA researcher and no language teacher can afford to ignore these distinctions.

The chapter begins with an exploration of how these distinctions have been treated in cognitive psychology. It then moves on to examining how they have been addressed in SLA research. Separate sections consider implicit/explicit L2 learning, implicit/explicit L2 knowledge and implicit/explicit language instruction. The issue of whether or not there is an interface between implicit and explicit learning and knowledge is also addressed, as this is of crucial importance when considering the role of instruction in L2 acquisition.

This chapter aims to provide an introduction to these key constructs together with the theoretical background that informs the empirical studies reported in subsequent parts of the book.

Chapter 1
Implicit and Explicit Learning, Knowledge and Instruction

ROD ELLIS

Introduction

The distinctions relating to implicit/explicit learning and knowledge originated in cognitive psychology, so it is appropriate to begin our examination of them with reference to this field of enquiry. Cognitive psychologists distinguish implicit and explicit learning in two principal ways:

(1) Implicit learning proceeds without making demands on central attentional resources. As N. Ellis (2008: 125) puts it, 'generalizations arise from conspiracies of memorized utterances collaborating in productive schematic linguistic productions'. Thus, the resulting knowledge is subsymbolic, reflecting statistical sensitivity to the structure of the learned material. In contrast, explicit learning typically involves memorizing a series of successive facts and thus makes heavy demands on working memory. As a result, it takes place consciously and results in knowledge that is symbolic in nature (i.e. it is represented in explicit form).
(2) In the case of implicit learning, learners remain unaware of the learning that has taken place, although it is evident in the behavioral responses they make. Thus, learners cannot verbalize what they have learned. In the case of explicit learning, learners are aware that they have learned something and can verbalize what they have learned.

The focus of research in cognitive psychology has been on whether implicit learning can take place, and, if it does, how it can best be explained. However, since Reber's (1976) seminal study of implicit learning, there has been an ongoing debate about the validity of his 'multiple learning systems' view of human cognition. Many researchers dispute the existence of multiple systems and argue in favor of a single system that is capable of achieving different learning outcomes.

This controversy within cognitive psychology is very clearly evident in a collection of papers addressing the role of consciousness in learning (Jimenez, 2003). In the opening paper, Shanks (2003) critiqued the research that used a technique known as 'sequential reaction time' to stake out the claim for multiple, differentiated learning systems. In studies using this technique, the time it takes for people to respond to an array of predictable visual information is compared to the time it takes when this array is suddenly disturbed. The claim here is that a difference in response times demonstrates that some learning must have taken place implicitly prior to the disturbance, even though the participants involved were unable to verbalize what they had learned. Shanks (2003: 38) argued that 'previous research has failed to demonstrate convincingly that above-chance sequence knowledge can be accompanied by null awareness when the latter is indexed by objective measures such as recognition'. He concluded that there was no convincing evidence that implicit learning is functionally or neurally separate from explicit learning and that it was misguided to look for such dissociation. He advanced the alternative view that there is a single knowledge source that underlies performance and that apparent differences in performance are due to 'subtle differences between the retrieval processes recruited by the tests' (p. 36).

In contrast, other papers in the same collection argued strongly for distinguishing the two types of learning. Wallach and Lebiere (2003), for example, developed a strong argument for a dual learning system based on the central concepts of ACT-R cognitive architecture (Anderson & Lebiere, 1998). This proposes a hybrid learning system consisting of a permanent procedural memory and a permanent declarative memory. The former consists of condition-action rules called 'productions' that enable a certain action to be performed provided that specific conditions have been met. Such 'productions' operate automatically. Declarative knowledge consists of factual knowledge stored as chunks organized into schemas. It operates in a more controlled fashion and with awareness. Wallach and Lebiere claimed that these two 'architectural mechanisms' could account for implicit and explicit learning and, crucially, the interplay between the two systems. They went on to demonstrate how they can account for the findings of a number of previous studies of implicit/explicit learning. The ACT-R model has also proved influential in second language acquisition (SLA) studies (see, e.g. DeKeyser, 2007).

In the same collection, Hazeltine and Ivry (2003) mustered neuropsychological evidence to support the existence of distinct learning systems. They reviewed studies of the neural activity when people are engaged in sequence learning. They noted that although such activity has been observed in regions across the whole brain, differences in task conditions result in distinct sets of neural regions becoming activated. When the learning task is complex (i.e. involves dual-task conditions) and thus favors implicit learning mechanisms, the medial supplementary motor area, parietal regions and the basal ganglia are involved. In contrast, when the task is simpler (i.e. involving single-task conditions), the prefrontal and premotor cortex are activated.

The controversy evident in cognitive psychology is mirrored in SLA. The clearest example of this can be found in the critique levelled against Krashen's (1981) distinction between 'acquisition' (the subconscious internalization of grammatical rules that occurs as a result of comprehending input that is slightly beyond the learner's current knowledge) and 'learning' (the conscious formulation of explicit rules of grammar). This was initially subjected to fierce criticism on the grounds that the distinction was not falsifiable. McLaughlin (1978: 21), for example, argued that Krashen failed to provide adequate definitions of what he meant by 'subconscious' and 'conscious' and 'provided no way of independently determining whether a given process involves acquisition or learning'. However, McLaughlin's distaste for the use of 'conscious' as a descriptor of the mental activity involved in L2 learning does not reflect mainstream thinking in either cognitive psychology or SLA. Schmidt (1990, 1994, 2001) has shown that consciousness is a useful construct if it can be carefully deconstructed into its several meanings. He distinguished consciousness in terms of intentionality (incidental versus intentional learning), attention (i.e. attended versus unattended learning), awareness (implicit versus explicit learning) and control (automatic versus controlled processing). Schmidt's work has reinstated the value of 'consciousness' for understanding the nature of second language (L2) learning and has had enormous influence on SLA theories and research. It at once acknowledged that Krashen might be right in trying to distinguish implicit and explicit processes and at the same time highlighted the fact that Krashen's initial distinction was simplistic (e.g. he failed to distinguish consciousness as intentionality, attention, awareness and control).

The importance of the implicit/explicit distinction for language learning (both first and second) was affirmed in the important collection of papers edited by Nick Ellis (1994). In his introduction, Ellis provided one of the clearest and most convincing statements of the distinction, which I provide in full:

> Some things we just come able to do, like walking, recognizing happiness in others, knowing that *th* is more common than *tg* in written English, or making simple utterances in our native language. We have little insight into the nature of the processing involved – we learn to do them implicitly like swallows learn to fly. Other of our abilities depend on knowing *how* to do them, like multiplication, playing chess, speaking pig Latin, or using a computer programming language. We learn these abilities explicitly like aircraft designers learn aerodynamics. (Ellis, 1994: 1)

Ellis drew on research in both cognitive psychology and language learning to spell out what he saw as the issues facing researchers. What aspects of an L2 can be learned implicitly? What are the mechanisms of explicit learning available to the learner? How necessary is explicit knowledge for the acquisition of an L2? What is the relationship between explicit and implicit L2 knowledge? How best can instruction aid L2 acquisition? So, rather than dismissing the distinction between implicit and explicit learning/knowledge and taking the lead from Schmidt and Ellis, SLA researchers have focused on trying to identify the processes involved in the two types of learning, how they interact, and how they can be externally manipulated through instruction. Thus, while acknowledging that doubts still remain (especially in cognitive psychology) about the legitimacy of a dual learning system, I am going to assume that a distinction can be made between the implicit and explicit learning of an L2 and between implicit and explicit L2 knowledge.

Following Schmidt (1994: 20), I will further assume that implicit/ explicit *learning* and implicit/explicit *knowledge* are 'related but distinct concepts that need to be separated'. Whereas the former refers to the *processes* involved in learning, the latter concerns the *products* of learning. It is possible, for example, that learners will reflect on knowledge that they have acquired implicitly (i.e. without metalinguistic awareness) and thus, subsequently develop an explicit representation of it. Also, it is possible that explicit learning directed at one linguistic feature may result in the incidental implicit learning of some other feature (an issue addressed in Chapter 11). In the case of SLA (less so perhaps in cognitive psychology), implicit and explicit learning have been examined by reference to the kinds of knowledge that result from conditions designed to favor one or other type of learning. That is, there have been relatively few studies that have tried to explore the actual processes involved, although the use of introspective techniques (see, e.g. the account of Leow's (1997) study below) offers a means of rectifying this gap. In general, studies have sought to infer the kind of learning that has taken place by examining the products of learning. For this reason, this book will focus on 'knowledge' rather than 'learning'.

Schmidt also argued that *learning* needs to be distinguished from *instruction*. It does not follow, for instance, that implicit instruction results in implicit learning or, conversely, that explicit instruction leads to explicit learning. Teachers might hope for such a correlation, but learners have minds of their own and may follow their own inclinations, irrespective of the nature of the instruction they receive (Allwright, 1984). This book is also concerned with the relationship between forms of instruction that can be described as 'implicit' or 'explicit' and the acquisition of implicit/explicit L2 knowledge.

MON 3/16: class // work // HIIT // scraBBle (?)
OR
RUN
[+ laundry?]
other

T 3/17: class // work // rball (?)

W 3/18: class // work // HIIT
OR
RUN(?)

R 3/19: class // work // rball (?)

F 3/20: → ① Applications (fellowship, summer job, etc.)
② Grade Exams
③

Sat 3/21: work for **3hrs** ~~4~~ + do sth fun ☺

SUN 3/22: → give Charlie to parents!

Mon 3/23: class // work // HIIT // start packing // laundry/etc
Mtg @ writing center

Tues 3/24: class // work // rball // pack

WED 3/25: class // work/gym // finish packing
HIIT

TH 3/26: class // bus @ 11am // flight @ 4pm-ish

FR 3/27 ↑ NJ
↳ spend day in Manhattan?
evening w/ G.

Sa 3/28
↳ day in Manhattan // evening?

Sun 3/29
↳ get outside! - naturish ②

MON 3/30 ⟶ walk around / work?

TUES 3/31 } SoCal
web 4/1
R 4/2
FRI 4/3 } *eve: G&T

SAT 4/4
*eve: G ☺
SUN 4/5:
flight @
745 am

FRE 101 & 102: Activities Manual Grade

Name: _____   Ensemble ____ Dossiers ____ & __

	Does not meet expectations	Meets expectations, weak	Meets or exceeds expectations
Task Completion Did you do all the required work and do so in a timely fashion?	0 1 2 3 4 5 Few exercises are attempted and evidence of self correction is absent	6 7 Most exercises attempted and some self correction may be evident	8 9 10 All or nearly all exercises completed and self corrected
Effort Did your work show that you attempted to do this work accurately and to the best of your ability?	0 1 2 3 4 5 Minimal amount of effort is demonstrated	6 7 Some effort is demonstrated, or effort varies depending on exercise	8 9 10 Sustained level of effort throughout work and self correction is demonstrated

Total: _____ / 20

Comments:

In the sections that follow, I will examine how SLA researchers have tackled the three distinctions: (1) implicit/explicit learning, (2) implicit/ explicit knowledge and (3) implicit/explicit instruction. This provides a basis for considering the interface position (i.e. the nature of the relationship between implicit and explicit knowledge). Finally, I will provide an overview of the contents of the rest of the book.

Implicit/Explicit L2 Learning

As defined above, implicit language learning takes place without either intentionality or awareness. However, there is controversy as to whether any learning is possible without some degree of awareness. This raises the important question of what is meant by 'awareness'. Schmidt (1994, 2001) distinguished two types of awareness: awareness as noticing (involving perception) and metalinguistic awareness (involving analysis). The former involves conscious attention to 'surface elements', whereas the latter involves awareness of the underlying abstract rule that governs particular linguistic phenomena. Schmidt argued that noticing typically involves at least some degree of awareness. Thus, from this perspective, there is no such thing as complete implicit learning and so a better definition of implicit language learning might be 'learning without any metalinguistic awareness'. That is, the processes responsible for the integration of material into the learner's interlanguage system and the restructuring this might entail take place autonomously and without conscious control. Other researchers (e.g. Williams, 2005), however, have argued that learning without awareness at the level of noticing is also possible. N. Ellis (2005: 306) has also claimed that 'the vast majority of our cognitive processing is unconscious'. Thus, there is no consensual definition of implicit learning although all theorists would accept that it excludes metalinguistic awareness.

Explicit language learning is necessarily a conscious process and is generally intentional as well. It is conscious learning 'where the individual makes and tests hypotheses in a search for structure' (N. Ellis, 1994: 1). As Hulstijn (2002: 206) put it, 'it is a conscious, deliberative process of concept formation and concept linking'.

The study of implicit and explicit learning in SLA draws heavily on cognitive psychology. The work of Reber (Reber, 1993; Reber *et al.*, 1991) has been seminal in this respect. Reber and colleagues investigated the two types of learning by means of studies involving artificial languages, where groups of participants were either instructed to memorize a set of letter strings generated by the artificial language without the help of any feedback (the implicit learning condition) or to try to figure out the underlying rules of the same letter strings (the explicit learning condition). Following training, both groups completed a judgement test that required them to decide if the strings of letters followed the same rules as the strings they saw during training. They were not forewarned that they would be tested in this way. The main findings of such studies were: (1) there was clear evidence of implicit learning; (2) there was no difference between the test scores of the implicit and explicit learning groups in the case of simple rules, but implicit learning proved more efficient for complex rules; and (3) the test scores of the explicit group demonstrated much greater individual variation than those of the implicit group, reflecting the fact that whereas analytical skills played a role in the former they did not in the latter. However, as we have already seen, the claim that implicit and explicit learning are dissociated has become a matter of controversy among cognitive psychologists. Also, disagreement exists regarding the nature of the knowledge that arises out of implicit learning, with some arguing that it consists of knowledge of fragments or exemplars, and others arguing that it is rule-based.

Much of the psychological research on implicit learning in language acquisition has followed Reber in employing artificial grammars. Rebuschat (2008), in his review of these studies, suggests that 'the most important finding to emerge in recent years has been the observation that infants, children and adults can use statistical cues such as transitional probabilities to acquire different aspects of language, including the lexicon, phonology and syntax'. Rebuschat also identifies a number of problems with these studies – many of the studies did not include a measure of awareness, often learners were exposed to the artificial language under conditions that were far from incidental, and the grammars involved were of the phrase-structure rather than fine-state kind.

In the case of SLA 'the amount of L2 research narrowly focused on the implicit-explicit distinction is quite limited, not only in the number of studies, but also in duration and in scope of the learning target' (DeKeyser, 2003: 336). The key issue (as in cognitive psychology) is whether implicit learning of an L2 (i.e. learning without conscious awareness) is possible. A number of studies have addressed this, including several that have examined the effects of enhanced input on language learning. In a series of studies, Williams examined whether learners are able to induce grammatical rules from exposure to input when their attention is focused on meaning (Williams, 1999, 2005; Williams & Lovatt, 2003). The studies showed that learning does take place, that the inductive learning of form (i.e. segmentation) is dissociable from the learning of the functions realized by the forms (i.e. distribution), that learner' differences in phonological short-term memory influence the extent to which learners are successful in inductive learning, and that language background (i.e. whether learners have prior experience of learning languages) impacts even more strongly on learning. However, Williams' tests of learning (translation or grammaticality judgement tests) may have favored those learners who attempted to construct explicit rules during the training and thus cannot convincingly demonstrate that implicit learning took place. Indeed, Williams (1999: 38) noted that the learners in this study 'had high levels of awareness of the product of learning', although, as he pointed out, awareness of the product of learning does not necessarily imply that conscious analysis occurred while learning. What is needed to resolve this issue are studies that obtain information about the microprocesses involved in the training (learning) phase of such studies.

One study that has attempted this is Leow (1997). Leow asked beginner learners of L2 Spanish to think aloud as they completed a crossword that exposed them to a number of morphological forms. Learning was measured by means of a multiple choice recognition task and a fill-in-the-blank written production task. The think-aloud protocols were analysed qualitatively to establish to what extent the learners demonstrated meta-awareness in the form of hypothesis-testing and conscious rule-formation. Leow reported that the level of awareness learners demonstrated correlated both with their ability to recognize and produce correct target forms. This study, together with Leow's (2000) follow-up study, demonstrated that online measures of meta-awareness are related to offline measures of learning, strongly suggesting that the learning that took place in these studies was explicit rather than implicit. DeKeyser (2003: 317), summarizing the results of a number of SLA studies concluded 'there is very little hard evidence of learning without awareness'. However, N. Ellis (2005) has argued differently on the grounds that studies investigating frequency effects in L2 acquisition have shown that these effects can only be explained if it is assumed that learning without awareness is possible.

One of the problems of studies that have compared implicit and explicit learning is that the two types of learning have been operationalized and measured in very different ways. A number of studies have shown that learning of some kind, intended by the researcher to be implicit, does take place (Doughty, 1991; Shook, 1994; Gass *et al.*, 2003), but whether or not the learners actually engaged in implicit learning is not demonstrated. Explicit learning is a lot easier to demonstrate – by asking learners to report what they have learned. A number of studies have sought to compare the relative effectiveness of implicit and explicit learning. The general finding is that explicit learning is more effective than implicit learning (N. Ellis, 1993; Rosa & O'Neill, 1999; Gass *et al.*, 2003). No study has shown that implicit learning worked better than explicit learning. However, two studies found no difference between implicit and explicit learning (Doughty, 1991; Shook, 1994). There is also some evidence to suggest that explicit learning is more effective with some linguistic features than others. Robinson (1996) reported that his explicit learners outperformed the implicit learners on a simple structure (subject-verb inversion), but not on a complex structure (pseudo-clefts). Gass *et al.* (2003) found that their focused condition (which involved explicit attention to form and meaning) proved more effective than the unfocused condition in the case of lexis than it did in the case of morphology or syntax.

Three studies investigated learners' awareness of the structures they were learning. Rosa and O'Neill (1999) replicated Leow's (1997) finding; learners who demonstrated high awareness during learning outperformed those with low awareness. N. Ellis and Robinson both tested the learners' ability to verbalize the rule they had been learning, but with different results. N. Ellis (1993) found that the most explicit group in his study were able to verbalize the rule, whereas Robinson reported that very few learners in any of his conditions could, although where the simple rule was concerned, the most explicit group (the one receiving an explanation of the rule) outperformed the rest. Finally, Gass *et al.*'s study raises the possibility that learners' level of proficiency may mediate the effects of explicit instruction; in this study, the focused condition proved most effective with the low-proficiency learners.

There is some evidence, therefore, of implicit L2 learning, but much clearer evidence of explicit learning. However, there are two reasons to reserve judgement. First, the treatments in the studies cited above were all of short duration, which arguably creates a bias against implicit learning. Second, the effects of the training were measured by the kinds of tests (e.g. grammaticality judgement tests) that were likely to favor explicit learning.

Implicit and Explicit L2 Knowledge

Before we consider the differences between implicit and explicit L2 knowledge, we need to examine what we mean by 'linguistic knowledge'? There are, broadly speaking, two competing positions. The first, drawing on the work of Chomsky, claims that linguistic knowledge consists of knowledge of the features of a specific language, which are derived from impoverished input (positive evidence) with the help of Universal Grammar (UG). This view of language is innatist and mentalist in orientation, emphasising the contribution of a complex and biologically specified language module in the mind of the learner. The second position, drawing on connectionist theories of language learning, as advanced by cognitive psychologists such as Rumelhart and McClelland (1986), views linguistic knowledge as comprised of an elaborate network of nodes and internode connections of varying strengths that dictate the ease with which specific sequences or 'rules' can be accessed. According to this view, then, learning is driven primarily by input and it is necessary to posit only a relatively simple cognitive mechanism (some kind of sensitive pattern detector) that is capable of responding both to positive evidence from the input and to negative evidence available through corrective feedback. These positions are generally presented as oppositional (see Gregg, 2003), but in one important respect, they are in agreement. Both the innatist and connectionist accounts of L2 learning view linguistic competence as consisting primarily of implicit L2 knowledge and see the goal of theory as explaining how this implicit knowledge is acquired. However, they differ in the importance that they attach to explicit knowledge, a point that I will return to later in this chapter.

In a series of articles (Ellis 1993, 1994, 2004, 2005), I have attempted to identify the criteria that can be used to distinguish implicit and explicit L2 knowledge. I will review these here.

Implicit knowledge is tacit and intuitive whereas explicit knowledge is conscious

Thus, it is possible to talk about intuitive and conscious awareness of what is grammatical. For example, faced with a sentence like:

*The policeman explained Wong the law.

a learner may know intuitively that there is something ungrammatical and may even be able to identify the part of the sentence where the error occurs, but may have no conscious awareness of the rule that is being broken. Such a learner has implicit but no explicit knowledge of the feature, dative alternation, in question. Another learner, however, may understand that the sentence is ungrammatical because the verb 'explain' cannot be followed by an indirect object without 'to'. A third learner (a linguist perhaps) might know that dative verbs like 'explain' that are of Latin origin and verbs like 'give' that are of Anglo-Saxon origin perform differently.

Implicit knowledge is procedural whereas explicit knowledge is declarative

Implicit knowledge is 'procedural' in the sense conferred on this term in the ACT-R cognitive architecture mentioned above. For example, for past tense verbs, learners behave in accordance with a condition-action rule along the lines of 'if the action to be referred to occurred in the past and is completed, then add -ed to the base form of a verb'. Explicit knowledge is comprised of facts about the L2. This is no different from encyclopedic knowledge of any other kind. I know, declaratively, that the Normans invaded England in 1066. Similarly, I know that verbs like 'explain' require an indirect object with 'to' and, further, that the indirect object usually follows the direct object. These facts are only loosely connected; they do not constitute a 'system' in the same way that the implicit knowledge of proficient L2 users does.

L2 learners' procedural rules may or may not be target-like while their declarative rules are often imprecise and inaccurate

The condition-action rules that learners construct as part of their implicit knowledge may or may not conform to the native speaker' rules. SLA research has shown that learners typically manifest developmental sequences when they acquire implicit knowledge (see Ellis, 2008). For example, the condition-action rule for the past tense described above would lead to both correct forms (e.g. 'jumped') and also overgeneralized forms (e.g. 'eated'). Such rules are continuously modified during learning. In the case of explicit knowledge, learners' knowledge is often fuzzy. For example, a learner who responded to the ungrammatical sentence above (*The policeman explained Wong the law) with the comment 'You can't use a proper noun after "explain"' clearly has some explicit understanding of what makes the sentence ungrammatical, but equally clearly does not have a very accurate notion. Sorace (1985) showed that much of learners' explicit knowledge is imprecise, but also that it becomes better defined as proficiency increases.

Implicit knowledge is available through automatic processing whereas explicit knowledge is generally accessible only through controlled processing

The 'procedures' that comprise implicit knowledge can be easily and rapidly accessed in unplanned language use. In contrast, explicit knowledge exists as declarative facts that can only be accessed through the application of attentional processes. One of the widely commented-on uses of explicit knowledge is to edit or monitor production, a process that is only possible in those types of language use that allow learners sufficient time to access the relevant declarative facts. For this reason, explicit knowledge may not be readily available in spontaneous language use where there is little opportunity for careful online planning. It is possible, however, that some learners are able to automatize their explicit knowledge through practice and thus access it for rapid online processing in much the same way as they access implicit knowledge. DeKeyser (2003) suggests that automatized explicit knowledge can be considered 'functionally equivalent' to implicit knowledge. Hulstijn (2002: 211), however, is doubtful, arguing that although practice 'may speed up the execution of algorithmic rules to some extent', it is still necessary to distinguish the automatization of implicit and explicit knowledge and that what appears to be the automatization of explicit knowledge through practice may in fact entail the separate development of implicit knowledge. N. Ellis (1994) suggests how this might come about; he proposes that sequences produced initially through the application of declarative rules can come to be performed automatically if they are sufficiently practised. That is, it is not the rules themselves that become implicit, but rather the sequences of language that the rules are used to construct.

Default L2 production relies on implicit knowledge, but difficulty in performing a language task may result in the learner attempting to exploit explicit knowledge

To borrow terms from sociocultural theory (see Lantolf, 2000), implicit knowledge can be viewed as knowledge that has been fully internalized by the learner (i.e. self-regulation has been achieved). In contrast, explicit knowledge can be viewed as a 'tool' that learners use to mediate performance and achieve self-control in linguistically demanding situations. Explicit knowledge manifests itself, for example, through the private speech that learners use to grapple with a problem. When learners are asked to make and justify grammaticality judgements in a think-aloud or dyadic problem-solving task, they typically try to access declarative information to help them do so, if they feel unable or lacking in confidence to make a judgement intuitively (R. Ellis, 1991; Goss *et al.*, 1994).

Implicit knowledge is only evident in learners' verbal behavior whereas explicit knowledge is verbalizable

Implicit knowledge cannot be described as it exists in the form of statistically weighted connections between memory nodes, and its regularities are only manifest in actual language use. This is why learners cannot explain their choice of implicit forms. In contrast, explicit knowledge exists as declarative facts that can be 'stated'. It is important to recognize, however, that verbalizing a rule or feature need not entail the use of metalanguage. As James and Garrett (1992) pointed out, talking about language can be conducted in a 'standard received language' or a 'nontechnical one'. Thus, the error in the double object sentence above might be explained nontechnically by saying 'You can't say "explain Wong". You've got to say "to Wong" after "explain"'. Alternatively, the explanation might call on extensive metalanguage, for example, 'In the case of dative alternation, there are some verbs like "explain" that require the indirect object to be realized as a prepositional phrase rather than as a noun phrase'. Although metalanguage is not an essential component of explicit knowledge, it would seem to be closely related.

There are limits on most learners' ability to acquire implicit knowledge whereas most explicit knowledge is learnable

Implicit knowledge is clearly learnable, but there would appear to be age constraints on the ability of learners to fully learn an L2 implicitly given that very few learners achieve native speaker proficiency. There are incremental deficits in our ability to learn implicit knowledge as we age (Birdsong, 2006). In contrast, as Bialystok (1994: 566) pointed out, 'explicit knowledge can be learned at any age', and it is not perhaps until old age that learning deficits become apparent. The constraints that exist on learners' ability to learn explicit facts about a language are of a different order, probably relating to individual differences in the analytical skills needed to memorise, induce or deduce them.

The learner's L2 implicit and explicit knowledge systems are distinct

An issue of considerable importance (and also controversy) is the extent to which a learner's L2 implicit and L2 explicit systems are distinct. We have already seen that Krashen (1981) viewed the two types of knowledge as entirely separate. Paradis (1994: 397, 2004) also postulated that the two types of knowledge reside in neuranatomically distinct systems. Explicit memory is stored diffusely over large areas of the tertiary cortex and involves the limbic system; implicit memory is 'linked to the cortical processors through which it was acquired' and does not involve the limbic system. The two memory systems are also susceptible to selective impairment. Paradis cited evidence to suggest that bilinguals who have learnt the L2 formally (and therefore can be assumed to possess substantial explicit knowledge), may lose the ability to use their L1 in the case of aphasia while maintaining the ability to speak haltingly in the L2.

Further evidence of the separateness of the two types of knowledge can be found in research based on Ullman's (2001) dual-mechanism model. Ullman argued that the brain is so organized as to support a mental model consisting of two largely separate systems – the lexicon and the grammar, each with distinct neural bases. He illustrated this model with reference to the processing of morphological forms such as regular and irregular past-tense verb forms. He proposed that procedural memory permits the computation of regular morphological features (e.g. V-ed) by concatenating the phonological forms of the base and an affix (e.g. walk + ed ? walked). In contrast, declarative memory handles irregular forms. Ullman (2001: 39) suggested that 'for a given morpho-syntactic configuration, both systems attempt to compute an appro-priately complex form', but that 'if a form is found in memory (*sang*), the rule-based computation is inhibited'.

Other researchers (e.g. Dienes & Perner, 1999), however, have viewed the distinction between implicit and explicit knowledge as continuous rather than dichotomous. Some evidence for this comes from Ullman himself. Ullman acknowledged that language cannot be so neatly divided into 'regular' and 'irregular' forms; there are also 'subregular' forms (i.e. forms that manifest some degree of regularity without being entirely regular). A good example can be found in the plural forms of German nouns. The default, regular form is -s, but other forms are partially regular (e.g. the -(e)n plural form that occurs predominantly with feminine nouns). Bartke *et al.* (2005) found that differences in brain responses depended on whether the stimulus was a complete irregular or a subregular form and suggested that the dual-mechanism account proposed by Ullman may need to be modified to incorporate a third processing component to explain how the brain processes subregular forms.

The view I have advanced in Ellis (2004) is that where representation (but not language use) is concerned we would do better to view the two types of knowledge as dichotomous. Adopting a connectionist account of implicit linguistic knowledge as an elaborate interconnected network, it is not easy to see how knowledge as weighted content (i.e. as a set of neural pathways of greater and lesser strength) can be anything other than separate from knowledge of linguistic facts. This book is predicated on the claim that the two knowledge systems are dissociated.

L2 performance utilizes a combination of implicit and explicit knowledge

The problem in determining whether implicit and explicit knowledge stores are separate or linked rests in part, at least, on the problem of determining precisely how learners draw on their linguistic knowledge when performing different language tasks. As Bialystok (1982) pointed out, language use typically involves learners drawing on *both* systems to construct messages. Furthermore, it is possible that learners will have developed both implicit and explicit knowledge of the same linguistic feature. For example, a learner may have internalized 'jumped' as a single item in explicit memory, but may also have developed the procedure for affixing -ed to the base form of the verb in implicit memory – as suggested by Ullman. Thus, the neurological distinctiveness of the two systems will be difficult to detect from simply examining a learner's linguistic behavior. This is a problem for the measurement of the two types of knowledge that will be considered in Chapter 2. The point at issue now is that irrespective of whether the two systems are psychologically and neurologically distinct, they will never be entirely distinct in performance.

The following is a summary of the main points that have emerged from this discussion of implicit and explicit L2 knowledge. These points constitute the assumptions that inform the contents of this book.

(1)   Explicit knowledge appears phylogenetically and ontogenetically later than implicit knowledge and it involves different access mechanisms.
(2)   Explicit knowledge is neurologically distinct from implicit knowledge.
(3)   The question of whether the two types of knowledge are to be seen as dichotomous or continuous is a matter of controversy, but neurological evidence and current connectionist models of linguistic knowledge point to a dichotomy.
(4)   The question of the separateness of the representation of the two types of knowledge is independent from the question of whether the processes of implicit and explicit learning are similar or different. This remains a controversial issue. It is likely, however, that learning processes and knowledge types are correlated to some degree at least.
(5)   While there is controversy regarding the interface of explicit and implicit knowledge at the level of learning, there is wide acceptance that they interact at the level of performance.

A number of studies have examined learners' implicit and explicit knowledge. These are considered in Chapter 2, where instruments designed to measure the two types of knowledge are described and validated.

Implicit and Explicit Instruction

The term 'instruction' implies an attempt to intervene in interlanguage development. Elsewhere, I have characterized language instruction in terms of 'indirect' and 'direct' intervention (Ellis, 2005). Indirect intervention aims 'to create conditions where learners can learn experientially through learning how to communicate in the L2 (p. 713). It is best realized through a task-based syllabus. Instruction as direct intervention involves the pre-emptive specification of what it is that the learners are supposed to learn and, typically, draws on a structural syllabus.

Implicit and explicit instruction do not correlate exactly with this basic distinction, but can be mapped onto it. Implicit instruction is directed at enabling learners to infer rules without awareness. That is, it seeks to provide learners with experience of specific exemplars of a rule or pattern while they are not attempting to learn it (e.g. they are focused instead on meaning). As a result, they internalize the underlying rule/pattern without their attention being explicitly focused on it. Clearly, then, indirect intervention is implicit in nature. But, it is also possible to envisage some types of direct intervention as being implicit. It is possible to determine a specific learning target (e.g. a grammatical structure), but to mask this from the learners so that they are not aware of the target. This type of implicit instruction involves creating a learning environment that is 'enriched' with the target feature, but without drawing learners' explicit attention to it. This is exactly what happens in the treatment found in studies that have sought to investigate implicit learning. Explicit instruction involves 'some sort of rule being thought about during the learning process' (DeKeyser, 1995). In other words, learners are encouraged to develop metalinguistic awareness of the rule. This can be achieved deductively (i.e. by providing the learners with a grammatical description of the rule) or inductively (i.e. by assisting learners to discover the rule for themselves from data provided). Explicit instruction, therefore, necessarily constitutes direct intervention. The relationships between direct/indirect intervention and implicit/explicit instruction are shown in Figure 1.1.

Housen and Pierrard (2006) provide a more elaborate definition of the two types of instruction in terms of a number of differentiating characteristics, as shown in Table 1.1.

This account of implicit and explicit instruction distinguishes different types of the two kinds of instruction. Implicit instruction can take the form of task-based teaching where any attention to linguistic form arises naturally out of the way the tasks are performed. In this case, attention to form is primarily reactive in nature. However, it can also be proactive, as when tasks are designed to elicit the use of a specific linguistic target, and performance of the task naturally creates opportunities for experiencing the target feature. Explicit instruction can also be reactive or proactive. Reactive explicit instruction occurs when teachers provide explicit or metalinguistic corrective feedback on learner' errors in the use of the target feature. Proactive explicit instruction occurs when the teacher offers a metalinguistic explanation of the target rule prior to any practice activities (direct proactive) or when the teacher invites learners

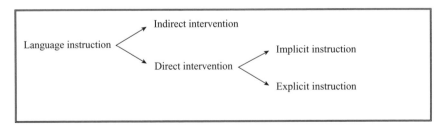

Figure 1.1 Types of language instruction

Table 1.1 Implicit and explicit instruction (Housen & Pierrard, 2006: 10)

Implicit FFI	*Explicit FFI*
• Attracts attention to target form	• Directs attention to target form
• Is delivered spontaneously (e.g. in an otherwise communication-oriented activity)	• Is predetermined and planned (e.g. as the main focus and goal of a teaching activity
• Is unobtrusive (minimal interruption of communication of meaning)	• Is obtrusive (interruption of communicative meaning)
• Presents target forms in context	• Presents target forms in isolation
• Makes no use of metalanguage	• Uses metalinguistic terminology (e.g. rule explanation)
• Encourages free use of the target form	• Involves controlled practice of target form

to discover the rule for themselves from data provided (indirect proactive).

It should be noted, however, that the terms explicit and implicit instruction can only be defined from a perspective external to the learner, i.e. the teacher's, material writer's or course designer's perspective. In contrast, the terms implicit/explicit learning refer to the learner's perspective. There is no necessary correlation between the two pairs of terms (Batstone, 2002). For example, the teacher may provide the learners with an explicit explanation of the use of the English definite and indefinite articles but, assuming that this explanation is provided through the medium of the L2 and that the learner is not motivated to attend to the teacher's explanation, the learner may end up acquiring implicitly and incidentally a number of lexical or grammatical items that happen to figure in the teacher's explanation. In other words, a learner can always elect to respond to what the teacher says as 'input' rather than as 'information'. In such a case, explicit instruction can result in implicit learning as a result of the incidental noticing of instances of language. Equally, in the case of direct intervention involving implicit instruction, learners may work out what the target of the instruction is and seek to make their understanding of it explicit. Thus, it does not follow that implicit instruction always results in implicit learning or that explicit instruction necessarily leads to explicit learning. It should also be noted that the aim of explicit instruction is not just to develop explicit knowledge but also, ultimately, implicit knowledge as well.

Given that the distinction between implicit and explicit instruction is not straightforward, it is not surprising to find that they have been operationalized in very different ways. Norris and Ortega (2000) conducted a meta-analysis of studies that had investigated the effects of the two types of instruction. They classified as implicit instruction studies where the treatment consisted of either enriched input (i.e. input that had been seeded with the target structure and which learners were asked to process for comprehension) or as a set of sentences containing the target feature which learners were simply asked to memorize. In the case of studies classified as explicit instruction, some of the treatments consisted solely of metalinguistic explanation while others also included production practice. A couple of examples of studies that have compared the relative effects of the two types of instruction on learning will illustrate the differences involved.

Doughty (1991) (in the study briefly considered earlier) compared the effects of 'meaning-oriented instruction' and 'rule-oriented instruction' on the acquisition of relative clauses by 20 intermediate-level ESL students from different language backgrounds. The materials consisted of computer-presented reading passages, specially written to contain examples of clauses where the direct object had been relativized. All the subjects skimmed the texts first. The meaning-orientated group received support in the form of lexical and semantic rephrasing and sentence clarification strategies (i.e. input enhancement). The rule-orientated group received instruction in the form of explicit rule statements and onscreen sentence manipulation. A control group simply read the text again. In this study then, implicit instruction was of the reactive kind, while the explicit instruction was of the direct proactive kind.

In Robinson (1996) there were four instructional conditions: (1) an implicit condition, which involved asking learners to remember sentences containing the target structures; (2) an incidental condition consisting of exposure to sentences containing the target structure in a meaning-centered task; (3) a rule-search condition involving identifying the rules; and (4) an instructed condition where written explanations of rules were provided. In terms of the definitions of implicit instruction above, both conditions (1) and (2) can be considered 'implicit' of the proactive kind, while conditions (3) and (4) are explicit, (3) involving direct explicit instruction and (4) indirect. Clearly, Robinson's operationalizations of implicit and explicit instruction differ considerably from those of Doughty.

It is not surprising, then, to find considerable differences in the results obtained by studies that have compared implicit and explicit instruction. These differences are reflected in Doughty's and Robinson's studies. Doughty reported that the meaning-orientated group and the rule-orientated group both outperformed the control group in their ability to relativize, but that there was no difference between the two experimental groups. Robinson, however, reported no differences in the scores on a grammaticality judgement test between his (1) and (2) conditions (both of which I classified as implicit). However, condition (3) (which I classified as direct explicit) outperformed the other three conditions, including condition (4) (which I classified as indirect explicit).

Overall, Norris and Ortega (2000) found that explicit instruction was more effective than implicit instruction in their meta-analysis. They reported an effect size for 29 implicit treatments of $d = 0.54$ and $d = 1.13$ for the 69 explicit treatments. Cohen (1988) considered effect sizes larger than .8 as 'large', sizes between .5 and .8 as 'medium', between .2 and .5 as 'small' and less than .2 as negligible. On this basis, the effect size for implicit instruction is 'medium' whereas that for explicit instruction is 'large', suggesting an advantage for explicit instruction. However, as might be expected, there was considerable variance from study to study, reflected in the relatively large standard deviations for the effect sizes (i.e. 0.86 in the case of the implicit treatments and 0.93 in the case of the explicit treatments).

There is also another problem with these studies. Many of the studies that investigated the relative effectiveness of implicit and explicit instruction relied on methods of measuring acquisition that favored explicit instruction. Norris and Ortega distinguished four types of measure: (1) metalinguistic judgement, (2) selected response, (3) constrained constructed response and (4) free constructed response. The first three are likely to allow learners to utilize their explicit knowledge of the target structures and thus can be thought to favor explicit instruction. (4), on the other hand, is more likely to tap implicit knowledge. Only 16% of the total studies in their meta-analysis included free constructed response measures. An inspection of the results for these measures indicates a slight advantage for implicit forms of instruction.

The problem of how to measure L2 acquisition is the focus of this book. Arguably, little progress can be made in investigating the effects of implicit and explicit instruction until we have valid measures of implicit and explicit knowledge. In Part 2 of this book, we report a series of studies designed to validate measures of these two types of knowledge.

The Interface Issue

The distinctions that we have now considered are all relevant to what has become known as the 'interface issue'. This concerns the extent to which implicit knowledge interfaces with explicit knowledge. The interface issue addresses a number of questions: to what extent and in what ways are implicit and explicit learning related? Does explicit knowledge convert into or facilitate the acquisition of implicit knowledge? Does explicit instruction result in the acquisition of implicit as well as explicit knowledge? These are key questions of both theoretical importance for SLA and practical importance for language pedagogy.

Three very different answers to the interface question have been offered; (1) the noninterface position, (2) the strong interface position and (3) the weak interface position. I will briefly consider each of these.

The noninterface position

This draws on research that shows that implicit and explicit L2 knowledge involve different acquisitional mechanisms (Krashen, 1981; Hulstijn, 2002), are stored in different parts of the brain (Paradis, 1994) and are accessed for performance by means of different processes, automatic versus controlled (R. Ellis, 1993). In its pure form, this position rejects both the possibility of explicit knowledge transforming directly into implicit knowledge and the possibility of implicit knowledge becoming explicit. However, in a weaker form of the noninterface position, the possibility of implicit knowledge transforming into explicit is recognized through the process of conscious reflection on and analysis of output generated by means of implicit knowledge (Bialystok, 1994).

The strong interface position

In contrast, the strong interface position claims that not only can explicit knowledge be derived from implicit knowledge, but also that explicit knowledge can be converted into implicit knowledge through practice. That is, learners can first learn a rule as a declarative fact and, then, by dint of practising the use of this rule, can convert it into an implicit representation, although this need not entail (initially, at least) the loss of the original explicit representation. The interface position was first formally advanced by Sharwood Smith (1981) and has subsequently been promoted by DeKeyser (1998, 2007). Differences exist, however, regarding the nature of the 'practice' that is required to effect the transformation, in particular whether this can be mechanical or needs to be communicative in nature.

The weak interface position

The weak interface position exists in three versions, all of which acknowledge the possibility of explicit knowledge becoming implicit, but posit some limitation on when or how this can take place. One version posits that explicit knowledge can convert into implicit knowledge through practice, but only if the learner is developmentally ready to acquire the linguistic form. This version draws on notions of 'learnability' in accordance with attested developmental sequences in L2 acquisition (e.g. Pienemann, 1989). The second version sees explicit knowledge as contributing indirectly to the acquisition of implicit knowledge by promoting some of the processes believed to be responsible. N. Ellis (1994: 16), for example, suggests that 'declarative rules can have "top-down" influences on perception', in particular by making relevant features salient, thus enabling learners to 'notice' them and to 'notice the gap' between the input and their existing linguistic competence. Such a position suggests that implicit and explicit learning processes work together in L2 acquisition and that they are dynamic, taking place consciously but transiently with enduring effects on implicit knowledge (N. Ellis, 2008). This is also the view that I have promoted in a series of publications (e.g. Ellis, 1993, 1994). According to the third version, learners can use their explicit knowledge to produce output that then serves as 'auto-input' to their implicit learning mechanisms (Schmidt & Frota, 1986; Sharwood Smith, 1981).

Neurolinguistic studies lend some support to the interface positions. Lee (2004: 67), for example, suggested that neuroanatomy allows for an interface between declarative and procedural memory:

> When (the learner) utters a sentence that violates the rule, his or her declarative memory may send a signal indicating that the utterance is wrong. This signal may prevent the formation of connections among neurons that could have represented the incorrect rule. On the other hand, when the speaker executes a correct sentence, this information aligns with that of declarative memory, and the connection that represents the sentence or the rule involved in the sentence may become stronger.

Lee's account appears to lend support to both a strong interface position (i.e. declarative memory can convert into procedural memory) and a weak interface position (i.e. declarative memory can help adjust the neural circuits in which procedural memory is housed). Other neuroscientific researchers, however, have rejected the possibility of a strong interface and emphasized the weak interface position. Paradis (2004) is adamant that explicit knowledge does not convert into implicit knowledge; acquisition may commence with an explicit rule (controlled processing) but subsequently, the learner acquires implicit computational procedures involving automatic processing. He proposed that metalinguistic knowledge can assist the development of implicit competence, but only indirectly through focusing attention on the items that need to be practised and through monitoring. Crowell (2004) also argued that declarative knowledge is not converted into procedural knowledge, but rather the two types of knowledge are learnt and stored separately and when activated involve different neural loops. Crowell (2004: 101) commented 'what would appear on the behavioral level to be a "conversion" is, in actuality, probably a strengthening of connections in the non-declarative loop that is sometimes accompanied by weakening of connections in the declarative loop'.

The different positions all have their adherents and have been the topic of much argument in the SLA literature. However, the evidence for them is largely indirect (e.g. cases of aphasia). They have not been subjected to empirical enquiry. One reason for this is the lack of agreed instruments for ascertaining whether what learners have learned as a result of instruction or exposure consists of implicit or explicit knowledge, or, of course, some amalgam of the two. Again, then, the importance of developing valid measures of the two types of knowledge is shown. No resolution of the interface question is possible until these are available.

Outline of the Book

The book is in five parts. Part 1 consists of this chapter, the purpose of which is to introduce readers to the key constructs of implicit/explicit learning, knowledge and instruction.

Part 2 contains four chapters, all of which address how to measure implicit and explicit knowledge. Chapter 2 (Rod Ellis) examines a number of studies that have attempted to measure implicit and explicit knowledge and then goes on to identify a set of criteria for operationalizing the distinction between the two types. It reports a study that investigated whether instruments based on the criteria were able to provide relatively separate measures of the two types of knowledge. Subsequent chapters in this section examine each of the instruments in greater detail. Chapter 3 (Rosemary Erlam) describes the development of the oral elicited imitation test, presenting a rationale for why elicited imitation was chosen as a means of accessing implicit language knowledge. Chapter 4 (Shawn Loewen) explores the construct validity of grammaticality judgement tests by examining the responses of both L1 and L2 English speakers to the test when administered in a timed and untimed condition. Chapter 5 (Catherine Elder) investigates the test of metalinguistic knowledge by forming a series of hypotheses regarding the nature of metalinguistic knowledge and then putting these hypotheses to the test, using data gathered in the context of trialling this instrument on a diverse population of L2 learners.

The purpose of the four chapters in Part 3 is to make use of the instruments for measuring implicit and explicit knowledge to examine a number of issues in SLA and teacher education. Chapter 6 (Rod Ellis) addresses the intriguing possibility that what constitutes grammatical complexity in terms of explicit knowledge may be very different from what constitutes complexity as implicit knowledge. It provides evidence to suggest that this is, in fact, the case and also that the notion of 'acquisitional sequences' applies only to implicit knowledge. Chapter 7 (Catherine Elder and Rod Ellis) asks to what extent the distinction between implicit and explicit L2 knowledge can account for proficiency as measured by standard tests such as TOEFL and IELTS. It suggests that, in fact, these tests seem to draw heavily on learners' explicit knowledge. Chapter 8 (Jenefer Philp), using a statistical technique known as cluster analysis, examines whether different types of learners can be distinguished in terms of the two types of knowledge (e.g. are there learners whose knowledge is predominantly implicit or explicit?) and also whether such variables as age and instructional experience can account for the differences in knowledge profiles. Chapter 9 (Erlam, Philp and Elder) investigates to what extent trainee teachers possess metalinguistic knowledge of English grammar. Three groups of trainee teachers were examined – a group of 94 highly proficient L2 learners of English from Malaysia enrolled in a Foundation program for preservice teachers, a group of TESOL teacher trainees in New Zealand and a similar group in Canada. These chapters demonstrate that the availability of instruments providing measures of implicit and explicit knowledge allows for a new perspective on a variety of current issues.

Part 4 examines the role that form-focused instruction plays in L2 acquisition. A major criticism of much of the research in this area of SLA is that it has failed to distinguish clearly between implicit and explicit knowledge in the way that acquisition is measured – as noted earlier in this chapter. Chapter 10 (Erlam, Loewen and Philp) examines whether output- and input-based instruction impacts on implicit language knowledge. This is an important question because strong claims have been made about the efficacy of input-based instruction (e.g. VanPatten, 1996, 2004) but, to date, there is little evidence that it benefits the acquisition of implicit knowledge (i.e. acquisition has typically been measured in controlled tests that favor explicit knowledge). Chapter 10 (Loewen, Erlam and Ellis) investigates the effects of instruction as 'enriched input' on learners' acquisition of third person -s. In this study, the learners' attention was focused on another grammatical feature (the use of the indefinite article for generic reference), so any acquisition of third person -s would be incidental. Again, acquisition was operationalized as both implicit and explicit knowledge. Chapter 12 (Reinders and Ellis) also investigated the effects of enriched input on acquisition. In this case, however, it compared the effects of enriched input alone with enriched input combined with a request for the learners to pay specific attention to the exemplars of the two structures that were the target of the instruction. This study used a timed and an untimed grammaticality judgement test to examine the effects of the instruction on the acquisition of implicit and explicit knowledge. The final chapter in this part of the book (Chapter 13 by Ellis, Loewen and Erlam) reports a study that compared the relative effects of implicit and explicit corrective feedback on L2 learners' acquisition of regular past tense. It found that explicit feedback seemed to have an effect on the development of learners' implicit as well as their explicit knowledge. The studies reported in this part demonstrate the value of using separate measures of implicit and explicit knowledge in research investigating form-focused instruction.

The final part of the book (Part 5) contains a single chapter (Chapter 14). In it, Ellis reviews the main issues discussed in previous chapters and the findings of the empirical research that they reported. It also discusses the limitations of the research and identifies areas for further study.

Conclusion

While acknowledging that the implicit/explicit distinctions are not without controversy, this book is predicated on the assumption that they are real, evidenced-based and useful. As N. Ellis (2008: 120) puts it:

> we know that implicit and explicit learning are distinct processes, that humans have separate implicit and explicit memory systems, that there are different types of knowledge of and about language, that these are stored in different areas of the brain, and that different educational experiences generate different type of knowledge.

This book is an exploration of these differences as they apply to L2 acquisition.

Part 2

The Measurement of Implicit and Explicit Knowledge

If it is assumed that second language (L2) acquisition involves both implicit and explicit learning and that the results of these learning processes is an amalgam of implicit and explicit L2 knowledge – and this is the fundamental claim we wish to make in this book – then it becomes essential to establish the means for measuring these two types of knowledge. The purpose of the chapters in Part 2 is to report a series of studies that investigated measuring instruments designed to provide relatively separate measures of implicit and explicit L2 knowledge. These studies comprised the first phase of the Marsden Project and constituted an essential preliminary for the next two phases – the application of the measures to investigate such issues as the nature of 'language proficiency' and the effect of instruction on the acquisition of implicit and explicit L2 knowledge.

Doughty (2003) provides a useful list of measures of L2 ability typically employed in instructed second language acquisition (SLA). Her list is organized in terms of four basic types of measures (taken from Norris & Ortega, 2000). These are:

(1) Constrained, constructed responses
    (a) Written production (e.g. correct sentences containing errors)
    (b) Oral production (e.g. recall of isolated sentences)
(2) Metalinguistic judgment responses
(3) Selected responses
    (a) Comprehension (e.g. matching pictures to sentences)
    (b) Production (choosing from a list of words to complete a sentence)
    (c) Other (e.g. recognition of words)
(4) Free responses
    (a) Comprehension (e.g. translate an L2 narrative into English)
    (b) Production (e.g. picture description)

This list reflects two general characteristics of the measures: (1) the extent to which the learner's use of language is controlled or free and (2) whether comprehension or production of L2 forms is involved. It serves as an excellent general guide for researchers interested in measuring L2 learners' linguistic knowledge.

Such a list, however, does not provide a basis for determining what *kind* of knowledge the different measures relate to. To achieve this, it is necessary to develop an operational framework that can inform the choice of measures. This is what Chapter 2 seeks to do. It identifies seven criterial features that can distinguish measures of implicit and explicit knowledge. On the basis of these features, five tests were designed, three of which were intended as primary measures of implicit knowledge and two as primary measures of explicit knowledge. These tests (which are described in detail in Chapter 2) can be mapped onto Doughty's list as shown in Table 1.

There is an important point to make about this analysis of the five tests. Whereas the ideal measure of implicit knowledge is probably 'free production', it is also possible to design tests of the constrained, constructed response and metalinguistic judgment types that can provide measures of implicit knowledge. This is important when the aim of the research is to measure knowledge of specific linguistic features, as was the case in the Marsden Project, which sought to investigate learners' knowledge of 17 grammatical structures. The problem with 'free production' is that learners can easily avoid using the target features. In contrast, constrained, constructed response and metalinguistic judgment tests oblige learners to demonstrate whether they have acquired the target features. The question arises, however, as to whether such tests afford valid measures of implicit knowledge. This is the question that is addressed in Chapters 2–4 of Part 2.

Explicit knowledge is perhaps easier to measure. Given the declarative nature of this type of knowledge and the fact that it typically requires time to access, measures that incorporate these two characteristics should

Table 1 Analysis of the five tests measuring implicit/explicit knowledge

Test	*Type of measure*	*Type of knowledge measured*
1. Elicited Oral Imitation Test	Constrained, constructed response – production	Implicit knowledge
2. Oral Narrative Test	Free production	Implicit knowledge
3. Timed Grammaticality Judgment Test	Metalinguistic judgment	Implicit knowledge
4. Untimed Grammaticality Judgment Test	Metalinguistic judgment	Explicit knowledge
5. Metalinguistic Knowledge Test	Selected responses	Explicit knowledge

provide valid measures of explicit knowledge. In accordance with the account of explicit knowledge provided in Chapter 1, we devised instruments that measured learners' knowledge of metalanguage and their ability to access analysed knowledge in a judgment test.

Chapter 2 (Ellis) introduces the theoretical rationale for the five tests and reports the results of a Confirmatory Factor Analysis that lends support to this rationale by demonstrating that the tests designed to measure implicit knowledge and those designed to measure explicit knowledge loaded onto separate factors. Chapter 3 (Erlam) examines the Elicited Oral Imitation Test in detail, relating it to previous work that has investigated such tests and identifying those features of the test that support the claim that it measures implicit knowledge. Chapter 4 (Loewen) examines the Timed and Untimed Grammaticality Judgment Tests. Through a number of analyses, Loewen was able to show that features of GJTs can be manipulated to predispose L2 learners to draw on different types of L2 knowledge. That is, GJTs with limited response times limit the ability of L2 learners to access their explicit knowledge in making a judgment, while ungrammatical sentences on an untimed test encourage learners to access explicit L2 knowledge. Chapter 5 (Elder) focuses on the Metalinguistic Knowledge Test. Elder presents a number of findings to support the validity of this test as a measure of explicit knowledge.

The research reported in Part 2 is central to the Marsden Project. Failure to successfully identify relatively separate measures of implicit and explicit L2 knowledge would have imperilled the second two phases of the project. That we were reasonably successful in developing separate measures made possible the investigation of L2 proficiency and of the effects of L2 instruction in Parts 3 and 4, respectively.

Chapter 2

Measuring Implicit and Explicit Knowledge of a Second Language

ROD ELLIS

Introduction

We have seen that there have been conflicting claims about the nature of implicit and explicit learning, with some theorists arguing that they involve separate learning systems and others disputing this. In part, this controversy has arisen because of the difficulty of ascertaining what processes are actually involved when learners engage in learning a second language (L2). That is, the controversy is, to a very considerable extent, methodological in nature. How do we know when learning is implicit and when it is explicit? This chapter will begin, therefore, with a brief examination of the methods that researchers have used to address these questions.

In cognitive psychology, a variety of approaches have been used. Eysenck (2001) distinguishes four general approaches, all of which have figured in second language acquisition (SLA) research.

(1) Experimental cognitive psychology – i.e. experiments are carried out on normal individuals, usually in a laboratory context.

In this approach, different groups of learners are given different learning tasks. A typical implicit learning task involves memorizing a set of sentences that have been constructed to exemplify a specific grammatical feature without being given any indication of what the feature is or even that the sentences illustrate a specific feature. The corresponding explicit learning task would involve presenting the same set of sentences with an instruction to study them in order to discover the underlying rule. The learning outcomes of such tasks have typically been measured in three ways: (1) by asking the learners to judge the grammaticality of sentences (where the sentences include both those contained in the task and novel sentences illustrating the same grammatical feature), (2) by examining the time individual learners take to make the grammaticality judgments and (3) by requesting the learners to verbalize what they know about the structure of the sentences. Implicit learning is considered to have occurred if (1) the learners are able to judge the grammaticality of the sentences (including the novel ones) correctly,

(2) they are able to do this rapidly and (3) they are unable to verbalize the underlying rule. Explicit learning is considered to have occurred if the learners are (1) able to judge the grammaticality of the sentences correctly, (2) require more time to make their judgments and (3) are able to verbalize the underlying rule. Examples of studies that adopted this approach in SLA research are N. Ellis (1993), Robinson (1996) and Williams (2005). It should be noted that this approach relies predominantly on measures of L2 knowledge as a basis for making inferences about the nature of the learning involved.

(2) Cognitive neuropsychology – i.e. the cognitive impairment of brain-damaged patients is studied with a view to understanding human cognition.

This approach has involved investigating bilingual aphasia in order to identify (1) which parts of the brain have been damaged in an individual learner and (2) which functions in which language(s) have been affected. In this way, it is possible to relate areas of the brain to particular linguistic functions. Studies of bilingual aphasia focus on both functional loss of language ability and patterns of recovery. The neuropsychological approach has produced evidence to suggest that impairment in one type of knowledge can occur independently of impairment in the other. For example, Ullmann (2001) produced evidence to show that the implicit memory system is damaged in the case of Parkinson's Disease, resulting in problems with grammatical processing, whereas the explicit memory system is impaired in Alzheimer's Disease and Williams' Syndrome, leading to difficulty in accessing items stored lexically. Paradis (2004), in his review of the neuropsychological research, distinguished between aphasia and amnesia, the former arising as a result of damage to the neural sites responsible for implicit memory and the latter occurring when there is neurological damage to the sites involved in explicit memory.

(3) Cognitive science – i.e. computational models are devised to account for human cognition and then tested.

Computerized connectionist simulation systems have been used to investigate the mechanisms involved in extracting regularities from sets of input data. Given that such systems are not supplied with explicit information about the target feature, it can be assumed that any learning evident is implicit in nature. A good example of this approach can be found in N. Ellis and Schmidt's (1997) connectionist simulation directed at the learning of plural forms. At the outset, the connection weights of the computer model were randomized. Initially, the model was trained in singular nouns followed by intensive training in plural forms. The model produced a very good simulation of the pattern of acquisition demonstrated by human subjects, including the same kind of overgeneralization of the regular plural form noted in natural language acquisition. In other words, this simulation replicated the implicit language learning that occurs in naturalistic acquisition.

(4) Cognitive neuroscience – i.e. neuroimaging techniques of various kinds are used to identify which regions and pathways in the brain are involved in different cognitive activities.

Gernsbacher and Kaschak (2003: 92) describe a typical neuroimaging study as one that 'relates stimulus- and task-related changes to changes in neural activity in an attempt to discern what brain regions underlie a particular type of processing and how these regions go about their work'. A variety of different techniques are available for examining brain activity, including magnetic resonance imaging (MRI) and electroencephalography (EEG). Lee (2004) summarized research based on this approach, in order to identify the neural mechanisms and pathways involved in implicit learning. She identified a major role for the basal ganglia. Crowell (2004) discussed studies that showed the role played by the hippocampus in explicit knowledge. Tokowicz and MacWhinney (2005: 174), in a study that employed EEG, found that 'learners are able to implicitly process some aspects of L2 syntax even in the early stage of acquisition'.

Our understanding of the processes and products of implicit and explicit learning will be best enhanced by studies that employ a combination of these approaches. It is clear that we need to investigate the actual processes involved in the two types of learning, and that approaches (2), (3) and (4) are best equipped to achieve this. However, to date in SLA it is (1) that has been pre-eminent – researchers have focused on the types of linguistic knowledge that result from different learning conditions. While there is a danger in trying to correlate 'learning processes' and 'learning outcomes' (see Chapter 1), it is not unreasonable to assume that implicit knowledge arises as a result of implicit processes, although it is perhaps less clear that explicit knowledge is inevitably the result of explicit processes, for, as Williams (2005) pointed out, awareness of the product of learning does not necessarily imply that conscious analysis occurred while learning.

This chapter will focus on the measurement of implicit and explicit knowledge, reflecting the primacy of approach (1) in SLA. There is another reason for this focus. SLA (as reflected in this book) is concerned with the role that instruction plays in L2 acquisition. As Doughty (2003) emphasized, it is important to establish whether instruction results not just in metalinguistic knowledge, but also in implicit knowledge, and this can only be achieved by ensuring that the instruments used to measure learning outcomes provide a valid measure of implicit knowledge. Doughty is rightly critical of many studies of form-focused instruction that have not only failed to ensure they include a measure of implicit knowledge, but have failed to address what their instruments are measuring. A premise of this book is that we will not be able to make progress in investigating the impact of instruction on L2 acquisition until we pay close attention to the validity of our measuring instruments, which entails the development of separate measures of implicit and explicit knowledge.

I will begin by examining a number of previous studies that have attempted to measure implicit and explicit L2 knowledge. This will provide a basis for developing operational definitions of the two types of knowledge. I will then briefly discuss an early study by Han and Ellis, which was the precursor of the Marsden Project, the main focus of this chapter.

Studies of Implicit and Explicit L2 Knowledge

A number of early studies examined the relationship between learners' implicit and explicit knowledge (e.g. Hulstijn & Hulstijn, 1984; Seliger, 1979; Sorace, 1985). In all of these studies, explicit knowledge was operationalized as learners' explanation of specific linguistic features, while implicit knowledge was determined by examining the learners' use of these features in oral or written language. The focus of this section will be on a number of later studies and how the 'measurement problem' has impeded the investigation of the interface question (see Chapter 1).

Green and Hecht (1992) presented 300 German school- and university-based learners of English with a set of sentences containing grammatical errors and asked them (1) to correct each sentence and (2) to state the rule that had been violated. They found that the learners could only state the correct rule in 46% of the cases (although the university learners in the sample were able to do so in 86% of cases), but were able to correct 78% of the sentences. In other words, the learners' ability to correct the errors exceeded their ability to explain the rules. Green and Hecht suggested that one interpretation of these results is that these learners' explicit rules constituted only a subset of their available implicit knowledge.

Macrory and Stone (2000) investigated British comprehensive school students' 'perceptions' of what they knew about the formation of the French perfect tense (measured by means of self-report), their 'actual knowledge' of the tense (measured by means of gap-filling exercises) and their ability to use the tense in an informal interview and in free written production. They found that the students had a fairly good explicit understanding of the perfect tense (e.g. they understood its function, they knew that some verbs used *avoir* and some *etre*, they were familiar with the forms required by different pronouns, and they were aware of the need for a final accent on the past participle). In general, this study found only weak relationships between students' perceptions, their performance in the gap-filling exercise and their use of the tense in free oral and written production. For example, whereas the learners typically supplied an auxiliary (not always the correct one) in the gap-filling exercise, they typically omitted it in free production except in formulaic expressions involving '*j'ai*'. Macrory and Stone concluded that what they term 'language-as-knowledge' and 'language-for-use', may have derived from different sources – instruction about the rule system and routines practised in class.

Hu (2002) conducted a study of 64 Chinese learners of English. His main purpose was to investigate to what extent explicit knowledge was available for use in spontaneous writing. He asked the learners to complete two spontaneous writing tasks and then to carry out an untimed error correction task and a rule-verbalization task before again completing two similar spontaneous writing tasks and a timed error correction task. The idea was that the correction and rule verbalization tasks would serve a consciousness-raising function, making the learners aware of the structures that were the focus of the study. Hu focussed on six structures, selecting a prototypical and peripheral rule for each structure (e.g. for articles, 'specific reference' constituted the prototypical rule and 'generic reference' the peripheral rule). Overall, when correct metalinguistic knowledge was available, the participants were more accurate in their prototypical use of the six structures. Also, accuracy in the use of the six structures increased in the second spontaneous writing task, suggesting that, when made aware of the need to attend to specific forms, the learners made fuller use of their metalinguistic knowledge. However, Hu admitted that it was not possible to claim that the participants actually used their metalinguistic knowledge in the writing tasks, although he did argue that the results are compatible with such an interpretation.

All of the above-mentioned studies were correlational in design. That is, they either sought to establish whether there was any relationship between learners' explicit and implicit knowledge (Green & Hecht, 1992; Macrory & Stone, 2000) or whether explicit knowledge was available for use in tasks that were hypothesized to require implicit knowledge (i.e. Hu, 2002). Such studies do not constitute tests of the interface position (nor were they intended to do so), as demonstrating a relationship does not show that knowledge that originated as explicit was subsequently transformed into implicit knowledge. To demonstrate this, it would be necessary to conduct an experimental study where learners were first taught a specific rule explicitly and as a result developed explicit knowledge of it and then, subsequently, as a result of opportunities to practise using the rule, developed implicit knowledge of it. Again, such a study is only possible if valid and reliable means of measuring explicit and implicit knowledge are available.

One study that has directly tested the interface position is DeKeyser (1995). DeKeyser's study examined the effects of two kinds of form-focussed instruction (explicit-deductive and implicit-inductive) on two kinds of rules in an artificial grammar ('simple categorical rules' and 'fuzzy prototypical rules'). Learning outcomes were measured by means of a computerized judgment test, which required the learners to say whether a sentence matched a picture, and a computerized production test, which required them to type in a sentence to describe a picture. DeKeyser suggests that the production test was, to some extent, 'speeded' (i.e. the learners had 30 seconds to respond). The learners were also asked to complete fill-in-the-blank tests to demonstrate their understanding of the grammatical rules. The learners in the explicit-deductive condition provided clear evidence of being able to produce the simple categorical rules in new contexts and did better than the learners in the implicit-inductive condition. Thus, on the face of it, this study suggests that, at least in the case of simple grammatical forms, learners who are taught explicit knowledge about the forms and then practise them, are able to use them. But, as DeKeyser admits, it was not clear to what extent the production task allowed for monitoring using explicit knowledge.

Another study that investigated the effects of form-focussed instruction on learners' implicit and explicit knowledge is De Jong (2005). This study was interested in the relative effects of receptive and mixed receptive/production training on the acquisition of Spanish noun-adjective agreement. There was also a control group that received just an explicit explanation of the target feature. Acquisition was measured by means of a battery of tests designed to discriminate between implicit and explicit knowledge. The tests included: (1) a self-paced listening test (i.e. learners were able to listen to a sentence one word at a time at a speed of their own choosing before deciding whether the sentence matched a picture), (2) a speeded grammaticality judgment test (i.e. the learners pressed a key as soon as they heard something wrong in a sentence), (3) an oral production test (OPT) conducted under a dual-task condition (i.e. the learners had to tap their fingers as they spoke) and (4) a questionnaire asking the learners to report their explicit knowledge of the target rule. De Jong is ambivalent as to the type of knowledge tapped by (1) and (2), but viewed the dual-task oral production task as likely to elicit implicit knowledge and, obviously, the questionnaire as an indicator of the learners' explicit knowledge. The results showed that all groups (including the control group) possessed explicit knowledge of the target structure (as demonstrated by the questionnaire). However, De Jong (2005: 229) concluded that 'no firm conclusions can be drawn as to the type of knowledge – implicit or explicit – that was acquired' from the results provided by the other tests.

How then did these studies operationalize the two types of knowledge? As in the earlier studies, explicit knowledge was typically elicited by asking learners to verbalize specific grammatical rules. In addition, Macrory and Stone used a blank-filling exercise to tap into explicit knowledge. The studies vary more in their means of determining implicit knowledge. Two of the studies used spontaneous production tasks, oral and written in the case of Macrory and Stone, and a fast-writing task in the case of Hu. Green and Hecht, however, used an untimed error correction task. DeKeyser used a cued sentence-based written production task. De Jong used a cued-production test conducted under a dual-task condition. There are some obvious problems with all these methods. Asking learners to verbalize rules requires at least some productive metalanguage and the ability to provide clear explanations of abstract phenomena, but learners' explicit knowledge exists independently of both the metalanguage they know and their ability to explain rules (R. Ellis, 2004).[1] Thus, as Bialystok (1979) pointed out many years ago, having learners verbalize rules provides a quite conservative picture of what they know explicitly. Likewise, a blank-filling exercise or a cued written production test may invite the use of explicit knowledge but it does not guarantee it, as learners are obviously able to complete the exercise by drawing on their implicit knowledge. Spontaneous production tasks are probably the best means of eliciting learners' implicit knowledge (R. Ellis, 2002), but again we cannot be sure that learners do not access at least some explicit knowledge, especially when the task involves writing. Hu, in fact, claims that, within certain constraints, metalinguistic knowledge is available for use in spontaneous production. De Jong also acknowledged this possibility. An error correction task, especially the kind of untimed task used by Green and Hecht, seems unlikely to produce a good measure of implicit knowledge, as the very nature of the task invites learners to access their explicit knowledge. As N. Ellis (2008: 128) noted 'this is a research area plagued with measurement problems'.

To date, then, there has been no empirical test of the interface positions for the simple reason that researchers have failed to give due consideration to implicit and explicit knowledge as constructs. Only DeKeyser and De Jong discuss the validity of their chosen instruments for measuring learning outcomes in terms of the type of knowledge they tap into, but both acknowledge their uncertainty as to what the instruments were actually measuring. As Douglas (2001: 447) noted, the failure to consider construct validity of testing instruments is widespread in SLA. In lamenting this, Douglas pointed to what is needed:

> construct validity may be demonstrated by the construction of theoretical arguments linking hypothesized aspects of language ability to features of the test tasks, demonstrating the appropriacy of the tasks for making interpretations regarding the construct, and then providing empirical evidence that the links are in fact present.

It is with a view to meeting Douglas' requirement that the next section attempts to examine the constructs of implicit/explicit knowledge, as a preliminary to the development of instruments designed to provide separate measures of them.

Operationalizing Implicit and Explicit Knowledge

Following R. Ellis (2004), explicit knowledge is conceptualized as involving primarily 'analyzed knowledge' (i.e. structured knowledge of which learners are consciously aware) and secondarily as 'metalanguage' (i.e. knowledge of technical terms such as 'verb complement' and semitechnical linguistic terms such as 'sentence' and 'clause'). Implicit knowledge is characterized as subsymbolic, procedural and unconscious. The operationalizations of these constructs is based partly on the theoretical differences between implicit and explicit L2 knowledge discussed in Chapter 1 and partly on insights gleaned from how these two types of knowledge have been operationalized in previous studies.

The operational definitions drew on seven criterial features:

(1) *Degree of awareness* (i.e. the extent to which learners are aware of their own linguistic knowledge). This clearly represents a continuum, but it can be measured by asking learners to report retrospectively whether they made use of 'feel' or 'rule' in responding to a task.

(2) *Time available* (i.e. whether learners are pressured to perform a task 'on-line' or whether they have an opportunity to plan their response carefully before making it). Operationally, this involves distinguishing tasks that are demanding on learners' short-term memories and those that lie comfortably within their L2 processing capacity.

(3) *Focus of attention* (i.e. whether the task prioritizes fluency or accuracy). Fluency entails a primary focus on message creation in order to convey information or attitudes, as in an information or opinion gap task. Accuracy entails a primary focus on form, as in a traditional grammar exercise.

(4) *Systematicity* (i.e. whether learners are consistent or variable in their response to a task). It is predicted that learners will be more

consistent in a task that taps their implicit knowledge than in a task that elicits explicit knowledge.

(5) *Certainty* (i.e. how certain learners are that the linguistic forms they have produced conform to target language norms). Given that learners' explicit knowledge has been shown to be often anomalous, some learners are likely to express more confidence in their responses to a task if they have drawn on their implicit knowledge. However, other learners may place considerable confidence in their explicit rules. Thus, this criterion of explicit knowledge needs to be treated with circumspection.

(6) *Metalanguage* (i.e. learners' knowledge of metalingual terms will be related to their explicit (analysed) knowledge, but not to their implicit knowledge).

(7) *Learnability* (i.e. learners who began learning the L2 as a child are more likely to display high levels of implicit knowledge, while those who began as adolescents or adults, especially if they were reliant on instruction, are more likely to display high levels of explicit knowledge).

It should be noted that these criteria refer to both the degree of awareness involved and to the conditions of use, reflecting the fact that the constitutive features of the two types of knowledge incorporate their manner of use. The criteria and their operationalizations in terms of implicit and explicit (analyzed and metalinguistic) knowledge are summarized in Table 2.1.

An Initial Study

In Han and Ellis (1998), an attempt was made to develop measures of L2 learners' implicit and explicit knowledge of verb complementation structures. This study employed the following instruments:

(1) An Oral Production Test (OPT). This consisted of 14 pictures devised to elicit oral responses containing English verb complements from the learners.

(2) A Timed Grammaticality Judgment Test (TGJT). This was computerized and allowed learners 3.5 seconds to indicate whether a sentence was grammatical, ungrammatical or they were not sure. This test was administered twice.

(3) An Untimed Grammaticality Judgment Test (UGJT). This contained the same 34 sentences as the TGJT, but learners were given as much time as they wanted to make a judgment.

(4) An interview. The same sentences as in the GJTs were written on cards and the learners asked to first judge the grammaticality of the sentences and then to state a rule to justify their decision. The

Table 2.1 Operationalizing the constructs of L2 implicit and explicit knowledge

Criterion	*Implicit knowledge*	*Explicit (analyzed) knowledge*
Degree of awareness	The task requires the learner to respond according to 'feel'	The task encourages the learner to respond using 'rules'
Time available	The task is time-pressured	The task is performed without any time pressure
Focus of attention	The task calls for a primary focus on meaning	The task calls for a primary focus on form
Systematicity	The task results in consistent responses	The task results in variable responses
Certainty	The task results in responses that the learner is certain are correct/ incorrect	The task results in responses the correctness/incorrect-ness of which the learner is uncertain about
Utility of knowledge of metalanguage	The task does not require the learner to use meta-linguistic knowledge	The task invites the learner to use metalinguistic knowledge
Learnability	The task favors learners who began learning as children	The task favors learners who have received form-focused instruction

interviews were transcribed and a score for each sentence was assigned using a rating scale based on whether their judgment was accurate and whether they could state a correct rule using appropriate technical language.

The OPT and the TGJT, both of which required learners to process sentences under a time constraint, were designed to measure implicit knowledge. The UGJT and the interview were designed to provide measures of explicit knowledge.

The four instruments were administered to 48 adult learners of English enrolled in a university Intensive English Language programme. A Principal Components Factor Analysis showed that scores from the OPT and the UGJT loaded on one factor, while the UGJT and the metalinguistic comments score loaded on a second factor. In accordance with the design of the study, Han and Ellis (1998) labeled these two factors 'implicit' and 'explicit L2 knowledge', respectively.

This study was limited, however, in that it focused on a single grammatical structure (verb complementation), although interestingly, despite its narrow scope, statistically significant correlations between the measures of implicit and explicit knowledge and measures from two widely used English language tests (i.e. the TOEFL and SPEAK tests) were obtained. A more serious limitation was the lack of a measure of the target structure in natural, unplanned language use. Also, the interview confounded metalinguistic knowledge with general oral proficiency, as it required learners to engage in an oral explanation of the rule involved. Nevertheless, the results provided by the study were intriguing and suggestive of the possibility of developing relatively separate measures of the two types of knowledge.

The Marsden Study

The Marsden study built on the Han and Ellis (1998) study. Its purpose was to develop a battery of tests that would provide relatively separate measures of implicit and explicit knowledge. It was acknowledged from the start, however, that even if task conditions could be identified that inclined learners to use one type of knowledge in preference to the other, it would be impossible to construct tasks that would provide pure measures of the two types of knowledge. As a number of researchers (e.g. Breen, 1989; Coughlan & Duff, 1994) have noted, there can be no guarantee that the 'task-as-workplan' (in this case the tests) will correspond to the 'task-as-process' (in this case learners' performance on the tests). Furthermore, learners are likely to draw on whatever resources they have at their disposal irrespective of which resources are best suited to the task at hand. Thus, the tests we designed were simply expected to predispose learners to access one or other type of knowledge.

Participants

A total of 111 participants completed the battery of tests described below. The participants were made up of 20 native speakers of English and 91 learners of L2 English.[2] The native speakers were either currently enrolled in undergraduate arts or engineering courses or graduate courses in a university in New Zealand or were former students of the university. Thirteen were male and seventeen female. Fifteen of them had studied a foreign language, including 11 who had studied it for more than two years. Ten of the native speakers had studied two or more foreign languages. The L2 learners were of mixed language proficiency. Some ($n = 21$) were enrolled in low-level courses in the university's English Language Academy, some were taking more advanced courses in English for Speakers of Other Languages (ESOL) as part of an under-graduate degree programme ($n = 30$), while others had sat the International English Language Testing System (IELTS), with an overall mean of 6.24 out of a possible 9.0 ($n = 44$). Thirty-six of the L2 learners were male and 58 were female (one participant failed to indicate gender). On average, they had been learning English for 10.0 years, mostly in a foreign language context – they had spent an average of only 1.9 years living in an English-speaking country. Most (70.5%) of the L2 learners came from China.

Test content

The tests were designed to provide measures of learners' knowledge of 17 English grammatical structures. The choice of the grammatical content was driven by a number of considerations. First and foremost, an attempt was made to select target language structures that were known to be universally problematic to learners (i.e. to result in errors). To this end, the SLA literature on error analysis was consulted (e.g. Burt & Kiparsky, 1972). Second, the structures were selected to represent both early and late acquired grammatical features according to what is known about the developmental properties of L2 acquisition (e.g. Pienemann, 1989). Third, the structures were selected to represent a broad range of proficiency levels according to when they were introduced in English as a Second Language (ESL) courses covering beginner, lower-intermediate, upper-intermediate and advanced levels. Fourth, the structures were chosen to include both morphological and syntactic features. Table 2.2 lists the structures and summarizes their properties in terms of the various selection criteria.

The test battery

A total of five tests were developed. The main properties of these tests were as follows:

(1) Elicited Oral Imitation Test

This consisted of a set of belief statements (involving both grammatical and ungrammatical sentences containing the target structures). In the original version of this test, there were 68 statements. However, in order to shorten the time it took to administer this test, this number was subsequently reduced to 34 statements (one grammatical and one ungrammatical sentence per structure) by selecting those sentences that correlated most strongly with total test scores in an initial sample of 50 L2 learners and 10 native speakers and, therefore, were considered the best measures of the underlying construct. The sentences were presented orally to test-takers, who were required to say first whether they agreed with, disagreed with or were not sure about the content of each statement. This was intended to focus their attention on meaning. Second, the test-takers were asked to repeat the sentences orally in correct English. The test-takers' responses were audiorecorded. The responses were then analyzed by identifying obligatory occasions

Table 2.2 Grammatical structures included in the tests

Structure	Example of learner error	When acquired	Pedagogic grading	Grammatical type
Verb complements	Liao says he wants *buying* a new car	Early	Lower intermediate	Syntactical
Regular past tense	Martin *complete* his assignment yesterday	Intermediate	Elementary/lower intermediate	Morphological
Question tags	We will leave tomorrow, *isn't it?*	Late	No clear focus at any level	Syntactical
Yes/no questions	Did Keiko *completed* her homework?	Intermediate	Elementary/lower intermediate	Morphological
Modal verbs	I must *to brush* my teeth now	Early	Various levels	Morphological
Unreal conditionals	If he had been richer, she *will* marry him	Late	Lower intermediate/intermediate	Syntactical
Since and *for*	He *has been living* in New Zealand *since* three years	Intermediate	Lower intermediate	Syntactical
Indefinite article	They had *the* very good time at the party	Late	Elementary	Morphological
Ergative verbs	Between 1990 and 2000 the population of New Zealand *was increased*	Late	Various levels	Syntactical
Possessive -s	Liao is still living in his rich *uncle* house	Late	Elementary	Morphological
Plural -s	Martin sold a few old *coin* to a shop	Early	No clear focus at any level	Morphological

Table 2.2 (Continued)

Structure	Example of learner error	When acquired	Pedagogic grading	Grammatical type
Third person -s	Hiroshi *live* with his friend Koji	Late	Elementary/lower intermediate	Morphological
Relative clauses	The boat that my father bought *it* has sunk	Late	Intermediate/advanced	Syntactical
Embedded questions	Tom wanted to know what *had I done*	Late	Intermediate	Syntactical
Dative alternation	The teacher explained *John the answer*	Late	No clear focus at any level	Syntactical
Comparatives	The building is *more bigger* than your house	Late	Elementary/intermediate	Syntactical
Adverb placement	She writes *very well* English	Late	Elementary/lower intermediate	Syntactical

for the use of the target structures. Test-takers' failure to imitate a sentence at all or to reproduce it in such a form that they did not create an obligatory context for the target structure of a sentence was coded as 'avoidance'. Each imitated sentence was allocated a score of either 1 (the target structure was correctly supplied) or 0 (the target structure was either avoided or attempted but incorrectly supplied). Scores were expressed as percentage correct. The sentences in the Elicited Oral Imitation Test can be found in Appendix A.

(2) Oral Narrative Test

The story used in this test was designed to elicit the use of a number of the target structures (i.e. regular past tense, modal verbs, third person -s, plural -s, indefinite article and possessive -s). Test-takers read a story twice. They were then asked to retell the story orally in three minutes. Their narratives were audiorecorded and subsequently transcribed. An obligatory occasion analysis was carried out to establish the percentage of correct suppliance of each target structure. A total score for each learner was calculated by averaging the percentage scores for each structure. The story used in the Oral Narrative Test can be found in Appendix B.

(3) Timed Grammaticality Judgment Test

This was a computer-delivered test consisting of 68 sentences, evenly divided between grammatical and ungrammatical. The sentences, which were different from those in the imitation test, were presented in written form on a computer screen. Thus, there were four sentences to be judged for each of the 17 grammatical structures. Test-takers were required to indicate whether each sentence was grammatical or ungrammatical by pressing response buttons within a fixed time limit.[3] The time limit for each sentence was established by timing native speakers' performance on the sentences in a pilot study, calculating an average response time for each sentence and then adding an additional 20% of the time taken for each sentence to allow for the slower processing speed of L2 learners. The time allowed for judging the individual sentences ranged from 1.8 to 6.24 seconds. Each item was scored dichotomously as correct/incorrect with items not responded to scored as incorrect. A percentage accuracy score was calculated. The sentences in the TGJT can be found in Appendix C.

(4) Untimed Grammaticality Judgment Test

This was a computer-delivered test with the same content as the TGJT (see Appendix C). Again, the sentences were presented in written form. Test-takers were required to (1) indicate whether each sentence was grammatical or ungrammatical, (2) indicate the degree of certainty of their judgment (as proposed by Sorace, 1996) by typing in a box a score on a scale marked from 0 to 100% and (3) to self-report whether they used 'rule' or 'feel' for each sentence. This test provided three separate measures; a percentage judgment accuracy score based on the participants' dichotomous responses, a percentage certainty score and a percentage score based on the participants' reported use of 'rule' in judging each item.

(5)   Metalinguistic Knowledge Test
This was an adaptation of an earlier test of metalanguage devised by Alderson *et al.* (1997). It consisted of an untimed computerized multiple-choice test in two parts. Part 1 presented test-takers with 17 ungrammatical sentences, based on the 17 structures, and required them to select the rule that best explained each error out of four choices provided. Part 2 consisted of two sections. In Section 1, the test-takers were asked to read a short text and then to find examples of 21 specific grammatical features from the text (e.g. 'preposition' and 'finite verb'). In Section 2, they were asked to identify the named grammatical parts in a set of sentences. A total percentage accuracy score was calculated. A copy of the Metalinguistic Knowledge Test can be found in Appendix D.

These tests were designed in accordance with four of the criteria for distinguishing implicit and explicit knowledge discussed above.[4] That is, it was predicted that each test would provide a relatively separate measure of either implicit or explicit knowledge according to how it mapped out on these criteria. Table 2.3 sets out these predictions. This shows that the Elicited Oral Imitation Test and the Oral Narrative Test were predicted to measure implicit knowledge because the test-takers would rely predominantly on feel, they would be under pressure to perform in real time, they would be focused primarily on meaning and they would have no reason to access their metalanguage. In contrast, the Metalinguistic Knowledge Test was predicted to measure explicit knowledge because it involved a high degree of awareness, was unpressured, focused attention on form and, obviously, required the use of metalinguistic knowledge. The two GJTs both required test-takers to focus attention primarily on form (as judging the correctness of sentences necessarily entails this). However, whereas the TGJT was predicted to measure primarily implicit knowledge because it encouraged the use of 'feel', was time-pressured and there was little need or opportunity to access metalinguistic knowledge, the UGJT was predicted to measure primarily explicit knowledge because it encouraged a high degree of awareness and was unpressured with the result that responses were more likely to involve metalinguistic knowledge.

Table 2.3 Design features of the tests in the test battery

Criterion	Oral Imitation	Oral Narrative	TGJT	UGJT	Meta-language
Degree of awareness	Feel	Feel	Feel	Rule	Rule
Time available	Pressured	Pressured	Pressured	Un-pressured	Un-pressured
Focus of attention	Meaning	Meaning	Form	Form	Form
Utility of knowledge of meta-language	No	No	No	Yes	Yes

Procedure

The tests were completed in the following order:

(1) Elicited Oral Imitation Test
(2) Oral Narrative test
(3) TGJT
(4) UGJT
(5) Metalinguistic Knowledge Test

All tests included a number of training examples for participants to practice on. The Elicited Oral Imitation Test was completed in one-on-one meetings between a researcher and a participant. Each participant listened to the sentences one at a time on a cassette recorder, completed an answer sheet indicating his/her response to the belief statement and then orally reproduced the sentence, which was audiorecorded. The Oral Narrative Test involved the participants listening to a narrative and then orally recording their retelling of it on a computer. The TGJT, the UGJT and the Metalinguistic Knowledge Test were completed individually on a computer in a private office. All the tests were completed in a single session lasting approximately two and a half hours.

The non-native participants also completed a background questionnaire that contained questions about their mother tongue, the age they started English, the number of years in an English-speaking country, other languages they had studied and the kind of instruction in English they had received at school.

Analysis

Descriptive statistics for the five tests were calculated. The reliability of the different test measures was calculated using Cronbach's alpha. Pearson Product Moment Coefficients were computed to examine the inter-relationships between the various test measures.

As reported in Ellis (2005), a Principal Component Factor Analysis (SPSS Version 11.5) was then carried out with a view to investigating the predictions about the type of knowledge each test measured. It was predicted that in a two-factor solution the Imitation Test, Oral Narrative Test and the TGJT would load on one factor (implicit knowledge) and the UGJT and Metalinguistic Knowledge Test (explicit knowledge) on the other factor. Isemonger (2007) criticized Ellis (2005) for using a Principal Components Factor Analysis on the grounds that the design of the study afforded precise predictions, which therefore needed to be tested using a Confirmatory Factor Analysis. Isemonger also suggested that an alternative solution to the one predicted by the design of the study (as shown in Table 2.3) needed to be tested. He argued that it was quite possible that the test scores would vary more significantly in terms of whether they constituted measures of production or of judgment. Responding to these criticisms, Ellis and Loewen (2007) carried out two Confirmatory Factor Analyses using AMOS 5.0 (Arbuckle, 2004). The first analysis tested the construct solution predicted by the design of the tests (i.e. that the Elicited Oral Imitation Test, the Oral Narrative Test and the UGJT would load on an 'implicit' factor and that the UGJT (ungram.) and the Metalinguistic Test would load on an 'explicit' factor). The second analysis tested the alternative method solution proposed by Isemonger.[5] In this solution, it was predicted that the Oral Imitation Test and the Oral Narrative Test would load on a 'production' factor, while the TGJT, the UGJT and the Metalinguistic Test would all load on a 'judgment' factor. In this chapter, only the Confirmatory Factor Analyses will be reported.

Results

Table 2.4 shows the measure of reliability for each test for the sample investigated. These varied between a high of 0.90 for the Metalinguistic Knowledge Test and 0.81 for the TGJT.

Table 2.5 presents the means and standard deviations for the five measures separately for the native speakers and L2 learners. The native speakers achieved scores close to 100% on all measures except TGJT (ungram.) and Metalinguistic Knowledge. Their scores exceeded those of the L2 learners on all measures except Metalinguistic Knowledge. The L2 learners scored highest on the UGJT measures. Both the native speakers and the L2 learners scored markedly higher on the grammatical than on the ungrammatical sentences in the TGJT. As might be expected, the L2

Table 2.4 Reliability measures for the five tests

Test	Number of items	Number of non-native participants	Reliability
Imitation Test	44	91	$\alpha = 0.88$
Narrative Test	Variable obligatory occasions	83	$r = 0.85$ (inter-rater agreement)
TGJT	68	91	$\alpha = 0.81$
UGJT	68	91	$\alpha = 0.83$
Metalinguistic Knowledge	41	91	$\alpha = 0.90$

Table 2.5 Descriptive statistics for the five tests

Test	Native speakers			L2 learners		
	Percentage	SD	n	Percentage	SD	n
Imitation	94	4.1	20	51	17.20	91
Oral Narrative	99	2.1	15	72	14.25	83
TGJT	80	10.02	18	54	11.80	91
UGJT	96	1.55	19	82	10.50	91
Metalinguistic Knowledge	57	7.37	20	53	20.73	91

learners manifested considerably greater intergroup variance than the native speakers on all the tests, as reflected in the standard deviations.

Table 2.6 shows the correlation matrix for the L2 learners' performance on the five tests. All the tests were intercorrelated with coefficients between all pairs of tests reaching statistical significance at the 0.05 level or higher. Metalinguistic Knowledge, however, was not as strongly related to the other measures as were the other tests.

A decision was taken to examine the psychometric properties of the grammatical and ungrammatical sentences in the UGJT separately. This was motivated by previous research (Bialystok, 1979; Hedgcock, 1993), which pointed to the fact that L2 learners respond differently to the grammatical and ungrammatical sentences in a GJT. Hedgcock (1993: 15) for example commented that although 'it would be ill-advised to claim that subjects rely on *different* L2 data bases or cognitive processes in

Table 2.6 Correlational matrix for the five tests (L2 learners)

Test	Imitation (n =91)	Oral Narrative (n =83)	TGJT (n =91)	UGJT (n =91)	Metalinguistic Knowledge (n =91)
Imitation		0.48**	0.58**	0.59**	0.28**
Oral Narrative			0.36**	0.36**	0.27*
TGJT				0.57**	0.24*
UGJT					0.60**

*$p = 0.05$.
**$p = 0.01$.

Table 2.7 Correlations between scores for the grammatical and ungrammatical sentences in the UGJT and other test measures

UGJT	Imitation	Oral Narrative	TGJT	Metalinguistic Knowledge
Grammatical	0.58**	0.37**	0.62**	0.27*
Ungrammatical	0.38**	0.26*	0.33**	0.63**

approving well-formed strings and in rejecting ungrammatical strings' nevertheless 'such a possibility is not entirely implausible'. He went on to suggest that 'positing autonomous L2 knowledge systems... is an attractive way of accounting for variable performance across learners and tasks'. Pearson Product Moment Coefficients were calculated between the grammatical and ungrammatical sentences in the UGJT and all other test measures. The results are shown in Table 2.7. The grammatical sentences' scores correlated significantly with the other tests. but more strongly with the Elicited Oral Imitation Test, Oral Narrative Test and TGJT than with the Metalinguistic Knowledge Test. In contrast, the ungrammatical sentences' scores correlated very strongly with the Metalinguistic Knowledge Test ($r = 0.67$) and less strongly with the other tests, especially the Elicited Oral Imitation and Oral Narrative Tests. This suggested that in the case of the UGJT the scores for the ungrammatical sentences would provide a better measure of explicit knowledge than the scores for the grammatical sentences or total scores.

Figures 2.1 and 2.2 show the results of the Confirmatory Factor Analyses. Figure 2.1 gives the implicit/explicit solution, while Figure 2.2 shows the production/judgment solution. Table 2.8 provides a summary of the model fit for both solutions, with the chi-square statistic testing the

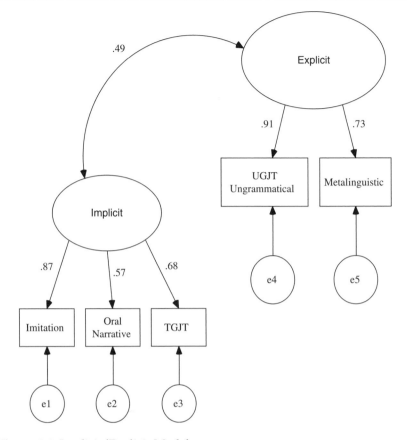

Figure 2.1 Implicit/Explicit Model

goodness of fit presented in the second left-hand column. A significant chi-square value indicates that the model is statistically *not* likely to occur, whereas, a nonsignificant value indicates an acceptable model (Byrne, 2001). In the current analysis, the chi-square value for the Implicit/Explicit model is not significant; however, the chi-square value for the Judgment/Production model is significant. Additionally, Byrne (2001) indicates that a Normed Fit Index (NFI) value of greater than 0.95 indicates a superior fit and that a root mean square error of approximation (RMSEA) value of less than 0.05 indicates a good fit for the model. Thus, according to these indicators, the Implicit/Explicit model is an acceptable model, while the Judgment/Production model is not.

These results can be summarized as follows:

(1) All five tests were shown to be reliable.
(2) The native speakers outscored the L2 learners on all tests except the Metalinguistic Knowledge Test.

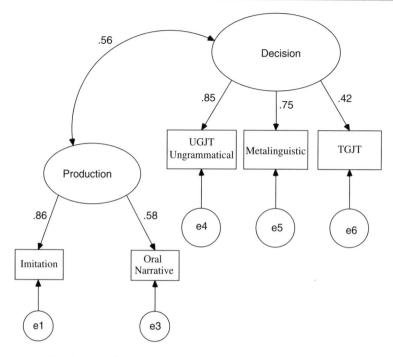

Figure 2.2 Production/Decision Model

Table 2.8 Summary of the model of fit for both solutions

Model	χ^2	NFI	RMSEA	df
Implicit/Explicit	1.191	0.991	0.000	4
Decision/Production	29.150**	0.784	0.259	4

Note: NFI = normed fit index, RMSEA = root mean square error of approximation.
**$p < 0.001$.

(3) All the tests were significantly intercorrelated. Correlations involving the Metalinguistic Knowledge Test were noticeably weaker.

(4) The grammatical and ungrammatical sentences in the UGJT behaved differently. The ungrammatical sentences correlated more strongly with the Metalinguistic Knowledge Test, while the grammatical sentences correlated more strongly with the Elicited Oral Imitation Test. It was decided to use the ungrammatical sentences as a measure of explicit knowledge.

(5) Confirmatory Factor Analysis supported the prediction that the Elicited Oral Imitation Test, the Oral Narrative Test and the TGJT would load strongly on one factor, while the ungrammatical UGJT

scores and Metalinguistic Knowledge Test would load on a second factor. The solution supported the claim that these tests were providing relatively separate measures of implicit and explicit knowledge.

(6) A Confirmatory Factor Analysis did not support a solution based on production versus judgment. That is, there was no evidence to show that the Elicited Oral Imitation Test and the Oral Narrative Test loaded on one factor and the other tests on a second factor.

Demonstrating the validity of the tests

Subsequent analyses explored the validity of the tests by examining to what extent they manifested the characteristics of implicit or explicit knowledge reflected in the criteria described in Table 2.1.

(1) Degree of awareness

It was predicted that the tests of explicit knowledge would encourage the conscious use of 'rule', while the tests of implicit knowledge would favor 'feel'. To test this prediction, Pearson Product Moment Coefficients of Correlation were computed between the measure of the learners' application of 'Rule' in the UGJT and all the other measures. It was predicted that Rule would correlate more strongly with accuracy of judgment in the UGJT (ungrammatical sentences) and also with scores on the Metalinguistic Judgment Test than with scores on the Elicited Oral Imitation Test, Oral Narrative Test and the TGJT (grammatical and ungrammatical sentences). Table 2.9 shows the results of this analysis. Low correlations between Rule and the measures of implicit knowledge were found, whereas statistically significant correlations (at the 0.01 level) were observed between Rule and UGJT (ungram.) and Metalinguistic Knowledge. Rule, however, was not related to UGJT (gram.) but, as we have already seen, this did not constitute a convincing measure of explicit knowledge.

(2) Time available

It was predicted that the time-pressured tests would require learners to rely on their implicit knowledge, whereas the unpressured tests would permit learners to draw on their explicit as well as their implicit knowledge. The time-pressured tests were the Elicited Oral Imitation Test, the Oral Narrative Test and the TGJT, while the unpressured tests were the UGJT and the Metalinguistic Test. As depicted in Figure 2.1 and Table 2.8, the Confirmatory Factor Analysis showed that the unpressured and pressured tests loaded on different factors. Also, if we assume that, in general, learners will perform better on the unpressured tests than the pressured tests because they will be able to supplement their implicit knowledge

Table 2.9 Correlations between Use of Rule and the Test Measures

	Imitation	Oral Narrative	TGJT (gram.)	TGJT (ungram.)	UGJT (gram)	UGJT (ungram)	Metalinguistic Knowledge
Rule	− 0.03	0.03	0.12	0.07	0.08	0.32**	0.37**

with their explicit knowledge, a difference in mean scores on the two groups of tests can be expected. The mean score for all learners' performance on the pressured tests was 57.3% and on the unpressured tests was 65.9%. This difference was statistically significant ($t = 4.54$; df $= 84$; $p = 0.001$). The effects of time pressure can be best assessed by comparing the TGJT and UGJT, as these tests were otherwise identical in content and method. The mean score for the TGJT was 53.9%, while for the UGJT it was 82.1%. Again, this difference was statistically significant ($t = 12.60$; df $= 87$; $p = 0.000$).[6]

(3) Focus of attention

It was predicted that the tests that required learners to focus on meaning would elicit implicit knowledge, whereas the tests that encouraged learners to focus on form would elicit explicit knowledge. Two tests required a focus on meaning – the Elicited Oral Imitation Test and the Oral Narrative Test. Both these tests loaded heavily on Factor 1 in the Confirmatory Factory Analysis reported in Figure 2.1 and Table 2.8. The TGJT, which requires a focus on form, also loaded on this factor but less heavily. The UGJT (ungrammatical), which requires a focus on form, loaded heavily on Factor 2. However, this hypothesis cannot be properly tested in this study as the focus and time-pressure variables were confounded in the design of the tests.

(4) Systematicity

It was predicted that the tests of implicit knowledge would elicit more systematic (less variable) responses than tests of explicit knowledge. Inspecting the standard deviations for the different measures tested this prediction. The prediction would be supported if it could be shown that the tests of implicit knowledge resulted in lower standard deviations than the tests of explicit knowledge. Table 2.5 shows that, on balance, the standard deviations were in fact higher on the tests of explicit knowledge, especially in the case of the Metalinguistic Knowledge Test. However, a direct comparison of the standard deviations of the TGJT and UGJT shows a higher standard deviation in the former (i.e. 11.80 versus 10.50), possibly because the pressured nature of the TGJT induced greater randomness in behavior. Thus, the evidence does not provide clear support for this hypothesis.

(5) Certainty

It was predicted that the tests of implicit knowledge would elicit more certain responses from learners than the tests of explicit knowledge. The UGJT asked participants to indicate the degree to which they were certain (on a percentage scale) of their judgments.

As we have seen, the grammatical and ungrammatical sentences in this test functioned somewhat differently, with the grammatical sentences correlating more strongly with the measures of implicit knowledge and the ungrammatical sentences with the measures of explicit knowledge. Pearson Product Moment Correlations between the measure of certainty and scores for the grammatical and ungrammatical sentences were computed. Both coefficients were statistically significant at the 0.01 level ($r = 0.32$ for the grammatical sentences and $r = 0.31$ for the ungrammatical). To further test the hypothesis, correlations between the participants' reported use of Rule and their Certainty scores for each item in the UGJT were calculated. It was predicted that these would be generally negative or very low (i.e. the participants would tend to be less certain when they used an explicit rule to make a judgment). However, most of the correlations (i.e. 55 coefficients out of 68) between Certainty and Rule were statistically significant at the 0.05 level or higher, indicating a generally strong relationship between the participants' level of certainty and their use of explicit knowledge in this test. Thus, the results did not support the prediction.

(6) Utility of metalinguistic knowledge

It was predicted that the tests of explicit knowledge would encourage fuller use of metalinguistic knowledge than the tests of implicit knowledge. The correlations reported in Tables 2.6 and 2.9 lend support to this prediction. Scores on the Metalinguistic Knowledge Test were more strongly related to scores on the UGJT Total ($r = 0.60$) and to UGJT Ungrammatical ($r = 0.64$) than to scores on the Elicited Oral Imitation Test ($r = 0.28$), the Oral Narrative Test ($r = 0.27$) and the TGJT ($r = 0.24$). However, it should be noted that although the correlations between Metalinguistic Knowledge and the tests claimed to measure implicit knowledge were weak, they were statistically significant.

(7) Learnability

It was predicted that scores on the tests of implicit knowledge would relate more strongly to the age the learners started learning the L2 than to years of classroom instruction, while the opposite would be the case for scores on tests of explicit knowledge. Table 2.10 shows the correlations for 'starting age' and 'years of formal instruction' and the different test measures. Starting age was related negatively to the TGJT (i.e. the older learners were when they began learning, the less well they performed on this test), but the correlations between starting age and the other tests deemed to measure implicit knowledge (i.e. the Elicited Imitation Test and the

Table 2.10 Correlations between starting age/years of formal instruction and test measures

	Imitation	Oral Narrative	TGJT	UGJT (gram)	UGJT (ungram)	Metalinguistic Knowledge
Starting age	− 0.11	0.03	− 0.23*	− 0.05	− 0.02	0.05
Years of formal instruction	0.10	− 0.05	0.17	0.03	0.27*	0.18

Oral Narrative Test) did not reach statistical significance. Correlations between starting age and the measures of explicit knowledge were all nonsignificant and very weak. Years of formal instruction was positively related to UGJT (ungram.), but not to the other measure of explicit knowledge (Metalinguistic Knowledge). No statistically significant relationship between this variable and the measures of implicit knowledge was observed.

The results of the validation analyses can be summarized as follows:

(1) The learners' awareness of the underlying rules of the grammatical structures related significantly to scores in the explicit tests but not to scores in the implicit tests.
(2) Learners' performance on the tests with and without time pressure differed significantly.
(3) Learners' performance on the tests where the focus was on meaning and where the focus was on form also differed significantly.
(4) There was only limited evidence to show that the learners' responses in the implicit tests were more systematic than their responses in the explicit tests.
(5) The tests of implicit knowledge did not elicit more certain responses from learners than the tests of explicit knowledge.
(6) The learners' metalinguistic knowledge was more clearly related to the test of explicit knowledge than to the tests of implicit knowledge.
(7) Starting age was related to one of the tests of implicit knowledge while years of formal instruction was related to one of the tests of explicit knowledge.

Discussion

The main purpose of the study was to demonstrate that tests could be designed to provide relatively separate measures of L2 implicit and explicit knowledge that were reliable and valid. To this end, operational definitions of the two types of knowledge were constructed. These served to draw up the specifications for five tests. With a view to establishing the validity of these specifications, the operational definitions that formed the basis for the tests were investigated using the scores obtained from the tests.

The reliability of four of the tests for the sample in this study was examined by computing the internal consistency of responses to the items that made up each test. The Cronbach's alpha coefficients all exceeded 0.80 (generally considered demonstrating a satisfactory level of reliability in social science research). The reliability of the Oral Narrative

Test was determined by means of inter-rater agreement. This was also above 0.80.

A comparison of the performance of the native speakers and L2 learners on the five tests lends support to the overall validity of the five tests. Whereas native speakers can be expected to possess higher levels of implicit knowledge than L2 learners, they cannot necessarily be expected to demonstrate higher levels of explicit knowledge, as L2 learners may have benefited in this respect from formal instruction in the L2. The results show that the native speakers outperformed the L2 learners on the three tests that measured implicit knowledge (the Elicited Oral Imitation Test, the Oral Narrative Test and the TGJT). They also outperformed the L2 learners on the UGJT, designed to measure explicit knowledge, but the difference in scores on this test was much smaller than the differences on the tests of implicit knowledge. Further, the native speakers and L2 learners performed very similarly on the other test of explicit knowledge, the Metalinguistic Knowledge Test.

The L2 learners' scores on all five tests were intercorrelated (see Tables 2.6 and 2.9). However, the shared variance between any pair of tests did not exceed 45% and was as low as 6.4%. Overall, then, the correlations do not support Oller's (1979) claim that L2 proficiency is unitary in nature. The Confirmatory Factor Analyses reported in Figure 2.1 and Table 2.8 demonstrated that the tests are, in fact, measuring two different constructs. Test scores loaded largely as predicted on two factors (i.e. the Elicited Oral Imitation Test, the Oral Narrative Test and the TGJT on one factor and the UGJT (ungrammatical sentences) and the Metalinguistic Knowledge Test on the other factor). The Elicited Oral Imitation Test and the Metalinguistic Knowledge Test can be seen as the 'best' respective measures of implicit and explicit knowledge (i.e. they load the heaviest on their respective factors). In short, there was congruence between the results of the factor analysis, the constructs underlying the test specifications and SLA theory. A second Confirmatory Factor Analysis was performed to examine whether the tests could be better understood in terms of the distinction between production (i.e. the Elicited Oral Imitation Test and the Oral Narrative Test) and judgment (i.e. the TGJT and UGJT and the Metalinguistic Knowledge Test). The judgment/production model, however, was found to be not acceptable. In short, these analyses suggest that the primary purpose of the study was largely achieved – that is, the tests afforded relatively separate measures of implicit and explicit knowledge.

The results also showed that it was important to distinguish between the grammatical and ungrammatical sentences in the GJTs. In the case of the UGJT, in particular, the grammatical and ungrammatical sentences appear to be measuring different constructs, with the latter providing a more convincing measure of explicit knowledge. A more detailed analysis of the GJT scores (see Chapter 4) indicates that they differ significantly on two dimensions (timed versus untimed; grammatical versus ungrammatical). This has important implications for the use of this kind of test in SLA research. In particular, it suggests that SLA researchers need to take great care to distinguish these two properties in both the design of GJTs and the analysis of scores obtained from tests, as they will influence what is being measured.

With a view to demonstrating the validity of the test constructs, a number of predictions were investigated. In general, the results support the construct validity of the tests. Thus, both tests of explicit knowledge were strongly related to the learners' reported use of Rule in the UGJT, while the tests of implicit knowledge were only weakly related to this measure. The three tests that incorporated time pressure all loaded on the implicit knowledge factor, while the two unpressured tests loaded on the explicit knowledge factor. The difference in the standard deviations of the Oral Imitation and Metalinguistic Knowledge Tests lent some support to the claim that there is greater systematicity in learners' implicit knowledge. The UGJT (ungram), as a measure of explicit knowledge, is more strongly related to metalinguistic knowledge than the other tests, as measures of implicit knowledge. One of the tests of implicit knowledge (the TGJT) was related to learners' starting age, while the test of explicit knowledge (UGJT – ungram.) was related to the number of years that learners had undergone formal instruction. Only one of the seven constructs investigated failed to receive any support; the learners appeared to be more certain of their responses to the test items when accessing their explicit knowledge. This may reflect the fact that many of the participants, especially those with lower levels of proficiency, lacked confidence in their implicit knowledge of many of the grammatical structures tested, as these are known to be late acquired (e.g. question tags and hypothetical conditionals). Also, one of the predictions (relating to the distinction between focus on form and meaning) could not be properly tested as these variables were conflated in the design of the tests. Overall, however, the construct validity of the tests receives empirical support from the analyses of the scores obtained from them.

Limitations

The Marsden Project is exploratory in nature. The challenge in the study reported in this chapter was to identify tests that provide relatively separate measures of implicit and explicit L2 knowledge. Although the results suggest that this challenge was largely successful, there are a number of limitations of the study.

The reliability of the tests for the sample investigated was established. However, it cannot be assumed that the instruments themselves are reliable, as reliability is a property of how a particular sample responded to the testing instruments, not of the instruments themselves. In the case of the present study, the sample was heavily biased towards Chinese learners.

The Oral Narrative Test did not provide a measure of all 17 structures, as it was not possible to design a narrative that would create obligatory occasions for all of them. Thus, the scores for the test were based on just five structures – regular past tense, modal verbs, third person -s, plural -s, indefinite article and possessive -s – all of which were morphological. This may explain why the loading for the Oral Narrative Test in the Confirmatory Factor Analysis (see Figure 2.1) was the lowest of the three implicit tests.

Isemonger (2007) queried whether the TGJT constitutes a measure of implicit knowledge given that the test invites a judgment of the correctness of sentences, which he considers 'metalinguistic'. To an extent, Isemonger seems to miss the point. Speakers of a language are perfectly able to decide whether a particular usage is grammatical without any explicit knowledge of the rule/feature involved. They do so on the basis of their implicit knowledge. Indeed, the plethora of studies that have utilized GJTs have been based on precisely this assumption. The rationale for the TGJT was that learners would only be able to judge the sentences on the basis of their implicit knowledge because the speed of the response required precluded them accessing their explicit knowledge. However, Isemonger's doubt is in part justified. Clearly, judging the grammaticality of sentences does invite a metalinguistic response, even if the test is time-pressured. Also, the results indicate that the TGJT was less clearly a measure of implicit knowledge than the Elicited Oral Imitation Test (i.e. it had a factor loading of 0.68 compared with 0.87 for the Elicited Oral Imitation Test).

Isemonger (2007: 110) also pointed out that 'constructs should be operationalized in as many ways as possible'. In the study, implicit knowledge was operationalized in three tests and explicit knowledge in two tests. Ideally, additional tests would have strengthened the study. However, the resources available for the project did not permit more extensive testing. Also, there is a limit to how many tests participants can be reasonably asked to complete. Hopefully, future studies will investigate further ways of operationalizing implicit and explicit knowledge.

Finally, it should be pointed out that the study only examined the distinction between implicit and explicit knowledge in relation to grammar. The distinction is also relevant to other areas of language (e.g. lexis and pragmatic knowledge). Whether it is possible to develop tests that distinguish the two knowledge types in these other areas remains to be shown.

Conclusion

There is an obvious need for tests that can provide relatively separate measures of implicit and explicit L2 knowledge. This need is evident both in the field of SLA and in language testing.

In the case of SLA, irrespective of one's theoretical orientation, it is important to be able to distinguish between learners' implicit and explicit knowledge of an L2. In particular, until this is achieved, it will not be possible to test the interface/noninterface hypotheses that lie at the center of so much current debate in SLA (see Chapter 1). Surprisingly, however, SLA researchers have made few attempts to develop instruments capable of distinguishing these two types of knowledge. Indeed, as Douglas (2001) has pointed out, researchers have conspicuously failed to make the effort to demonstrate the validity (and reliability) of their testing instruments. This constitutes a major weakness in the discipline.

In contrast, in language testing, there has been a constant and sophisticated examination of the reliability and construct validity of instruments designed to measure language proficiency. However, the models of L2 proficiency that have informed test construction have generally not been supported by psychometric analyses of the tests designed to investigate them. Oller's (1979) Unitary Competence Hypothesis, which claimed that language proficiency is comprised of a single underlying construct ('pragmatic expectancy grammar'), was rejected on the grounds that Oller failed to include an oral test of proficiency and also that the factorial analyses he employed were inconclusive (see Baker (1989) for a discussion). Subsequent attempts to validate models of proficiency based on a modular view of 'communicative competence' have not fared much better. For example, Harley *et al.* (1990) examined the validity of Canale and Swain's (1980) model of communicative competence by developing a battery of tests for measuring different components of competence (grammatical, discourse and sociolinguistic) using three different methods (oral, written and multiple choice), but a confirmatory factor analysis failed to support the model. Attempts to build models of proficiency based on the construct of 'ability to use' as mediating between underlying competence and performance conditions (e.g. Bachman, 1990; Bachman & Palmer, 1996) have also failed to find clear empirical support. More recently, Skehan (1998) has attempted to build a psycholinguistic model of proficiency that incorporates both a language dimension (where lexically based and rule-based knowledge of language are distinguished) and a language-processing dimension (based on a limited-capacity short-term memory) and to explore how different tasks affect the fluency, complexity and accuracy of learners' production. However, Iwashita *et al.*'s (2001) attempt to validate Skehan's (1998) model in the context of a tape-based test of oral proficiency failed to show the expected differences in the quality of language produced when various dimensions of tasks were manipulated. Obviously, the choice of a model of language proficiency to serve as the basis for the development of language tests must take account of a number of factors (e.g. the purpose of the test, the target domain of language use and the likely backwash effect). One such factor, however, ought to be the psycholinguistic validity of the underlying model, as this can be demonstrated empirically. In this respect, the models referred to above have not been conspicuously successful.

The development of tests, whether in SLA or in language testing, depends on a clear and theoretically based description of the constructs involved. To this end, this chapter has examined previous L2 studies of implicit/explicit knowledge and reported two studies (Ellis, 2005; Han & Ellis, 1998) that investigated the psychometric properties of tests based on theoretically derived criteria for distinguishing the two types of knowledge. Both studies indicate that it is possible to develop tests that successfully discriminate between implicit and explicit knowledge of L2 grammar. The study reported in this chapter, in particular, demonstrated that an Elicited Oral Imitation Test afforded a convincing measure of implicit knowledge, while the ungrammatical sentences in a UGJT provided a solid measure of explicit knowledge.

The following chapters in this section of the book provide a closer study of four of the tests in the Marsden Study. Chapter 3 examines the Elicited Oral Imitation Test. Chapter 4 analyzes the results for the TGJT and UGJT. Chapter 5 reports on a validation study of one part of the Metalinguistic Knowledge Test.

Notes

1. Green and Hecht's finding that there was a gap between their learners' ability to correct errors and to verbalize the rules involved was interpreted as reflecting a difference between implicit and explicit knowledge. However, another equally valid interpretation could be that it reflected the difference between what the learners knew explicitly and what they could actually verbalize.
2. Not all the participants completed all tests. The actual numbers completing each test are shown in Table 2.4.
3. A reviewer of a draft version of the article on which this chapter is based expressed concern that the participants were not asked to correct the sentences in the TGJT, thus making it difficult to know exactly what they were responding to in the sentences. This must be acknowledged as a weakness of the test. However, in piloting the test, it was felt that the pressured nature of test made it extremely demanding and that to have required test-takers to also produce corrections would have overloaded the resources of many of them.
4. The other three criteria were systematicity, certainty and learnability. Systematicity did not constitute a design feature for any of the tests although

it was examined in a *post-hoc* analysis of the test scores (see Results section). Certainty was a design feature in only one of the tests (the UGJT) and for this reason is not included in Table 2.4. Learnability is a characteristic of learners, which was also considered *post-hoc*.

5. In fact, the solutions of the Principal Components and the Confirmatory factor analyses were more or less identical.

6. In fact, a detailed analysis suggests that time-pressure in the two GJTs interacted with the grammaticality of the sentences. A univariate ANOVA found a significant difference in the four sets of scores ($F = 253.33$; df = 3; $p = 000$) while a *post hoc* Scheffe test indicated three subsets; (1) TGJT (ungrammatical), (2) TGJT (grammatical) and UGJT (ungrammatical) and (3) TGJT (ungrammatical) and UGJT (grammatical). In other words, the learners' responses in the GJTs were not solely the product of time-pressure. A more detailed analysis of results obtained from the two GJTs is provided in Chapter 4.

Chapter 3

The Elicited Oral Imitation Test as a Measure of Implicit Knowledge[1]

ROSEMARY ERLAM

Introduction

At first sight, it may seem rather surprising that, in designing a test of implicit language knowledge, we should choose to turn to elicited imitation (EI), a method of language testing with a rather chequered history and one which Gallimore and Tharp (1981: 369) say is viewed with a 'certain disquiet'. Whatever happened to the oral production test? the reader may ask. Why would we choose a testing method that has participants listening to and then repeating statements that someone else has produced, statements that are, furthermore, usually decontextualized? Surely, in terms of validity, such a test compares unfavorably with a spontaneous production test where participants have to produce their own language according to their own resources. Furthermore, a spontaneous production test seems more obviously to satisfy the criteria that have been established in Chapter 2 for a test of implicit knowledge, that is, the learner responds according to 'feel' in a context where the focus is on meaning, and there is time-pressure. A key problem, however, with measures of free language production is that, while they may provide a large sample of natural speech, there is no way of predicting which particular language structures will be elicited. This means that relying on spontaneous language production as a method of eliciting language production is limited, most notably in research contexts, where there is often the need to test for acquisition of the specific language features that have been targeted as the research focus. These difficulties perhaps explain why, as has already been noted in Chapter 2, most research to date that has investigated the effectiveness of second language (L2) instruction has employed measures that tap controlled language use and that therefore may permit learners to use their explicit knowledge (Norris & Ortega, 2000), rather than measures that allow students to use spontaneous, fluent and contextualized language (Ellis, 2002). Clearly, there is a need for alternative and more practical measures of implicit knowledge.

The Elicited Imitation Test

The EI test is not 'new'; according to Vinther (2002) it has a 35-year history and has been used within three major areas, that is, child language research, neuropsychological research and second language (L2) research. I was first introduced to EI while working as a speech-language therapist in the 1980s. EI was used as a means of assessing children who were suspected of having either delayed or disordered language. The technique used, one that is, furthermore, typical of most EI tests, involved reading aloud an utterance to the test participant and having him/her repeat it as exactly as possible. Some researchers (e.g. Kelch, 1985) have further extended the use of this basic technique and applied it to written imitation. This chapter will, however, limit itself to a discussion of oral EI only.

The use of EI is not without controversy. I have already referred to Gallimore and Tharp's 'certain disquiet' (1981: 369); Vinther (2002) documents that throughout its history, EI has at times been accepted and at other times rejected. She documents that EI has been described as too 'slippery'. The 'slipperiness' of EI is explained by the uncertainty surrounding the neurolinguistic processes involved in having test participants repeat a given stimulus. The crucial question is whether imitation requires them to decode and interpret the stimulus before they reproduce it, or whether they can merely repeat the stimulus verbatim without having comprehended it. This dilemma was encapsulated by Markman *et al.* (1975) who used EI to investigate the French language competence of English learners in a French immersion context. They concluded that there were two factors at play in the data that they obtained. The first they termed a 'memory factor', where those students with reasonable exposure to French were able to reproduce whole sentences exactly as presented, replicating both correct and deviant target features. The second they termed an 'internalised grammar factor', where they found evidence that students had manipulated grammatical structures in a manner that was consistent with their own internal grammar. The second of these factors is, of course, crucial for our defense of the use of an EI as a measure of implicit knowledge. It is important to ascertain that EI does require the learner to process the stimulus that they receive and that correct imitation of a specific target language structure is evidence that it is part of the learner's internal grammar or interlanguage system. In summary, we need to be able to claim that EI is reconstructive, requiring the learner to process the stimulus, and that it does not allow for the simple rote imitation of stimuli presented.

The Reconstructive Nature of Elicited Imitation Tests

In order to examine the question of whether EI tests are reconstructive, it is important to consider evidence from research in cognitive psychology and from research in EI itself. Over the last 30 years, within the field of cognitive psychology, there has been a considerable focus on memory. The concept of working memory has replaced the traditional concept of static short-term memory in which the emphasis was on the ability to store information passively (Carroll, 1962). According to Baddeley (1999), working memory is responsible for both manipulating and temporarily storing information. The ability of working memory to process language is believed to be influenced by the knowledge a learner already has about that language (Speciale *et al.*, 2004). Evidence for this claim comes from research conducted by Gathercole and Baddeley (1993) who asked speakers of English to repeat lists of English words and lists of Aymara words (see Table 3.1). Their participants had had no exposure to Aymara. Unsurprisingly, Gathercole and Baddeley found that they did significantly better at repeating the lists of English words.

N. Ellis (2001) gives a convincing explanation of why this should be the case: participants had not had any experience with the material they were being asked to repeat and so had not had the opportunity to build up long-term memory representations. N. Ellis (2001: 48) adds: 'this is why elicited imitation tests serve so well as measures of second-language competence'. The results of such research has demonstrated that, in processing language, the capacity of working memory is determined by the stored knowledge that already exists about the language (Baddeley *et al.*, 1998).

Additional evidence for why EI tasks may be reconstructive in nature comes from research conducted by Sachs (1967), demonstrating that memory for the *meaning* of a sentence is retained for longer than memory for the *form* of a sentence. Sachs asked participants to remember the following (original) sentence:

> There he met an archeologist, Howard Carter, who urged him to join in the search for the tomb of King Tut.

Table 3.1 Gathercole and Baddeley's (1993) lists of Aymara and English words

Aymara	*English*
wayna	sick
usuta	leg
cayu	new
machaka	this
aca	flower
pankara	but
uncampisa	to sleep

After a short interval, she then presented them with the following sentence and asked whether it was the same as or different to the original sentence:

There he met an archeologist, Howard Carter, and urged him to join in the search for the tomb of King Tut.

Seven of eight participants noticed that the two sentences were different. Sachs then repeated the procedure showing participants the original sentence, and presenting them, after a short interval, with the following:

There he met an archeologist, Howard Carter, who urged that he join in the search for the tomb of King Tut.

This time, only one in eight students noticed that the two sentences were different. Sachs concluded that while memory for details of syntax and vocabulary are lost soon after a sentence has been comprehended, memory for meaning is retained for longer.

In another study, Potter and Lombardi (1999) presented participants with sentences, each of which contained a critical word. In the following example, the critical word, unknown to the participants, was *home*.

They moved into their new home a week after he started his job.

Participants were then shown a list of words, one of which was synonymous with the critical word. In the case of the example given above, one of the words which participants saw was *house*. When they were then asked to recall the sentence they had read, participants typically used either of these two words (i.e. *home* or *house*). These results again demonstrate that memory for details of vocabulary and, by extension, syntax are lost soon after a sentence has been comprehended. Potter and Lombardi concluded that when a sentence is recalled it is regenerated from a representation of its meaning.

Additional evidence for the fact that EI tasks can be reconstructive and that responses reflect the degree to which participants are able to assimilate a given stimulus into an internal grammar (Munnich *et al.*, 1982) come from EI studies themselves.

Bley-Vroman and Chaudron (1994) document evidence from EI studies that corroborates the results from research in cognitive psychology, which have been reviewed above. They state that the more you know of a foreign language, the better you can imitate the sentences of that language. Scott's research (1994), looking at the relationship between auditory memory and success on an imitation task, provides convincing evidence of this. Scott found that success in repeating words, phrases and sentences of increasing length in Spanish was greater for 'bilingual' participants who had some knowledge of Spanish than for participants who hadn't and who were thus unable to use meaning to aid retention. Bley-Vroman and Chaudron (1994: 247) also document evidence for what they term an 'abstract meaning level' that can be assessed in EI, when messages are not repeated word for word but when participants produce a different sentence that captures the same meaning as the original.

Arguably the most convincing evidence for the fact that utterances that participants are given to repeat pass through a 'filter of existing grammatical knowledge' (Vinther, 2002: 57) rather than just being reproduced verbatim, comes from an innovative adaptation of the standard EI test, where participants are given ungrammatical as well as grammatical sentences to imitate. Slobin and Welsh (1968) were perhaps the first to do this, and found that their participant imitated ungrammatical sentences as long as they did not exceed her memory span, but that she changed them into correct sentences if they were longer. In two other studies (Hamayan *et al.*, 1977; Munnich *et al.*, 1994), learners were also presented with a group of sentences, some of which were grammatical and some of which were ungrammatical. They were simply asked to repeat the sentences that they had heard. In both studies, significant numbers of participants converted the ungrammatical to grammatical sentences. Hamayan *et al.* (1977) refer to this as the normalization of sentences. In yet another study (Markman *et al.*, 1975), native speakers of French and learners of French were given both grammatical and ungrammatical sentences in French to repeat. While learners did correct ungrammatical sentences, the native speakers corrected significantly more deviant sentences. Munnich *et al.* (1994) conclude that if EI simply involved rote imitation, participants would 'parrot' ungrammatical sentences rather than spontaneously correcting them. Their acceptance or rejection of grammatical violations was, they claim, a powerful indication of their knowledge of constraints on grammar. Hamayan *et al.* (1977) called for further investigation of the empirical relationship between elicited repetition and normalizations.

From the literature to date, evidence suggests that EI tests may be reconstructive, requiring learners to process language stimuli, rather than allowing them to repeat verbatim what they have heard:

(1) The capacity of working memory is determined by the stored knowledge that learners already have (Baddeley *et al.*, 1998; Gathercole & Baddeley, 1993; Scott, 1994).
(2) Memory for the meaning of a sentence is retained longer than memory for form (Potter & Lombardi, 1990; Sachs, 1967).
(3) Grammatically incorrect sentences are spontaneously corrected (Markman *et al.*, 1975; Munnich *et al.*, 1994; Slobin & Welsh, 1968).

It must be acknowledged at this point, however, that EI is not always reconstructive. Bley-Vroman and Chaudron (1994) point out that possessing the appropriate linguistic knowledge is not always necessary for candidates to be able to imitate stimuli successfully. They point to evidence that learners can accurately imitate sentences with linguistic features that they have not mastered. Similarly, they document examples of repetition that are not only accurate for meaning, but also for particular wording and even for details of pronunciation. They argue that these suggest that a lower level of representation can be involved and not just one that involves processing for meaning. The dilemma is that if EI does operate in different ways, in some instances allowing for stimuli to be repeated verbatim and in others requiring that the stimuli be internally processed, is there any way in which the likelihood that EI will be reconstructive can be maximized? To use the terminology of Markman *et al.* (1975), it is the 'internalised grammar factor' that needs to be tapped, rather than the 'memory factor'. In other words, the 'slipperiness' of EI needs to be minimized. In this chapter, I aim to demonstrate that this can be done through careful attention to the design of an EI task and through manipulation of those features which are more likely to require participants to process stimuli and thus access their interlanguage.

The Characteristics of a Reconstructive Elicited Imitation Test

Perhaps the most obvious feature of an EI test that can be manipulated and that would appear to impact crucially on performance is the length of stimuli. As Bley-Vroman and Chaudron (1994: 252) point out, it is to be expected that accuracy will be better when length is short and that as the 'limits of memory' are approached, accuracy will decrease. Hameyer (1980) found in his study that the length of correctly repeated sentences strongly correlated with the number of syntactic and semantic errors participants made, as well as with the years that they had spent learning the L2 (German). Bley-Vroman and Chaudron (1994) conclude that a test that was a good measure of global proficiency would include stimuli of various lengths and complexities. In this discussion, however, I am going to stress other design features that can enhance the likelihood that participants attend to and process stimuli rather than engaging in rote repetition. Stimuli length will be dealt with again later when outlining the design of the test used in this study.

The design of an EI test that focuses participants' attention on meaning is more likely to be reconstructive than one that focuses attention or allows a focus of attention on language form. While the research that has been reviewed above suggests, for example, that information about the form of a sentence is lost shortly after it has been comprehended, Murphy and Shapiro (1994) argue that memory recall is greatly affected by attentional allocation. Listeners will attend to those aspects of a text that are most relevant to the goals they have for listening. Murphy and Shapiro were able to demonstrate that memory for form improves when task demands require a focus on form rather than on content. Hulstijn and Hulstijn (1984) demonstrated that learners can and will attend to form if asked to do so. Clearly, an EI test can be designed to enhance the likelihood that participants focus on meaning rather than on form.

Evidence also suggests that whether memory is reconstructive or whether participants are able to perform an EI test relying simply on rote repetition, may depend on whether there is a time interval between presentation of the stimulus and the elicited response. Sach's (1967) tests of recognition for the memory of sentences found that memory was essentially verbatim immediately after the sentence was heard or read, but that details of form were lost if even one sentence intervened between the presentation of the sentence and repetition of it. McDade *et al.* (1982) found that participants could repeat sentences they did not understand as long as imitation was immediate, but that after a three-second delay they were unable to do so.

Once an EI test intended to be reconstructive had been designed, what would be the evidence that would support these claims? It is to be anticipated that results would clearly differentiate it from a test that allowed participants to engage in rote repetition. Should such a test, for example, contain ungrammatical sentences, it is to be expected that there would be some spontaneous correction of these (Hamayan *et al.*, 1977; Munnich *et al.*, 1994). Secondly, there would be some evidence that participants were focusing on meaning rather than on form in completing the test. Finally, in an EI test that did not allow for test-takers to engage in role repetition, there would be no significant correlation between the length of the sentence and test-takers' success at repeating it. Bley-Vroman and Chaudron's (1994) claims with respect to sentence length have been referred to at the beginning of this section, as has the role that sentence length plays in precluding the possibility that participants repeat verbatim what they have heard. In an EI test that was reconstructive, success should not simply be a function of sentence length.

Elicited Imitation Tests as Measures of Implicit Language Knowledge

This discussion has thus far concerned itself with identifying the criteria to establish that EI tests require learners to process language stimuli rather than simply to imitate by rote. I will now consider the criteria that need to be satisfied in order to be able to conclude that a specific EI test is a likely measure of implicit language knowledge. It may initially appear that the two are one and the same thing, that is, that a test that is reconstructive must also be a measure of implicit language knowledge. Certainly, a measure of implicit language knowledge must be reconstructive and not simply a measure of rote repetition. An EI test that allowed participants time to monitor their responses, however, could allow them recourse to explicit language knowledge. It is clear from the criteria set out in Chapter 2 that for an EI test to be a measure of implicit knowledge, it must be performed under time pressure and not allow test-takers time to plan or monitor responses.

Furthermore, if an EI test is measuring implicit knowledge, there should be some relationship between participants' EI ability and other measures of production that do not allow test-takers to monitor their performance (i.e. other measures of implicit language knowledge). This relationship should be stronger than that between the EI measure and measures of explicit language knowledge. There is some evidence for this in the research literature. Chaudron and Russell (1990) report 'primarily general correlations' between EI performance and various other measures of production in L2 learners (Bley-Vroman & Chaudron, 1994: 252). Losey (1986) reports a 'moderate relationship' between EI and spontaneous language. Interestingly, she found that, for most learners, percentages of correct production were higher in spontaneous language than in elicited language. Gallimore and Tharp (1981) compared performance on an EI test and children's production of plural noun forms in a natural communicative play setting (the EI test did not assess plurals). They found that those who performed well on the EI test (the 'high' group) formed nearly twice as many correct plural forms as those who performed poorly on the EI test (the 'low' group). They thus concluded that EI scores are related to language behavior in natural settings. Munnich *et al.* (1994) report strikingly convergent results between EI and grammaticality judgment (GJ) tasks in their study, especially when the GJ tasks were taped, rather than read and so allowed participants less opportunity to monitor responses.

In summary, an EI test that is reconstructive in nature would have certain features that distinguish it from a test that might allow learners to rely on simple rote repetition of target stimuli. It would be designed to require a primary focus on meaning rather than on form and it would include some delay between the presentation and repetition of the stimulus. It would also produce results that would differentiate it from a test where participants engaged in rote repetition of stimuli: namely, there would be some spontaneous correction of ungrammatical sentences and there would be a nonsignificant relationship between length of stimuli and success at repetition. Similarly, an EI test that is a likely measure of implicit language knowledge would be different in design and in results from a test that is a likely measure of explicit language knowledge. It would be completed under time pressure and there would be some relationship between performance on the EI test and other 'time-pressured' measures of language use. These features are presented in Table 3.2, along with those features of a test that is, in contrast, a measure of rote repetition and a likely measure of explicit language knowledge.

The Present Study

I will now report on the development and validation of the Oral EI Test that was used in the Marsden study and that has already been described in Chapter 2. This Oral EI Test is innovative in that it can be distinguished from most other tests of EI with respect to two key design features:

(1) it requires students to focus on meaning rather than form;
(2) it includes both grammatical and ungrammatical stimuli.

Table 3.2 Features of an Elicited Imitation Test that is reconstructive and a likely measure of implicit language knowledge

	Design	*Results*
Reconstructive	Task design requires primary focus on meaning Delay between presentation of stimuli and repetition	Ungrammatical sentences corrected No correlation between length of sentence and success
Implicit knowledge	The test is time-pressured	Relationship between performance on EI test and other measures of 'on-line' language use
Rote repetition	Task design allows primary focus on form No delay between presentation of stimuli and repetition	Ungrammatical sentences repeated verbatim Correlation between length of sentence and success
Explicit knowledge	Test is preformed without time pressure	Relationship between performance on EI test and measures that allow for planned and/or monitored language use

In discussing the validation of this test, the evidence which would suggest that, as a test, it is reconstructive and a likely measure of implicit knowledge will be considered. Bley-Vroman and Chaudron (1994: 258) identify the need for research that considers how performance on EI tests compares with performance on other measures and, in particular, stress that 'free production and grammaticality judgments be employed consistently to cross-validate elicited imitation performance on specific structures and sentence characteristics'. In actual fact, Chapter 2 has already compared participant performance on the Oral EI Test in relation to performance on other tests and found evidence to support claims that it is indeed a measure of implicit language knowledge: a Confirmatory Factor Analysis demonstrated that the Oral EI Test loaded strongly along with other likely measures of implicit knowledge, also developed as part of the Marsden study, namely, the Oral Narrative Test and the Timed Grammaticality Judgment Test. On the other hand, the Untimed Grammaticality Judgment Test (ungrammatical sentences) and the Metalinguistic Knowledge Test, designed as measures of explicit language knowledge, loaded on a second factor. Furthermore, the solution supported the claim that these tests were providing separate measures of explicit and implicit knowledge.

This chapter will present additional evidence that would validate claims that the Oral EI Test is a likely test of implicit language knowledge. In particular, the following two research questions will be addressed.

(1) Is there a positive relationship between participants' ability to repeat grammatical structures correctly and their ability to correct ungrammatical structures in the Oral EI Test?

   The rationale for asking this research question is to establish whether there is evidence to suggest that the test is reconstructive. If the participants in this study were processing stimuli presented to them, rather than repeating verbatim what they heard, they would be correcting ungrammatical structures as well as repeating grammatical structures correctly. In this case, there would be a positive correlation between the two. On the other hand, if participants were engaging in rote repetition of grammatical statements, then they would also be repeating ungrammatical statements verbatim and not correcting them. In this case, there would be an inverse correlation, rather than a positive correlation, between their ability to repeat grammatical structures correctly and their ability to correct ungrammatical structures.

(2) Is there a relationship between participants' performance on the Oral EI Test and performance on other 'time-pressured' tests of L2 language use?

Tests of 'time-pressured' language use are operationalized as the listening and speaking components of the International English Language Testing System (IELTS) test and as an Oral Narrative Task. (The Oral Narrative Task has already been described in Chapter 2; its role in validating the Oral EI Test will be dealt with more fully in this chapter.)

Method

Participants

One hundred and fifteen participants took part in the trialing of the Oral EI Test. This group of participants was the same as that described in Chapter 2 ($n = 111$) with the addition of an extra four participants who had been removed from the data set described in Chapter 2 because of missing data on other tests.

Participants were asked to complete a background questionnaire that required them to give information about their L1 and to give a self-reported measure of proficiency. Twenty participants were native speakers of English, included in the trialing for validation purposes (see Chapter 2 for background information about this group). The remaining 95 participants were L2 learners of English, all of them studying and living in New Zealand. Of these, 78% were Chinese speaking. Thirty were enrolled as students at the University of Auckland and completing an ESOL paper, that is, a credit-bearing EAP undergraduate course. The self-reported average English proficiency level of this group of students was higher-intermediate. Other students were studying English in private language schools in Auckland. The self-reported average English proficiency level of this second group of students was lower-intermediate. Forty-four of these 95 participants had sat IELTS within the last year prior to their involvement in this study. These students scored an overall average of 6.24 on IELTS. IELTS describes a score at band 6 (scores range between bands 1 and 9) as signifying competent language use. The language user had 'generally effective command of the language despite some inaccuracies, inappropriacies and misunderstandings. Can use and understand fairly complex language, particularly in familiar situations' (IELTS, 2005).

Target structures

The Oral EI Test, like the other tests used in the Marsden study, was designed to provide information about participants' knowledge of specific language structures, 17 in total. The rationale for the choice of these 17 specific structures has already been outlined in Chapter 2 (see Table 2.2).

Test content

For each grammatical structure, four statements were initially constructed. In two of these, the particular target structure was used grammatically and in the other two, it was used ungrammatically. Examples of grammatical and ungrammatical statements to test for the use of the correct verb complement with 'want' are given below:

(1)   *Many overseas students **want coming** to New Zealand to study.
(2)   New Zealanders **want to keep** their country clean and green.
(3)   Good students **want to work** hard to pass their exams.
(4)   *People in love usually **want getting** married as soon as possible.

Some grammatically correct statements contained two instances of the target structure used correctly. For these statements there were thus two items testing participants' ability to correctly repeat the target structure used in a grammatically correct context. An example designed to test use of comparatives is given below:

New Zealand is **greener** and **more beautiful** than other countries.

Some grammatically incorrect sentences contained one instance of the target structure used correctly followed by another example of it used incorrectly or vice versa. Such statements thus contained one item testing for participants' ability to repeat the target structure when it was presented in a grammatically correct context and one testing their ability to correct the target structure when it was presented in a grammatically incorrect context. An example, again designed to test the use of the comparative, is given below:

Girls are usually **quieter** and **more nicer** than boys.

The original test consisted of 68 statements and 81 items testing participants' ability to repeat and correct statements. A total of 47 of these items presented target structures in a grammatically correct context, 34 in a grammatically incorrect context. This original version of the test was subsequently shortened, as described in Chapter 2. This was because administration was too time consuming, especially given the fact that this test was only one of a number that the participants who were involved in this project were taking. Administration of this original test took around 40 minutes of both the participant's and administrator's time (the test was administered one-on-one, see below). An abridged version of the test was therefore created. In this subsequent version of the test, one grammatical and one ungrammatical statement testing each target structure was retained from the original. The selection was made after a trial with 50 second-language learners and 10 native speakers. Those statements that correlated most strongly with total test scores and that were considered to be best measures of the underlying construct were retained. This abridged version of the test consisted of 34 statements and

44 items testing participants' ability to repeat and correct statements. In 27 of these items, the target structures were presented in a grammatically correct context, in 17 they were presented in a grammatically incorrect context. A copy of this abridged version of the test is included in the Appendix (targeted structures are bolded). The results presented in this chapter relate to this second and abridged version of the test.

Beliefs questionnaire: Focus on meaning

As has already been discussed, the EI test used in the Marsden study was designed to maximize the possibility that participants would be attending to the meaning rather than the form of the sentences that they heard. Murphy and Shapiro (1994) demonstrated that memory is influenced by the way that listeners allocate their attention. The EI test was therefore described to participants as a 'Beliefs Questionnaire' and they were told that they would be asked to give their opinion about a range of topics. More specifically, they were told that they would hear a statement and would first be required to decide whether it was true or not true for them or whether they were not sure, and that they were to circle their choice on the test sheet they were given. See example below:

True/Not True/Sure

The sentences used in the Oral EI Test were therefore designed as statements that participants could agree with or not. As much as possible, these statements were loosely organized around themes; for example, statements 12 to 16 dealt with issues related to education while statements 31 to 34 dealt with issues related to relationships (see Appendix). It can be hypothesized that the grouping together of thematically similar sentences had the effect of reducing participants' attention to form. Peterson and McIntyre (1973) found that surface information was less available in thematically organized sentences than it was in seemingly unrelated sentences. They suggested that this may be because thematic information changed less rapidly than form and so received greater attentional allocation.

Requiring participants to make decisions about the truth value of the statements they heard not only focused their attention on meaning rather than on form, it also had the added benefit of delaying repetition. This meant, of course, that information about the surface structure of the statement, that is, its form, was less available to participants when they did repeat the statements (McDade *et al.*, 1982; Sachs, 1967).

Repetition of statements in *correct English*

Participants were told that after they had indicated their belief about each statement they had heard, they were then to repeat it in *correct* English. The training that they received prior to commencing the test gave them practice in both aspects of the task, that is, in indicating their 'beliefs' on the test sheet and in repeating each statement in correct English. They were given eight statements to practice with, four grammatically correct and four grammatically incorrect. They were told (during the training only) what their response should have been. The correction of ungrammatical items was therefore modeled for them.

As has already been discussed, the rationale for including grammatically incorrect statements in the test was to ascertain whether learners would spontaneously correct these as they had in research conducted by Hamayan *et al.* (1977) and Munnich *et al.* (1994). It was hypothesized that their acceptance or rejection of grammatical violations in spoken stimuli presented in real time would be an indication of their internalization of targeted language structures. Hamayan *et al.* (1977) and Munnich *et al.* (1994) simply asked learners in their studies to repeat grammatically incorrect sentences. However, this approach was considered problematic in that, as Vinther (2002) points out, grammatical errors may prompt a range of different reactions. As well as conscious corrections, unconscious 'normalizations' (Vinther, 2002: 65) or unconscious repetitions of the error, these could also include conscious repetitions of the error. It was deemed important, therefore, to prevent the situation where higher-level learners, in particular, could succeed in remembering and repeating grammatically incorrect sentences because this is what they thought that they were being asked to do. For this reason, participants in this study were told that they were to repeat the statements in *correct* English. It is important to point out that test-takers were at no time explicitly told that they would be hearing ungrammatical statements.

Syllable length and sentence complexity

While a number of researchers have suggested that sentence length is an important issue in the design of an EI test, it is usually discussed as a variable that needs to be considered in relation to a specific population and test design rather than as a specified absolute. For example, Munnich *et al.* (1994) used sentences of 15 syllables in length in a study with advanced ESL learners, while Hamayan *et al.* (1977) used sentences that averaged 9 syllables in length with Arabic learners of English across several age levels. In the test used in this study, sentences varied between 8 and 18 syllables in length, with the mean length being 13.53 syllables. In designing the test, we did not control for sentence length beyond this, because structures that are both simple and complex were targeted and length was a feature that was intrinsic to some of the grammatical structures targeted. For example, to test for acquisition of the unreal conditional, a sentence containing both a subordinate and main clause was needed. The statements used therefore represented a range of difficulty for the learners participating in the test and broadly sampled 'stimuli of various lengths and complexities' as recommended by Bley-Vroman and Chaudron (1994: 253).

Gallimore and Tharp (1981) claim that structures that are placed at the beginning of sentences are easier to imitate than those placed at the end, which are, in turn, easier than those placed in the middle. No structures in the test used in the Marsden Project were placed in statement initial position. However, it was impossible to avoid placing some structures in statement final position. One example, as given below, was question tags:

Spending 10 hours in an aeroplane isn't much fun, **is it**?

Time pressure

The test was designed to be completed under time pressure. The test was time pressured in that participants listened to each statement only *once* and in *real time*. The training session and test were administered by audiocassette and participants' answers were recorded. The test administrator regulated the presentation of test stimuli. Test-takers could produce their belief evaluation and repeat the statement in their own time (i.e. self-paced). However, the test administrator would move to the next test item when the test-taker had either repeated the statement, attempted to or when it was obvious that he/she was unable to attempt the particular item. The test administrator ensured that participants did not attempt to repeat the statement before they had indicated their 'beliefs' choice on the test sheet.

In summary, it can be seen from this description of the design and administration of the test that the criteria for a test that was both reconstructive and a measure of implicit language knowledge have been met. In summary, the test first focused test-taker attention on meaning, it did not allow for immediate repetition of the stimulus, it gave participants the opportunity to correct ungrammatical statements as well as repeat grammatical statements and it was performed under time pressure.

Scoring

Participants' responses were scored according to three criteria:

(1) obligatory occasion created – supplied;
(2) obligatory occasion created – not supplied;
(3) no obligatory occasion created.

The first criterion describes a response where the participant created an obligatory occasion for use of the target structure and used it correctly.

A response was correct if the target structure was used correctly irrespective of lexical accuracy. For example, the following response was scored correct.

Target structure: modals/specific error tested was double marking of modals
Stimulus: People **can win** a lot of money in a casino
Response: People **can earn** a lot of money in a casino

The second criterion describes a response where the participant created an obligatory occasion for use of the target structure, but used it incorrectly. These responses were scored as incorrect. An example is given below:

Target structure: possessive 's'
Stimulus: Princess **Diana's** death shocked the whole world
Response: Princess **Diana** death shocked the whole world

The third category describes those responses where participants did not create an obligatory occasion for the use of the target structure. This includes responses where the participant did not attempt the section of the sentence that contained the target structure(s). The following is an example.

Target structure: placement of adverb in sentence
Stimulus: Children play rugby **well** and soccer **badly** in New Zealand
Response: Children play rugby

This category also includes responses where the participant substituted another linguistic form for the target structure, as in the example below:

Target structure: possessive 's'
Stimulus: Princess **Diana's death** shocked the world
Response: The death of Princess Diana shocked the world

All responses in this third category were also scored as incorrect. The rationale behind this was that failure to create an obligatory occasion for use of the target structure could be seen as evidence that this structure had not been internalized.

To some extent this scoring was problematic, as not allowing for structural modifications of the original utterance that excluded the target utterance cannot be considered as conclusive evidence that participants are 'avoiding' the structure because they have not acquired it. As one anonymous reviewer of the paper on which this chapter is based (Erlam, 2006) pointed out, the instructions to 'repeat each statement in correct English' would suggest that structural modifications are not disallowed.

There are, however, a number of factors that would suggest that the decision to score these responses as incorrect is defensible. The first is that in the training that the participants received, they were given eight statements to practice with. For each of these statements they were told what the response should have been. These modeled responses did not allow for structural modifications of the original stimulus. They were either exact replications of the original (i.e. where the statement was correct) or they were corrections to the original structure of the statement. Two examples of the latter are given below (note that these statements are focusing on linguistic structures that were not among those targeted in this project):

Stimulus: A good doctor always listens what patients say
Modeled response: A good doctor always listens **to** what patients say
Stimulus: English spoken in many different countries
Modeled response: English **is** spoken in many different countries

Secondly, in the designing of the test, all statements were piloted on native speakers. Only those items for which native speakers produced the targeted structure were retained as test items. This was seen as a precedent for scoring structural modifications of target structures as incorrect and also as evidence of the validity of items in this test. Finally, the possibility of scoring responses in this category as missing data was not seen as a reasonable alternative, as it was considered that a large source of data would be missing, that is, responses that indicated that participants had not internalized target structures.

Those responses that were impossible to score because the sound recording was not clear enough for a judgment to be made were coded as missing data.

Test reliability

Test reliability was initially estimated on the original version of the test, comprising 68 statements and a total of 81 items (see above). Internal consistency was calculated using the Kuder-Richardson Formula 20, on the performance of 61 participants. The reliability estimate was 0.98.

Reliability of the abridged version of the test, which subsequently replaced the original, was estimated on the performance of the 95 non-native speakers who took part in the study that this chapter reports on. Internal consistency was once again calculated using the Kuder-Richardson Formula 20, yielding a reliability estimate of 0.87.

Measures of 'time-pressured' language use

(1) Oral Narrative Task

In this test (see Chapter 2), participants were given a short story to read that was 'seeded' with seven structures: verb complements, third person -s, plural -s, indefinite article, possessive -s, yes/no questions, regular past tense. These seven structures were a subset of the 17 structures included in the EI test, chosen because they were easily incorporated together into a cohesive narrative. A copy of this story with targeted structures highlighted is included in the Appendix.

This test was computer administered. Participants were told that they would see a story presented on a computer screen and that they were to read it twice. They were told that they would need to read it carefully because they were going to be asked to retell the story in as much detail as possible. They were not allowed access to pen and paper during this test, so could not take notes. After they had finished reading the story (they were allowed as much time as they liked), they clicked on a button whereupon the story was removed and an instruction told them that they had only three minutes to tell the story and that they needed to keep as close to the original as possible in retelling it, using direct speech where appropriate. As they retold the story, a series of boxes appeared on the computer screen to indicate the passing of time. It was hoped that this, as well as the instruction that they had only three minutes, would create time pressure.

For each target structure, participants were scored for the number of correct instances of use out of the total obligatory occasions that they created for use of that particular structure. Twenty scripts (i.e. 19%) were rated by an independent rater and correlation coefficients were calculated to give an estimate of inter-rater reliability, yielding $r = 0.85$.

(2) The speaking and listening components of the IELTS

The speaking subtest of the IELTS consists of an oral interview that lasts between 10 and 15 minutes and is made up of three components. For two of these three components, test-takers must answer questions for which they have had no time to plan responses. For one component, they are given 1 minute to plan a topic about which they must speak for 1 to 2 minutes. One would argue that this limited amount of planning time would allow them to focus on content but not on language form. The listening subtest of the IELTS requires participants to process language in real time, that is, participants must answer questions as they listen to taped mono-logues and a series of dialogues. It can, therefore, be hypothesized that the speaking and listening subtests of the IELTS draw on greater amounts of implicit language knowledge in contrast to the reading and writing subtests, which do not require participants to process and/or use language in real time and therefore may allow participants the chance to monitor language performance, thereby accessing their explicit knowledge.

IELTS scores were available for 44 of the 95 non-native speaker participants. These participants had sat IELTS prior to their involvement in this project; these data were not collected as part of the present study.

Results

Items were grouped according to whether they tested participants' ability to repeat grammatically correct structures or the ability to correct ungrammatical structures. Individual total scores for each of these categories were averaged, that is, divided by the total number of items. The decision to report scores as proportions was made because, as outlined above, the sound quality of the recording at times meant that a decision about some responses could not be made. These were thus scored as missing data. Therefore, this meant that participants' total scores had to be averaged over the items for which there were data so that they were not penalized for those responses that could not be coded. Maximum scores for each category were thus 1.0. Descriptive statistics were calculated for native speakers and L2 learners. The results are presented in Table 3.3.

The results show that native speakers performed highly, repeating 97% of grammatical items correctly and correcting 91% of ungrammatical items. This is evidence of the validity of the test as a measure of implicit knowledge. The L2 learners repeated 61% of grammatical items correctly. Therefore, 39% of grammatical items were repeated incorrectly or no obligatory occasion was created for use of the target structure. Results also show that L2 learners did correct ungrammatical items. A total of 35% of

Table 3.3 Descriptive statistics for performance at repeating grammatical statements and correcting ungrammatical statements

	Native speakers (n = 20)		L2 learners (n = 95)		Total – NS and L2 (n = 115)	
	M	*SD*	*M*	*SD*	*M*	*SD*
Repeat grammatical	0.97	0.04	0.61	0.19	0.67	0.22
Correct ungrammatical	0.91	0.08	0.35	0.17	0.45	0.26
Total	0.94	0.04	0.51	0.17	0.58	0.23

ungrammatical items were corrected. Thus, 65% of ungrammatical items were either repeated incorrectly or no obligatory occasion was created for use of the target structure.

Individual L2 learner scores for repeating grammatical statements were correlated with scores for correcting ungrammatical statements. The significance level was set at 0.05 for all correlations. There was a significant positive correlation, $r = 0.73$, $p < 0.00$, $n = 95$. The correlation for the performance of all participants, native speakers included, was $r = 0.83$, $p < 0.00$, $n = 115$.

In Table 3.2, it was established that an EI test that was reconstructive (i.e. a likely measure of learner interlanguage) would need to require participants to focus on meaning. To check that the participants in this project had, indeed, focused on the meaning of the statements that they heard, rather than simply 'going through the motions' when it came to indicating their beliefs, the author took two statements that she believed participants would be likely to consider 'true' (statements 1 and 2, Table 3.4) and two which they would be more likely to consider 'not true' or which would elicit the response 'not sure' (statements 3 and 4, Table 3.4). She compared responses to these four statements. Results for all participants, presented in Table 3.4, demonstrate that the 'belief' responses to the four statements are as would be expected given the propositional nature of these statements. This is evidence that the participants were indeed focusing on meaning as intended in the design of the test.

In Table 3.2 it was also established that in an EI test that was reconstructive there would also not be a significant correlation between syllable length of items and success at performance on these items. Correlations were therefore carried out to establish whether there was a significant relationship between syllable length of individual test items ($k = 34$) and participants' ability to repeat grammatical structures

Table 3.4 Participants' (NS and NNS) responses to the meaning of selected statements

	Student responses	
Statement	*True*	*Not true/not sure*
1. A good teacher makes lessons interesting and cares about students.	108	7
2. People should report the police stolen money.	85	30
3. Everyone loves comic books and read them.	24	90(1 no response)
4. Young women like cigarettes and fast car.	15	100

correctly and correct ungrammatical structures. Results show that there was a small and nonsignificant negative correlation; $r = -0.28$, $p = 0.11$.

Performance on the Oral EI Test was compared with performance on the Oral Narrative Test. Table 3.5 presents descriptive statistics for L2 learners for each of the seven structures that were common to both the EI and the Oral Narrative Test. While all participants completed the test, due to recording error, data were obtained for only 86 out of the 95 L2 learner participants. The scores for the EI test are combined scores for grammatical and ungrammatical items. The *n* sizes for the oral narrative vary because the number of participants who created obligatory occasions for the use of these structures varies.

In order to compare the relationship between overall performance on the oral EI measure and performance on the Oral Narrative Test, Pearson Product Moment correlations were performed on scores of the Oral EI Test (all 17 target structures included) and overall scores of the Oral Narrative Test (individual total scores on this test were calculated by averaging scores on those items for which participants created obligatory occasions). Correlations are presented for both L2 learners only and for the total participant group, which included the 20 native speakers. Results are presented in Table 3.6. There was a significant correlation ($r = 0.47$) between the L2 learners' overall scores on the EI test and the Oral Narrative Test. It is interesting to note that the correlation was stronger for the total participant group ($r = 0.68$), presumably because of the greater variance contributed by the native speakers.

One of the problems with tasks where test-takers are asked to tell a story from memory is that they may create few obligatory occasions for

Table 3.5 Descriptive statistics for L2 participants' performance on the Elicited Imitation and Oral Narrative Task according to target structure

Structure	*Elicited imitation*			*Oral narrative*		
	M	*SD*	*N*	*M*	*SD*	*N*
Verb complements	.80	.33	95	.88	.27	51
Third person -s	.58	.39	95	.41	.34	81
Plural -s	.46	.37	95	.80	.21	86
Indefinite article	.36	.33	95	.79	.24	86
Possessive -s	.77	.30	95	.89	.23	83
Yes/no questions	.56	.33	95	.89	.30	31
Regular past tense	.55	.33	95	.59	.27	86

Table 3.6 Correlations between scores of Imitation Test and Oral Narrative Test

	Oral narrative total L2 learners	Oral narrative total L2 learners and NS
Oral EI Test Total		
Pearson Correlation	0.47	0.68
Sig. (two-tailed)	0.00	0.00
n	86	103
EI total for repeating grammatical structures		
Pearson Correlation	0.43	0.63
Sig. (two-tailed)	0.00	0.00
n	86	103
EI total for correcting ungrammatical structures		
Pearson Correlation	0.45	0.68
Sig. (two-tailed)	0.00	0.00
n	86	103

use of the structures that the task is designed to test. Therefore, correlations were also calculated for the total scores of those target structures for which L2 learners established a mean of four or more obligatory occasions (i.e. third person -s, plural -s, indefinite article, regular past tense). Correlations (for L2 learners) were slightly higher, Oral EI Test total, $r = 0.48$; EI total for repeating grammatical structures, $r = 0.44$; EI total for correcting ungrammatical structures, $r = 0.48$.

Correlations were performed between scores for individual target structures on both tests (i.e. scores on the Oral Narrative Test were correlated with scores on the EI test for each structure). Results for L2 participants are presented in Table 3.7 (n sizes again vary because the number of participants who created obligatory occasions for use of these structures varies). Correlations vary significantly according to target structure; those that produce the highest correlations are third person singular -s and regular past tense.

Individual scores for the Oral EI Test were correlated with IELTS scores for the 44 participants for whom scores were available. Results are presented in Table 3.8. Results show that the shared variance between

Table 3.7 Correlations between scores on the Elicited Imitation Test and Oral Narrative Test for specific language structures

Structure	Verb comp.	Third person -s	Plural -s	Indefinite article	Possessive -s	Yes/no question	Regular past tense
Pearson correlation	0.26	0.42*	0.19	0.09	0.07	− 0.02	0.36**
Sig (two-tailed)	0.06	0.00	0.08	0.43	0.52	0.91	0.00
n	51	81	86	86	83	31	86

Table 3.8 Pearson's correlations performed on overall scores of the elicited imitation task and IELTS scores

	IELTS listening	IELTS reading	IELTS writing	IELTS speaking	IELTS overall
EI total					
Pearson	0.72	0.51	0.46	0.67	0.76
Sig. (two-tailed)	0.00	0.00	0.00	0.00	0.00
n	44	44	44	44	44
EI total grammatical					
Pearson	0.67	0.47	0.40	0.61	0.70
Sig. (two-tailed)	0.00	0.00	0.01	0.00	0.00
n	44	44	44	44	44
EI total ungrammatical					
Pearson	0.71	0.52	0.51	0.68	0.76
Sig. (two-tailed)	0.00	0.00	0.00	0.00	0.00
n	44	44	44	44	44

total scores on the EI test and the IELTS speaking test was 45% ($r = 0.67$), and 52% between total scores on the EI and the listening test ($r = 0.72$). These percentages of shared variance were higher than those between scores on the EI and the reading test, 26% ($r = 0.51$) and between scores on the EI and the writing test, 21% ($r = 0.46$).

Discussion

The high performance of the native speakers on this test (97% of grammatical items correctly repeated and 91% of ungrammatical items corrected, see Table 3.3) in relation to that of non-native speakers (61% of grammatical items correctly repeated) is evidence of the validity of the test as a measure of implicit knowledge.

The results suggest that the EI test described in this study is reconstructive, according to the criteria established in Table 3.2. First of all, in Table 3.4, participants' 'belief' responses to four statements are as expected given the propositional nature of these statements. These results show that the participants did initially focus on the meaning of the statements with which they were presented, as intended in the design of the test. Requiring participants to first respond to the meaning of these statements meant, of course, that there was also a delay between presentation and the repetition of the stimulus. Secondly, the fact that L2 test-takers did correct 35% of ungrammatical statements is evidence that this test is reconstructive. If these participants were engaging in rote repetition of grammatical state-ments, then it would be expected that they would repeat ungramma-tical statements but not correct them. Research question one asked whether there would be a significant positive relationship between participants' ability to repeat grammatical structures correctly and their ability to correct ungrammatical structures. There was a significant positive correlation ($r = 0.73$, $p < 0.00$, $n = 95$). The fact that the ability to correct ungrammatical structures was positively correlated with the ability to repeat grammatical structures correctly is further evidence that the test is reconstructive and that participants were processing stimuli presented to them. While other studies (Hamayan *et al.*, 1975; Munnich *et al.*, 1995) have had test-takers repeat grammatically incorrect sentences, they have not looked at the relationship between test-takers' performance in repeating correct sentences and their performance in correcting incorrect sentences.

There is, furthermore, incidental evidence to suggest that at least some participants were not conscious of correcting ungrammatical sentences. One examiner asked participants at the end of the test whether they were aware of correcting the incorrect sentences (regrettably, this debriefing procedure had not been thought of earlier so that it could be incorporated into the original research design). Some participants were not sure, while results showed, however, that on a number of occasions these learners had. For example, one participant who said that he was not sure if he had corrected the sentences had in fact corrected 5 out of the 17 incorrectly used target structures.

The nonsignificant relationship between syllable length and success at repetition and normalization in this study ($r = -0.28$, $p = 0.11$) suggests that the task did not allow participants to rely on rote memory (Bley-Vroman & Chaudron, 1994) to any significant degree and is further suggestive evidence that the test is reconstructive in nature. This contrasts with Hameyer's (1980) finding that the length of correctly repeated sentences strongly correlated with the number of syntactic and semantic errors that participants made in the study he conducted.

It is important, however, to consider alternative interpretations of how the different design features of the test may have impacted learner performance. The question may be asked to what extent it was possible that test-takers may have been memorizing individual statements knowing that they would have to produce them later. Or, we can ask whether the instructions to repeat statements in 'correct English' and the training that participants received alerted them to the need to focus on form. With respect to the memorization issue, research that demonstrates that the capacity of working memory is determined by the stored knowledge that already exists about the language, would suggest that those participants who had the ability to memorize stimuli were indeed those who had internalized language, and, therefore, that their superior performance on the test was an indication of this. Furthermore, responding both to the meaning of the belief statements and memorizing them would require a dual focus on both meaning and form, which is difficult if not impossible for all but the highest level learners (VanPatten, 1989). The difficulty that learners experience in processing linguistic stimuli for both meaning and form can also explain why it is unlikely that even if the training did alert participants to the need to focus on form, they were unable to do this unless they had high levels of linguistic competence (evidence for the fact that test-takers did focus on meaning during the test has been presented above).

The inclusion of ungrammatical statements in the test was an innovative feature that did produce interesting results in line with predictions. However, it is important to remain tentative to some extent about the effect of this feature of the test on test-taker performance and whether failure to correct sentences can indeed, as the literature suggests, be seen as evidence that structures have not been internalized. In particular, it would be interesting in future research to incorporate into the test design a more consistent check of how aware participants were of this feature of the test and to examine the relationship between awareness and performance.

The issue of scoring was discussed in the section focusing on the design of the test. Scoring, as incorrect, those responses where partici-pants did not create an obligatory occasion for suppliance of the target structure is inferential rather than conclusive evidence that the structure has not been internalized. It is recognized that this is a possible source of error in the test. However, native speakers scored an average of 94% on combined scores for repetition of grammatical sentences and correction of ungrammatical sentences, suggesting that the margin of error may not have been high.

Another question that could be asked is the extent to which test-takers were able to monitor their output in repeating stimuli. If, however, learners were able to access explicit knowledge in this way, we would expect that the results of this test would not correlate with language measures that were 'time-pressured' (i.e. likely measures of implicit language knowledge). This issue will be dealt with below.

The second research question asked whether there was a significant relationship between participants' performance on the Oral EI Test and on other measures of 'time-pressured' L2 use. The answer to this question is yes. There is a significant positive correlation ($r = 0.47$)

between overall scores on the EI test and the Oral Narrative Test (see Table 3.6). Correlations between L2 learners' scores for individual structures on these two tests showed small but statistically significant correlations for two of the four structures for which learners created a mean of four or more obligatory occasions for use of that target structure (third person -s, $r = 0.42$; regular past tense -ed, $r = 0.36$). For verb complementation the correlation approached significance, $r = 0.26$, $p = 0.06$.

Descriptive statistics show that for all but one, third person −s, of the seven target structures elicited by the Oral Narrative Test, participants performed better on the spontaneous language production test than on the Oral EI Test (see Table 3.5). Losey's study (1986) produced similar results. Connell and Myles-Zitzer (1982), in a study that used EI with linguistically normal children, found that imitated productions were linguistically simpler than spontaneously produced language. Fujiki and Brinton (1987), in a study with children with language disorder, found that there were significant correlations for certain structures, but not for others, on an EI task and a spontaneous production task. Further research is indicated in order to establish to what extent and how performance on an EI test predicts spontaneous language production.

Correlations were calculated between participants' performance on the Elicited Oral Imitation Test and on the IELTS scores. Results show moderately high correlations between total scores on the EI test and scores on the IELTS speaking test ($r = 0.67$) and scores on the listening test ($r = 0.72$). Correlations are stronger for those components of the IELTS that require learners to process language in real time, that is, the speaking and listening components of the test, than for those components of the test that are more likely to allow learners time to monitor their responses, that is, the reading and writing tests ($r = 0.51$, $r = 0.46$). This is evidence that suggests that the EI test may be accessing implicit language knowledge.

It is interesting to note, however, that there is an even stronger correlation between scores on the EI test and overall IELTS scores, $r = 0.76$ (see Table 3.7). An anonymous reviewer of the paper on which this chapter is based pointed out that this stronger correlation may also be a psychometric effect, for the full IELTS test includes more items and therefore contributes more reliable scores and possibly greater variance, both of which are favorable conditions for correlations.

In summary, Table 3.2 established that an EI test that was a likely measure of implicit language knowledge would demonstrate significant correlations with other measures of 'time-pressured' language use. This criterion has been fulfilled for the test described in this chapter.

The development of the Oral EI Test was crucial for the Marsden Project because, as explained in Chapter 1, as a measure of implicit language knowledge it allows for questions about the role of form-focused instruction in L2 acquisition to be addressed. The test described in this chapter was therefore adapted and used as a measure of implicit language knowledge in a number of studies that are presented in Part 4. In each case, the test was designed to test the acquisition of the target feature that was the specific focus of the study. The principles of design outlined in this chapter were adhered to.

Conclusion

The results of this study indicate that there are a number of grounds on which it can be claimed that an Oral EI Test that requires participants to first process statements for meaning and then to repeat those statements that are grammatically correct and correct those statements that are ungrammatical, is reconstructive, requiring participants to process, rather than repeat verbatim, language stimuli. The first of these is the strong positive correlation between participants' performance at repeating grammatically correct items and their correction of ungrammatical items. Results that indicate no significant relation between statement syllable length and performance suggest that the test did not allow participants to rely on rote memory to any significant extent when repeating and correcting items.

The moderately high, significant correlations between performance on this test and other measures of 'time-pressured' language use, in particular the components of the IELTS test, is evidence to suggest that the Oral EI Test, which required participants to perform under time pressure, is a likely measure of implicit language knowledge.

There are a number of features of this test that require further investigation. The first relates to the scoring of the test. We need further research to establish the extent to which test-takers' failure to create obligatory occasions for the suppliance of target structures can be considered as evidence that these structures have not been internalized. The second relates to the incorporation in the test of the ungrammatical sentences. Further research is needed to corroborate evidence that the correction of ungrammatical sentences in the context of EI is a reliable indication of internalized constraints on grammar.

The advantages of this EI test as a measure of implicit knowledge are, however, considerable. It is, first of all, practical, in that it is easily administered and scored. Furthermore, unlike other measures of implicit language knowledge, it allows for the targeting of specific language structures. And, lastly, results suggest that as a measure of implicit language knowledge, it has both validity and reliability.

Acknowledgements

The author wishes to thank Nick Ellis for his initial help with the planning of the paper on which this chapter is based. The constructive comments of the anonymous reviewers of this earlier paper were also much appreciated.

Notes

1. This chapter is based on a previously published paper by Erlam (2006).

Chapter 4

Grammaticality Judgment Tests and the Measurement of Implicit and Explicit L2 Knowledge

SHAWN LOEWEN

Introduction

Grammaticality Judgment Tests (GJTs) have been frequently used in second language acquisition (SLA) research to provide information about second language (L2) learners' linguistic ability, particularly with regards to morphosyntactic proficiency. GJTs have a relatively long history of use in SLA, and they continue to be popular, as evidenced by their use in numerous, recent studies (Bley-Vroman & Joo, 2001; De Jong, 2005b; Flege & Liu, 2001; Helms-Park, 2001; Inagaki, 2001; Montrul, 2005; Nabei & Swain, 2002; Sorace & Shomura, 2001; Toth, 2006). However, questions continue to be raised about the construct validity and reliability of GJTs (Han, 2000; Han & Ellis, 1998) as it is not always clear what type of linguistic knowledge is being measured, whether implicit, explicit or some combination of the two. If SLA researchers are to continue using GJTs, it is important to know more about what type(s) of linguistic knowledge GJTs measure (Douglas, 2001; Purpura, 2004). This article investigates the construct validity of GJTs by evaluating them against criteria for measuring explicit and implicit linguistic knowledge.

What are GJTs?

A GJT[1] can be defined as a task in which participants are involved in 'deciding whether a sentence is well-formed or deviant' (Ellis, 1991: 162). Early uses of GJTs include those by Chomsky and other Universal Grammar (UG) linguists to provide intuitions about first language (L1) sentences. The method has been carried over into L2 research, with learners' judgments often being compared to native speakers' judgments to provide a baseline against which to measure the nativeness of learners' judgments. One reason for the popularity of GJTs is that they allow researchers to investigate grammatical structures that may be difficult to investigate in learner production because they do not occur frequently (Ellis, 1991; Mackey & Gass, 2005).

GJTs have a number of optional features, apart from the central task of judging a sentence's well formedness, such as (1) making preference judgments; (2) limiting the amount of response time (Han & Ellis, 1998); (3) providing learners with dichotomous or multiple-choice response options; (4) locating, correcting and describing the errors (Ellis, 1991); and (5) indicating the degree of confidence in the judgment (Gass, 1994). These task features may influence the type(s) of knowledge learners draw on in performing the central task of a GJT, namely making a decision about the correctness/well formedness of a linguistic stimulus.

What do GJTs measure?

Having briefly described the features of GJTs, it is important to consider their construct validity. What do GJTs measure and what can they tell SLA researchers about learners' linguistic ability? In the past it has been suggested that GJTs provide a direct measure of linguistic competence; however, it is now acknowledged by many researchers that GJTs do not provide a direct window into L2 learners' linguistic competence (Bard *et al.*, 1996; Birdsong, 1989; Chaudron, 1983; Davies & Kaplan, 1998; Ellis, 1991; Hedgcock, 1993). Instead, it is argued that GJTs provide a performance measure of L2 learners' linguistic abilities. 'What is observed instead is a particular kind of linguistic behavior, an overt response to the subject's opinion about characteristics of the sentence' (Bard *et al.*, 1996: 33). Researchers who argue that GJTs constitute a measure of L2 performance are not, however, necessarily rejecting GJTs. Many argue that GJTs can still provide useful information about L2 learners' linguistic ability (Hedgcock, 1993); the important issue is to determine the nature of the linguistic knowledge, whether implicit, explicit or some combination of both, that participants draw on in their performance on GJTs.

In fact, it was recognized early on (Chaudron, 1983) that the nature of learners' knowledge, whether implicit or explicit, can affect their judgments about the grammaticality of a sentence. There are several options that learners have in performing a GJT. In GJTs that only ask learners to discriminate between well-formed and deviant sentences, it is possible for them to respond 'purely intuitively' (Ellis, 1991). On the other hand, other options in the design of GJTs, such as locating, correcting and/or describing errors, require 'some degree of conscious analysis' (Ellis, 1991).

Ellis (2004) proposes that participants potentially undergo a three-step process when performing GJTs:

(1) Semantic processing (i.e. understanding the meaning of the sentence).
(2) Noticing (i.e. searching to establish if something is formally incorrect in the sentence).

(3) Reflecting (i.e. considering what is incorrect about the sentence and, possibly, why it is incorrect).

Ellis argues that giving participants unlimited time to perform a GJT allows them potentially to perform all three operations; however, he and others point out that participants are not necessarily obliged to reflect on the correctness of the sentence (step (3)), and that even with unlimited time, participants may rely on intuition (implicit knowledge) to judge a sentence. Nevertheless, with unlimited time, learners have the opportunity to reflect on the sentence, and thus to draw on their explicit knowledge. In order to ensure that learners rely only on their implicit knowledge, a GJT must not allow time to reflect on the sentence. Typically, studies employing GJTs have allowed unlimited time, although there are some exceptions (Bialystok, 1979; Han & Ellis, 1998; Mandell, 1999), which will be discussed later.

Several studies have attempted to investigate how participants respond to GJTs by examining learners' discourse as they make their judgments (Davies & Kaplan, 1998; Ellis, 1991; Goss *et al.*, 1994). For example, Ellis (1991), in a study using a think-aloud protocol, identified the following learner' strategies for judging sentences: use 'feel', rehearse, rehearse alternate versions, try to access explicit knowledge, use analogy, evaluate a sentence, and guess. Other studies have investigated the discourse of dyads involved in GJTs (Davies & Kaplan, 1998; Goss *et al.*, 1994). Goss *et al.* (1994) found that L1 speakers did not produce talk about rules when making judgments, but the authors suggest that this may have been due to the abstract nature of the structures under investigation. The L2 learners however, did produce talk that involved translation and reference to rules. Although more advanced learners had a tendency to rely on feel, both advanced and elementary learners relied on strategies such as translation and explicit metaknowledge to make accurate judgments. Goss *et al.* conclude that while advanced learners may be more able to draw on implicit knowledge during GJTs, there is no guarantee that they will not also draw on their explicit knowledge. Similarly, Davies and Kaplan (1998) in their study of L1 and L2 participants judging sentences in French and English, found that L1 speakers relied primarily on feel to make their judgments, while L2 speakers also used feel, although to a lesser degree, and they also made use of their explicit knowledge.

One other means for investigating the type of knowledge learners draw on in making grammaticality judgments is to examine GJTs' concurrent validity by comparing the results of GJTs to other tests. For example, Han and Ellis (1998) included three GJTs among a battery of tests to investigate learners' knowledge of English verb complementation. In a factor analysis of the various tests, they found two factors that they labelled implicit and explicit knowledge, respectively. The time-pressured GJT (3.5 second response time) and the Oral Production Test both loaded on the same (implicit) factor, while the delayed response GJT and the Metalingual Comments loaded highly on the other (explicit) factor. Han and Ellis also found that a repetition of the time-pressured GJT resulted in a somewhat even distribution between the two factors. They suggest that although this GJT was timed, learners' familiarity with the test due to their previous performance on it, allowed them to access more explicit knowledge. They have suggested that administering GJTs under time constraints may affect the type of knowledge that learners access in making their responses. GJTs with limited response times predispose learners to draw more on implicit knowledge, while unlimited response times can allow learners to access more explicit knowledge.

Response times

The previous discussion has highlighted that one of the more influential design features of a GJT as regards the type of knowledge participants can access is the amount of time they are given to perform the judgment (Ellis, 1991). If learners are given limited time to respond, this may encourage them to rely on implicit knowledge; in contrast, unlimited time may allow them to access explicit knowledge (Bialystok, 1979). In much previous research, GJTs were generally untimed. However, some researchers have imposed a time limit. Studies have ranged from allowing 3 or 3.5 seconds (Bialystok, 1979; Han, 2000) to 10 seconds (Mandell, 1999) for participants to respond to each sentence. It should be pointed out that although the first two studies arrived at the times by trialling the test (it is unclear how Mandell arrived at 10 seconds), these studies have still not investigated whether this amount of time is (a) adequate for learners to process the sentence semantically or (b) short enough to limit learners' ability to draw on explicit knowledge. Additionally, it is possible that some learners, particularly very advanced learners, may still be able to draw on highly proceduralized explicit knowledge, even with such short response times. The complexity of the sentence may also affect how much time it takes to process the sentence (Ellis, 2004). In addition, Purpura (2004) cautions that limited response times on test items can heighten learners' anxiety and thereby introduce irrelevant variability into the test.

Related to the amount of time learners are given to make a judgment is the issue of the speed with which learners actually perform the judgment. Response time scores (also termed latency scores) may provide an indication of the processes learners undertake in making their judgments (Juffs, 2001). The response times of GJTs have been examined in L1 research to investigate child language acquisition and impaired or abnormal language development (see, e.g. the investigation by Blackwell *et al.* (1996) into GJTs and their implications for aphasia research).

As far back as the mid-1980s, a rapid response time to L2 GJT items was argued to indicate a high degree of availability and automaticity of the required knowledge. That is to say, the faster the response time, the more 'automatic' the decision (Lehtonen & Sajavarra, 1985, cited in Alanen, 1997). Building on this assertion, Alanen (1997) used GJTs and response time data to examine the nature of L2 learners' linguistic knowledge, particularly the relationship between the speed and accuracy of L2 learners' judgments and their L2 proficiency. His results revealed weak but statistically significant correlations between the speed and accuracy of the GJTs and the grammar section of an L2 proficiency test. English L2 learners, whose English language background had been primarily in formal settings, obtained more accurate GJT scores than those who had received immersion-type English language education. These findings suggest that a degree of metalinguistic skill, particularly with respect to form, was involved in performing the GJTs.

Task stimulus

Another issue that may affect the type of linguistic knowledge learners draw on in making grammaticality judgments relates to the well formedness of the task stimuli, that is whether the sentences being judged are grammatical or ungrammatical. Hedgcock (1993), in a discussion of grammatical and ungrammatical sentences, admits that L2 learners may rely on different L2 databases or cognitive processes in approving well-formed strings and in rejecting ungrammatical strings; however, such an idea, he proposes, needs more investigation. If we consider the three-step process suggested by Ellis (2004) that learners may go through in making a grammaticality judgment (semantic processing, noticing, reflecting), then it is possible that learners may differ in these processes for grammatical and ungrammatical sentences. With both grammatical and ungrammatical sentences, learners need to process for meaning and to notice if there are any incorrect elements. But, if the sentence is grammatical, they may finish processing at this point. If, however, the sentence is ungrammatical, they may need to reflect on that sentence in order to locate the erroneous parts. Alternatively, if the error is immediately obvious to the learner, they may make their judgment at that point and not process the sentence further. Finally, in his use of think-aloud protocols, Ellis (1991: 178) observed that 'sentences that learners judged to be ungrammatical or that they were not sure about often invoked attempts to make use of declarative knowledge'.

Studies have found conflicting results as to whether grammatical or ungrammatical sentences are more likely to be judged accurately. Ellis (1991) found that learners were better at judging grammatical sentences correctly, but Gass (1983) found the opposite. Ellis suggests that 'different tests are likely to produce different results depending on the structure under investigation and the proficiency of the learners'. Han (2000) discusses accuracy asymmetry in which participants judge either grammatical or ungrammatical sentences more accurately. She says that 'it is not yet clear what causes accuracy asymmetry' (Han, 2000: 179).

Additionally, Juffs (2001) suggests that judging ungrammatical sentences may take longer than judging grammatical ones, as learners attempt to match the sentence to their internal grammar. Failing to find such a match, learners may continue to search; however, if the sentence is grammatical, then such a match will be found sooner.

Difference between L1 and L2 speakers' judgments

Another issue that arises in GJTs is whether the respondents are L1 or L2 speakers of the language. It can be argued that the type(s) of knowledge that L1 and L2 speakers draw on may differ. For example, it is acknowledged that L2 learners' linguistic knowledge may be partial and incomplete. In fact, numerous studies have commented on the indeterminacy of L2 learners' knowledge as an issue in GJTs (Birdsong, 1989; Davies & Kaplan, 1998; Ellis, 1991; Gass, 1994). Davies and Kaplan (1998: 199) suggest that indeterminacy of L2 learners' proficiency may be an important issue, and that 'GJ tasks are only going to provide valid and reliable data when the subjects being tested have attained sufficient proficiency in the L2 (where defining "sufficient proficiency" then becomes an important issue.)'.

The reliability of GJTs

Finally, in considering the construct validity of GJTs, it is also important to consider their reliability. In fact, Douglas (2001: 447) argues that 'performance consistency is a prerequisite for construct validity'. However, researchers have looked at GJT reliability independently of construct validity, with some researchers questioning the reliability of GJTs (Ellis, 1991; Han, 2000). Ellis (1991) found 'considerable inconsistency' in the test-retest results of his study with learners. However, others have suggested that GJTs are reliable. For example, Gass (1994), using a test-retest method, argues that learners were generally consistent in the judgments they made, with an overall correlation coefficient of $r = 0.598$. However, she makes the point that reliability is linked to the indeterminacy of learners' knowledge. To test this, she gave learners sentences based on an accessibility hierarchy for relative clauses. She found that learners were more indeterminate and consequently less reliable on the structures at the advanced end of the hierarchy. The correlations for the various relative clauses ranged from $r = 0.48$ to 0.76. At the very least, these conflicting results suggest that it is important for studies using GJTs to investigate their reliability.

While these previously mentioned studies have added to our understanding of the construct validity and reliability of GJTs in SLA, the current study attempts to investigate what type(s) of linguistic knowledge GJTs measure by asking the following research questions:

(1) Is there a difference between L1 and L2 speakers' performance on the GJTs in terms of
     (a) accuracy?
     (b) response time?
(2) What is the relationship between L2 learners' performance on timed and untimed GJTs in terms of
     (a) accuracy?
     (b) response time?
(3) What effect does task stimulus (grammatical versus ungrammatical) have on L2 speakers' performance on a GJT in terms of
     (a) accuracy?
     (b) response time?
(4) Is there a relationship between L2 learners' performance (both accuracy and response time) on an Untimed GJT and
     (a) the certainty of their judgments?
     (b) their self-reported use of rules in making judgments?

Method

The present study examines participant performance on two GJTs, one timed and one untimed.

Participants

One hundred and fifty-eight participants took part in this study; 42% were male and 58% were female. Of the participants, 18 were L1 speakers of English who were students at the University of Auckland. The remaining 140 participants were L2 learners of English, who were also studying in New Zealand. Some of them were studying in undergraduate and graduate university programs, while others were studying in private language schools. Most of the learners were Chinese language speakers (76%). Other Asian languages, such as Japanese, Korean and Vietnamese, accounted for 16% of the L1s, and European languages, such as French, Russian and Serbian, for the remaining 8%. The average age for starting to learn English was 12 years. On average, students had been studying English for nine years, and had lived in an English-speaking country for almost two years.

Instruments

The study involved the use of two GJTs, one speeded (Timed GJT) and the other unspeeded (Untimed GJT). Both the Timed and Untimed GJTs were computer-delivered using Illuminatus Opus Pro, and contained 68 sentences, covering 17 grammatical structures. For each of 17 structures (see Table 2.2 in Chapter 2 for a complete list), two grammatical and two ungrammatical sentences were included in the GJTs, resulting in 68 items. (The items are listed in the Appendix.) The sentences were identical in both the Timed and Untimed GJTs. No attempt was made to control the length of the sentences. Because different structures were being targeted, it was not possible to control for grammatical complexity; however, the level of lexical complexity was controlled by choosing words only from the 2000 most frequent English words list (Nation, 1990). The sentences were all decontextualized, and in an attempt to control for order of item presentation (Chaudron, 1983), three different, randomized versions of the test were used.

As has been mentioned, the Timed GJT was a speeded test. In order to determine the length of time necessary to judge each sentence, the test was trialled on 20 L1 English speakers. These participants were encouraged to respond to each item as quickly as possible, and, unknown to them, the computer recorded their response times (in tenths of a second). In order to reduce the effects of outliers, the median response time was calculated for each item. To take into account the fact that L2 learners would be taking these tests, an additional 20% was added to the median response time for each item. Thus, the amount of time that each item remained on the computer screen ranged from 1.8 seconds for Item 8 (Did Keiko completed her homework?) to 6.24 seconds for Item 2 (I think that he is nicer and more intelligent than all the other students.).

The instructions for the test were as follows: 'decide if each sentence is grammatically correct or incorrect for written English. You need to respond quickly based on your first impression'. Before the actual Timed GJT, participants were given eight practice sentences to familiarize them with the speeded nature of the test; these practice sentences were followed by a reminder: 'Remember: there is a time limit for each question so you will need to respond as quickly as possible'. During the Timed GJT, participants were given two 10-second breaks. Participants indicated their judgments on the computer keyboard by pressing either the right-hand shift key that was labelled 'incorrect' or the enter key that was labelled 'correct'.

As has been previously stated, the Untimed GJT used the same 68 sentences as the Timed GJT; however, participants were allowed as much time as they wished to respond, again by pressing keys on the keyboard labelled either 'correct' or 'incorrect'. In addition to judging the acceptability of sentences on the Untimed GJT, participants were asked to indicate the certainty with which they made their judgments by typing in a number from 0 to 100%. Finally, participants were asked to indicate how they made their judgment, whether by 'rule' or by 'feel'.

Procedure

The Timed and Untimed GJTs were administered as part of a larger battery of tests. An Elicited Oral Imitation Task and an Oral Narrative Task preceded them. Participants then took the Timed GJT followed immediately by the Untimed GJT. The final test was a Metalinguistic Knowledge Test. (See Chapter 2 for a full description of the other tests and procedures.)

Analysis

The computer recorded the grammaticality judgments and response times of each participant. For both the Timed and the Untimed GJTs, one point was awarded for each correct judgment, and no points were awarded for incorrect judgments. Additionally, the Timed GJT recorded if a judgment was not made within the allotted time. This inability to respond in time counted against the participants in terms of their overall accuracy scores; however, such cases were recorded differently from the incorrect judgments in order to separately analyze 'incorrect' responses that were due to a lack of response and those that were due to an incorrect judgment. For both GJTs, the learners' accuracy scores were calculated for the entire test (out of a possible 68 points), as well as separately for the grammatical and ungrammatical items (with 34 points possible on each section). In addition to the accuracy scores on the Untimed GJT, the average percentage certainty scores were also calculated. Finally, on the Untimed GJT, participants were asked to indicate the way in which they made their judgments, whether by 'rule' or 'feel'. One point was awarded each time 'rule' was chosen, and a total was calculated. Thus, a high score on this variable (labelled 'Rule') represents a high self-report of 'rule', while a low score, conversely, represents a high self-report of 'feel'.

Reliability

Cronbach's Alpha was used to calculate reliability for the 68 items in the GJTs. Scores were calculated twice, once for the entire sample

Table 4.1 Reliability scores

	L1/L2	*L2 Only*
Timed GJT	.875	.803
Untimed GJT	.855	.831
Certainty	.944	.941
Rule	.965	.935

(i.e. both L1 and L2 speakers), and once for L2 speakers only. The results shown in Table 4.1 indicate that all alpha scores were above .80.

Statistics

Descriptive statistics, consisting of raw frequencies and percentages, were calculated for each GJT as a whole, as well as for the grammatical and ungrammatical sections. The difference between L1 and L2 respondents was not investigated using inferential statistics, given the large difference in sample size between the two groups. However, in order to investigate the effects of the other independent variables, that is time pressure (timed/untimed) and task stimulus (grammatical/ungrammatical), a repeated measures ANOVA was performed on just the L2 sample ($n = 140$). In order to investigate the relationship between certainty and self-reported use of rules and the accuracy scores, Pearson Product Moment correlations were calculated. An alpha level of .05 was set for both the ANOVAs and the correlations. SPSS 12.0 was used to calculate all statistics.

For the response time data, the computer recorded the participants' response times. In the Timed GJT, if participants did not respond to a sentence within the allocated response time, their response time was entered as the maximum allocated time for that sentence. Repeated measures ANOVAs, similar to the ones described above, were also performed on the response time scores.

Results

The results of the GJTs, shown in Table 4.2, reveal that L1 speakers had an average accuracy score of almost 80% on the Timed GJT and over 96% on the Untimed GJT. In contrast, L2 speakers' accuracy scores on the Timed GJT averaged less than 55%, and just over 80% on the Untimed GJT. Table 4.2 also shows that L1 speakers performed at or above 90% on the Timed and Untimed grammatical items and for the Untimed ungrammatical items; however, on the Timed ungrammatical items, L1 speaker' accuracy rates dropped to under 70%. It should also be noted

Table 4.2 Accuracy scores

	L1			L2		
	Mean	*SD*	*%*	*Mean*	*SD*	*%*
Timed GJT total	54.3	10.0	79.9	37.2	7.9	54.7
Timed grammatical	30.9	3.6	90.8	25.9	5.2	76.1
Timed ungrammatical	23.4	7.4	68.9	11.3	5.6	33.4
Untimed GJT total	65.6	1.6	96.4	56.2	7.1	82.6
Untimed grammatical	33.3	1.1	98.0	28.4	4.1	83.6
Untimed ungrammatical	32.2	1.4	94.8	27.7	4.8	81.6

that the standard deviations for the L1 speakers on both sections of the Timed GJT were considerably higher than their standard deviations on the Untimed GJT. For the L2 speakers, the most noticeable result was their very low accuracy score on the Timed ungrammatical items, just under 35%; however, for the Timed grammatical items, their accuracy scores were almost 80%. On the Untimed GJT, the L2 speakers' accuracy scores were just over 80% for both grammatical and ungrammatical sections. Note that the standard deviations were relatively high for all L2 speakers' scores. In summary, one of the more notable results from this section is the poorer performance of both L1 and L2 speakers on the ungrammatical section of the Timed GJT.

One of the reasons for the poor performance on the Timed GJT was obviously incorrect judgment. However, Table 4.2 does not distinguish between judging a sentence incorrectly and failing to respond to the item quickly enough. An analysis of the frequency of missed items (i.e. those that were not responded to quickly enough) for the L1 and L2 participants reveals that L1 speakers missed on average just over 7 of the 68 items (11%), while L2 speakers missed on average 12 of the 68 items (19%).

Regarding the participants' response times, Table 4.3 shows that the overall mean response times of the L1 and L2 participants were relatively comparable on the Timed GJT; however, the response times were much less comparable on the Untimed GJT, with L1 speakers making their judgments considerably more rapidly. Thus, the answer to research question 1 is that L1 speakers performed more accurately than L2 speakers on both GJTs and they performed more quickly than L2 speakers on the Untimed GJT.

The remaining research questions focus only on the L2 participants; therefore, the L1 speakers have been excluded from the following analyses. The answers to questions 2 and 3 will be considered together

Table 4.3 Response time scores (in seconds)

	L1		L2	
	Mean	*SD*	*Mean*	*SD*
Timed GJT total	2.20	.44	2.38	2.34
Untimed GJT total	5.58	1.40	7.47	2.34

Table 4.4 Repeated measures ANOVA for L2 speakers' accurate judgments

Variable	*df*	*F*	*p*	*Partial Eta-squared*
Time pressure	1	982.770	.000	.876
Task stimulus	1	315.116	.000	.694
Time pressure*task stimulus	1	435.989	.000	.758

through the use of repeated measures ANOVAs, with time pressure and task stimulus as independent variables. The results in Table 4.4 show that there was a significant effect for both time pressure and task stimulus. The significant effect for time pressure indicates that learners were significantly more accurate on the Untimed GJT than on the Timed GJT. The significant effect for task stimulus indicates that the learners performed significantly more accurately on the grammatical items than on the ungrammatical ones. The results also indicate that there was a significant interaction between time pressure and task stimulus. Figure 4.1 indicates that the difference between the grammatical (dotted line) and ungrammatical (solid line) items was much greater on the Timed GJT than on the Untimed GJT, meaning that the ungrammatical items were more difficult on the Timed GJT than on the Untimed GJT.

A similar analysis was conducted for the response time data. The descriptive statistics in Table 4.5 reveal that response times for the grammatical and ungrammatical sentences on the Timed GJT were roughly equal, while those on the Untimed GJT differed by almost one second, with the ungrammatical items being responded to more quickly. The results of the repeated measures ANOVA in Table 4.6 show that there are significant main effects for both time pressure and task stimulus. The significant effect for time pressure indicates that the participants were significantly faster on the timed test (not surprisingly) and the significant effect for stimulus indicates that, overall, participants responded more quickly to the ungrammatical items than to the grammatical items. Furthermore, there is an interaction effect between time pressure and task stimulus, indicating that the response times were

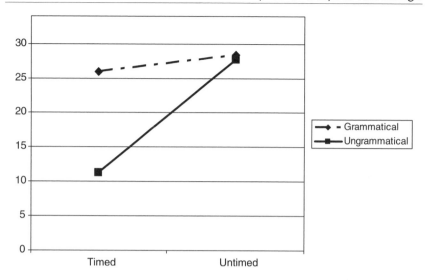

Figure 4.1 Accuracy scores for Timed and Untimed GJTs by task stimulus

Table 4.5 Response time scores (in seconds)

	Mean	SD
Timed grammatical	2.39	.36
Timed ungrammatical	2.37	.30
Untimed grammatical	7.98	2.56
Untimed ungrammatical	7.01	2.47

Table 4.6 Repeated measures ANOVA for L2 speakers' response times

Variable	df	F	p	Partial Eta-squared
Time pressure	1	510.668	.000	.852
Task stimulus	1	26.844	.000	.232
Time pressure*task stimulus	1	24.562	.000	.216

affected by both of these variables. As Figure 4.2 demonstrates, while the response times on the Timed GJT do not differ considerably between the grammatical and ungrammatical items, the same is not true of the Untimed GJT, in which the grammatical items have a slower response time.

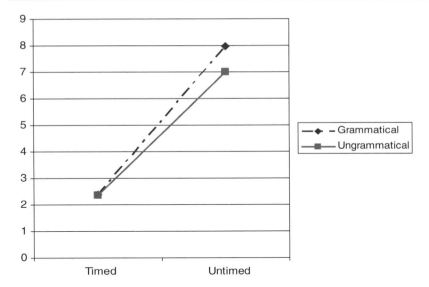

Figure 4.2 Response times for Timed and Untimed GJTs by task stimulus

Thus, in terms of accurate performance, the answer to research questions 2 and 3 is that time pressure had the effect of significantly lowering L2 speakers' accuracy scores on the GJTs and that task stimulus also affected L2 learners' scores, with grammatical sentences having higher accuracy scores than ungrammatical ones. In addition, there was a significant interaction effect between time pressure and task stimulus, with timed, ungrammatical items have a significantly lower accuracy rate.

In terms of response times, time pressure and task stimulus both significantly affected L2 speakers' scores, with the Timed GJT and the ungrammatical items being responded to more quickly. In addition, there was an interaction effect, with the untimed, grammatical items being responded to at a significantly slower rate.

The fourth and final research question addresses the relationship between learners' performance on the Untimed GJT and their certainty and rule scores. The descriptive statistics in Table 4.7 indicate that, in making their judgments, L2 speakers had an overall average certainty of 91% and this number was similar for both grammatical and ungrammatical sentences. In addition, learners reported using rules on average 72%, but the use of rules on ungrammatical sentences was higher than on grammatical ones by more than 10%.

In order to investigate the relationship between accuracy and response scores on the one hand and learners' certainty and use of rules on the other, correlations were calculated. The results in Table 4.8 show several

Table 4.7 Reported certainty and use of rules on the Untimed GJT

	Mean	*SD*
Certainty total	91.3	8.3
Certainty grammatical	91.5	7.2
Certainty ungrammatical	93.0	6.7
Rule total	72.2	20.0
Rule grammatical	66.0	24.9
Rule ungrammatical	78.3	15.0

Table 4.8 Untimed GJT correlations

	Accuracy		*Response time*	
	Grammatical	*Un-grammatical*	*Grammatical*	*Un-grammatical*
Certainty	.383**	.248**	− .018	− .175
Rule	.146	.323**	.326**	.226**

significant, albeit weak, positive correlations. First, learners' accuracy scores correlated with their certainty scores, indicating that learners who were more certain were also more accurate. There was also a relationship between accuracy and self-reported use of rules on the ungrammatical items, indicating that learners who reported using more rules had higher accuracy levels, but only on the ungrammatical items. As for response times, there was a relationship between the reported use of rules and the speed with which learners judged sentences; the more frequently learners relied on rules the more time they took in judging the sentences.

Discussion

The analysis of the GJT data suggests several implications for the use of such tests in measuring implicit and explicit L2 knowledge. The rest of this chapter will consider these implications in relation to each of the research questions.

When considering the difference between L1 and L2 speakers' performances on the GJTs, it is perhaps not surprising that L1 speakers were more accurate and faster in their judgments, given their implicit knowledge of their L1; nevertheless, these results speak to the construct validity of the GJTs. If there were no differences between L1 and L2 speakers' performances then it might be considered that the tests were measuring some other construct, perhaps some type of test-taking ability that was independent of language knowledge. Furthermore, the considerably lower scores of the L2 speakers on the Timed GJT supports the assertion that implicit knowledge is better measured on GJTs with limited response times (Bialystok, 1979; Ellis, 2004; Han & Ellis, 1998). In this instance, participants with arguably high levels of implicit knowledge (e.g. the L1 speakers) did significantly better on the test that was hypothesized to favor the use of implicit knowledge. However, when participants were given unlimited time, the advantage of implicit knowledge was mitigated somewhat, as L2 speakers potentially had time to draw on their explicit knowledge and thereby compensate for limited implicit knowledge.

When considering time pressure on the results of only the L2 speakers, it is also possible to explain the data in terms of access to implicit and/or explicit knowledge. The results indicate that learners performed significantly better on the Untimed GJT than on the Timed one. The Timed GJT was hypothesized to favor participants with higher levels of implicit linguistic knowledge, while the Untimed GJT encourages (though does not require) the use of explicit linguistic knowledge. Thus, it would be expected that L2 speakers, particularly those with extensive amounts of classroom instruction such as those in this study, would perform better on the test that favors the use of explicit linguistic knowledge, and that was in fact the case. Arguably, the time pressure of the Timed GJT does not allow L2 speakers to draw on their explicit knowledge, and they do not have sufficient implicit knowledge to help them on the test. Similar to the differences between L1 and L2 speakers, these results suggest that limited response time may necessitate a reliance on implicit linguistic knowledge.

Although the relationship between time pressure and linguistic knowledge seems probable given the current data, it is important to consider alternative explanations for these results. For example, it is possible that the results are primarily due to the speeded nature of the test, which did not allow participants to react quickly enough, regardless of the type or amount of L2 knowledge they possessed. One piece of supporting evidence for this explanation is that L1 speakers scored roughly 16% lower on the Timed GJT than on the Untimed GJT, which would give some indication that the speeded nature of the Timed GJT did decrease accuracy scores, regardless of the amount of implicit linguistic knowledge possessed by the participants. It would seem, as Purpura (2004) suggests, that the speeded nature of the test is introducing some construct irrelevant variability. At the moment, the ideal response time for discouraging the use of explicit knowledge is not clear, with previous studies ranging from 3 to 10 seconds (Bialystok, 1979; Han, 2000; Mandell, 1999). Further investigation into this issue is warranted.

The third research question considers learners' performances on the grammatical and ungrammatical sections of the GJTs. The results indicate that learners performed significantly better on the grammatical sections of both GJTs, which supports Hedgcock's (1993) assertion that learners may differ in judging grammatical and ungrammatical stimuli. Further differences between the grammatical and ungrammatical sentences were found in examining the interaction effect between time pressure and task stimulus, which revealed that the L2 learners did significantly worse on the ungrammatical section of the Timed GJT. A possible explanation for these differences may be found in the three steps that learners may go through in making a grammaticality judgment (Ellis, 2004): (1) semantic processing, (2) noticing and (3) reflecting. For each sentence, learners must process semantically in order to understand the sentence. Next, learners need to notice if there are any ungrammatical elements. If learners do not notice anything ungrammatical, they can make their judgment at this point. However, if learners detect something ungrammatical, they may reflect in order to determine what is incorrect in the sentence. On the Untimed GJT, there is plenty of time for learners to go through all three steps for both grammatical and ungrammatical sentences if they wish. Thus, we would not expect to see large differences in learners' judgments of the grammatical and ungrammatical sentences, and in fact the results show only a 3% difference. However, on the Timed GJT, learners do not have unlimited time to make their judgments; therefore, they may have time for steps 1 and 2, which would allow them to indicate a judgment of a grammatical sentence, but they may not have time for step 3 to consider what is incorrect about the sentence. Thus, we would predict considerable differences in learners' ability to judge grammatical and ungrammatical sentences on the Timed GJT, and in fact the results show a 41% difference.

While the accuracy scores support the above interpretation, the response time data do not indicate that learners took longer in judging the ungrammatical items. In fact, contrary to Juffs' (2001) observation, learners took longer to judge the grammatical items on the Untimed GJT. One possible explanation for this phenomenon is that once learners encountered the ungrammatical element in the sentence, they were immediately able to make their judgment. However, if a sentence was grammatical, the learners had to read the entire sentence and then perhaps check through it again to see if they might have missed an ungrammatical element. Obviously, such examination of the sentence would take longer.

The results of the correlation analyses provide some corroboration for the above explanation regarding the difference in response times between grammatical and ungrammatical items on the Untimed GJT. The self-reported use of rules correlated positively with response times on both grammatical and ungrammatical items, indicating that longer response times were related to more reported use of rules. The correlation was stronger for the grammatical items, accounting for almost 11% of the variance, as compared to 5% for ungrammatical items. The difference is explainable if we consider the process that learners might engage in when judging both types of sentences. For example, in judging the sentence 'Did Martin visited his father yesterday?', the learners' knowledge of past tense formation rules could be invoked when making a decision. Conversely, when judging the sentence 'Rosemary reported the crime to the police', learners would need to call upon multiple rules, concerning past tense, dative alternation, article use, etc., to account for the sentence's grammaticality. Clearly, being able to rely on one rule to judge a sentence as ungrammatical would take less time than considering multiple rules.

Finally, Ellis (2004) suggests that learners will be more certain of their judgments when they are drawing on their implicit knowledge, and conversely less certain when relying on explicit knowledge. The correlations from the present data indicate that certainty correlated significantly with accurate judgments, but did not do so with response times. Furthermore, the correlation with the grammatical items was slightly higher than with the ungrammatical ones ($r = .383$ and $.248$, respectively), suggesting that learners were somewhat more certain on the grammatical items, but they were also certain on the ungrammatical items.

Conclusion

In summary, the results of this study suggest that features of GJTs may be manipulated to predispose L2 learners to draw on different types of L2 knowledge. GJTs with limited response times seem to limit the ability of L2 learners to access their explicit knowledge in making a judgment, while ungrammatical sentences on an untimed test appear to encourage learners to access explicit L2 knowledge. Nonetheless, it is clear that the results of the investigation into both the concurrent and construct validity of the GJTs do not suggest that these tests are pure measures of either implicit or explicit linguistic knowledge. That being said, the differing design features in these tests may predispose L2 learners to draw on different types of linguistic knowledge in making their judgments, and such differences may help SLA researchers interpret more clearly the results of subsequent GJTs.

Further investigation into the design and construct validity of GJTs is still warranted. Future research could use a time course design (Blackwell *et al.*, 1996) in which sentences are presented word-by-word on a computer. Learners' reaction times can be captured, as can the precise moment of decision-making in relation to the words in the sentence. Information provided by this type of design could indicate whether learners make a decision immediately when an ungrammatical element is encountered or if they first process the entire sentence before making a decision. For both ungrammatical and grammatical sentences, a time course design could help distinguish between the amount of time learners take to read the sentences (i.e. semantic processing) and to make their judgments (i.e. reflecting). Another method that could be employed to provide additional information about GJTs would be to present sentences in an oral rather than written form. An oral GJT would be similar to an oral elicited imitation test, but instead of responding to the semantic content of the sentence and then repeating it, learners would judge the grammaticality of the sentences. The online processing required for the oral modality would arguably encourage learners to draw upon their implicit L2 knowledge, while avoiding the possible stress of a computerized timed GJT. Such suggestions, nevertheless, remain speculative and await further empirical investigation.

Notes

1. Bard *et al.* (1996) prefer to use the term 'acceptability judgment' to refer to the response made by the speaker, while grammaticality is 'a characteristic of the linguistic stimulus itself' (p. 33). In the current paper, the more widely used term 'grammaticality judgment' will be used, although the author acknowledges the distinction made by Bard *et al.*

Chapter 5

Validating a Test of Metalinguistic Knowledge

CATHERINE ELDER

Introduction

This chapter reports in detail on one component of the test battery designed to operationalize the constructs of implicit and explicit knowledge for the Marsden study described in Chapter 2.

The chapter begins with an attempt to define the construct of metalinguistic knowledge and then describes in some detail the content and format of the instrument that was developed to measure this knowledge (the Metalinguistic Knowledge Test; MKT). There follows a series of hypotheses regarding the nature of metalinguistic knowledge and its relationship to other variables. These hypotheses were generated for the purpose of eliciting the necessary chain of argument and evidence required to explore the validity of this instrument. They were then tested using trial data gathered from a diverse population of candidates, including both native speakers (NS) of English and second language (L2) learners. The findings, which offer tentative support for some but not all of the validation hypotheses, serve as a basis for discussing both the validity of the instrument and the nature of metalinguistic knowledge and its relationship to the broader constructs of implicit and explicit language knowledge and L2 proficiency.

Defining the Construct of Metalinguistic Knowledge

The term knowledge is used here to refer to 'a set of informational structures available for use in long-term memory' (Purpura, 2004). Metalinguistic knowledge is a particular area of knowledge to do with the attributes of language. It potentially encompasses a range of language features, including morphosyntax, lexis, semantics and pragmatics at both the subsentential and suprasentential (discourse) level. While the research described here is limited to the area of morphosyntax, we would argue that the characteristics of metalinguistic knowledge, as described by Ellis (2004, 2005, Chapter 1) and elaborated in the pages that follow, could be extended to cover all the above-mentioned aspects of language.

The criterial features of the metalinguistic knowledge construct as conceptualized in the Marsden study are listed below.

Type of knowledge

Metalinguistic knowledge is different from the widely used term 'metalinguistic awareness'. Metalinguistic awareness has been defined by Masny (1987: 59) as 'an individual's ability to match, intuitively, spoken or written utterances with his or her knowledge of language'. To the extent that intuitions are involved, metalinguistic awareness can be said to involve implicit rather than explicit knowledge. Metalinguistic knowledge, on the other hand, as defined in the current study, is analytical rather than intuitive in nature, in the sense that it involves explicit declarative facts (whether rules or fragments of information) that a person knows about language. The analytical nature of metalinguistic knowledge is supported by Roehr's (1997) findings, which revealed a close relationship between metalinguistic knowledge and language analytic ability as measured by tests traditionally used to assess components of language learning aptitude.

A strong view of the cognitive difference between metalinguistic knowledge and implicit linguistic awareness or understanding is proposed by Paradis (2004), who claims that the neuroanatomical processes involved in learning and retrieval of linguistic facts are quite different from those implicated in the acquisition and use of implicit knowledge. Further support for the distinctness of implicit and explicit knowledge constructs is presented in Chapter 1.

Awareness

As metalinguistic knowledge is analyzed and requires deliberate attentional focus, learners will be aware of it. This means that they will know when they are drawing on it (e.g. to make judgments about the grammaticality of a sentence or to edit a piece of writing). Support for this contention is found in Roehr's (2006) study, which showed that learners were able to offer detailed accounts of the explicit knowledge base that they were drawing on while resolving form-focused tasks. If learners are able to provide such accounts, it seems reasonable to assume that they may also be able to estimate their level of metalinguistic knowledge more accurately than would be the case with implicit, automated knowledge of which they may not be conscious.

Metalanguage

Being explicit rather than implicit, metalinguistic knowledge is, at least potentially, verbalizable (Butler, 2002). To verbalize the rules of target language grammar, or even to distinguish a correctly formulated rule from an inaccurate one, a learner may benefit from a command of technical or semitechnical terminology (James & Garrett, 1992). However, even though a command of this subject-specific lexis (verb, noun etc.)

may assist the learner to display his/her metalinguistic knowledge, the knowledge of such terminology is independent of grammatical knowledge per se (N. Ellis, 1994) and indeed of any cognitive or analytical skills associated with such knowledge (Roehr, 2007). An analogy can be drawn with architecture, where the knowledge required to design or construct a building is clearly independent of the ability to label its parts.

Learnability

Unlike implicit knowledge, metalinguistic knowledge is alleged to be learnable at any age (Bialystok, 1994). Thus, if appropriate instructional opportunities are provided, an individual's metalinguistic knowledge may continue to grow throughout the lifespan, falling off only with the advent of old age (Kemp, 2001).

Growth in metalinguistic knowledge is most likely to occur in instructed contexts and is often associated with the onset of literacy (Donaldson, 1978), and with formal learning of a second language. Bialystok (1991: 130) explains the process thus:

> Becoming literate in a second language forces the language learner to examine the structure of the second language through the process of analysis so that the language is represented as a formal system. This means that bilingual children who are also biliterate have had the experience of analyzing two linguistic systems, the results of which must translate into a more powerful and more analytic conception of language in general.

However, the extent of a person's metalinguistic knowledge may vary according to the type of instruction received, with traditional grammar-based courses more conducive to building learners' explicit language knowledge than more experiential communicative approaches. Elder and Manwaring (2004), for example, found significantly higher levels of metalinguistic knowledge among *ab initio* L2 learners of Chinese who had been exposed to one year of intensive grammatical instruction at university than among fellow students who had spent several years studying Chinese in more meaning-focused secondary school classrooms.

Accessibility

An important feature of metalinguistic knowledge, which is the subject of considerable debate in the literature, is that it may not be readily accessible in the context of language use. Many studies (e.g. Alderson *et al.*, 1997; Elder *et al.*, 1999; Green & Hecht, 1992; Roehr, 2007; Seliger, 1979) have shown either weak or modest relationships between metalinguistic knowledge and L2 output on a range of performance measures. Han and Ellis (1998), on the other hand, make somewhat stronger claims for the role of metalinguistic knowledge in performance, suggesting that variations in the knowledge proficiency relationship across studies may have to do with how proficiency is operationalized. Their study revealed that learners' explicit knowledge of a single grammatical feature (verb complements) was significantly associated with performance on both the Secondary Level English Proficiency Test (SLEP) and the pencil-and-paper version of the Test of English as a Foreign Language (TOEFL), but that the strength of this relationship varied according to test type. Scores on an untimed grammaticality test of sentences containing verb complements were more strongly associated with performance on the discrete-item TOEFL test than on the SLEP, which gives relatively less weighting to reading and grammar.

Bialystok and Ryan (1985) proposed a psycholinguistic model that accounts for such variation in terms of the demands that different tasks make on the cognitive processes of analysis and control. As metalinguistic knowledge makes high demands on controlled processing and analysis, it is said to be implicated in literacy-related tasks. However, it is not always retrievable during performance on conversational tasks that rely on automatized knowledge, which can be accessed under real-time performance conditions. Renou (2001) subsequently invoked this model in her study of the relationship between metalinguistic knowledge and task performance among 64 university level L2 learners of French. Her results are, however, difficult to interpret in light of this model given that there were some significant associations between scores on tasks deemed to be rather different in their processing demands whereas scores on tasks making similar cognitive demands did not in all cases converge. Elder and Manwaring's (2004) study, on the other hand, offered some support for the Bialystok and Ryan model in that metalinguistic knowledge of the target language (Chinese), as measured by a test very similar to the instrument used for the current study, was more strongly associated with performance on classroom achievement tasks involving reading and writing skills than with scores obtained for listening and speaking, as might be predicted.

The findings of both the Renou (2001) and Elder and Manwaring (2004) studies point to a further variable that may affect learners' access to metalinguistic knowledge during production. Their respective results reveal that learners instructed via communicatively oriented methodologies (which presumably place greater value on spontaneous language production than on language analysis) may be less able to retrieve their metalinguistic knowledge in performance than those who have been exposed to predominantly form-focused instruction.

A more elaborate characterization of the constraints on the use of metalinguistic knowledge in L2 production is offered by Hu (2002), who suggests that learners' ability to apply their knowledge may vary significantly not only according to the degree of attention to form and time pressure imposed by a task, but also according to how the relevant target structures are used in production (whether prototypically or otherwise). Hu's participants produced prototypical uses of a form (e.g. the use of simple past to refer to a definite past event, or second-mention use of the definite article) more accurately than peripheral uses. The author argues that the greater frequency and cognitive prominence of prototypical uses can account for these findings.

The study described below draws on the criterial features of meta-linguistic knowledge, as outlined above, to address the question: how valid is the MKT as a measure of the metalinguistic knowledge construct? The MKT is one of the measures used in the Marsden study to capture the implicit and explicit knowledge constructs (see Chapter 2 of this volume).

Method

Test design

The MKT, which is an adaptation of a previous measure developed by Alderson *et al.* (1997) and subsequently used by Elder *et al.* (1999) in a partial replication study, is divided into two parts (see Appendix E for the full version of the test). Part 1 focuses on learners' knowledge of the rules of the target language and presents test-takers with 17 ungramma-tical sentences. The errors in the sentences relate to the same structures targeted in each of the other tests in the Marsden battery (see Table 2.2, Chapter 2) and the justification for the choice of these structures was provided in that chapter. The target structures include those that involve item learning (e.g. verb complements) and those that are rule-based (each third person -s).

As indicated in the example below, learners are not required to judge the grammaticality of each sentence or even to supply the correct form because this is the focus of the other explicit and implicit measures in the test battery. The sentences are all incorrect and the erroneous part of each sentence is underlined. Learners are told that the sentences are ungram-matical and presented with multiple-choice options offering explanations (accurate and inaccurate) of the target language rule that has been violated in each case. In this respect, the test format departs from that used by Alderson *et al.* (1997) in that it measures passive metalinguistic knowledge rather than the ability to actively verbalize target language rules. An item from the test with its accompanying distractors is shown below.

For each sentence choose which statement best explains the error

4. If Jane had asked me, I <u>would give</u> her some money.

(a) 'would' is conditional so it should appear in the 'if' clause not the main clause.

(b) The first clause tells us that this is an impossible condition, so use the subjunctive.

(c) We must use 'would have given' to indicate that the event has already happened.

(d) When 'if' clause is in the past perfect tense, main clause verb is in the past conditional.

It should be noted that the distractors for each item are based loosely on inaccurate explanations offered by learners at the pilot stage of test development. The wording of the 'key' or correct answer (shaded) was designed to approximate the way such rules are rendered in English as a second language (ESL) textbooks or by ESL teachers. A pedagogical grammarian checked all correct answer statements in the test for accuracy and plausibility. It will be noted that most of the options contain basic metalinguistic terminology (*conditional, clause, subjunctive, past perfect tense, verb*) both because such terminology is often central to explicit grammar teaching and also because it is often difficult to formulate explanations without the use of such terms.

Part 2 of the MKT is based very closely on the corresponding component of Alderson *et al.*'s (1997) test and requires learners to match items from a list of grammatical terms to their corresponding exemplars in an English sentence. Modifications were made to the original version to ensure that the terminology relevant to the 17 grammatical structures in Part 1 was included. A portion of the modified sentence and some sample terms indicating what is required of the test-taker is set out below. (See the Appendix E for the entire contents of this part of the test.)

Read the sentence below. Find ONE example in the passage for each of the grammatical features listed in the table. Write the examples in the spaces provided. The first item has been done for you.

The materials are delivered to the factory by a supplier, who usually has . . .

Grammatical feature	*Example*
Definite article	*the*
Verb	
Noun	_____
Preposition	_____
Passive verb	_____

Responses to both parts of the MKT are scored dichotomously.

Validation hypotheses

As the prime aim of this chapter is to offer evidence for the MKT's validity, a series of validation hypotheses have been formulated, as is normal practice in test validation research (e.g. see Chapelle, 2000; Davies & Elder, 2004; Messick, 1989). These hypotheses (listed below) arise out of earlier research reviewed above and offer a basis for eliciting an appropriate chain of evidence to determine whether the MKT is indeed capturing the construct of metalinguistic knowledge, as it has been conceptualized above.

Type of knowledge

As metalinguistic knowledge is a kind of explicit knowledge that is rule-based and declarative rather than procedural in nature, it is hypothesized that:

(1) Scores derived from the MKT will be more strongly associated with scores obtained from the other measures of explicit knowledge in the Marsden test battery (such as the Untimed Grammaticality Judgment Task) than with those derived from the operational measures of implicit grammatical knowledge (the Elicited Oral Imitation Test and the Timed Grammaticality Judgment Task described in detail in Chapters 3 and 4, respectively).

(2) There will be a significant relationship between self-reported use of rule in the Untimed Grammaticality Judgment Test (UGJT) and performance on Part 1 of the MKT, which independently measures knowledge of these rules.

Awareness

Since, as argued above, the application of explicit knowledge is deliberate and conscious rather than automated:

(3) There will be a significant relationship between self-reported grammatical knowledge and (whole and part) scores on the MKT. This will not be the case with respect to the measures of implicit knowledge.

Metalanguage

As we have argued that knowing about the rules of the target language grammar is cognitively independent of knowing the meta-linguistic terminology associated with these rules, we can hypothesize that

(4) Scores on Part 1 of the MKT designed to measure knowledge of grammar rules will not be related to scores on Part 2 designed exclusively to measure understanding of metalinguistic terminology.

Learnability

As explicit knowledge of a language, unlike implicit knowledge, is often learned via formal instruction rather than through exposure, it is hypothesized that:

(5)   Greater amounts of formal English study will be associated with higher scores on the MKT.

(6)   Exposure to formal (gra~~~~ ~~~~unicative) instruction will be associ~~~~ ~~~~MKT.

[handwritten: Assumption that there is no form focus instruction in CLT]

Further, as NS acquire their ~~~~re (in the first instance) and as explicit grammatical instruction tends to be the exception rather than the rule in English mother tongue classrooms, it seems reasonable to predict that

(7)   The NS/NNS differential on the MKT will be smaller than is the case for the implicit knowledge tests in the Marsden battery.

Accessibility

Given the documented constraints on the accessibility of metalinguistic knowledge on tasks performed under time-pressured conditions with little opportunity for focus on form we might expect that

(8)   Scores on the MKT will not be related to accuracy of performance on the Oral Narrative Test (described in Chapter 2).

Conversely, when ample time is allowed for learners to monitor their production and attend not only to meaning but also to form, it is anticipated that explicit knowledge may come into play. Accordingly

(9)   Scores on the MKT will ~~~~ and writing tasks on standardized t~~~~ing tasks.

[handwritten: This is of interest for FL programmes!]

Participants

To gather the necessary data to test the above hypotheses, the MKT was administered to a total of 249 learners. Twenty members of the group were NS and the remaining 229 were L2 learners drawn from both New Zealand and overseas institutions. On average, the L2 learners in the sample had been learning English for 10 years, mostly in a foreign language context, although some learning environments were more English-rich than others.

Other tests of implicit and explicit knowledge

The MKT was administered alongside all the other tests in the implicit/explicit knowledge battery described in Chapter 2. Because the administration of some tests was labor-intensive, requiring a one-to-one encounter between test administrator and candidate, not all

Table 5.1 Size of test candidatures for explicit and implicit knowledge measures used for this study

Tests	Type of knowledge measured	n
Timed Grammaticality Judgment Test (TGJT)	Implicit	226
Untimed Grammaticality Judgment Test (UGJT)	Mainly explicit	229
Metalinguistic Knowledge Test (M-C Version) (MKT)	Explicit	229
Elicited Oral Imitation Test (EI)	Implicit	229
Oral Narrative Task (ONT)	Implicit	158

candidates took the entire test battery. However, nearly all undertook a common core consisting of those tests (marked with an asterisk in Table 5.1) that our piloting and preliminary analyses had indicated were the best measures of implicit and explicit knowledge. A sizeable number also did the Oral Narrative Task, a further measure of implicit knowledge referred to in Hypothesis 8 above.

Language proficiency tests

Data on the language proficiency of 118 of the above-mentioned participants was also gathered using an institutional version of the computer-based TOEFL (CBT), a standardized English language test used for admissions to English-medium universities in the USA and elsewhere. Trained TOEFL test personnel scored this test, and scores are reported for Listening Comprehension, Reading Comprehension and Structure/Writing, respectively. A total of 125 test-takers from Malaysia took the Diagnostic English Language Needs Assessment (DELNA) ($n = 125$), a professionally validated measure used to diagnose academic language needs following entry to the University of Auckland (Elder *et al.*, 2003, Read, 2008). This test yields scores on five different skills, namely Vocabulary, Text-editing, Listening Comprehension, Reading Comprehension and Writing. Recent band scores on the Listening, Reading, Writing and Speaking components of the International English Language Testing System (IELTS) test, widely used for admission to UK and Australasian universities, were available for a further 96 of the MKT candidates.

Questionnaire

Before completing the various tests mentioned above, all participants filled out the background questionnaire (see Appendix A). The reader is reminded that this questionnaire canvassed details of the participants' learning history, including the total time spent studying English formally and the type of instruction received (whether communicative or grammatical or a combination of the two). The questionnaire also included a self-assessment component in which learners were asked to rate their level of grammatical competence on a 5-point rating scale. In addition, when taking the UGJT, which like the MKT is designed to offer learners the opportunity to access their explicit knowledge about language, learners were asked to report on the processes they drew on when responding to test items (whether by *rule* (i.e. drawing on their explicit knowledge) or by *feel* (i.e. drawing on intuitions or implicit knowledge)). Responses to this questionnaire yielded useful information for test validation purposes.

Analysis

All MKT test scripts were marked and total scores for each test as well scores on the individual test items were entered into a database together with questionnaire and language proficiency test results.

MKT reliability was calculated using both Cronbach's alpha and the case reliability estimated by a Rasch analysis using Quest software (Adams & Khoo, 1993). The various validation hypotheses formulated above were tested using a range of statistical techniques, including a confirmatory factor analysis (CFA) (using the AMOS program), the Pearson Product Moment correlation and the ANOVA statistic as appropriate (using SPSS statistical software). These analyses will be described in more detail in the results section.

Results

Reliability

The internal consistency of the MKT was very high (alpha = 0.90). The case reliability estimate yielded by the Rasch analysis was likewise high at 0.88, indicating an acceptably high level of discrimination between candidates at different ability levels.

The results of the various data analyses will be reported in relation to each of the validation hypotheses formulated above.

Hypothesis 1

Scores derived from the MKT will be more strongly associated with scores obtained from other tests of explicit knowledge in our test battery than with those derived from our measures of implicit grammatical knowledge.

This hypothesis was explored via a CFA of scores on those tests in the battery which previous analyses had revealed to be the best measures of the targeted constructs of implicit and explicit knowledge. For the UGJT, only responses to ungrammatical items were used in this analysis because, as indicated in Chapter 2 (and see also Chapter 4), these had been found to have greater discriminatory power in measuring the target construct of explicit knowledge than those relating to grammatical sentences. The factor solution against which the data were evaluated is depicted in Figure 5.1. The CFA analysis was initially run using total score on the MKT and subsequently with component scores on Parts 1 and 2, respectively. The resultant model fit statistics are presented in Table 5.2.

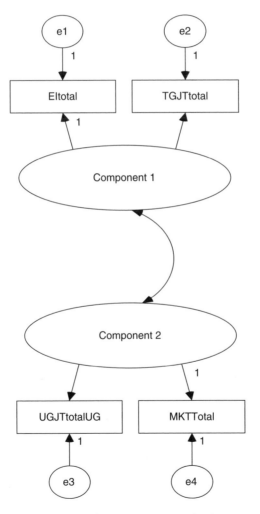

Figure 5.1 Posited relationship between MKT and other measures

Table 5.2 Summary of the model fit for three CFA solutions

Model	*X2*	*NFI*	*RMSEA*	*df*
Implicit/explicit (using MKT total score)	0.046 ns	1.000	0.000 (95% CI: 0.000–0.109)	1
Implicit/explicit (using MKT Part 1 score)	0.688 ns	0.997	0.000 (95% CI: 0.000–0.164)	1
Implicit/explicit (using MKT Part 2 score)	0.002 ns	1.000	0.000 (95% CI: 0.000–0.000)	1

Note: NFI = normed fit index, RMSEA = root mean square error of approximation, CI = confidence interval.

As explained in Chapter 2, the indicators of good model fit are a low and nonsignificant chi-square value, a high normed fit index (NFI) and a high root mean square error of approximation (RMSEA) value (preferably at or above 0.95). It can be seen from Table 5.4 that, according to these indicators, a model that couples metalinguistic knowledge with other explicit knowledge measures and distinguishes it from those eliciting implicit knowledge achieves acceptable fit to the data. This is true not only when the model is run with the total score on the MKT (Row 1, Table 5.4), but also when the two components of the test, Part A and B, are considered separately (Rows 2 and 3).

Hypothesis 2

There will be a significant relationship between self-reported use of rule in the UGJT and performance on Part 1 of the MKT.

Self-report data generated by learners while performing the UGJT, indicating whether they used 'rule' or 'feel' when making decisions about the grammaticality of test items, were correlated with scores on Part 1 of the MKT. Self-reports were on a 3-point scale, with 1 indicating that the learner's choice was based on intuition, 2 indicating the use of both rule and intuition and 3 indicating a reliance on the relevant rule. Thus, higher scores on this item indicate greater use of rule. The analysis (see Table 5.3) revealed a very weak but statistically significant correlation with these self-reports and performance on the rule-based component of the MKT ($r = 0.173$, $p \leq 0.027$), confirming that those more prone to using rules when judging the correctness of sentences on the UGJT were also marginally more likely to perform better on the rule choice component of the MKT. (There was also, as one might predict, a statistically significant relationship between use of rule and performance on the UGJT ($r = 0.183$, $p < 0.032$), whereas this was not true for the

Table 5.3 Relationship between self-reported use of rule in making grammaticality judgments and performance on the MKT and other implicit and explicit knowledge measures

	n	r	p
EI	137	− 0.042	0.626
TGJT total	137	0.035	0.684
UGJT total	137	0.183	0.032
MKT Part 1	137	0.173	0.027
MKT Part 2	137	0.070	0.371
MKT Total	137	0.100	0.205

Table 5.4 Relationship between self-assessed knowledge of English grammar and performance on implicit and explicit knowledge measures ($n = 249$)

	n	r
EI total	143	0.147 ns
TGJT total	141	0.088 ns
UGJT total	136	0.363*
MKT Total	141	0.311*

*Significant at the 0.001 level.

implicit knowledge measures (Oral Elicited Imitation Test (EI) and Timed Grammaticality Judgment Test TGJT).)

Hypothesis 3

There will be a significant relationship between self-assessed grammatical knowledge and overall scores on the MKT. This will not be the case for the measures of implicit knowledge.

Correlations were also performed between self-assessed grammatical knowledge (on a scale of 1 (very poor) to 5 (excellent) and performance on the various tests in the battery (for results see Table 5.4). As anticipated, learners' self-assessed grammatical ability proved to be more accurate in relation to Part 1 of the MKT ($r = 0.311, p < 0.001$) and to total scores on the UGJT, than to learners' performance on the two implicit knowledge measures, (EI and TGJT), which are designed to measure an automated or proceduralized form of language knowledge of which learners may not be conscious.

Hypothesis 4

Scores on Part 1 of the MKT designed to measure knowledge of grammar rules will not be related to scores on Part 2 designed to measure understanding of metalinguistic terminology.

It will be recalled that Part 1 of the MKT measures knowledge or rules, whereas Part 2 measures the ability to match metalinguistic terms with exemplars of those terms in the context of a sentence. A correlational analysis revealed a moderate relationship between these two components ($r = 0.553$, $p < 0.01$). However, while there is clearly some overlap between the two components of the MKT, there are also areas of difference that become evident if we compare the relative difficulty of items assessing the ability to identify metalinguistic terms with those involving rule explanation. Whereas the most difficult item on the rule component (Part 1) was the item measuring a rule about adverb placement (only 9% of candidates got this right), the majority of candidates (73%) were able to pick out an adverb from the sentence provided in Part 2. In fact, this was one of the easier items on this part of the MKT. Similarly, most test-takers were able to identify a subject (84%) and a verb (100%) in the sentence, but far fewer (only 50%) were able to identify the correct rule regarding subject–verb agreement. However, there were a number of other rules that learners were able to identify successfully without knowing the relevant terminology. One example is the rule regarding ergative verbs, knowledge of which was tested in the sentence 'His school grades *were improved* last year'. Choosing the correct answer to this question did not appear to relate to ability to recognize the passive form, although there was reference to this terminology in two of the multiple-choice options. In fact, only 13% of test-takers were able to identify the passive form in Part 2, whereas the correct explanation for the above ergative verb item was selected correctly by 30% of the candidature.

Hypothesis 5

Greater amounts of formal English study will be associated with higher scores on the MKT.

Contrary to our prediction, the relationship between total scores on the metalinguistic test and years of English study was nonsignificant and this was also the case for the other tests in the battery (see Table 5.5). However, when scores for Part 2 (ability to match metalinguistic categories with the corresponding words in an English sentence) were considered separately, a weak but statistically significant relationship ($r = 223$, $p = \leq 0.05$) was found, with higher scores on this component of the MKT associated with years of formal study of English. There was no such relationship between length of formal study and performance on Part 1.

Table 5.5 Relationship between years of formal learning and MKT ($n = 249$)

	n	r
EI total	95	0.152 ns
TGJT total	93	0.165 ns
UGJT total	88	0.190 ns
MKT total	93	0.182 ns
MKT Part 1	94	0.086 ns
MKT Part 2	94	0.223*

*Significant at the 0.05 level.

Table 5.6 Relationship between type of formal instruction and MKT ($n = 249$)

	n	r
EI total	143	− 0.014 ns
TGJT total	141	0.063 ns
UGJT total	137	− 0.153 ns
MKT Total	141	− 0.144 ns
MKT Part 1	141	− 0.046 ns
MKT Part 2	141	− 0.141 ns

Hypothesis 6

Exposure to formal (grammar-based rather than communicative) instruction will be associated with higher scores on the MKT.

Responses to the questionnaire item about type of English language instruction were coded on a scale of 1–3, with 1 indicating that learners had undergone mainly formal grammar-based instruction, 2 indicating that they had experienced a mixture of formal and informal instruction and 3 indicating that instruction was mainly informal and communicative in its orientation. While the correlations between this variable and performance on the MKT was negative as predicted (− 0.144 ns) (i.e. the lower scores associated with formal language instruction were associated with higher scores on the metalinguistic test), the relationship was very weak and statistically nonsignificant, and this was true of all measures in the battery, whether implicit or explicit (see Table 5.6).

Table 5.7 NS versus NNS performance on implicit and explicit knowledge measures

Name of test	Knowledge type	NS mean	NNS mean	F
EI	Implicit	92	49	35.9**
TGJT (Total)	Implicit	53	43.8	22.8**
UGJT (Ungrammatical)	Explicit and implicit	32	26	4.3**
Meta Part 1	Explicit	10	9.5	0.8 ns
Meta Part 2	Explicit	10	11.3	3.7**
Meta Total	Explicit	20	21	2.8*

*Significant at 0.05 level.
**Significant at 0.01 level.

Hypothesis 7

The NS/NNS differential on the MKT will be smaller than is the case for tests of implicit knowledge.

An ANOVA analysis was computed to compare mean differences in the performance of NS and NNS candidates on all tests in the explicit/ implicit knowledge battery. It can be seen from Table 5.7, that, as predicted, the NS candidates outperform all the NNS groups on all measures *except* the MKT. On the implicit knowledge measures in particular (i.e. EI and TGJT), the NS outperform the NNS by a very wide margin. In contrast, on the MKT, the NNS group significantly outperformed the NS ($F = 2.8$, df 6, $p = 0.001$). The NNS advantage occurs on Part 2 (Terminology) ($F = 4.19$, df 6, $p = 0.000$) but not on Part 1, where there is no difference between the two groups ($F = 0.8$, df 6, $p = 0.098$).

Hypothesis 8

Metalinguistic knowledge will not be associated with the accuracy of performance on a Timed Oral Narrative Task.

This hypothesis was tested by correlating total scores on Part 1 of the MKT and total scores on the Oral Narrative Task. The scoring procedures for the Oral Narrative Task are described in Chapters 2 and 3. The result, presented in Table 5.8, was nonsignificant. Item-by-item correlational analyses were also undertaken comparing MKT scores measuring knowledge of particular structures to scores from scores for these same structures as displayed in performance on the Oral Narrative Task. The results of those structures for which there is parallel evidence from each instrument are also presented in Table 5.8.

Table 5.8 Relationship between MKT Part 1 and accuracy on STTO (total and item scores) ($n = 158$)

Feature	r
Oral Narrative Test score	0.181 ns
Subject verb agreement (third person -s)	0.136 ns
Plural −s	0.128 ns
Regular past -ed	0.148 ns
Indefinite article	0.028 ns

Hypothesis 9

Scores on the MKT will relate more strongly to reading and writing tasks on standardized English proficiency tests than to speaking and listening tasks.

This hypothesis was tested by correlating scores on the MKT with those on the various components of the IELTS, DELNA and TOEFL (as described above). These analyses were carried out for both Part 1 and Part 2 of the MKT as well as for overall MKT scores. Results are reported in Tables 5.9 –5.11, with those tasks deemed to meet the unpressured and form-focused conditions identified in bold.

The above results present a mixed picture regarding the MKT/ proficiency relationship, with correlations generally stronger for the TOEFL than for the IELTS and DELNA. In the case of DELNA, there are only four significant correlations. One of these is between vocabulary and MKT scores and the remaining three show a link between the MKT and DELNA Reading Comprehension. Interestingly, Reading is in all cases the test component that correlates most closely with MKT scores. The correlations with Listening scores are, as predicted, weaker relative to Reading, but not markedly different in strength than those obtained for Writing. The only exception is the TOEFL CBT, where scores for

Table 5.9 Correlations between MKT and IELTS ($n = 96$)

	IELTS Listening	IELTS Speaking	IELTS Reading	IELTS Writing	IELTS Overall
MKT Part 1	0.473**	0.353**	0.567**	0.391**	0.547**
MKT Part 2	0.371**	0.266**	0.475**	0.319**	0.440**
MKT Total	0.436**	0.332**	0.540**	0.388**	0.523**

**Significant at the 0.001 level.

Table 5.10 Correlations between MKT and DELNA ($n = 54$)

	DELNA text-edit (speeded)	DELNA Vocabulary	DELNA Listening	DELNA Reading	DELNA Writing
MKT Part 1	0.164 ns	0.283*	0.253 ns	0.271*	0.210 ns
MKT Part 2	0.130 ns	0.062 ns	0.053 ns	0.318*	0.200 ns
MKT Total	0.175 ns	0.187 ns	0.166 ns	0.363**	0.248 ns

*Significant at the 0.05 level.
**Significant at the 0.01 level.

Table 5.11 Correlations between MKT and TOEFL ($n = 115$)

	TOEFL CBT Listening	TOEFL CBT Reading	TOEFL CBT Structure/Writing	TOEFL CBT Total
MKT Part 1	0.435**	0.575**	0.558**	0.589**
MKT Part 2	0.440**	0.485**	0.492**	0.529**
MKT Total	0.490**	0.574**	0.573**	0.613**

**Significant at the 0.001 level.

Structure (selection of the most appropriate forms to fill gaps in a written text) are included in the Writing total. The correlation between the IELTS Speaking score and the MKT, while statistically significant, is weaker than that for Reading and Writing as predicted.

Discussion

Results are summarized in Table 5.12. These results offer some useful validity evidence in relation to the MKT. The extent to which the evidence gathered corresponds to our original hypotheses is now discussed.

Type of knowledge

The initial claim that the declarative knowledge to be elicited by this test would be different in nature from the proceduralized knowledge required for language use is strongly supported by the factor analysis, which offers confirmatory evidence of two different factors (which have

Table 5.12 Results summary

Hypothesis	Method	Sustained?	Result
1. Scores derived from the MKT will be more strongly associated with scores obtained from other tests of explicit knowledge in our test battery than with those derived from our measures of implicit grammatical knowledge.	Confirmatory factor analysis (AMOS)	Yes	• Good model fit with posited two-factor solution (i.e. with EI and TGJT as one component and factor and UTGT untimed and MKT as the second) • Model fit is acceptable for both part and whole MKT scores
2. There will be a significant relationship between self-reported use of rule in the UGJT and performance on Part 1 of the MKT.	Correlation (Pearson)	Yes	• Very weak but statistically significant correlation between MKT Part 1 and self-reported use of rule
3. There will be a significant relationship between self-assessed grammatical knowledge and overall scores on the MKT. This will not be the case for the measures of implicit knowledge.	Correlation (Pearson)	Yes	• Moderately low but statistically significant correlation between MKT and self-reported use of rule • Correlations with implicit knowledge measures were nonsignificant
4. Scores on Part 1 of the MKT designed to measure knowledge of grammar rules will not be related to scores on Part 2 designed to measure understanding of metalinguistic terminology.	Correlation	No	• Modest correlation between scores on Part 1 and Part 2 of the MKT • Knowledge of *particular* rules did not always imply understanding of relevant metalinguistic terminology or the ability to identify parts of speech associated with that rule

Table 5.12 (*Continued*)

Hypothesis	Method	Sustained?	Result
5. Greater amounts of formal English study will be associated with higher scores on the MKT.	Correlation	Yes, partially	• Weak but statistically significant correlation between years of formal study and understanding of metalinguistic terminology (MKT Pt 2) • Correlations between Part 1 and with the overall MKT score were nonsignificant
6. Exposure to formal (grammar-based rather than communicative) instruction will be associated with higher scores on the MKT.	Correlation (Pearson)	No	• All correlations were nonsignificant
7. The NS/NNS differential on the MKT will be smaller than is the case for tests of implicit knowledge.	ANOVA	Yes	• NS outperformed NNS by a wide margin on implicit knowledge measures • No significant difference between NS and NNS on Part 1 of the MKT. • NNS outperformed NS on Part 2
8. Metalinguistic knowledge will not be associated with the accuracy of performance on a timed Oral Narrative Task.	Correlation	Yes	• Nonsignificant correlation between whole and part scores on each test
9. Scores on the MKT will relate more strongly to Reading and Writing scores on standardized English proficiency tests than to Speaking and Listening scores.	Correlation	Yes, partially	• Correlations between MKT and Reading skill were consistently stronger than those for Listening. Not true for Writing, except for CBT (which includes grammar component) • MKT scores more weakly correlated to IELTS Speaking than to IELTS Reading and Writing

been labeled explicit and implicit knowledge) with the different tests lining up on one or other factor. The fact that the MKT loads on the same factor as the ungrammatical sentences in the UGJT, rather than on the timed version of this test (TGJT) or the EI, conforms with the notion that explicit knowledge is elicited in contexts where time is available for reflection and analysis, whereas implicit knowledge is automated and therefore accessible under time-pressured or meaning-focused conditions.

The notion that metalinguistic knowledge is measuring rule-based, analyzed knowledge however, derives only marginal support from the results reported above regarding the relationship between self-reported use of rule on the UGJT and performance on the rule explanation component of the MKT. The correlation coefficient, while statistically significant as predicted, is very weak. One reason for this may be that self-report is not a very reliable means of indicating what knowledge base learners are drawing on, first because they may be reluctant to admit to intuiting or even guessing an answer, and also because, when both implicit and explicit knowledge are implicated (as is possible in responding to the UGJT), learners may be unable to determine which knowledge type prevails. A more effective means of determining the extent to which learner responses rely on application of rules, rather than intuition or guesswork, would be to conduct a think-aloud study in which learners are asked to explicate (preferably in their L1) the reasoning they use when selecting between multiple-choice distractors on the MKT.

Awareness

The hypothesis that learners are more aware of their level of explicit metalinguistic knowledge than of their implicit knowledge is confirmed by the correlations between self-assessments of grammatical knowledge (which were made before the tests began) and scores on the various tests in the battery. The correlations were modest but significant for both the MKT and the UGJT, but were not so for the tests of implicit knowledge, indicating that, as was anticipated, learners are able to estimate their level of metalinguistic knowledge with a greater degree of accuracy with respect to the explicit knowledge measures. This also adds further weight to the claim that the knowledge measured by the MKT is analytic rather than intuitive in nature.

Metalanguage

It was hypothesized that learners' ability to display their knowledge of target language rules would be independent of their command of metalinguistic terminology, and therefore that there would be no relationship between scores on the two parts of the MKT. The evidence reported above did not sustain this hypothesis, although there was some evidence that the two areas of knowledge did not always go hand in hand. Thus, metalinguistic knowledge appears not to be entirely unitary in nature, and, as Clapham (2001), Ellis (2004) and others have suggested, a learner can have explicit knowledge of target language rules without having command of the technical language that is often used by teachers and textbook writers to communicate such rules to language learners. However, it is difficult to reach any firm conclusion on this issue on the basis of the data presented here, given that the multiple-choice distractors used for the MKT varied considerably from one another in the amount of technical terminology used and also in the extent to which this terminology was crucial for understanding the rule. Further insights about the role of metalanguage in rule formulation may be gleaned from an alternative, constructed-response version of the MKT, which was also developed as part of the Marsden project. This version requires learners to supply their own rules, rather than selecting from options provided. These open-ended responses are then scored using a system that separates the conceptual and the technical aspects of learner explanations (see Chapter 9).

Learnability

There were a number of hypotheses relating to the instructed nature of metalinguistic knowledge, most of them sustained at least partially by our results. Type of foreign language instruction was the one exception. Being exposed to grammar-based instruction did not appear to be associated with higher performance on the MKT or any other tests in the battery for that matter. While we must be wary of discounting evidence that does not support the validation hypotheses, it may well be that this result is due to the dubious reliability of self-reports regarding the nature of L2 instruction. Learners may either have lacked understanding of our nomenclature for the different instructional methods and/or have lacked insight into the nature of their L2 instruction.

In contrast, length of formal English instruction was, as predicted, associated with higher MKT performance, although this manifested only on the Terminology section and not on the Rules section of the test.

More convincing evidence of the distinct, instructed nature of the knowledge elicited by the MKT comes from the comparison of NS and NNS performance across the various tests in the battery, which revealed a consistent and statistically significant advantage for NS on all tests except the MKT, where the gap between the two groups is much narrower and not statistically significant. The relatively poor performance of NS on the latter test is almost certainly due to their limited access to formal grammatical instruction, which is more often a characteristic of second or foreign language classrooms than of mother tongue education. The fact that NNS actually outperform the NS on the MKT offers further support for our hypothesis, although at first glance it seems odd that this advantage is only present on Part 2 of the test. There may be a number of reasons why the NNS students do relatively less well on Part 1 (Rules). One may be that L2 learners learn grammatical terminology from their teachers, whereas rule explanations are less well taught in L2 classrooms and indeed in some cases poorly understood by L2 teachers. Another possibility to be entertained is that the MKT measures not only metalinguistic knowledge, but also English reading ability and that some L2 learners' responses are limited by their inability to decipher the meaning of the multiple-choice options. The latter was found to be true of a small cohort of lower-intermediate learners from Japan, who were unable to do this section of the test at all. This possibility and its implications for MKT validity will be discussed further below.

Accessibility

The lack of any significant correlation between total scores on the MKT and those on the Oral Narrative Task is in keeping with the contention that learners will be unable to access their MKT under time-pressured performance conditions. The nonsignificant results for the feature-by-feature comparison also confirms the inaccessibility hypothesis, although we must be wary of analyses based on a single exemplar of each particular structure on the MKT and a quite limited number of obligatory occasions for these same structures on the story-telling task. The limited frequency of each structure in the Oral Narrative Task also precludes any further subcategorization, for example using the proto-typical versus peripheral distinction investigated by Hu (2002). Thus, we are unable to determine whether the finding of inaccessibility of metalinguistic knowledge under time-pressured condition holds for all structures, regardless of their cognitive salience, or whether it is confined to particular grammar features.

The evidence derived from the proficiency test data likewise permits only tentative conclusions about the nature of the MKT construct. Comparisons across different proficiency tests are always complex (see further discussion of this issue in Chapter 7), all the more so when there are different populations involved in each trial. All the tests used as outcome measures in this study had in common the fact that they measured academic language skills. However, they differed from one another in their method of testing the various skills and, to some extent, in the nature and scope of the academic proficiency construct. The

TOEFL CBT for example is made up of largely discrete-point items, whereas the IELTS is more performance-based and includes a separate writing and speaking component. DELNA lacks a speaking test but in other respects is more akin in both format and content to the IELTS than TOEFL.

These differences in format may go someway towards explaining the variable strengths of the correlations between the MKT and TOEFL on the one hand and between the MKT and IELTS on the other. Format or test method differences do not however account for the much weaker relationship between the DELNA test scores and the MKT compared to the results obtained for the IELTS. This is more likely to be a function of the Malaysian population who took this test, all of whom have fairly high levels of English proficiency and are schooled in what is a relatively English-rich environment. The limited spread of proficiency scores among this group may have affected the size of the correlations. It may also be the case that the advanced communicative skills of these students, all of whom had been handpicked at interview for an overseas English language teacher trainee program, made them more prone to use implicit rather explicit language knowledge in test performance. As already noted both by Renou (2001) and Elder and Manwaring (2004), learners with higher levels of communicative skill may rely on these resources when carrying out language proficiency tasks and may have less need to draw on their metalinguistic knowledge during performance.

One result that is consistent across all three tests is the *relative* strength of the MKT/Reading correlations compared to those obtained for other skills. This conforms with our hypothesis and Bialystok's contention that literacy-based and metalinguistic tasks make similar cognitive demands in that they both require controlled processing and analysis. Support for this hypothesis is, however, weakened by the fact that correlations between the MKT and Writing are in fact no stronger than those for Listening and Speaking. In fact, it seems that metalinguistic knowledge is implicated to the same extent across all three skills, which is contrary to our prediction and also to the findings of Han and Ellis (1998) and Elder and Manwaring (2004) reported earlier. We may surmise that what all tests components have in common is their academic nature, and that the knowledge and skills required to perform even the listening and speaking tasks are cognitive and analytical as well as communicative. This explanation may also account for the fact that significant correlations emerged between the MKT and IELTS Speaking, but not between the MKT and the Oral Narrative Task, which is less formal and academic in its orientation. Further insights into the relationship between implicit and explicit knowledge and language proficiency will be presented in Chapter 7.

Conclusion

This paper has reported the findings of an investigation into the validity of a test of metalinguistic knowledge, based on a series of hypotheses derived from previous research into the nature of the construct. This kind of enquiry is seldom conducted by SLA researchers, who have been accused by Douglas (2001), Sorace and Robertson (2001) and others of paying too little attention to the validity and reliability of the measures on which their research claims are founded.

Previous research reviewed in this paper has revealed that metalinguistic knowledge, while not unitary in nature, is distinct from implicit knowledge in the following respects: (a) it is learned in a piecemeal fashion via formal instruction rather than acquired systematically via naturalistic exposure, (b) it is analytical and subject to conscious control rather than intuitive and (c) it is not automatized and therefore difficult to access during spontaneous language production. The majority of the hypotheses derived from this conceptualization was sustained by the current investigation and thus attest to the construct validity of the MKT.

Perhaps the most convincing evidence of the MKT as a measure of explicit rather than implicit knowledge is the finding from the CFA, which supported the appropriateness of a two-factor solution in which the MKT was aligned with the other test purporting to measure explicit language knowledge (UGJT). The fact that self-assessed ability was more strongly linked to scores on the MKT than to those derived from the implicit knowledge measures supports the notion that the knowledge elicited via this test is conscious and analytic. The finding that NNS test-takers as a group performed on a par with the NS and sometimes outperformed them is in keeping with the notion that metalinguistic knowledge is learned though formal instruction of the kind characteristic of L2 rather than L1 (English) classrooms and therefore provides further support for the validity of the MKT as a measure of this knowledge. This conclusion is also corroborated by the fact that the longer learners had studied English formally, the higher their scores were on the MKT and UGJT, the only other explicit knowledge measures in the test battery.

With regard to the vexed question of the accessibility of metalinguistic knowledge during L2 production, this study has yielded ambiguous evidence. It may be that our accessibility hypothesis was inappropriate, given the conflicting findings of previous research on this issue. In any case, it is hard to know whether the results, which provide only tentative support for the notion that access to explicit knowledge is restricted under time-pressured performance conditions, are a reflection of the validity of the MKT or rather whether they are an artifact of the standardized English proficiency instruments used to elicit language performance data. As noted above, the academic nature of the measures used for concurrent validation purposes in this study may mean that they are unsuitable as measures of automated language production. Or indeed it may be that all language tests, by their very nature, encourage a focus on self-monitored rather than spontaneous performance, as Elder *et al.* (2002) have surmised.

On the other hand, as already noted, the stronger shared variance between the MKT and reading (as opposed to writing) may be due to the fact that the MKT it is at least partly a measure of reading proficiency. To the extent that this is true, it constitutes a threat to the validity of the MKT as a 'pure' measure of the metalinguistic knowledge construct. However, while the limitations of this instrument are acknowledged, it is hard to know how to get around the problem, which incidentally also emerges in relation to the Grammaticality Judgment tests described in Chapter 4, which assumes an ability to understand the meaning of the target sentences, whether these are delivered orally or in writing. Validity is a relative rather than absolute test quality and all elicitation tools are subject to method effects that restrict, to some degree, the inferences that can be drawn from test scores. This is all the more true of language tests where the method and object of measurement are inevitably intertwined. On balance, however, given the weight of argument and evidence provided above, it seems reasonable to conclude that the MKT described in this chapter is an acceptably valid measure of the underlying construct of metalinguistic knowledge as conceptualized both here and in Chapter 1 of this volume.

Part 3

Applying the Measures of Implicit and Explicit L2 Knowledge

The initial plan for the second phase of the Marsden Project was directed at investigating to what extent tests of language proficiency could be explicated in terms of the distinction between second language (L2) implicit and explicit knowledge. However, as is often the case with large research projects, once we had obtained measures of the two types of knowledge, we began to see a number of different ways in which they could be applied. This part of the book reports four studies that made use of the measures to investigate the following issues:

- the learning difficulty of different grammatical structures;
- the nature of language proficiency;
- individual differences in language proficiency;
- the metalinguistic knowledge of teacher trainees.

The aim was two-fold: (1) to explore to what extent the distinction between implicit and explicit knowledge could shed light on these issues and (2) by demonstrating that our measures of the two types of knowledge could illuminate these issues, to provide further evidence of the validity of the tests used to obtain the measures.

Chapter 6 investigates whether learning difficulty differs for implicit and explicit knowledge. Scores for 17 grammatical structures were obtained using two tests of implicit knowledge and two tests of explicit knowledge. The results indicate that structures that are easy in terms of implicit knowledge may be difficult in terms of explicit knowledge and vice versa. The chapter also explores what factors might explain the differences in learning difficulty of the two types of knowledge. In particular, it examines whether Pienemann's (1989, 2005) Processability Theory is able to predict learning difficulty for the two types of knowledge. It was found that whereas the theory successfully predicted the learning difficulty of grammatical structures as implicit knowledge, it did not do so for the same structures as explicit knowledge. This result testifies to the validity of the Elicited Oral Imitation Test as a measure of implicit knowledge as Processability Theory is a theory of implicit knowledge. In other words, the Elicited Oral Imitation Test appears capable of producing data with the same essential characteristics as free constructed response data, which previous research based on the Processability Theory has utilized.

Chapter 7 examines the relationship between implicit/explicit L2 knowledge and L2 proficiency, as this is conceptualized and measured by means of two standardized tests. In this respect, therefore, this chapter realizes one of the main aims of the Marsden Project – namely, to establish a bridge between the fields of second language acquisition (SLA) and language testing. However, whereas SLA is pre-eminently a psycholinguistic enterprise, language testing currently is not, electing to emphasize ways of assessing what learners can *do* with language rather than what they *know* of or about language. Even so, it seems reasonable to assume that what learners can do with a language depends to a very considerable extent on their implicit and explicit knowledge of it, with different uses of language drawing differentially on the two types of knowledge. The results of the two studies reported in this chapter support such a position. In the first study, only measures of explicit knowledge were related to scores on the Tests of English as a Foreign Language (TOEFL). In the second study, measures of both implicit and explicit knowledge were found to be related to scores on the International English Language Testing System (IELTS). While there are a number of possible explanations for these different results, it is tempting to conclude that it reflects the different types of language use that these tests tap into, with the TOEFL eliciting primarily academic language use and the IELTS both academic and more interactive, interpersonal use of language. Seen in this way, the relationship between the tests of implicit and explicit knowledge and the standard tests of language proficiency constitutes evidence of the concurrent validity of the former.

Chapter 8 explores to what extent L2 learners' implicit and explicit knowledge differs according to their language learning experiences. This was made possible by the fact that the participants in the Marsden Project were quite varied in their backgrounds. They included native speakers of English, students of varied levels of proficiency enrolled in both pre-sessional and university-level English courses in New Zealand, a group of Japanese university students with no experience of English outside Japan and a group of Malaysian trainee teachers living in Malaysia where English is quite widely used. The learners in this sample varied on such dimensions as the age at which they had started learning English, the number of years they had been learning English, the number of years they had lived in an English-speaking country, the type of instruction they had experienced and the extent to which they used English in their daily lives. Cluster analysis was used to distinguish different clusters of participants in terms of their implicit and explicit knowledge of English. Each cluster was then examined to see whether the differences in their learning experiences matched the pattern of implicit and explicit knowledge that characterized that cluster. This method of analysis proved profitable in two ways. First, it was able to show that the differences in the learners' background could account for their implicit and explicit knowledge. Second, it confirmed the findings of the Confirmatory Factor Analysis in Chapter 2 by showing that the tests used to measure implicit and explicit knowledge were able to distinguish learners in terms of these two types of language knowledge and that there were identifiable 'best' measures for each type of knowledge (e.g. the Elicited Oral Imitation Test provided the best measure of implicit knowledge).

The final chapter in this Part of the book (Chapter 9) makes use of a revised version of the Metalinguistic Knowledge Test and the Untimed Grammaticality Judgment Test to investigate the explicit knowledge of grammatical rules of two groups of trainee English teachers – one consisting of native speakers and the other non-native speakers. The study of their explicit knowledge was motivated by the conviction that teachers need to be able to explain grammatical rules to students when conducting form-focused instruction, whether this involves incidental attention for form in communicative activities or planned grammar lessons. A key finding of the study was that both groups manifested relatively low levels of metalinguistic knowledge, especially when asked to provide explanations of grammatical errors (i.e. to use their explicit knowledge productively). This study also reinforces some of the findings of Chapter 6; high levels of explicit knowledge are evident in some grammatical structures (e.g. plural -s) but much lower levels in other structures (e.g. ergative verbs). Not surprisingly, this study also found that the non-native speaker teacher trainees demonstrated higher levels of metalinguistic knowledge than the native-speaker trainees, reflecting the fact that language learners are more likely to be exposed to explicit grammatical explanations than native speakers. This finding lends support to the construct validity of the Metalinguistic Knowledge Test.

These chapters are indicative of the utility of the tests of implicit and explicit knowledge in addressing a range of issues. Clearly, there are many more issues that such tests might usefully be used to study – the role of individual difference factors such as language aptitude in language learning and the nature of L1 transfer are two that come to mind. In Part 4 of the book, the tests are applied to the study of form-focused instruction in order to investigate which type of L2 knowledge (implicit, explicit or both) grammar instruction impacts on.

Chapter 6

Investigating Learning Difficulty in Terms of Implicit and Explicit Knowledge

ROD ELLIS

Introduction

DeKeyser (2003) distinguishes the 'objective' and 'subjective difficulty' of grammatical features. Objective difficulty concerns the inherent difficulty of different grammatical features. It is determined by reference to some theory of grammar that allows predictions to be made about which features will be easy and which difficult to learn. Subjective difficulty refers to the actual difficulty that individual learners experience when learning a second language (L2). The concern of this chapter is entirely with subjective difficulty, although, undoubtedly, learning difficulty is likely, in part at least, to reflect objective difficulty.

Clearly, 'subjective difficulty' is a relative concept, as what is 'difficult' for one learner may not be for another. A whole host of learner variables (e.g. developmental stage, motivation, intelligence) potentially impact on whether a particular learner at a particular time finds structure x easy or difficult.[1] There will also be a number of contextual variables (e.g. the availability and the type of form-focused instruction) that may influence whether feature x is easy or difficult to learn in this or that situation. However, it would seem reasonable to assume that to some degree at least, some features are easier to learn than others for all learners, reflecting how the human mind grapples with their intrinsic properties. In other words, learning difficulty is, in part at least, a universal phenomenon. The 'natural order' (Dulay & Burt, 1973; Krashen, 1977), one of the earliest findings in second language acquisition (SLA) research, is evidence in support of this claim.[2]

There is, however, a major problem with the notion of difficulty in this absolutist and universalist sense. This problem is reflected in the fact that the natural order and the order of presentation of grammatical features in traditional structural syllabuses are not the same. For example, English third person -s is a late acquired feature, but typically figures early in structural syllabuses. Irregular past tense verb forms are acquired quite early, but often figure much later than third person -s in structural syllabuses. It would seem, then, that there are very different meanings being attached to the idea of 'difficulty'. These different senses of 'difficulty' may reflect whether difficulty is being treated in relation to implicit knowledge or explicit knowledge of a L2.

What, then, are the criteria that respectively determine the learning difficulty of grammatical features as implicit and explicit knowledge? These criteria are a mixed bag, drawing on factors relating to the linguistic environment (e.g. input frequency), the nature of the grammatical features themselves (i.e. linguistic factors) and learnability (i.e. psychological difficulty).

The Learning Difficulty of Grammatical Structures as Implicit Knowledge

Theories of L2 acquisition, whether of the symbolist or connectionist types, seek to explain how learners develop implicit knowledge, not explicit knowledge (Hulstijn, 2002; Selinker, 1972). L2 acquisition, then, is equated with the development of implicit knowledge.

Drawing on the work of N. Ellis (1996), Goldschneider and DeKeyser (2000), Hulstijn and De Graaf (1994) and Pienemann (1998), the following criteria are proposed as determinants of what makes different grammatical features easy or difficult as implicit knowledge:

(1) Frequency (i.e. how frequently does the grammatical feature occur in the input?)
(2) Saliency (i.e. is the grammatical feature easy to notice in the input?)
(3) Functional value (i.e. does the grammatical feature map onto a clear, distinct meaning?)
(4) Regularity (i.e. does the grammatical feature conform to some identifiable pattern?)
(5) Processability (i.e. is the grammatical feature easy to process?)

I will briefly examine each.

Frequency

N. Ellis (1996: 113) argues that the long-term representations that result from implicit learning are 'tuned by the regularities and relative frequencies in the relevant perceptual domain'. In a later article, N. Ellis (2002) musters an impressive array of evidence to support this claim. He suggests that learners have the neural capacity to unconsciously count the elements of language they are exposed to. According to this view, features that occur frequently in the input will be easier to acquire than features that occur infrequently. However, although frequency clearly does contribute to learning difficulty, it cannot by itself account for the order in which implicit knowledge of different grammatical features is developed (see, e.g. Gass & Mackey, 2002). English articles, for example, occur with extremely high frequency in the input but are certainly not easy to acquire.

Saliency

Some grammatical features are inherently more salient (easy to notice) than others. Goldschneider and DeKeyser (2000) carried out a *post-hoc* analysis of the morphemes that figure in the natural order with a view to identifying what factors might account for the consistency of the order across multiple studies. They concluded that 'saliency' (broadly defined) was the primary factor. For example, verb -ing (more phonologically salient) is acquired before third person -s (less phonologically salient). The value of their analysis is that it provides a clear operational definition of saliency in terms of a number of other factors that make one morpheme more salient than another. These factors include 'perceptual salience', 'morphophonological regularity', 'syntactic category' (i.e. whether a morpheme is free or bound) and frequency.

Functional value

Grammatical forms typically realize discoursal, semantic or pragmatic functions, although some forms (e.g. third person -s) are entirely redundant and other forms (e.g. plural -s) can be redundant in specific contexts. Also, some forms realize multiple functions – for example, the present simple tense in English can convey a general truth, a habitual activity and a future event. Forms that realize a single function and that are typically nonredundant cater to the learner's One-to-One Principle (Andersen, 1984), and thus can be considered easier to learn than forms that realize multiple functions or that are always or often redundant.

Regularity

Regular features will be easier to acquire than irregular features. Hulstijn and Graaf (1994) distinguished two aspects of regularity. 'Scope' concerns the number of cases that are covered by a particular rule. 'Reliability' concerns the extent to which a rule holds true. For example, the plural -s rule is large in scope because it applies to a large number of nouns in English and also is high in reliability because it applies to a large percentage of all nouns. In contrast, the pattern verb + direct object + verb (as in 'My father made me work') is small in scope and low in reliability given that few verbs take this pattern – the more general pattern being verb + direct object + infinitive (as in 'My father persuaded me to work').

Processability

Pienemann's Processability Theory seeks to explain what is known about acquisitional orders/sequences in terms of a set of processing procedures. As Pienemann (2005: 2) put it 'once we can spell out the sequence in which language processing routines develop we can delineate those grammars that are processable at different points of development'. Drawing on Levelt's work on speech production, he proposed that language production, whether in the L1 or the L2, can only be explained with reference to a set of basic premises: (1) speakers possess relatively specialized processing components that operate autonomously and in parallel; (2) processing is incremental (i.e. a processor can start working on the incomplete output of another processor); (3) in order to cope with nonlinearity (i.e. the fact that the linguistic sequence may not match the natural order of events as in 'Before the man rode off, he mounted his horse'), speakers need to store grammatical information in memory; and thus it follows that (4) grammatical processing must have access to a grammatical memory store, which Pienemann saw as task-specific and as involving 'procedural' rather than 'declarative' memory.[3]

Processability Theory is a theory of language production. However, it can also lay claim to being a theory of language acquisition in that it proposes that the processing procedures are hierarchical and are mastered one at a time. As Pienemann (2005: 13) put it, 'it is hypothesized that processing devices will be acquired in their sequence of activation in the production process'. Thus, the failure to master a low-level procedure blocks access to higher-level procedures and makes it impossible for the learner to acquire those grammatical features that depend on them.

Pienemann (1998, 2005) identified the following language generation processes:

(1)   word/lemma;
(2)   category procedure (lexical category);
(3)   phrasal procedures (head);
(4)   S-procedure and word order rule;
(5)   matrix/subordinate clause.

What distinguishes these processes is the nature of the grammatical information that the learner needs to deposit and exchange in what Pienemann calls 'feature unification'.

Initially, learners are unable to control any of the processes involved. At this stage, learners are able to access L2 words, but these are invariant in form and are used in single constituent utterances. The learners' lexicon is not annotated while transfer of L1 annotation is blocked because the learner has not yet developed the specialized procedures to hold L2 grammatical information. Thus, the beginning learner 'is unable to produce any structures which rely on the exchange of specific grammatical information using syntactic procedures' (Pienemann, 2005: 11).

The first procedure to be mastered is the 'category procedure'. Lexical entries are now annotated with a number of diacritic features (e.g. 'possessive' and 'number'). These can be accessed but only within a single constituent and are matched directly with the underlying conceptual content of a message so no exchange of grammatical information is required. At this stage, the learner is still not able to handle structures where diacritic features need to be matched across elements in a constituent or between constituents.

The ability to handle this begins at the next stage – the level of phrasal constituents. Thus, it is now possible for learners to handle such structures as articles, plural agreement (e.g. 'many children') and do-fronting (e.g. 'Do he like it?'). Exchange of information in the phrasal procedure is required to check the value of a diacritic feature of one lexical entry (e.g. 'child' – plural) with that of another (e.g. 'many' – plural) to ascertain that they match and thus enable the production of a structural phrase (e.g. 'many children').

At this stage, however, exchange of information *between* structural phrases is still not possible. This is activated at the next stage – the S-procedure. This involves exchange of information between heads of different phrases, as in subject-verb agreement, which entails the unification of features such as person and number *across* constituent boundaries. The features of one constituent (the subject noun phrase) are deposited in the S-procedure and subsequently placed in another constituent (the verb phrase). When this becomes possible, learners are able to mark the third person of the present simple tense with the -s morpheme.

The final procedure to be acquired enables learners to process the word order of subordinate structures such as that found in embedded questions in English (e.g. 'He asked where I lived') and verb-end in German (e.g. 'Er fragt warum ich traurig war').

Pienemann argues there is a basic difference between the first three procedures and the last two in the hierarchy, in that structures appearing in levels 1–3 cannot be represented by constituent structure rules because the S-procedure has not been developed. Thus, in the early stages 'sentences are formed using simplified procedures based on a direct mapping of argument structure onto functional structure' (Pienemann, 2005: 14). According to this theory, then, learning difficulty and the sequence of acquisition is determined by the nature of the processing procedure required to produce a specific grammatical feature. In contrast to the other criteria listed in Table 6.1, processability is precisely defined and affords highly specific predictions about learning difficulty – but only as implicit knowledge.

Applying the criteria

It is not yet clear how such criteria can be applied to determine the learning difficulty of different grammatical features. Goldschneider and

DeKeyser (2001) proposed a scoring method for the criteria they examined. They drew on a range of previous studies (e.g. semantic complexity was evaluated in terms of Brown's (1973) assignment of meanings to grammatical functors). However, a key question is whether these criteria are independent or overlapping. As noted above, Gold-schneider and DeKeyser (2001: 35) argued that there is a common factor underlying all the criteria they investigated – 'saliency in a broad sense of the word' – but their study did not consider 'processability' (a criterion that covers both morphological and syntactical features). This relates to output rather than input and thus is distinct from saliency. A second question concerns the relative contribution of the specific criteria to overall learning difficulty. Goldschneider and DeKeyser do not directly address this in their study. In short, we are still a long way from being able to algorithmically predict the relative learning difficulty of different grammatical elements.

Learning Difficulty as Explicit Knowledge

Robinson (1996) distinguishes two dimensions of 'pedagogic rule complexity': complexity of the structural regularity itself and complexity of the accompanying explanation. Clearly though, these are related in that a complex feature will require a complex explanation and, vice-versa, a simple feature a simple explanation. In fact, Hulstijn (2002) suggests that explicit knowledge should be operationalized as 'knowledge that can be verbalized with the use of labels for concepts'. This definition suggests that learning difficulty as explicit knowledge needs to be understood in terms of how easy or difficult it is to *verbalize* a declarative rule and that this will depend on two principal factors; the concepts involved and the labels (metalanguage) needed to express them. Thus, the difficulty of declarative rules of grammar will be considered under two general headings: conceptual clarity and metalanguage.

Conceptual clarity

Where conceptual clarity[4] is concerned, a basic distinction can be drawn between structures that are formally or functionally simple (Krashen, 1982). Articles, for example, constitute a relatively simple formal system (i.e. there are only three forms), but are functionally very complex (i.e. they perform a number of different functions relating to both the category of the noun they determine, the situational context and the discourse context). In contrast, wh-interrogatives are functionally simple but formally complex in that they involve the auxiliary system and subject-verb inversion. Fairly obviously, features that are easy to learn as explicit knowledge (in the sense that descriptions of them are easy to understand) will be those that are both formally and functionally simple, as the rules can be expressed in accordance with Hammerly's (1982) 'design criteria' – i.e. rules should be concrete, simple, nontechnical, close to popular/traditional notions and in rule-of-thumb form.[5] It can be hypothesized, then, that features that are more difficult to learn will be those that are either formally or functionally complex. The most difficult structures to understand will be those that are both formally and functionally complex.

A second distinction important for understanding conceptual clarity concerns whether there is some kind of transparent, general rule (e.g. how to make the past tense of regular verbs in English) or whether there is no such rule (e.g. how to make the past tense of irregular verbs). This distinction relates to the distinction Hulstijn and De Graaf (1994) make between 'rule learning' and 'item learning'. Of course many structures for which there are clear rules (such as past tense -ed) can also be learnt as items ('moved', 'drowned', 'jumped' etc.), but structures for which there are no clear rules probably have to be mastered as items. We can assume that structures for which clear (and true) rules can be formulated can
be more easily learned as explicit knowledge than structures that necessarily involve item learning.

Where rules are expressible, conceptual complexity can be defined in terms of 'the <u>number</u> of different formal or functional grammatical features that contribute to the specific form of a target structure and the specific function it performs' (De Graaf, 1997: 41). These features determine the 'complicatedness' of the declarative rule. Thus, a pedagogic rule for the choice of third person singular pronouns in English ('he', 'she', 'it') can be considered relatively simple in that it addresses only three forms that are transparently related to three functions (human male, human female, inanimate). In contrast, the rule for the choice of articles in English is more complex in that there are four forms ('the', 'a', 'an' and zero) while a whole host of formal and functional factors are involved (e.g. whether the following noun is countable or uncountable, definiteness, specificity, whether the noun begins with a vowel or consonant). Of course, it may still be possible to formulate some relatively simple rules of thumb for articles (e.g. use 'a/an' with a first mentioned noun and 'the' when the noun is mentioned subsequently) but such rules will, at best, be anomalous as they correspond only loosely to actual use. De Graaf suggests that his definition of complexity can be applied quantitatively. However, this may not be easy, partly because it is not always clear what constitutes the scope of a rule (e.g. we could formulate a rule for the use of all articles or just for one particular article) and because it may not always be easy to specify the number of forms and functions involved.

Another factor influencing the conceptual clarity of declarative rules concerns the prototypicality of the rule. Hu (2002) distinguished rules that specify the prototypical function of a form and rules that specify a more peripheral use. For example, the present simple tense can be used to refer to general truths or habitual actions (prototypical functions) or to planned future actions (peripheral function). Hu found that Chinese learners of English were better able to employ declarative rules relating to prototypical functions of six English structures than rules relating to peripheral functions. This suggests that they found the former easier than the latter, although it is also possible that they had received explicit instruction in the prototypical but not the peripheral rules.

Metalanguage

Metalanguage can be 'semitechnical' or 'technical' (James & Garrett, 1992). For example, the rule for the use of the indefinite article with uncountable nouns in English can be expressed quite simply with minimal metalanguage ('Don't "use a/an" before a word that cannot be made plural') or much more technically, involving substantial metalanguage ('Don't use the indefinite article before an uncountable noun'). However, it would seem likely that the rules for some grammatical structures will require more extensive and technical metalanguage than the rules for other structures. For example, it is difficult to see how the rule for dative alternation with verbs like 'give' and 'send' can be formulated without reference to 'direct' and 'indirect object'. In general, we can assume that the more technical the metalanguage needed to formulate a rule, the more difficult that rule will be to learn.

Applying the criteria

It is clearly possible to establish some general guidelines for determining the difficulty of grammatical structures as explicit knowledge. However, it may prove impossible to arrive at criteria that will ensure a reliable and valid assessment of the difficulty of different declarative rules. It may be necessary, therefore, to employ empirical rather than theoretical means to distinguish grammatical structures in terms of their difficulty as explicit knowledge. Two such empirical means are to examine the order in which different pedagogical rules are introduced in language syllabuses (if we assume that structures are primarily graded on the basis of learners' ability to understand and 'learn' them in Krashen's (1981) sense) and to rely on the judgments of 'experts' (e.g. applied linguists or experienced language teachers). Robinson (1996) serves as an example of the second of these.

The approach that is adopted in the study reported below is to examine learning difficulty in terms of learners' performance on the tests of implicit and explicit L2 knowledge described in Section 2 of this book. Thus, investigating learning difficulty in terms of implicit knowledge will draw on tests that tap into what learners intuitively feel is correct, that are time-pressured, that call for a primary focus on meaning and that make no call on the learners' metalinguistic knowledge. In contrast, to investigate learning difficulty in terms of explicit knowledge, the tests employed will be those that encourage learners to respond using 'rules', are performed without any time pressure, call for a primary focus on form and invite the use of metalinguistic knowledge.

The Study

Research questions

(1) Are there some grammatical structures that are easy in terms of implicit knowledge but difficult in terms of explicit knowledge?
(2) Conversely, are there some grammatical structures that are difficult in terms of implicit knowledge but easy in terms of explicit knowledge?

Grammatical structures

A total of 17 grammatical structures were investigated. These are listed with examples of learner errors in Table 2.2 in Chapter 2. The structures were chosen based on a number of criteria. They were all known to be problematic to learners, resulting in identifiable production errors. They included structures that were likely to involve both item learning (e.g. verb complements) and system learning (e.g. third person -s). They included both morphological and syntactical structures. They were representative of the full range of structures covered in a typical teaching syllabus and were drawn from all levels of such a syllabus.[6]

Participants

Over 220 L2 learners[7] took the battery of tests described below. The sample was made up of a number of different groups. The majority ($n = 147$) were international students of mixed language proficiency who were studying English as a L2 in either a language school in New Zealand, or as part of an undergraduate degree programme at the University of Auckland. The majority of learners in this group were from China. Some of these were taking presessional English courses at various language schools, while others were already enrolled in university degree programmes. A small group ($n = 28$) were first-year Japanese students at an all women's university in Tokyo, Japan. With a few exceptions, these students had very limited procedural ability in English. A third group ($n = 54$) were students enrolled in a four-year BEd TESOL program in Malaysia. These students had undergone an intensive English preparation course and generally spoke and wrote English fluently and with confidence. Overall, the English proficiency of the learners in this sample was very mixed, ranging from false beginners to advanced learners displaying high levels of linguistic competence and fluency. All the participants agreed to complete the tests and signed an ethics consent form.

Tests of implicit/explicit knowledge

Four of the tests described in Chapter 2 were used in this study. Two of the tests (the Elicited Oral Imitation Test and the Timed Grammaticality Judgment Test; GJT) were designed to measure implicit knowledge of the 17 grammatical features, and the other two tests (the Untimed GJT (ungrammatical sentences only) and the Metalinguistic Knowledge Test) were designed to measure explicit knowledge. The chapters in Section 2 of the book provide a detailed description of these tests together with the results of various correlational analyses that demonstrate their validity as relatively separate measures of implicit and explicit knowledge. For convenience sake, brief descriptions of the four tests are provided below.

(1) Elicited Oral Imitation Test
     This consisted of a set of 34 belief statements (involving both grammatical and ungrammatical sentences containing the target structures). There were 68 statements in the original version of this test. Examples of the belief statements for dative alternation were as follows:
       People should report a car accident to the police.
     * People should report the police stolen money.
     The participants were required to say first whether they agreed with, disagreed with or were not sure about each statement and then to repeat the sentences orally in correct English. Their responses were audiorecorded. Each imitated sentence was allocated a score of either 1 (the target structure was correctly supplied) or 0 (the target structure was either avoided or attempted but incorrectly supplied). Scores were expressed as percentage correct. (See Chapter 3 for a detailed account of this test.)

(2) Timed Grammaticality Judgment Test
     This was a computer-delivered test consisting of 68 sentences, evenly divided between grammatical and ungrammatical. The sentences, which were different from those in the Elicited Oral Imitation Test, were presented in written form on a computer screen.

Thus, there were four sentences to be judged for each of the 17 grammatical structures. Test-takers were required to indicate whether each sentence was grammatical or ungrammatical by pressing response buttons within a fixed time limit. Each item was scored dichotomously as correct/incorrect (reflecting the responses of native speakers of English on whom the sentences in this test were repeatedly trialled) with items not responded to scored as incorrect. A percentage accuracy score was calculated. (See Chapter 4 for a detailed account of this test.)

(3) Untimed Grammaticality Judgment Test
This test had the same content as the Untimed GJT. The sentences were again computer-delivered in written form. Test-takers were required to indicate in their own time whether each sentence was grammatical or ungrammatical. This test provided a percentage judgment accuracy score based on the participants' dichotomous responses. Total accuracy scores as well as scores for the grammatical and ungrammatical sentences were calculated. (See Chapter 4 for a detailed account of this test.)

(4) Metalinguistic Knowledge Test
This test consisted of two parts, but only the scores from Part 1 were used in this study. This presented test-takers with 17 ungrammatical sentences, based on the 17 structures in Table 2.2, and required them to select the rule that best explained each error out of four choices provided. A total percentage accuracy score was calculated. (See Chapter 5 for a detailed account of this test.)

Procedure

The tests were completed in the following order:

(1) Elicited Oral Imitation Test
(2) Timed GJT
(3) Untimed GJT
(4) Metalinguistic Knowledge Test

All tests included a number of training examples for participants to practise on. The Elicited Oral Imitation Test was completed in one-on-one meetings between a researcher and a participant. Each participant listened to the sentences one at a time on a cassette recorder, completed an answer sheet indicating his/her response to the belief statement and then orally reproduced the sentence, which was audiorecorded. The Timed GJT, the Untimed GJT and the Metalinguistic Knowledge Test were completed individually on a computer in a private office. The complete test battery was completed in a single session lasting approximately two and a half hours.

Analysis

Descriptive statistics for the four tests were calculated. The reliability of the different test measures was calculated using Cronbach's alpha. The alpha for the Elicited Oral Imitation Test was 0.88, for the Timed GJT 0.96, for the Untimed GJT 0.83 and for the Metalinguistic Knowledge Test 0.79. Mean scores on the Elicited Oral Imitation Test and the Timed GJT for each of the 17 grammatical structures were calculated and then averaged to produce a single score for implicit knowledge. A combined mean explicit knowledge score using the ungrammatical sentences on the Untimed GJT[8] and the scores from the Metalinguistic Knowledge Test was calculated for each of the 17 structures. Difference scores for explicit and implicit knowledge for each grammatical structure were calculated by subtracting the mean implicit knowledge score from the mean explicit knowledge score.

Two separate analyses were based on these scores. First, the implicit and explicit scores for the entire sample were compared to identify to what extent there were differences in learning difficulty.

Second, four of the 17 structures were chosen to represent each of the hierarchical processing operations that distinguished the Processability Theory. Details of these four structures will be provided in the Results section. Research based on the Processability Theory has used 'emergence' as the measure of acquisition (i.e. a feature is considered 'acquired' if a learner has used it in two nonformulaic utterances). It is also clear that the theory addresses acquisition in relation to learner production. For this reason, only the Elicited Oral Imitation Test scores were used as the measure of implicit knowledge. Also, only the scores for the ungrammatical sentences of the Untimed GJT served as the measure of explicit knowledge. Mean accuracy scores for each grammatical structure were calculated. Also, implicational scaling was used to identify whether the predicted learning difficulty of the four structures was evident in the scores for the two types of knowledge.

Results

This section first reports a Principal Component Factor Analysis for the four tests. This is necessary in order to show that the larger sample used in the study reported in this chapter performs in a similar way on the tests as the smaller sample reported in Chapter 2. Next, the results for the whole sample on all 17 structures are provided. This is followed by the results for the randomly selected subsample of 20 learners on four of the structures.

Table 6.1 Principal Component Analysis of four measures (Rotated Component Matrix)

Component	Total	% Variance	Cumulative%
1	2.113	53.256	53.256
2	0.894	22.338	75.594
Test		*Component 1*	*Component 2*
Imitation Test		0.856	0.211
Timed GJT		0.878	0.159
Untimed GJT (ungram.)		0.202	0.819
Metalinguistic Knowledge		0.153	0.846

Table 6.2 Descriptive statistics

Elicited Oral Imitation Test (n =228)		Timed GJT (total) (n =227)		Untimed GJT (ungram.) (n =225)		Meta-linguistic Test (n =228)	
Mean	*SD*	*Mean*	*SD*	*Mean*	*SD*	*Mean*	*SD*
50.44	18.91	56.21	11.88	80.67	13.13	54.61	15.56

The results of the factor analysis are shown in Table 6.1. The Elicited Oral Imitation Test and the Timed GJT loaded on factor 1, while the Untimed GJT (ungrammatical) and the Metalinguistic Knowledge Test both loaded only on factor 2. This solution, then, mirrors the results of the Confirmatory Factor Analysis reported in Chapter 2, and lends support to the claims that the tests provide relatively separate measures of implicit and explicit knowledge.

Table 6.2 shows the means and standard deviations for the participants who completed the Elicited Oral Imitation Test, the Timed GJT, the Untimed GJT (ungrammatical sentences) and the Metalinguistic Test.

Table 6.3 shows the means for the explicit and implicit scores together with the differences between the two sets of scores for each of the 17 grammatical structures in the whole sample ($n = 224$). The explicit scores are generally higher than the implicit scores, although this may simply reflect the differences in the test methods. As can be seen from the standard deviations (SD), the scores for all the structures displayed considerable variance in both implicit and explicit measures. In the case of the implicit knowledge scores, 'easy' structures (i.e. structures with

Table 6.3 Difference between explicit and implicit scores for 17 grammatical structures

	Explicit knowledge		Implicit knowledge		Difference between means
	Mean	SD	Mean	SD	
Verb complement	0.77	0.27	0.65	0.23	0.12
Third person -s	0.64	0.28	0.46	0.200	0.18
Plural -s	0.79	0.29	0.51	0.22	**0.28**
Indefinite article	0.79	0.27	0.40	0.20	**0.39**
Possessive -s	0.81	0.25	0.61	0.22	0.20
Regular past tense -ed	0.77	0.28	0.50	0.22	**0.27**
Yes/no questions	0.56	0.32	0.50	0.22	0.06
Comparative	0.73	0.33	0.54	0.23	0.19
Hypothetical conditionals	0.50	0.26	0.37	0.19	0.13
Modals	0.71	0.29	0.72	0.21	− 0.01
Ergative verbs	0.47	0.30	0.53	0.27	− 0.06
Embedded questions	0.57	0.33	0.45	0.21	0.12
Adverb placement	0.47	0.25	0.63	0.20	− 0.16
Question tags	0.75	0.29	0.41	0.20	**0.34**
Since/for	0.72	0.30	0.52	0.24	**0.20**
Dative alternation	0.49	0.31	0.57	0.22	− 0.12
Relative clauses	0.84	0.28	0.63	0.26	**0.21**

mean scores higher than 0.60) were verb complement, possessive -s, modals, adverb placement and relative clauses, while 'difficult' structures (i.e. structures with scores lower then a mean of 0.45) were indefinite article, hypothetical conditionals and question tags. In the case of explicit knowledge, the 'easy' structures (i.e. structures with scores higher than 0.75) were plural -s, indefinite article, possessive -s, regular past tense and relative clauses. 'Difficult' structures for explicit knowledge (i.e. structures with scores of 0.50 or lower) were adverb placement, ergative verbs and hypothetical conditionals. The difference column shows that there were some structures that varied very little in ease/difficulty for implicit and explicit knowledge – verb complements, yes/no questions, modals, and ergative verbs all scored almost the same for both types of knowledge. Other structures (i.e. those shown in bold in Table 6.3) manifested a marked difference between implicit and explicit scores. Indefinite article and question tags, for example, were among the easiest structures where explicit knowledge was concerned, but the most difficult for implicit knowledge. Other structures where the difference between implicit and explicit scores was notable were plural -s, third person -s, indefinite article, regular past -ed, since/for with present perfect and relative clauses.

These results suggest that there are clear differences in the difficulty of grammatical structures as implicit and explicit knowledge. These differences are revealed more clearly in Figure 6.1, which shows the rank ordering of the 17 structures for explicit and implicit knowledge based on the scores for the whole sample. As might be expected, the Spearman Rank Order Correlation for the two sets of scores was weak and statistically nonsignificant ($r = 0.08$; $p = NS$).

To investigate whether predictions about the learning difficulty of grammatical structures based on the Processability Theory were borne out in the data, four structures were chosen to represent each of the hierarchical processing operations distinguished by the theory. Information about these four structures can be found in Table 6.4.

For the category procedure, possessive -s was chosen. Pienemann (2005) claims that possessive-s is a feature marked diacritically in lexical entries and thus can be accessed directly from the learner's lexicon. For the phrasal procedure, 'since/for' was chosen. Here, the selection of preposition depends on the nature of the following noun phrase. If this refers to a specific point in time, 'since' is required (e.g. 'since 1985'), whereas if this refers to a period of time, 'for' is required (e.g. 'for five years'). Thus, choice is entirely dependent on information contained within the phrasal constituent. For the S-procedure, third person -s was chosen. Pienemann (2005) gives this as an example of this procedure. Finally, for subordinate clause procedure, question tags were chosen; the form of a question tag depends on information contained in the main clause that precedes it.

Two analyses are reported. The first is based on mean accuracy scores for the whole sample. The second used implicational scaling of the scores of 20 participants who were randomly selected from the total sample. In both

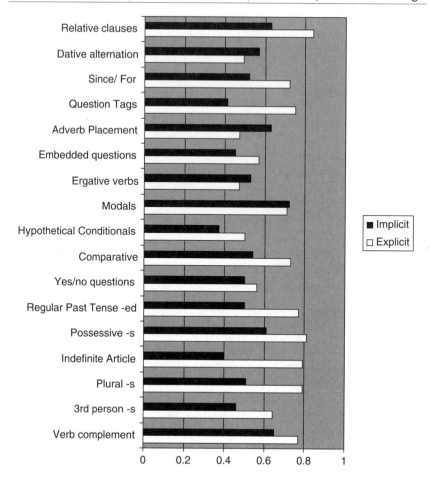

Figure 6.1 Rank orders for explicit and implicit scores of the of 17 grammatical structures

cases, it was expected that the theory would successfully predict learning difficulty as implicit knowledge, but not necessarily as explicit knowledge.

Table 6.5 shows the mean implicit and explicit scores for each of the four structures for the whole sample. The rank order of difficulty of the four structures, as shown in the implicit scores, conforms to the order of difficulty predicted by the Processability Theory. That is, possessive -s emerges as the easiest structure, 'since/for' as next, third person -s as next and question tags as the most difficult. However, a very different order of difficulty is evident for the explicit scores. While possessive -s was still the easiest (not surprisingly perhaps as the rule for this structure is conceptually simple and requires little metalanguage), question tags proved the next easiest, with third person -s and 'since/for' more difficult.

Table 6.4 The four grammatical structures used in the processability analysis

	Description	*Typical learner error*
Possessive -s	-s is attached to a modifying noun to signal it is the possessor	*Liao is still living in his rich uncle house.
Question tags	The choice of auxiliary in a question tag is dependent on the form of the main verb (e.g. if the main verb contains an auxiliary then the same auxiliary must be chosen in the question tag)	*We will leave tomorrow, isn't it?
Since/for	'Since' denotes a period of time commencing at a specific point in the past and continuing into the present; 'for' is used when the period is denoted in terms of a number of time units	*He has been living in New Zealand since three years.
Third person -s	-s is attached to the base form of the verb in the third person of the present simple tense	*Hiroshi live with his friend Koji.

Table 6.5 Means implicit and explicit scores for four structures

Processing procedure	*Structure*	*Mean implicit score*	*Mean explicit score*
Subordinate clause procedure	Question tags	0.41(4)	0.75(2)
S-procedure	Third person -s	0.46(3)	0.64(4)
Phrasal procedure	Since/for	0.52(2)	0.72(3)
Category procedure	Possessive -s	0.61(1)	0.81(1)

Mean scores, however, can be misleading. It does not always follow that individual learners will experience the same order of difficulty as the sample as a whole. It is for this reason that research based on the Processability Theory has invariably examined the sequence of acquisition of individual learners. Accordingly, a second analysis using implicational scaling was undertaken. A structure was considered acquired as implicit knowledge if a learner used it correctly in both of the two items measuring it in the Elicited Oral Imitation Test. This scoring decision reflected Pienemann's use of 'emergence' as a criterion of acquisition. A structure was considered acquired as explicit knowledge only if the learner judged both of the two ungrammatical sentences measuring it correctly.[8] The results of the implicational scaling are shown in Table 6.6. The coefficient

Table 6.6 Implicational scaling of 20 learners' implicit and explicit knowledge

Learner	Q tag		Third person -s		Since/ for		Poss -s	
	Impl	Expl	Impl	Expl	Impl	Expl	Impl	Expl
30	−	+	−	+	−	−	−	−
71	−	+	−	+	+	+	−	−
121	−	+	−	−	+	−	−	+
133	−	+	−	−	−	−	−	−
187	−	−	−	−	−	−	−	−
98	−	+	+	+	−	+	+	−
179	−	+	−	+	−	+	+	−
5	−	+	−	+	+	+	+	+
18	−	+	−	−	+	+	+	+
42	−	+	−	+	+	−	+	+
143	−	+	−	+	+	+	+	−
171	+	+	−	+	+	+	+	+
10	−	+	+	−	+	−	+	+
16	−	+	+	+	+	+	+	−
27	−	+	+	−	+	−	+	+
39	−	+	+	+	+	−	+	+
216	−	+	+	+	+	+	+	+
169	+	+	+	+	+	+	+	+
198	+	+	+	+	+	+	+	+
208	+	+	+	+	+	+	+	+
Total	4	19	9	15	15	12	15	12

of scalability for the measure of implicit knowledge was 0.80, reaching the criterion level recommended by Hatch and Farhady (1982).

The four structures scaled as predicted for the Elicited Oral Imitation Test scores. That is, with very few exceptions, learners who have acquired question tags have also acquired the other three structures, learners who have acquired third person -s have also acquired the other two structures, and learners who have acquired 'since/for' have also acquired possessive -s. The reverse is clearly not true. Acquisition of possessive -s, for example, does not implicate acquisition of the other structures. In contrast, the structure predicted to constitute the greatest difficulty in learning (question tags) emerged as the simplest of the four structures in the Untimed GJT, with 19 of the 20 learners judging the ungrammatical sentences correctly.

The difference between the measures of implicit and explicit knowledge is also evident in other ways. For example, whereas 15 of the 20 learners had acquired the two simplest structures (possessive -s and 'since/for') as implicit knowledge, only 12 had acquired these structures as explicit knowledge. In contrast, whereas only four and nine learners, respectively, had acquired the two most difficult structures as implicit knowledge, 19 and 15 learners had acquired these structures as explicit knowledge. One learner (No. 187) demonstrated neither implicit nor explicit knowledge of any of the four structures. Three learners (Nos. 169, 198, 208) demonstrated both implicit and explicit knowledge of all four structures. Four learners (Nos. 30, 71, 121, 133) had no implicit knowledge, but explicit knowledge of at least one of the structures. Many learners (e.g. Nos. 5 and 216) had explicit knowledge of a structure without implicit knowledge, and somewhat fewer had implicit knowledge without any explicit knowledge of a structure.

Discussion

The research questions addressed whether there are some grammatical structures that are easy in terms of one type of knowledge (implicit or explicit), but difficult in terms of the other type. To address these questions, the tests described in Part 2 of the book were administered to learners of mixed levels of proficiency. The psychometric properties of the tests (as shown in Chapter 2) support the claim that they were measuring two separate constructs – which we labelled L2 implicit and explicit knowledge.[9]

A comparison of the mean scores for implicit knowledge (based on a combined score for the Elicited Oral Imitation Test and the Timed GJT) and for explicit knowledge (based on a combined score for the Untimed GJT ungrammatical sentences and the Metalinguistic Knowledge Test) indicates that learning difficulty is indeed different depending on which type of knowledge is involved. This is evident in the scores for individual grammatical structures (e.g. regular past tense -ed has a high explicit score and relatively low implicit score, whereas adverb placement has a moderately high implicit score but a low explicit score) and also, overall, in the different rank orders of difficulty for the implicit and explicit scores (see Figure 6.1).

Taking 45% (somewhat arbitrarily) as a cut-off point, implicit scores were low for four structures; hypothetical conditionals, indefinite article, question tags and embedded questions. What factors might explain the difficulty the learners experienced with performing these structures in the Elicited Oral Imitation Test and Timed GJT? Five factors that potentially contributed to the ease/difficulty of structural features for implicit knowledge were considered (see Learning Difficulty as Implicit Knowledge section). Table 6.7 attempts an assessment of the difficulty of the four structures with low implicit scores in terms of these factors. It must be acknowledged, however, that this analysis is *post hoc* and that the application of these factors as criteria of learning difficulty is not always straightforward. By way of illustration, their application to two of the structural features will be considered. The indefinite article can be considered easy to learn in terms of frequency (it is one of the most frequently occurring grammatical items in English), but difficult in terms of the other four factors. It has low saliency (e.g. it is perceptually nonsalient), it realizes several different discourse functions, it is irregular in the sense that it only applies to countable nouns (Butler (2002) reported that learners find distinguishing countable and uncountable nouns problematic) and it is difficult to process in that selection depends on exchanging information across constituents.[10] In the case of question tags, the point tested was the choice of auxiliary verb. This can be considered low in frequency (in so far as different auxiliary verbs occur in questions tags), but perceptually quite salient as it occurs at the end of the sentence and constitutes a free morpheme. Also, it can be considered to meet the regularity criterion in that the rule determining which auxiliary to choose is highly reliable. However, it has low functional value in that the choice of auxiliary form is determined entirely formally (i.e. with reference to the verb form in the main clause) and it is difficult to process in that it involves subordinate clause procedures in Piene-

Table 6.7 Explaining the grammatical complexity of four structures

Grammatical structure	Frequency	Saliency (low/ high)	Functional complexity (complex/ simple)	Regularity (regular/ irregular)	Easy/ difficult to process
Indefinite article	High	Low	Complex	Irregular	Difficult
Embedded questions	Medium	Low	Complex	Regular	Difficult
Hypothetical conditionals	Low	Low	Complex	Regular	Difficult
Questions tags	Low	High	Complex	Regular	Difficult

mann's (1999) hierarchy of processing procedures. The analysis shown in Table 6.6 suggests that two of the criteria (functional value and processability) may be especially important in determining learning difficulty as implicit knowledge. However, clearly, these (and other) factors need to be more thoroughly tested.

Scores for explicit knowledge of the grammatical structures were generally high, but this reflects the format of the tests used to measure this type of knowledge (i.e. they involved selected responses). In this case, the cut-off point will be fixed at 50%. Three structures scored at or below 50% – hypothetical conditionals, ergative verbs and dative alternation. The conceptual complexity of all three structures can be considered high. Hypothetical conditionals are clearly formally and functionally complicated, involving compound verb tenses, making it difficult to formulate a simple rule-of-thumb. Ergative verbs are also highly problematic as they are difficult to distinguish conceptually from verbs that permit a passive form (see discussion in Westney, 1994). Dative alternation does permit a reasonably transparent rule (e.g. verbs that derive from Latin or Greek do not permit dative alternation while Anglo-Saxon verbs do), but such a rule does not figure in typical pedagogic grammars and, in any case, rests on learners' knowledge of the etymology of individual verbs. Finally, all three structures cannot be easily explained without reference to metalanguage of a technical nature. For example, a verbal account of hypothetical conditionals ideally requires the use of terms like 'main clause', 'subordinate clause', 'past perfect', 'modal verb', 'past participle'. In short, all three structures appear difficult in terms of both conceptual complexity and the metalanguage required.

It is also noticeable that the grammatical features where the difference between the implicit and explicit scores was notably large (e.g. plural -s, indefinite article, regular past tense -ed and question tags) are all features for which ready rules-of-thumb are available and which many of the learners in this study had probably been formally taught. It is clear, then, that a feature easy to 'grasp' does not guarantee its accurate use as implicit knowledge. Conversely, there are some features (e.g. dative alternation and adverb placement) that the learners perform better as implicit knowledge. Such features are difficult to render as rules-of-thumb and are probably not taught explicitly.

The second analysis focused exclusively on just one of the factors predicted to influence learning difficulty as implicit knowledge – processability. This examined four structures selected to represent the hierarchical stages of acquisition in Processability Theory, using implicational scaling of the scores from the Elicited Oral Imitation Test and the ungrammatical items of the Untimed GJT. The implicational scaling of scores for the four structures on the measure of implicit knowledge lends strong support to the claims about learning difficulty derived from Processability Theory. The data obtained from the Elicited Oral Imitation Test proved comparable to the unplanned language use data that processability researchers have traditionally collected. That is, they allowed predictions based on the theory to be successfully tested. In contrast, as expected, Processability Theory failed to predict learning difficulty as explicit knowledge. This analysis then indicates that processability can account for implicit knowledge but not explicit knowledge and confirms the central claim that learning difficulty needs to be considered separately for the two types of knowledge.

Conclusion

The study reported in this chapter was exploratory. It explored the relative difficulty of a range of grammatical features in terms of learners' implicit and explicit knowledge of them. Like all exploratory studies of this kind, the main findings must be considered cautiously. The main findings were:

(1)   The difficulty of grammatical structures varies according to whether one is considering implicit or explicit knowledge of the structures. Structures that are easy in terms of implicit knowledge may be difficult in terms of explicit knowledge and vice versa.
(2)   Different factors are needed to predict learning difficulty as implicit and explicit knowledge. For example, processability is able to predict learning difficulty as implicit knowledge but not as explicit knowledge.

These findings are compatible with a view of language learning that distinguishes the acquisitional processes involved in the development of implicit L2 knowledge from the general deductive learning strategies involved in the development of explicit language (Krashen, 1981; Schwartz, 1993; Zobl, 1995). It seems that whereas adult learners will depend on general acquisitional processes to learn some structures, they may draw on 'a general problem solving module' (Felix, 1985) to learn others.

It is important to take into account the limitations of the study reported in this chapter. A major limitation lies in the fact that the implicit and explicit scores obtained for the different structures were derived from only a limited number of items – six items in the case of the Elicited Oral Imitation Test/Timed GJT and only three items in the case of the UGJT (ungrammatical)/Metalinguistic Test. Furthermore, the response to the UGJT was dichotomous while the Metalinguistic Test offered four choices, allowing for guesswork to influence the scores obtained.

The results of this study, however, are of significance for SLA research. The generally preferred means for investigating L2 acquisition has been to tap learners' unplanned communicative language use – what Norris and Ortega (2000) call 'free constructed response'. Surprisingly however, few published SLA studies have been based on such data; many studies continue to measure acquisition by means of untimed metalinguistic judgments, selected responses or constrained constructed responses. One reason for this is the difficulty in obtaining adequate exemplars of the specific structures targeted for study from tasks designed to elicit free constructed responses. However, as the results of the analysis reported in this chapter suggest, tests such as the Untimed GJT that encourage learners to focus on formal accuracy rather than message conveyance, permit learners to access their explicit knowledge and, therefore, cannot convincingly shed light on their interlanguage development. What is needed is an instrument that will gather information about learners' implicit knowledge of specific linguistic features. The Elicited Oral Imitation Test is promising in this respect. This test appears capable of producing data with the same essential characteristics as the free constructed response data that processability research has utilized.

The Elicited Oral Imitation Test may also provide a much-needed means of determining the stage of development that individual learners have reached. The need for some general index of development has long been recognized (Larsen-Freeman, 1978), but none of those suggested to date has been adopted. It might be possible to design an Elicited Oral Imitation Test to measure learners' implicit knowledge of grammatical features that have been carefully chosen to represent the different processing procedures that Pienemann has shown characterize L2 development. If this does prove possible, it would enable SLA research-ers to describe a learner's developmental stage in much more precise terms than the currently crude way it is described in so many studies (i.e. as 'beginner', 'intermediate' or 'advanced').

Notes

1. DeKeyser (2003) neatly suggests that rule complexity for the individual learner is 'the ratio of the rule's inherent linguistic complexity over the student's ability to handle the rule' – i.e. an amalgam of subjective and objective complexity.
2. It is also interesting to note that there appears to be an established order for teaching grammatical features in traditional structural syllabuses. In part, this reflects the designers' views about what features are easy or difficult to learn but, as a reviewer of a draft of this paper pointed out, it also reflects grading criteria other than difficulty (e.g. frequency and communicative value).
3. Eysenck (2001) notes that the procedural/declarative memory and implicit/explicit memory cannot be clearly distinguished. That is, for all intents and

purposes, they should be considered as referring to the same mental phenomena.

4. A reviewer of the paper on which this chapter is based pointed out that some of the factors identified as contributing to conceptual clarity (e.g. proto-typicality) may also determine learning difficulty as implicit knowledge. The reviewer also argued that, ideally, the criteria for distinguishing the difficulty of the two types of knowledge need to be separate. I disagree. The same factor may contribute to difficulty as implicit knowledge because it influences the saliency and processability of a grammatical feature, and to difficulty as explicit knowledge because it influences the ability of the learner to understand and/or construct a declarative rule. In other words, it is entirely possible that some features will be difficult in terms of *both* types of knowledge.

5. Drawing on Vygotskyan theory, Lantolf and Johnson (2007) refer to the kinds of rules-of-thumb that Hammerley describes as 'nonspontaneous concepts'. They argue, however, that they are inadequate and that learners require 'scientific concepts' (i.e. concepts that are 'systematic, coherent, and general-izable', p. 880) as 'these allow them to function appropriately in any concrete circumstance in which they find themselves' (p. 881). Clearly, understanding 'scientific concepts' presents a significant challenge for many learners. Clearly, too, it will be easier to construct such concepts for some grammatical structures than for others.

6. To ensure that the structures chosen were representative of the full range of structures in a teaching syllabus, a number of course books were inspected to see which structures figured at different levels of proficiency.

7. The number of participants completing each test varied slightly. A total of 248 completed the Elicited Oral Imitation Test, 245 the Timed GJT, 244 the Untimed GJT and 248 the Metalinguistic Test.

8. Only the ungrammatical sentences from the Untimed GJT were used to derive explicit knowledge scores because the factor analysis reported in Chapter 2 showed that a measure based on these loaded much more heavily on the explicit factor than a measure derived from either the grammatical sentences of the same test or a total test score.

9. A reviewer of the paper on which this chapter was based pointed out that an alternative way of viewing the four tests might be in terms of whether they required oral or written production. However, such a proposal lacks evidence as the Timed and Untimed GJTs loaded on different factors even though both involved responding to written sentences. See also the Confirmatory Factor Analysis in Chapter 2, which tested the two solutions and found that only the implicit/explicit solution was satisfactory.

10. Another factor making the indefinite article difficult was the lack of an equivalent form in the L1s (Chinese, Korean and Japanese) of many of the learners in the sample investigated. Harley (1994), among others, has identified incongruency with the L1 as an important factor determining learning difficulty.

Chapter 7

Implicit and Explicit Knowledge of an L2 and Language Proficiency

CATHERINE ELDER and ROD ELLIS

Introduction

In this chapter, our interest is in exploring the extent to which standardized tests of second language (L2) proficiency can be explicated in terms of the distinction between implicit and explicit knowledge using the measures of the two types of knowledge described in Chapters 2 to 5. We see this as one way of increasing our understanding of what standard proficiency tests are actually measuring. We also see the study as a demonstration of the potential for synergy between language testing and SLA research.

We will address the relationship between implicit and explicit L2 knowledge in two ways. In the first study reported in this chapter, we will examine the relationship between measures of the two types of knowledge and measures obtained from a standardized proficiency test (TOEFL). In the second study, we will explore whether implicit and explicit knowledge of specific grammatical structures (the 17 grammatical structures described in Chapter 2 and investigated in Chapter 6) are related to and can predict scores on another standardized proficiency test (IELTS). There are two assumptions that underlie our approach. The first is that knowledge of grammar (of whatever kind) is an important component of L2 proficiency. The second assumption is that L2 proficiency can be accounted for in terms of a model based on the distinction between implicit and explicit knowledge.

Regarding the first assumption, there is ample evidence to support the claim that grammar is a central component of L2 proficiency. Upshur (1976; cited in Oller, 1979) has suggested that the grammatical system of the learner can account for a substantial proportion of the variance on a wide range of tests. Oller (1979) reports a study of 145 L2 learners who completed the UCLA English as a Second Language Placement Examination and two dictations (the latter serving as general measures of L2 proficiency). Scores on the two grammar components of the UCLA test strongly correlated with the dictation scores (between $r = 0.69$ and $r = 0.61$). McNamara (1996) reports a study that shows 'grammar' accounted for a large proportion (60%) of the variance in scores on an impressionistically scored writing test, greater than any other measure. He also notes a number of studies which found that raters' assessment of learners' grammatical accuracy was central to their overall ratings of speaking ability. As for reading proficiency, Alderson's work on the English Language Testing Service (ELTS) Revision project (Alderson, 1993), found strong correlations between a grammar test and tests of academic reading, as high as 0.80 in one case. However, he acknowledged that the high correlations might have been partly due to contamination between the semantic sentence processing requirements of both the grammar and reading tests. Conflicting findings have emerged from componential analyses of L2 reading proficiency, with some studies (e.g. Bosser, 1992; Brisbois, 1995) indicating that vocabulary knowledge may be more important for predicting reading performance than syntactic or grammatical knowledge. However, a careful critique of this work by Shiotsu and Weir (2007) and their own research findings with a large sample of Japanese EFL students, suggest that, in fact, the reverse is true and that syntactic knowledge is a stronger predictor of reading performance than vocabulary.

With regard to listening skills, Clapham and Alderson (1997) found that there was no evidence from the ELTs-IELTS revision project that the new Listening Test was indeed measuring listening rather than grammatical ability. Davies (2008: 81), commenting on this finding, offers the following insight:

> If it is indeed the case. . . that listening cannot be distinguished from grammatical knowledge/ability, then we need to ask a further question: is this because the ways in which the listening and the grammatical components were presented was not sufficiently different, or, is it that tests inevitably reduce to a grammatical mean. . . That is one possibility, that it is the fault of the test construction that it has not teased out the underlying differences between listening and grammar. But there is a second, more profound possibility which needs to be countenanced, reminiscent of the position championed by John Oller in the 1970s. . . . – the position that all proficiency is reducible to one underlying ability/factor (the Unitary Competence Hypothesis or UCH). This goes to the very heart of both the proficiency construct and of proficiency testing, pointing as it does to the dilemma of our understanding of language competence. If by language competence we focus on that narrow aspect of ability which concerns the manipulation of structures, then the UCH position appears tenable, and there really is not much point in testing anything other than grammar. Indeed, from this point of view, it doesn't have to be grammar that is being tested: since everything reduces to the same thing, it doesn't really matter which feature is being tested.

This is not a fashionable argument given the current preference in the field of language testing for models based on some theory of communicative competence (e.g. Bachman, 1990; Bachman & Palmer, 1996) and for performance-based models (e.g. McNamara, 1996) or the model promulgated by Skehan (1998) based on information processing theories. However, it is certainly worth revisiting, given the weight of evidence about the role of grammar in the studies reviewed above, and also because of the failure of current models to produce firm psychometric evidence for the components they claim to be central. For example, Harley *et al.* (1990) failed to find support for a Bachman-like model of proficiency in a confirmatory factor analysis of the test performance of 175 Grade 6 early French immersion students on a battery test designed to measure the different components of communicative competence in Canale's (1983) model. Likewise, Iwashita *et al.* (2001), in a large-scale study, failed to find support for the factors that Skehan (2001) has hypothesized influence learners' performance of tasks either in relation to test scores or in relation to quantified features of discourse produced on a monologic oral narrative task.

Since Oller's early findings were discredited on the grounds that he used inappropriate statistical techniques, language testers have shown little interest in grammar testing generally (but see Rea-Dickins (2000) and Purpura (2004)) and have paid scant attention to the distinction between implicit and explicit L2 knowledge, which lies at the centre of current enquiry in second language acquisition (SLA). We believe, however, that the implicit/explicit distinction is an important one for modelling L2 learners' language proficiency, perhaps more subtle a model based on unified grammar. Han and Ellis's (1998) findings provide tentative support for the explanatory power of such a distinction. They found that measures of implicit and explicit grammatical knowledge correlated significantly with learners' scores on both the Secondary Level English Proficiency Test (SLEP) and the Test of English as a Foreign Language (TOEFL), with measures of implicit knowledge correlating more strongly with the SLEP test and a measure of explicit knowledge with the TOEFL, and offered reasons why each test might be engaging different types of knowledge. With the exception of Han and Ellis, and Chapter 5 in this book, however, we have been unable to find any studies that have investigated the relationship between the two types of knowledge and L2 proficiency.

This review of the previous research indicates that there are clear grounds for believing that grammar is an important component of any model of L2 proficiency and that the implicit/explicit distinction may also be important for understanding the nature of proficiency and our ability to measure it. However, we acknowledge that grammar can only constitute one of several components of proficiency and thus we cannot necessarily expect to find the two constructs strongly correlated. Ideally, to investigate the extent to which the implicit/explicit distinction can explain (and predict) L2 proficiency, we would need to look at how this distinction applies to other aspects of language, including vocabulary and pragmatic knowledge. However, this was not possible in the context of the Marsden Project as this only examined grammatical knowledge. With this limitation in mind, we will now report the two studies.

Study 1

Research questions

(1) Can expert judges classify standardized proficiency tests using the implicit/explicit knowledge distinction?
(2) What relationship is there between the performance on tests designed to measure L2 implicit knowledge and scores derived from standardized proficiency tests?
(3) What relationship is there between the performance on tests designed to measure L2 explicit knowledge and measures derived from standardized proficiency tests?
(4) Do these score relationships provide support for judges' classifications?

Design

To answer the first research question an expert panel of judges (see details under Participants) used a rating designed expressly to assist them in making judgments about the test components and the likelihood that these were eliciting implicit and explicit knowledge. The second two questions were addressed via a correlational design, drawing on the scores of 111 test-takers on a subset of the battery of tests described in Chapter 2 as well as on two further proficiency tests, the computer-based TOEFL and a pilot version of the recently launched internet-based TOEFL used in an international field study conducted at the end of 2002. Factor analyses were then computed to investigate the explanatory power of a psycholinguistic processing model (based on a distinction between implicit/explicit knowledge).

Participants

Five expert judges who had completed at least a Masters degree in Applied Linguistics, including a course on Language Testing, were recruited to participate in a training session during which they were briefed about the implicit/explicit knowledge constructs and familiarized with an expressly devised rating scale (described below). There were three males and two females in the group.

The test-taker group was made up of almost equal numbers of male ($n = 55$) and female ($n = 56$) students enrolled either in presessional English classes or in tertiary academic courses in New Zealand. The vast majority of the students were from Mainland China, and spoke Chinese as their first language. Most were recent arrivals – 96 had lived in an English-speaking country for a year or less. As for the duration of their English study, the group varied widely, although the majority reported having studied English for 10 years or more in formal grammar-based classrooms.

Instruments

Three kinds of instruments were used in the current study.

Rating scheme

A rating scheme (see Table 7.1) was devised to enable experts in language testing to evaluate each component of two standardized tests (the computer-based and internet-based TOEFL) in terms of the kind of knowledge (explicit or implicit) they were likely to draw on. The underlying assumptions of this scheme were (1) test tasks by their very nature are likely to predispose learners to deploy one type of knowledge to a greater extent than the other type; and (2) test tasks will not constitute 'pure' measures of implicit/explicit knowledge, but rather will call on both types of knowledge, but in differing proportions, depending on the nature of the task.

As in the design of the battery of tests described below, the rating scale drew on three criteria for distinguishing explicit and implicit knowledge, as shown in Table 7.1. These criteria are based on discussions of the nature of implicit and explicit knowledge in the SLA literature (see Ellis, 2004, and Chapter 1). To reflect assumption (2), the description of each criterion is presented in terms of four levels, ranging from 'very explicit' (Level 1) to 'very implicit' (Level 4). The intervening two levels can be glossed as 'somewhat explicit' (Level 2) and 'somewhat implicit' (Level 3). The criteria are accompanied by lists of relevant task characteristics to assist the expert judges in determining what features of the tests they should focus on in evaluating the test task. The scheme is designed to elicit an overall rating for each type of task in the proficiency tests against each of the three criteria and also an overall implicit/explicit score for each skill component.

In the first version of the rating scheme there were four different criteria, including a metalanguage criterion designed to assess the extent to which the various tests drew on metalinguistic knowledge, or knowledge about the rules of the target language. The expert judges, however, felt that this criterion was irrelevant to the task, because neither

Table 7.1 Rating scale for analyzing test components in terms of implicit/explicit knowledge

Criteria	Level descriptors	Relevant task characteristics
Degree of awareness	1. The test task calls for learners to reflect carefully on their response.	**Channel of input:** *aural* or *visual* or both
	2. The test task encourages learners to reflect to some extent on their response.	**Length of input:** *short* or *extended*
	3. The test task makes it difficult for learners to reflect on their response.	**Type of input:** *item* requiring selected or limited production response or *prompt* requiring extended production
	4. The test task makes it more or less impossible for learners to reflect on their response.	**Flexibility of input display:** e.g. capacity to scroll back and forward through text in the case of online reading input
		Degree of reactivity of response: *reciprocal* (e.g. dialogue) or *nonreciprocal* (e.g. dictation, composition, reading)
Time available	1. The test task allows learners as much time as they want.	**Instructions:** to test-takers, relating to time allocation before task (planning allowed?) time allocation for entire task (speeded test or power test?) and time between questions
	2. The test task sets a generous time limit to enable learners to finish the task comfortably.	**Speed of input:** rate at which test-taker has to process the information
	3. The test task sets a restricted time limit designed to pressure learners to work quite quickly.	**Number of repetitions:** in the case of a listening input
	4. The test task sets a very restricted time limit designed to pressure learners to respond rapidly and automatically.	**Degree of adaptivity:** i.e. the extent to which the interlocutor on a speaking test is permitted to adjust his/her behavior acccording to the test-taker's response, e.g. by repeating a question, asking a candidate to repeat or elaborate

Table 7.1 (*Continued*)

Criteria	Level descriptors	Relevant task characteristics
		Flexibility of response: e.g. opportunity to rerecord an answer
Focus of attention	1. The test task specifically calls for learners to attend to accuracy of form.	**Type of scoring method:** *objective/analytic* or *holistic*, relative weightings accorded to accuracy, fluency and content
	2. The test task encourages learners to attend to accuracy of form.	**Explicitness of scoring criteria:** e.g. do test-takers know that accuracy is valued over fluency?
	3. The test task encourages learners to focus attention on message content.	**Scope of relationship between input and response:** *broad* (e.g. reading for gist) or *narrow* (e.g. focused on identifying or using specific language items)
	4. The test task is intended to lead learners to focus more or less exclusively on meaning (message content).	**Directness of relationship between input and response:** *direct* (i.e. response relates directly to information or language supplied in the input) or *indirect* (i.e. response is open-ended and not dependent on the input)

Note: Low scores indicate that the test task favors explicit knowledge; high scores indicate that the test task favors implicit knowledge.

of the two tests elicited such knowledge. Therefore, this metalanguage criterion was removed.

Tests of implicit/explicit knowledge

For this study, for practical reasons, we were obliged to select a subset from the battery of tests designed expressly to measure L2 implicit/explicit knowledge. The subset was made up of the following:

(a) Timed Grammaticality Judgment Test (TGJT)
(b) Untimed Grammaticality Judgment Test (UGJT)
(c) Metalinguistic Knowledge Test (MKT)

All three tests measured learners' knowledge of the same 17 grammatical structures described in Chapter 2. Test (a) (see further information in Chapter 4) was designed to measure implicit knowledge and tests (b) and (c) targeted learners' explicit knowledge of English grammar (see full descriptions in Chapters 4 and 5, respectively).

Tests of L2 proficiency

(a) The computer-based TOEFL (TOEFL CBT)

The computer-based TOEFL (no longer in operation) is very similar to the pencil-and-paper TOEFL and consists of the following sections:

Section 1: Listening comprehension

In Parts A and B, the test-takers hear short conversations between two people (typically no more than three turns). Each conversation is followed by a question. The conversations and questions are repeated once only. Test-takers indicate their answers to the questions by selecting from multiple-choice options. In part C, they hear a number of short talks of around 100 words in length. Each talk is given once only and is followed by a question, again requiring multiple-choice responses.

Section 2: Structure of written expression

This contains two types of multiple-choice questions. In one type (referred to as 'Structure'), test-takers are asked to complete an incomplete sentence. In the second type (referred to as 'Written Expression'), test-takers have to identify which of four underlined parts of a sentence is erroneous. Included in this section is an essay-writing task very similar to that used for the Test of Written English. Test-takers write a short essay on a general writing topic, which is evaluated in terms of their ability to organize information and to use standard written English.

Section 3: Reading comprehension

The test-takers read a series of short passages (about 100 words in length) and answer a number of multiple-choice questions following each passage, designed to test the their understanding of what is stated or implied in the passage.

(b) The pilot version of the internet-based TOEFL (TOEFL iBT)

This pilot version of the recently launched TOEFL iBT closely resembles the current operational version and consists of four different sections measuring reading, listening, speaking and writing, respectively.

Section 1: Reading (60–100 minutes)

The reading section is made up of three to four academic texts, each with 12–14 questions. The question types are similar to those on the TOEFL CBT, but there are also some additional 'reading to learn' items requiring candidates to retrieve and synthesize information from different parts of the passage using an organization chart or a summary. This component has a glossary feature that allows candidates to view definitions and explanations of particular words.

Section 2: Listening (60–90 minutes)

The listening section is made up of a number of both monologic lecture-type passages and mini-conversations with between five and six questions per text. The texts are longer than on the TOEFL CBT. Unlike the TOEFL CBT, there are opportunities to take notes while listening and, in some cases, parts of a lecture or conversation are replayed.

Section 3: Speaking (20 minutes)

This section contains six different tasks, two of which are independent and focus on topics familiar to the test-taker and three of which are integrated, involving a spoken response to some reading and listening input. All tasks are spoken into a microphone and digitally recorded. The tasks are analytically scored for Delivery, Language use and Topic development on a 4-point scale. Each candidate is scored by at least three different raters who take responsibility for evaluating different test tasks.

Section 4: Writing (50 minutes)

Like the Speaking section, this component of the test includes integrated tasks, in this case in response to Reading and Listening stimuli as well as an independent essay task very similar to the one used on the CBT. Again, each candidate's writing sample is scored by more than one rater on a scale that includes the following categories: Development, Organization and Appropriate and Precise Use of Grammar and Vocabulary.

Procedures

Expert judges were paid to attend a training session at which they were familiarized with the rating scale and the constructs of implicit and explicit knowledge that the scale was designed to embody. Some tasks from a practice version of the IELTS test were presented during the training process, and judges rated these on the scale and discussed the reasons for their ratings with other panel members. After 2.5 hours, the judges were deemed to be ready to undertake the rating task on their own and, after signing confidentiality statements, completed a trial version of the TOEFL CBT and iBT under test conditions. Immediately after completing each test, they independently filled out the rating sheets as they had been trained to do and handed them to a research assistant.

One hundred and eleven test-takers, as described in 'Participants', were recruited to take part in the TOEFL iBT field trials, which also involved them taking a version of the TOEFL CBT test. The administration took around six hours (with a break in between each test). The following day, these test-takers were recalled to undertake the three implicit/explicit knowledge tests. The order of these tests was rotated for different subgroups of test-takers.

Data from the judges and test-takers were entered into a database and analyzed using descriptive statistics in the first instance. A Principal Components Factor Analysis with a forced two-factor solution was also computed on the scores for the various tests to determine the relationship between implicit and explicit knowledge and language proficiency and, by implication, the extent to which the data accorded with our prediction that different tasks/skills will elicit different kinds of knowledge.

Results and discussion

Results of the study will be presented and discussed in relation to each of the research questions posed above.

Research Question 1: Can expert judges classify standardized proficiency tests using the implicit/explicit knowledge distinction?

Table 7.2 presents the mean ratings assigned by the panel of five judges to each test component on a scale of 1–4, where 1 = high explicit and 4 = high implicit knowledge. More precisely, a rating of 1 on each of the criteria in the table indicates that the task requires of the test-taker a high degree of reflection, offers a generous time allowance and encourages a strong focus on accuracy. A rating at the opposite end of the scale indicates that this component of the test is performed in the absence of awareness, under time pressure and without attention to form.

The total explicit/implicit knowledge score for each test is 8.80 (TOEFL CBT) and 11.0 (TOEFL iBT), indicating that, in the opinion of the judges, no test measured implicit or explicit knowledge exclusively, except the Structure section of the CBT with its explicit focus on form. The TOEFL iBT, in the opinion of the judges, came closer to measuring implicit knowledge than the CBT, as might be expected given the more communicative and integrated nature of the former test. The rank order of the skill components on the explicit-implicit continuum is set out in Table 7.3. The totals are based on the average score across the same skill on both tests, except in the case of Structure, which appears in the TOEFL CBT only.

While the mean ratings shown in Table 7.3 are very close to one another, the continuum is in the expected order with Speaking, which might be expected to elicit more spontaneous language production, falling at the more implicit end, and Writing, where there is likely to be greater opportunity for self-monitoring, and Structure, which obviously requires a focus on form, at the more explicit end.

The answer to the first question is therefore that 'yes', the trained judges recruited for this study can, with the guidance provided for them by the rating scale, classify test tasks according to the degree of implicit or explicit knowledge that they perceive to be elicited through performance. In addition, it could be said that their ratings provide support for the theoretical model in that those skills that one would expect to elicit implicit or explicit knowledge were rated as doing so by the judges.

Table 7.2 Mean ratings assigned by expert panel for each test component

	CBT Listening	CBT Reading	CBT Writing	CBT Structure	iBT Listening	iBT Reading	iBT Writing	iBT Speaking
Degree of awareness	3	1.5	2	1	3	1.5	2.5	3.25
Time allowance	3	3	2.5	1.5	3	2.5	2.5	2.5
Focus on Form	4	2.5	1.5	1	3	3.5	1.5	4
Overall mean	3.3	2.3	2	1.2	3	2.5	2.2	3.3

Table 7.3 Rank order of judges' mean ratings by skill

Test component	Mean rating
Structure	1.2
Writing	2.1
Reading	2.4
Listening	3.2
Speaking	3.3

Research Question 2: What relationship is there between the performance on tests designed to measure L2 implicit knowledge and scores derived from standardized proficiency tests?

Research Question 3: What relationship is there between the performance on tests designed to measure L2 explicit knowledge and measures derived from standardized proficiency tests?

The results of the Principal Components analysis with Varimax rotation and a forced two-factor solution are presented in Table 7.4. It can be seen that this solution accounted for a respectable 68% of the test variance, with the UGJT (grammatical and ungrammatical sentences) loading on one factor (Component 2) and all the other variables loading on the other.

The strongest loadings on Component 1 were, interestingly, for the TOEFL iBT Reading test (0.91) and for the CBT TOEFL Structure section (0.87). The weakest loadings (apart from the TGJT components that loaded on Component 2) were CBT Writing (0.66) and the two parts (grammatical and ungrammatical sentences) of the UGJT (0.54 and 0.69), respectively.

There are a number of possible explanations for these results. One is that the tests loading on Component 2 are measuring implicit knowledge as they were designed to do, and all the other test components are measuring explicit knowledge, or at least are more strongly oriented to eliciting explicit knowledge than implicit knowledge. If this is the case, the answer to Research Question 2 is that there is no relationship or an extremely weak relationship between implicit knowledge and language proficiency as measured by the TOEFL tests. The relationship between language proficiency and explicit knowledge, on the other hand, is strong (Research Question 3). It seems that there is something about standardized proficiency tests, or perhaps simply about the tests of advanced academic language proficiency used for the current study, that is not conducive to eliciting unanalyzed automated language knowledge. This

Table 7.4 Rotated component matrix for all test components ($n = 97$)

Component	Eigenvalues	% of Variance	Cumulative %
1	7.783	56.591	55.591
2	1.713	12.234	67.825
		Component 1	Component 2
TGJT Ungrammatical		0.21	**0.83**
TGJT Grammatical		0.23	**−0.82**
UGJT Ungrammatical		**0.69**	**0.36**
UGJT Grammatical		**0.55**	**−0.36**
Metalinguistic knowledge		**0.72**	− 0.07
CBT Structure		**0.88**	− 0.02
CBT Writing		**0.66**	0.24
iBT Writing		**0.81**	− 0.06
CBT Reading		**0.86**	− 0.02
iBT Reading		**0.91**	− 0.03
CBT Listening		**0.85**	− 0.09
iBT Listening		**0.86**	− 0.09
iBT Speaking		**0.76**	0.00

may be because, as suggested elsewhere (Elder *et al.*, 2002), language tests encourage a focus on display that invites self-monitoring at the expense of more spontaneous language performance. Such an interpretation does not, strictly speaking, discredit the implicit-explicit model as a predictor of language proficiency, but rather suggests that language proficiency in all its facets is not well measured by language tests such as the ones used for this investigation.

Another possible factor that may explain the stronger role played by explicit knowledge in predicting language proficiency is the fact that the test-takers involved in this study were recent arrivals from countries like China, where there are limited opportunities for exposure to English other than in formal classrooms where the focus tends to be on grammar, as the respondents themselves reported. A more diverse population of test-takers may be needed, including long-term residents in English-medium environments, before we can draw definitive conclusions about the relationship between implicit language knowledge and language proficiency.

An alternative explanation for the above results is that the factor analysis is identifying a method effect associated with the TGJT, which was performed under speeded conditions, and that this is what distinguishes the measures derived from this test most powerfully from all the other measures obtained from the test battery. A multitrait, multimethod analysis (Cambell & Fiske, 1959), using a broader range of implicit and explicit knowledge measures – each with a different format – would be needed to determine if this is indeed the case. In particular, a measure of implicit knowledge provided by the Elicited Oral Imitation Test, which was shown to be the best measure of this type of knowledge, would have been desirable.

Whatever the explanation, in answer to Research Question 4: 'Do these score relationships provide support for judges' classifications?', we must conclude that the judgmental analysis, which gave us grounds for predicting that speaking and listening components of both the TOEFL CBT and iBT would load on one factor and that the reading and writing and structure components would load another, was not supported by the empirical data Thus, although there seems to be some intuitive appeal in the explicit/implicit model as way of classifying different test tasks, there is no evidence from this study that the judges' insights reflect what knowledge L2 test-takers actually draw on when responding to test tasks.

Study 2

Research questions

In Study 2, the research questions were investigated in a different way. Whereas Study 1 examined total scores on the battery of Marsden tests, Study 2 examines the scores obtained for each of the 17 grammatical structures. The research questions were:

(1)   To what extent is implicit/explicit knowledge of specific grammatical features related to general L2 proficiency?
(2)   To what extent does implicit and explicit knowledge of specific grammatical structures predict general L2 proficiency?

Participants

The participants were a subgroup of the participants in the study reported in Chapter 6. They were composed of 50 learners from the international student group in New Zealand, with 30 females and 20 males. Thirty-four came from China and the rest from a wide mix of Asian and European countries. They were predominantly instructed learners, 24 indicating they had relied mainly on formal instruction for learning English, 22 claiming a mixture of formal instruction and exposure and only four indicating they had learnt English naturalistically. Most were enrolled in foundation courses to prepare for entry to university or in courses in private language schools. The mean IELTS score for this sample was 6.22 (SD = 0.80) with the minimum score 4.5 and the maximum 8.00.

Instruments

The learners completed four of the battery of tests used to measure implicit and explicit knowledge. Two of these tests (Elicited Oral Imitation Test and TGJT) were designed to measure implicit knowledge and two (UGJT and MKT) were designed to measure explicit knowledge. These tests and the 17 grammatical structures they were designed to measure are described in Chapter 2. In addition, the participants completed the International English Language Testing System (IELTS), which has four parts. The Listening part has four sections that involve answering multiple-choice questions after listening to a conversation or a monologue. The Reading part has three sections; typical tasks are completing a summary, matching information in two columns and true/false questions. The Writing part is in two parts, one involving a functional writing task (e.g. writing a letter to a house rental agency) and the other is a more formal writing task (e.g. an argument). The Speaking part consists of three sections (a general interview, a short talk on a general topic and a discussion on a more abstract topic). Scores are based on nine bands and are available for each part and for the total test.

Procedures

The battery of tests designed to measure implicit and explicit knowledge were completed in the following order:

(10) Imitation Test
(11) TGJT
(12) UGJT
(14) MKT

The procedures for administering these tests are described in Chapter 2. The complete test battery was completed in a single session lasting approximately two and a half hours.

Official IELTS scores were obtained from the learners who agreed to complete the battery of tests referred to above. In general these were recent IELTS scores, but in some cases there was a gap of one or two months between the date of the IELTS and the date the learners completed the test battery.

Analysis

Descriptive statistics for the tests of implicit and explicit knowledge were calculated. Mean implicit and explicit scores for each of the 17 grammatical structures were calculated. Difference scores for explicit and implicit knowledge for each grammatical structure were also calculated. The method used to calculate these scores is described in Chapter 6. Finally, multiple regression analyses were run with the implicit and explicit scores for selected grammatical structures as the independent variables and the IELTS scores as the dependent variables.

Results

Table 7.5 shows the means and standard deviations for the participants who completed the Oral Imitation Test, the TGJT, the UGJT (ungrammatical sentences) and the Metalinguistic Test.

Table 7.6 shows the mean explicit and implicit scores together with the differences between the two sets of scores for each of the 17 grammatical structures. The results for the 50 participants in this study were very similar to those of the larger sample reported in Chapter 6. They suggest that there are clear differences in the difficulty of grammatical structures as implicit and explicit knowledge. As with the larger sample, the Spearman Rank Correlation for the two sets of scores was very weak ($r = 0.09$; $p = $ NS).

To establish whether the within-group variance justified conducting correlational analyses, measures of skewness and kurtosis for all test scores (Implicit, Explicit and IELTS total, oral and written) were calculated for the IELTS. Only two scores (Conditional Implicit and Plural Explicit) failed to meet the criterion levels for normal distribution. The results of these analyses, therefore, indicate that, overall, the test scores were normally distributed.

Table 7.7 shows the means and standard deviations for the IELTS scores. Tables 7.8 and 7.9 give the correlations between the implicit/ explicit knowledge scores for the 17 grammatical structures and the IELTS scores (Total, Listening, Reading, Speaking, Writing). The measures of implicit and explicit knowledge both correlate significantly with IELTS

Table 7.5 Descriptive statistics ($n = 50$)

Elicited Oral Imitation test (%)		Timed GJT (total) (%)		Untimed GJT (ungram.) (%)		Metalinguistic Test	
Mean	*SD*	*Mean*	*SD*	*Mean*	*SD*	*Mean*	*SD*
45.26	15.11	55.50	10.12	82.36	14.33	55.18	15.80

Table 7.6 Difference between explicit and implicit scores for 17 grammatical structures ($n = 50$)

	Explicit UGJT ungram. +metalanguage (mean (SD))	Implicit Imitation +TGJT (mean (SD))	Difference between means
Verb complement	0.81(0.27)	0.67(0.37)	0.14
Third person -s	0.68(0.25)	0.47(0.18)	**0.21**
Plural -s	0.85(0.27)	0.48(0.20)	**0.37**
Indefinite article	0.76(0.31)	0.37(0.19)	**0.39**
Possessive -s	0.78(0.24)	0.62(0.19)	0.16
Regular past tense -ed	0.79(0.26)	0.48(0.21)	**0.31**
Yes/no questions	0.60(0.32)	0.50(0.28)	0.10
Comparative	0.75(0.30)	0.54(0.21)	**0.21**
Hypothetical conditionals	0.52(0.22)	0.37(0.20)	**0.15**
Modals	0.75(0.31)	0.77(0.17)	− 0.02
Ergative verbs	0.53(0.29)	0.54(0.26)	− 0.01
Embedded questions	0.64(0.32)	0.46(0.20)	0.18
Adverb placement	0.46(0.25)	0.64(0.18)	− 0.18
Question tags	0.76(0.29)	0.40(0.21)	**0.36**
Since/for	0.72(0.31)	0.49(0.25)	**0.23**
Dative alternation	0.52(0.35)	0.57(0.17)	− 0.05
Relative clauses	0.84(0.27)	0.63(0.22)	**0.21**

scores. A total of 46 statistically significant correlations involve implicit knowledge and a total of 40 involve explicit knowledge. Thus, just over half of the total possible correlations reached statistical significance.

There were some marked differences in the grammatical features correlating with IELTS scores in terms of implicit and explicit knowledge. The implicit scores for comparative, unreal conditionals and *since/for*

Table 7.7 Descriptive statistics for IELTS scores

IELTS	Mean	Standard deviation
IELTS Listening	6.25	1.00
IELTS Reading	5.98	0.87
IELTS Writing	6.22	1.12
IELTS Speaking	6.12	0.85
IELTS Total	6.22	0.80

were all strongly related to the IELTS scores, whereas the explicit scores for the same features were only weakly related. In contrast, the explicit scores for indefinite article, regular past tense and, in particular, relative clauses were strongly related to the IELTS scores, whereas the implicit scores for these structures were only weakly related. However, for some grammatical features (e.g. embedded questions and adverb placement), both the implicit and explicit scores correlated with the IELTS scores. There were also some grammatical features (e.g. modals) where neither kind of knowledge showed much of a relationship with the written IELTS scores.

Implicit scores were, in general, more strongly related to the oral IELTS measures (Listening and Speaking) than to the written measures (Reading and Writing). There were 23 statistically significant correlations between the implicit measures and oral IELTS, whereas there were only 15 between the implicit measures and written IELTS. The reverse pattern is evident with the explicit scores. Whereas there were 13 statistically significant correlations between the explicit measures and oral IELTS, there were 17 for oral IELTS.

The grammatical features for the stepwise regression analyses were selected using two criteria: (1) strong correlations across the range of IELTS scores and (2) significant correlations with IELTS were found for one type of knowledge but not the other. The three implicit features selected were comparative, unreal conditionals and *since/for*. The three explicit features were indefinite article, regular past and relative clauses. Tables 7.10 and 7.11 report the results of a series of stepwise regression analyses with IELTS Total, IELTS Listening, IELTS Reading, IELTS Speaking and IELTS Reading as the dependent variables. For the implicit measures, comparative and unreal conditional accounted for 34% of the variance in Total IELTS scores, while for the explicit measures, relative clause and indefinite article accounted for 39% in the variance of Total IELTS scores. The best overall implicit measure was comparative, which figured in the regression analyses for Total IELTS, IELTS Listening and

Table 7.8 Correlations between implicit knowledge of the 17 grammatical structures and the IELTS scores

	IELTS Total	IELTS Listening	IELTS Reading	IELTS Speaking	IELTS Writing
Verb complement	0.28	0.31*	0.30*	0.37**	0.19
Third person -s	0.34*	0.35*	0.15	0.37**	0.28*
Plural −s	0.35*	0.26	0.29*	0.42**	0.19
Indefinite article	0.29*	0.43*	0.16	0.13	0.18
Possessive -s	0.19	0.33*	0.11	0.37**	0.13
Regular past tense −ed	0.19	0.24	0.12	0.45**	0.23
Yes/no questions	0.05	0.19	0.08	− 0.07	0.00
Comparative	0.47**	0.44**	0.40**	0.35*	0.45**
Unreal conditionals	0.41**	0.54**	0.38**	0.35*	**0.32***
Modals	0.04	0.13	0.07	− 0.01	0.09
Ergative verbs	0.28	0.34*	0.25	0.14	0.28*
Embedded questions	0.42**	0.47**	0.30*	0.46**	0.44**
Adverb placement	0.35*	0.49**	0.44**	0.41**	0.27
Question tags	0.25	0.43**	0.14	0.26	**0.24**
Since/for	0.43**	0.43**	0.43**	0.40**	**0.37****
Dative alternation	0.33*	0.33*	0.37**	0.10	0.33*
Relative clauses	0.23	0.27	0.26	0.31*	0.15

*p > 0.05.
**p > 0.01.

IELTS Writing. The best overall explicit measure was relative clause, which figured in the regression analyses for all the IELTS measures except Speaking.

Finally, Table 7.12 reports the regression analyses for the two grammatical features that emerged as the best predictors of IELTS scores. In the case of implicit knowledge it was comparative, while for explicit

Table 7.9 Correlations between explicit knowledge of the 17 grammatical structures and the IELTS scores

	IELTS Total	IELTS Listening	IELTS Reading	IELTS Speaking	IELTS Writing
Verb complement	0.43**	0.38**	0.47**	0.17	0.39**
Third person -s	0.21	0.26	0.12	0.23	0.08
Plural -s	0.26	0.37**	0.29*	0.21	**0.16**
Indefinite article	0.46**	0.41**	0.33*	0.46**	0.32*
Possessive -s	0.33*	0.27	0.20	0.40**	0.25
Regular past tense -ed	0.37**	0.32*	0.32*	0.23	0.36*
Yes/no questions	0.32*	0.24	0.46**	0.13	0.19
Comparative	0.10	0.16	0.26	0.00	0.03
Unreal conditionals	0.26	0.07	0.08	0.37**	**0.22**
Modals	0.24	0.27	0.36*	0.20	0.22
Ergative verbs	0.29*	0.28*	0.44**	0.01	0.25
Embedded questions	0.42**	0.37*	0.54**	0.20	0.29*
Adverb placement	0.47**	0.35*	0.50**	0.22	0.42**
Question tags	0.29*	0.26	0.28*	0.16	**0.16**
Since/for	0.25	0.36*	0.20	0.22	**0.05**
Dative alternation	0.01	0.23	0.17	0.01	0.09
Relative clauses	0.52**	0.53**	0.50**	0.31*	0.42**

$*p > 0.05$.
$**p > 0.01$.

knowledge it was relative clause. In these analyses, both the implicit and explicit scores for both grammatical features were entered. This analysis allows us to see the extent to which both implicit and explicit knowledge of specific features can account for variance in IELTS scores and the relative contribution of each type of knowledge. It shows that the

Table 7.10 Stepwise regression coefficients for the implicit measures of three grammatical structures

Features	IELTS Total		IELTS Listening		IELTS Reading		IELTS Speaking		IELTS Writing	
	Beta	*Sig*	*Beta*	*Sig*	*Beta*	*Sig*	*Beta*	*Sig*	*Beta*	*Sig*
Comparative	0.466	0.001	0.352	0.004					0.432	0.002
Conditional	0.350	0.005	0.462	0.000						
Since/for					0.408	0.003	0.396	0.004		
	$r = 0.58$		$r = 0.62$		$r = 0.41$		$r = 0.40$		$r = 0.43$	
	$r^2 = 0.34$		$r^2 = 0.38$		$r^2 = 0.17$		$r^2 = 0.16$		$r^2 = 0.18$	
	Excluded: since/for		Excluded: since/for		Excluded: comparative conditional		Excluded: comparative conditional		Excluded: conditional since/for	

Table 7.11 Stepwise regression coefficients for the explicit measures of three grammatical structures

Features	IELTS Total		IELTS Listening		IELTS Reading		IELTS Speaking		IELTS Writing	
	Beta	Sig	Beta	Sig	Beta	Sig	Beta	Sig	Beta	Sig
Indefinite article	0.360	0.003	0.327	0.009			0.464	0.001		
Regular past										
Relative clause	0.517	0.000	0.435	0.000	0.488	0.000			0.399	0.004
	$r = 0.63$		$r = 0.60$		$16r = 0.49$		$r = 0.46$		$r = 0.40$	
	$r^2 = 0.39$		$r^2 = 0.36$		$r^2 = 0.24$		$r^2 = 0.22$		$r^2 = 0.16$	
	Excluded: regular past		Excluded: regular past		Excluded: indefinite article; regular past		Excluded: regular past; relative clause		Excluded: indefinite article; regular past	

Table 7.12 Regression coefficients for the best implicit and explicit predictors of IELTS scores

Features	IELTS Total		IELTS Listening		IELTS Reading		IELTS Speaking		IELTS Writing	
	Beta	Sig	Beta	Sig	Beta	Sig	Beta	Sig	Beta	Sig
Implicit comparative	0.304	0.024					0.353	0.012	0.432	0.002
Explicit relative clause	0.391	0.004	0.508	0.000	0.488	0.000				
	$r = 0.59$		$r = 0.51$		$r = 0.49$		$r = 0.35$		$r = 0.43$	
	$r^2 = 0.34$		$r^2 = 0.26$		$r^2 = 0.24$		$r^2 = 0.12$		$r^2 = 0.19$	
	Excluded: none		Excluded: implicit comparative		Excluded: implicit comparative		Excluded: explicit relative clause		Excluded: explicit relative clause	

measures of both implicit and explicit knowledge contribute significantly to IELTS Total scores. The two features accounted for 34% of the variance in IELTS Total scores.

For the individual IELTS components' scores, it is *either* the implicit score *or* the explicit score that emerges as a statistically significant predictor (i.e. not both). The implicit feature is a significant predictor for both productive skills (IELTS Speaking and IELTS Writing), while the explicit feature predicts both receptive skills (IELTS Listening and IELTS Reading).

Discussion

The research questions concerned the relationship between the measures of implicit and explicit for specific grammatical structures and general language proficiency, as measured by a standardized test (IELTS) and also the extent to which the implicit/explicit measures predicted IELTS scores.

A number of moderately strong, statistically significant correlations between measures of implicit and explicit grammatical knowledge and IELTS scores were found. A key finding was that, generally, the implicit and explicit measures of the *same* structure were not *both* related to proficiency. Rather, it was the implicit measures of one set of structures and the explicit knowledge of a different set that correlated with the IELTS measures. In other words, the extent to which the variance in the individual structure scores matched the variance in the proficiency scores depended to a considerable extent on the type of knowledge being measured. However, there is no easy explanation for the results. Neither the morphological nor the syntactic differences between the grammatical features can explain why it was that implicit knowledge of some structures and explicit knowledge of others was related to proficiency. Nor can the grammatical structures related to the two types of knowledge be distinguished in terms of the learners' level of knowledge. Not all the implicit features had high scores (unreal conditionals scored only 0.10 on the implicit measure). Similarly, not all the explicit features had notably high explicit scores (indefinite articles scored 0.75, in the mid-range).

A more insightful line of enquiry might be to look for differences in the patterns of correlations involving oral and written language. It is not unreasonable to suppose that oral IELTS will favor implicit knowledge and written IELTS explicit knowledge. Oral language use draws more on automatic processing (a key feature of implicit knowledge), whereas written language allows for more controlled processing (a feature of explicit knowledge). The expert panel whose judgments were canvassed in relation to TOEFL in Study 1 also supported this supposition. This is borne out by the general pattern of correlations. Implicit knowledge of the grammatical features was more strongly related to oral IELTS than to written IELTS, while the reverse was the case for explicit knowledge.

Overall, the correlational analyses demonstrate that both implicit and explicit knowledge are implicated in language proficiency, as measured by IELTS. This conclusion is supported by the results of the regression analyses. Just two implicit structures (comparative and conditional) were able to predict 34% of the variance in the IELTS Total scores, while two different explicit structures (indefinite article and relative clause) predicted 39% of the variance in the IELTS Total scores. When one implicit (comparatives) and one explicit (relative clause) variable was entered into the same regression analysis, the two features predicted 34% of the variance in IELTS Total scores. Clearly, then, as other studies reviewed at the beginning of this chapter have also shown, knowledge of grammar serves as a relatively powerful predictor of general proficiency and, importantly for the theoretical model this study is based on, both implicit and explicit knowledge of grammar predict proficiency. Importantly, also, it is implicit and explicit knowledge of different rather than the same structures that function as predictors of overall proficiency. However, for individual IELTS components, it was either the implicit feature (in the case of IELTS Speaking and IELTS Writing) or the explicit feature (in the case of IELTS Listening and IELTS Reading) that emerged as significant predictors in the stepwise regression analyses. In the case of this analysis, therefore, it was the receptive/productive distinction rather than the modality distinction that accounted for the pattern of results. A possible explanation for this finding is that the particular measures of implicit and explicit knowledge (comparative and relative clause, respectively) are differentially important for input and output processing. For example, learners cannot avoid having to process relative clauses in oral and written input, but can avoid using them in oral and written output. Such an interpretation is supported by the results from Han and Ellis (1998). They found that measures of implicit knowledge correlated with performance on the SLEP test (which consists of tests in listening and reading only), whereas their measures of explicit knowledge correlated with the TOEFL (which includes production tests).

Conclusion

This chapter reports on two studies that examined the relationship between measures of L2 implicit and explicit knowledge and measures of general language proficiency, with a view to exploring the extent to which language proficiency can be explicated in terms of the two types of knowledge. The results of the two studies, however, differed markedly. The first study, in which the proficiency measures were the computer-based TOEFL and the pilot version of the internet-based TOEFL, found that these measures were related only to the measure of explicit knowledge (based on the UGJT and the MKT). In this study, the measure of implicit knowledge (the TGJT) was not related to the proficiency measures. In the second study, where the proficiency measures were derived from the IELTS, measures of both implicit and explicit knowledge of specific grammatical structures were found to be related to proficiency. Interestingly, in this second study, the measures of both implicit and explicit knowledge correlated with all four language skills, although implicit knowledge was seen to be more strongly related to the oral skills and explicit knowledge to the written skills.

The question arises as to why the results of the two studies were so different. To answer this question, we will consider the major differences between the two studies:

(1)   The proficiency tests – TOEFL as opposed to IELTS.
(2)   The measure of implicit knowledge – Study 1 measured implicit knowledge using the TGJT only, whereas Study 2 used both the Elicited Oral Imitation Test and the TGJT.
(3)   Study 1 looked at total scores for the 17 grammatical structures, whereas Study 2 looked at scores for specific grammatical structures.

It is worth noting, however, that there was no difference in the composition of the two samples (i.e. both were predominantly Chinese/Asian).

It is tempting to look to (1) as the main explanation for the difference in the two studies. That is, TOEFL really does encourage the use of explicit knowledge, whereas IELTS requires both types of knowledge. There is a difference in the TOEFL and IELTS Speaking and Listening tasks. IELTS is often criticized for failing to capture academic competence on these two skills – that is, it is really a general proficiency test. It could also be argued that the monologic nature of the TOEFL speaking task allows for monitoring, whereas the IELTS Speaking task is interactional, making monitoring more difficult. However, it is perhaps the academic/general distinction that provides the more convincing explanation. Even though the new TOEFL requires integrated skills and does not have structure sections as in the old TOEFL, it is still primarily a measure of cognitive academic language proficiency, whereas IELTS more clearly involves basic interpersonal interactional skills.

However, (2) might also explain the differences in the results of the two studies. In Chapter 2, we noted that the best single measure of implicit knowledge was the Elicited Oral Imitation Test. The TGJT did load on the same implicit factor, but not so strongly. It is possible, then, that the failure of Study 1 to find a clear relationship between implicit knowledge and the TOEFL was because the measure of implicit knowledge was inadequate. An inspection of the factor analysis in Table 7.4 suggests that what distinguished the two factors was automaticity – that is, all the unspeeded measures loaded on factor 1, whereas only the TGJT loaded on factor 2. Automaticity, however, is only one of several characteristics of implicit knowledge (see Chapters 1 and 2).

Difference (3) can also provide an explanation for the different results. As grammatical structures vary in the extent to which they draw on implicit and explicit knowledge, as shown in Study 2, it could be argued that the subtleties are lost when everything goes into the same pot, as happened in Study 1. Learners may well draw on whatever type of knowledge they have in order to perform the tasks used to measure proficiency and, as is now clear, they are likely to have implicit knowledge of some structures and explicit knowledge of others.

A plausible theoretical case for viewing language proficiency in terms of implicit and explicit L2 knowledge can be made. However, the studies reported in this chapter do not provide overwhelming empirical evidence for this case. Clearly, this is an area in need of further study.

Chapter 8

Pathways to Proficiency: Learning Experiences and Attainment in Implicit and Explicit Knowledge of English as a Second Language

JENEFER PHILP

Introduction

As outlined by Ellis in Chapter 1 of this volume, the linguistic competence of a language learner is characterized as comprising both implicit and explicit knowledge (see also N. Ellis, 2005). Implicit knowledge is described as intuitive or tacit knowledge of language that comes through implicit learning. It is the knowledge that enables a person to understand what is being said and to respond with fluency in real time, without conscious recourse to rules and without the need to consciously monitor comprehension or production (Bialystok, 1979). In other words, it is automatic. Explicit knowledge, in contrast, is described as 'all the conscious facts the learner has about the language and the criterion for admission to this category is the ability to articulate those facts' (Bialystok, 1979). That is, the learner has a degree of awareness of the regularities or patterns of a language and is able to verbalize these, though not necessarily by using metalinguistic terms (Green & Hecht, 1992). R. Ellis (2004, 2005) notes that, unlike the systematicity evident in implicit knowledge (Tarone, 1988), second language (L2) explicit knowledge is disparate, anomalous knowledge and is often inaccurate and inconsistent (Sorace, 1985). Yet, this is the kind of knowledge learners employ to help them out when their implicit knowledge is inadequate (N. Ellis, 2005), and particularly when engaged in a task that presents some difficulty (Bialystok, 1982; R. Ellis, 1991, 2005). It is knowledge that may be employed as a monitor on performance. Typically, we would predict that native-speakers or very fluent users of a second language operate primarily by using implicit knowledge, whereas those who have learnt the language in formal instructed settings might need to rely on a base of explicit knowledge. Focusing on utility, others have contrasted explicit and implicit knowledge in terms of 'language-as-knowledge' and 'language-as-use' (Macrory & Stone, 2000), or 'knowledge *about* language' and 'knowledge *of* language' (Andrews, 2003).

As noted in Chapter 1, the relationship between these two types of knowledge is under debate, yet there is general consensus for a distinction between them. This study explores support for this distinction by considering the degree to which performance on tests of implicit and explicit knowledge match expectations based on testees' learning profiles. A second aim of the study is to consider the extent to which L2 English users' implicit and/or explicit knowledge of certain morphological or syntactic structures relates to their experience of language learning.

Individual differences in cognitive and affective aptitudes, learning context and age are all identified as contributing factors to relative success in language acquisition among adult learners (DeKeyser, 2005). Individual differences of personality, aptitude, motivation and learning style (Dornyei, 2005) impact on the potential effectiveness of various types of input and instruction for any one learner. Starting age of instruction or age of first exposure appears to shape the kinds of knowledge representations of the L2 that L2 users hold (for a review see Birdsong, 2004; DeKeyser, 2000; Hyltenstam & Abrahamsson, 2003; Ioup, 2005). The present study thus focuses on the effects of L2 learning experience on different kinds of L2 knowledge.

Measuring Implicit and Explicit Knowledge

While previous research has characterized implicit and explicit knowledge based on articulating rules versus language use (Green & Hecht, 1992; Hu, 2002; Hulstijn & Hulstijn, 1984; Macrory & Stone, 2000; Seliger, 1979; Sorace, 1985), and has investigated the relationship between the two, few studies have focused on the validity of the constructs and the measurement of these two types of knowledge (see Ellis, 2005). Chapter 2 of this volume provides a detailed description and discussion of the tests developed for this purpose. Five tests were developed as measures of knowledge of 17 structures in English: an Elicited Oral Imitation Test (EIT) (testees repeated in correct English a correct or incorrect belief statement containing the targeted structure); an Oral Narrative Test (testees read a short story seeded with six target structures, then orally reproduced the story themselves); two Grammaticality Judgment Tests, one timed and one untimed (each containing equal numbers of grammatical and ungrammatical sentences) and a Metalinguistic Knowledge Test. In Chapter 2, R. Ellis distinguished the tests according to four principal criteria: time available, focus of attention, degree of awareness and metalinguistic knowledge. Explicit knowledge is operationalized as requiring time, attention to form, consciousness and metalinguistic knowledge. In contrast, implicit knowledge does not require awareness, operates under time pressure, gives focus to meaning and does not require metalinguistic knowledge.

None of the tests was claimed to be a measure of purely implicit or purely explicit knowledge (Ellis, 2004). However, through manipulation of speed and normality of the structure, as well as degree of awareness and metalinguistic knowledge, some tests were argued to be more likely to entail explicit knowledge, while others were more likely to elicit use of implicit knowledge. Based on the results of a factor analysis of performance on the tests by native and non-native speaker university students ($n = 20$ and 91, respectively), R. Ellis argues that the EIT and the Timed Grammaticality Judgment Test (TGJT), particularly the grammatical items, provide better measures of implicit knowledge, while the Metalinguistic Knowledge Test and the Untimed Grammaticality Judgment Test (UGJT), particularly the ungrammatical items, provide clearer measures of explicit knowledge (see Chapters 2 to 5 in Part Two).

Ellis (2005: 165) also found some support for the hypothesis that scores on tests of implicit knowledge would relate more strongly to the age at which the learners started to learn English, whereas scores on tests of explicit knowledge would relate more strongly to years of formal instruction. Results were based on data from 91 non-native speakers and 20 native speakers. All participants were university students in New Zealand, therefore all had experience of learning English in L2 contexts. The current study adds an additional set of 100 L2 users to this database; including L2 users who are studying and using English in a foreign language (FL) context, that is, Malaysia.

As noted above, learning experience encompasses many different factors, including starting age of instruction, context of learning, L2 use and type of instruction. The question of how age might contribute to language knowledge is one that has primarily been explored in terms of ultimate attainment, based on L2 users who are living in a country in which the majority speak L2 as a first language. Research indicates a strong relationship between ultimate attainment and age of arrival (AOA), and a somewhat weaker relationship for years of education and length of residence (LOR) in the target language country (e.g. Birdsong, 1992; DeKeyser, 2000; Flege *et al.*, 1999; Johnson & Newport, 1989, 1991; McDonald, 2000; Weber-Fox & Neville, 1996). Little of this research discusses the nature of the knowledge measured by tests of ultimate attainment (typically, grammaticality judgment tests), however, it appears that the researchers focused on or assumed implicit knowledge.

Individual Differences and Contextual Factors

Studies have examined variables associated with AOA, length of education and LOR. This review focuses on studies concerned with the effects of these factors on morphosyntactic knowledge.

Age of arrival

AOA studies demonstrate a correlation between AOA and performance on GJTs (morphosyntax), suggesting a long-term advantage for child starters (for a review, see Birdsong, 2004); that is, those who start using the L2 or being exposed to L2 input from an early age, develop a high degree of implicit L2 morphosyntactic knowledge.

Length of education

Flege *et al.* (1999) examined age and age-related factors and attainment in acquisition of morphosyntactic structures, based on the GJT scores of 240 native speakers of Korean who differed according to AOA in the USA (1 to 23 years). They found that once AOA was controlled for, the number of years of education completed in the USA was a significant factor. Differences in length of education in an English-speaking country (USA) predicted performance on rule-based items (morphosyntax), while reported language use predicted performance on lexically based items. Both correlated with AOA.

Length of residence

In a subsequent study, providing further exploration of the effects of education, Flege and Lui (2001) examined LOR as a factor influencing attainment. They conducted a study involving 60 Chinese students and non-students living in the USA. LOR predicted performance on GJTs for those learners who were students and who had lived in the USA for over 3.9 years, but not for nonstudents. The authors attributed this divergence to differences in provision of L2 input, suggesting that the frequency and type of input that students received (whether through formal instruction and/or some other aspect of student life), contributed to their knowledge of English morphosyntax.

A significant negative correlation was found between nonstudents' LOR and their performance on the GJT. That is, the longer they had lived in the USA, the lower their grammaticality judgment test scores tended to be. Flege and Liu (2001: 545) suggest that long-term residents 'forgot what they had learned about English grammar in school in China'. This explanation hints at the use of both explicit and implicit knowledge, suggesting that long-term residents may forget their explicit knowledge and become more reliant on their implicit knowledge.

In a study of native Korean and Chinese speakers who were US university academic staff or graduate students, Johnson and Newport (1989) found, for L2 morphosyntax, correlations between high scores on GJTs and AOA, but not LOR. The authors suggest that this supports the notion of a critical or sensitive period for L2 acquisition (DeKeyser, 2000; Patkowski, 1980, 1990; Scovel, 1988). Alternatively, Flege and Liu

(2001: 531), considering both these results and their own findings for students versus nonstudents, suggest that while 'the amount or the nature of L2 input, or both, does influence L2 learning, (...) length of residence provides a good index of L2 input only for certain individuals'. Experiences of children (at school), for example, clearly differ from those of adults (at home or work), both in terms of opportunity for L2 input and the type of L2 input available (see also Jia & Aaronson (2003) on differences between older and younger children).

The research reviewed above suggests a possible relationship between the type of knowledge acquired and the type and length of L2 learning experience, including when L2 exposure began. The study reported in this chapter compared the implicit and explicit knowledge of 17 grammatical structures in English of different populations of L2 users. Some had recently arrived in an L2 context, others had never been in an L2 context, some had lived all or the greater part of their lives in an L2 context.

Research Questions

(1) Do the participants group similarly according to performance on 'best measures' of implicit knowledge versus 'best measures of explicit knowledge?

(2) Is there a relationship between performance on measures of implicit and explicit knowledge and particular participant and contextual factors, specifically:
     (a) starting age of instruction;
     (b) length of instruction;
     (c) number of years in an English-speaking country;
     (d) type of instruction?

The first research question is examined by investigating whether students will cluster similarly according to performance on measures of implicit knowledge, on the one hand, and explicit knowledge on the other hand. Following discussion of the tests in Chapter 2, it is hypothesized that performance on the two best measures of implicit knowledge will match, while performance on the best measures of explicit knowledge will match, and there will not necessarily be concord between the two types of knowledge.

The second research question focuses on the degree of relationship between one learner factor (age) and contextual factors (length and type of instruction and number of years in an English-speaking country) on the one hand and type of linguistic knowledge on the other. It was hypothesized that those who scored high on measures of implicit knowledge would be those who had had high exposure to the target language from an early age and/or experienced high L2 use (i.e. native speakers and non-native speakers who had substantial experience using the L2). Conversely, those who scored high on measures of explicit knowledge would be those who had learnt the L2 primarily through formal instruction. If L2 users clustered according to performance on implicit measures on the one hand, and explicit measures on the other, this would provide further support for the tests as measures of different types of knowledge. Clustering in relation to type of learning experience may provide additional insights about how these two types of knowledge develop.

Method

Participants

The 211 participants were all students enrolled in tertiary institutions or private language schools and comprised three distinct groups:

(1) Twenty native speakers of English who were university students. These participants were enrolled in university undergraduate courses in Engineering, Education and Applied Linguistics in Auckland.
(2) One hundred and thirty-seven non-native speakers who were students enrolled in English language classes in universities or private language schools in Auckland. Proficiency levels ranged from lower-intermediate to advanced levels, by self-report. International English Language Testing System (IELTS) scores were available for a subset of 52 participants and these ranged substantially from 4 to 8.
(3) Fifty-four non-native and native speaker students enrolled in a Bachelor of Education programme at a university in Malaysia, studying to be English language teachers. These students ranged from lower-intermediate to advanced level, by self-report. Five students were native speakers. Performance on a Diagnostic English Language Needs Assessment (DELNA)[1] indicated that the greater majority had sufficient English skills to meet the academic language demands of an English-medium university.

Of the 211 participants, 80 were male and 131 were female. Reported L1s were: Bengali (1), Cantonese (6), Chinese (99)[2], English (23), French (2), German (1), Gujarati (1), Hebrew (1), Hindi (1), Indonesian (2), Japanese (1), Korean (7), Macedonian (1), Malay (36), Mandarin (8), Portuguese (1), Punjabi (1), Russian (5), Serbian (1), Tamil (5), Telugu (1), Thai (3) and Vietnamese (4). The majority were L1 Mandarin or Cantonese speakers. Regarding country of origin, the largest group represented was from China (45.7%), followed by Malaysia (24.4%), New Zealand (9%) and Korea (4.1%).

Background questionnaire

All participants were given a background questionnaire to fill out, requesting information regarding their experience of language learning, including the length of time they had been learning English, when they first began learning English, the number of languages they had learned and the type of instruction they had received. Participants who self-reported as native speakers did not complete two of the questions: length of time learning English and type of instruction. Each participant then completed a series of tests.

The test battery

A battery of tests targeting 17 grammatical structures was used (see Chapter 2 for a detailed description). The range of structures were selected as being those reported to be problematic for learners, ones that appeared in English as a second language (ESL) course texts across a range of levels and which represented both early and late acquired forms (Pienemann, 1989). A brief description of the tests follows.

The EIT, described in detail in Chapter 3, consisted of 34 statements, one grammatical and one ungrammatical for each structure. The statements were presented on audiotape to participants who sat one-on-one with an interviewer, who observed task compliance. After each statement, the participant was required to respond to the veracity of the statement according to personal belief, checking one of three boxes: true, not true, not sure. They then had to repeat the statement in correct English. In this way, the participant was first required to focus on meaning, before repeating or reformulating the statement correctly. Correct suppliance of the targeted form in the utterance was scored as 1, while incorrect suppliance or avoidance in using the targeted form was scored as 0.

The TGJT, described in detail in Chapter 4, consisted of 68 sentences and was computer-administered to all participants. There were four sentences on each of the 17 structures, two grammatical and two ungrammatical. Participants viewed each sentence separately and were asked to indicate whether the sentence was grammatical or ungrammatical. The time allowed for judging each sentence varied according to length, from 1.8 to 6.24 seconds, timing was established according to native-speaker baseline data. Scoring was dichotomous. Unanswered items were scored as incorrect.

The UGJT consisted of the same 68 sentences, presented in the same way, but with no time limit. Participants were also asked to indicate, for each sentence, how certain they were about their judgment (on a scale of 0–100%) and whether they had arrived at their answer predominantly by rule or by feel.

The Metalinguistic Knowledge Test, described in Chapter 5, was adapted from the test created by Alderson *et al.* (1997). It was computer-administered, except for the Malaysian group who completed a paper-and-pencil version. It consisted of two parts: recognition of a rule and recognition of grammatical features. The first part of the test consisted of 17 ungrammatical sentences (one sentence for each targeted structure) and a multiple choice of four items, each consisting of a rule. The test required the participants to choose the rule that explained the underlined error in the sentence. The second part of the test consisted of two sections: in section 1, participants identified examples of 21 grammatical features (e.g. adverb or a finite verb) in a short written text. In section 2, participants identified the features in a set of sentences. A total percentage accuracy score was calculated for each part of the Metalinguistic Knowledge Test.

Participants obtained seven different scores from these tests. As noted above and in Chapter 2, of the seven scores, a subset of these scores were identified as distinct measures of either explicit or implicit knowledge: scores on the EIT and the grammatical items on the TGJT were identified as best measures of implicit knowledge; scores on part 1 of the Metalinguistic Knowledge Test (recognition of rules) and the ungrammatical items on the UGJT were identified as best measures of explicit knowledge.

Scoring of tests was completed by hand (EIT and the Metalinguistic Knowledge Test) and by computer (UGJT and TGJT). Reliability for these tests, based on data for all 221 participants, including native speakers, is recorded in Table 8.1. Overall, Cronbach's alpha score encompassing all

Table 8.1 Individual items' and total reliability scores for the tests

Tests	Cronbach's alpha if item deleted
Timed Grammatical Judgment Test – grammatical items	.0653
Timed Grammatical Judgment Test – ungrammatical items	.0632
Untimed Grammatical Judgment Test – grammatical items	.0614
Untimed Grammatical Judgment Test – ungrammatical items	.0607
Metalinguistic Knowledge Test – Part 1	.0636
Metalinguistic Knowledge Test – Part 2	.0651
Elicited Imitation Test	.0690
All tests	.0677

tests is 0.677, which is considered acceptable (Kline, 1999). As separate scores were entered in the cluster analysis for grammatical and ungrammatical items, TGJT and UGJT, these scores were analyzed separately for reliability, as were the scores for each part of the Metalinguistic Knowledge Test.

Analysis of the data

Test responses and responses to the background questionnaire were entered into the Statistical Package for the Social Sciences (SPSS) for cluster analysis. Cluster analysis partitions participants into 'relatively homogenous subsets based on the [inter-participant] similarities' (Kachigan, 1991: 261). In this case, using hierarchical clustering, participants were clustered based on similarities in their test performances, made up of the seven subscores on the four tests. Clusters were arrived at on the basis of 'small within-cluster variation but larger between-cluster variation' (Kachigan, 1991: 262). While number of clusters can be manipulated, 'best fit' was found for nine clusters, made up of four individual outliers (i.e. there was only one individual in each of four of the clusters), and five main clusters. 'Best fit' was based on examination of dendograms and spread of participants.[3] The five main groups produced by cluster analysis were then characterized using descriptive statistics for (a) mean scores on best measures of implicit and explicit knowledge and (b) homogeneous features of the participants and their language learning experience.

Identification of the best measures were based on a factor analysis, as reported in Chapter 2 and described above. Combined mean scores of the two best measures for explicit knowledge and two for implicit knowledge were calculated for each cluster grouping. This composite score was then characterized as 'High', 'Medium' or 'Low' in relation to performance across groups, based on comparison across groups and consideration of histograms for performance on individual tests across the whole population. These composite scores and their classification are presented in Table 8.3. For implicit knowledge, high scores were those over 90%, and low range scores were less than 60%. For explicit knowledge, high scores were those over 70%, and low range scores were less than 60%.

A number of features based on the self-report data were explored through descriptive statistics and compared for each cluster, including: L1 and country of origin; starting age of instruction; type of instruction (whether informal, formal or mixed); length of time spent learning English, years spent in an L2 context and language most used.

Each cluster of participants was characterized descriptively for these nine features.

Results

Research Question One: Do participants group similarly according to performance on 'best measures' of implicit knowledge versus 'best measures' of explicit knowledge?

The cluster analysis grouped participants according to their performance on the measures of explicit/implicit knowledge. Of the 211 participants, all but four clustered into five main groupings, with outliers falling into an additional four separate clusters (one individual in each cluster). Upon examination, it is evident that the participants generally clustered according to high, medium or low performance on the different measures. The five main clusters are compared in Table 8.2. Details of the mean and standard deviation for each cluster group on each measure are provided in Table 8.3. Figures 8.1 and 8.2 provide a comparison of performance across the two best measures for implicit knowledge and explicit knowledge, respectively. In terms of performance on measures of

Table 8.2 Composite percent mean scores for best measures of implicit and explicit knowledge by cluster

	n	Implicit knowledge		Explicit knowledge	
Cluster 1	15	95.13	(H)	77.44	(H)
Cluster 2	117	70.75	(M)	71.89	(H)
Cluster 3	37	64.75	(M)	67.925	(M)
Cluster 4	26	52.80	(L)	74.04	(H)
Cluster 5	13	58.06	(L)	57.41	(L)

Table 8.3 Raw scores on best measures of implicit and explicit knowledge by cluster

		Implicit				Explicit			
		Imitation%		TGJT (gram.) 34		UGJT (ungram.) 34		Meta 1 17	
	n	M	SD	M	SD	M	SD	M	SD
Cluster 1	15	94	.04	32.7	1.33	33.87	.35	10.33	1.84
Cluster 2	117	58	.17	28.39	3.18	28.73	3.9	10.08	2.47
Cluster 3	37	52	.18	26.35	3.38	27.81	1.86	9.19	1.86
Cluster 4	26	43	.15	21.62	3.36	29.69	3.04	9.81	2.12
Cluster 5	13	41	.17	25.54	3.91	18.38	2.06	5.92	2.06

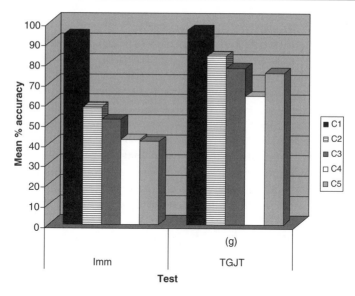

Figure 8.1 Performance by cluster on best measures of implicit knowledge

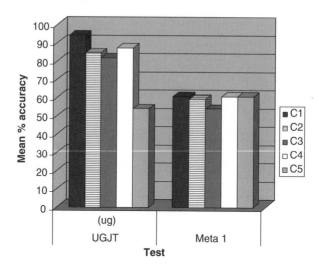

Figure 8.2 Performance by cluster on best measures of explicit knowledge

implicit knowledge, Cluster 1 (native and near-native speakers) clearly performs better than any other group, particularly on the EIT, a measure of implicit knowledge. Generally, performance is poorer from Clusters 1 to 5. In terms of performance on measures of explicit knowledge, the difference in performance between Cluster 1 and other clusters is far less clear.

Research Question Two: Is there a relationship between performance on measures of implicit and explicit knowledge and particular participant and contextual factors, specifically:
(a) starting age of instruction;
(b) length of instruction;
(c) number of years in an English-speaking country;
(d) type of instruction?

Each cluster is now described in turn, and general trends are further explored in the Discussion section.

Cluster 1

The 15 participants in this cluster were all native or near-native speakers. Twelve were from New Zealand, one from Fiji, one from France and one from Malaysia. Thirteen of the fifteen self-reported as native speakers and had started learning English before the age of six.

The participants scored high on measures of both implicit and explicit knowledge. As seen in Table 8.3, these learners consistently produced the highest scores on all tests, with near perfect scores. The exception was Part 2 (Identification of sentence parts) of the Metalinguistic Knowledge Test in which their mean scores were exceeded by Clusters 2 and 4. Figure 8.3 provides a comparison of this group's performance against the mean of the entire population. The results here fulfill expectations that the native speakers would achieve the highest scores on all tests and that

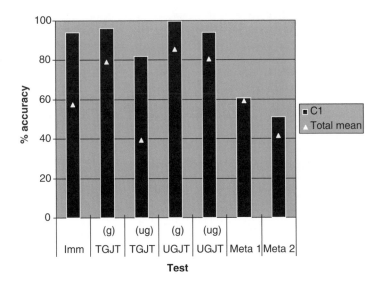

Figure 8.3 Comparison of percentage accuracy on all subtests for Cluster 1

the differences among the learners would most clearly be seen on measures of implicit knowledge.

Cluster 2

The largest number of participants ($n = 117$) fell into the second cluster. This included virtually all (94%) of the Malaysian students who were studying in the BEd programme in their own country. In addition, there were eight L1 English speakers and 51 L1 Chinese speakers in this group, while 23% was made up of L1 speakers of other languages.

As seen in Table 8.3, mean scores in Cluster 2 were in the mid range on measures of implicit knowledge and high on measures of explicit knowledge. While scores appear to be much lower on implicit measures compared to those of Cluster 1, particularly for the EIT, they are still consistently higher than those of the other three clusters. Note that within this group, despite the wide range of scores, standard deviations are relatively small, indicating a reasonably homogenous group with most scores clustering around the mean. As seen in Figure 8.4, this group was consistently a little higher than average for all tests, with the highest scores on Part 2 of the test of metalinguistic knowledge (parsing), an indication of higher metalinguistic knowledge.

In this cluster, roughly a third (32.5%) of participants learnt English before age six, 27% started learning English in primary school, 34% in junior high school, and the remainder (6%) in the final years of schooling or as adults. This group, then, is characterized by relatively early

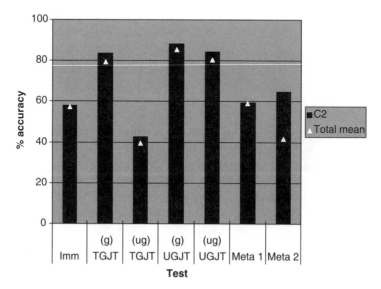

Figure 8.4 Comparison of percentage accuracy on all subtests for Cluster 2

language instruction (mean age = 8.33, SD = 4.74). In terms of type of instruction, 39% reported having had mainly formal instruction, 52% a mixture. Length of time learning English ranges from 2 to 25 years, with a mean length of 11.81 years[4] (SD = 5.63). While the majority of the Malaysian students had not lived in an English-speaking country, of the other L2 users, 32.5% had lived in New Zealand for one year at the time of the study and 12% had been there for less than a year. Almost half the group (47%) noted English as their most spoken language.

Cluster 3

Cluster 3 comprised 37 participants, of whom 24 were Chinese speakers (54%), four Korean, and three L1 English speakers. As seen in Figure 8.5, this group scored in the mid range on all tests, achieving mean or below mean scores, with slightly higher scores on one of the best measures of explicit knowledge (UGJT, ungrammatical items) (mean = 84.26). The group ranged in terms of starting age of instruction from 0 to 17 years, however the mean was 10.7 years. Half (54%) had begun learning English in their early teens, seven had begun before the age of 6. Type of instruction was reported as formal (30%) or a mixture (49%); 21% of this group reported having received mostly informal instruction. There was also considerable variation in their experiences of using English; 51.3% had been in an English-speaking country for one to two years, while five learners had never been in such an environment. Length

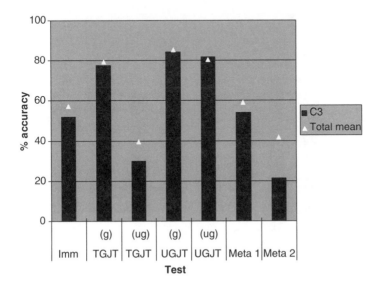

Figure 8.5 Comparison of percentage accuracy on all subtests for Cluster 3

of time spent learning English ranged from 3 to 18 years. Less than half (40.5%) reported English as their most spoken language.

Cluster 4

Cluster 4 comprised 26 participants, characterized by good explicit knowledge of the structures, but low implicit knowledge, as seen in Figure 8.6. This group scored above average on measures of explicit knowledge and also had good formal metalinguistic knowledge as evidenced by performance on Part 2 of the Metalinguistic Knowledge Test (parsing). Twenty-three of the twenty-six participants were L1 Chinese speakers, in addition to two speakers of L1 Russian and one L1 Malay speaker. The mean starting age of instruction for this group was relatively late, 13.73. Half (50%) of this group had begun learning English in their early teens, as 11–13 year olds, 15% in primary school and 15% as adults. Two thirds (65.4%) reported a language other than English as their most spoken language. Type of instruction was reported as being either mixed (58%) or mainly formal (34%), with just two learners reporting having received mainly informal instruction.

Cluster 5

Cluster 5 was the smallest group. The 13 participants who clustered together in this group tended to score low on all tests, as seen in Figure 8.7, with the exception of an average score on Part 1 of the Metalinguistic

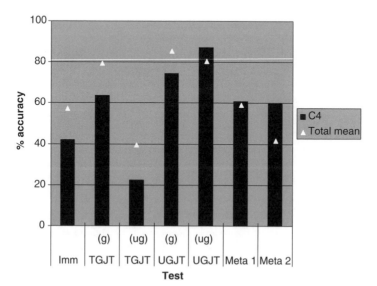

Figure 8.6 Cluster 4: Comparison of percentage accuracy on all subtests

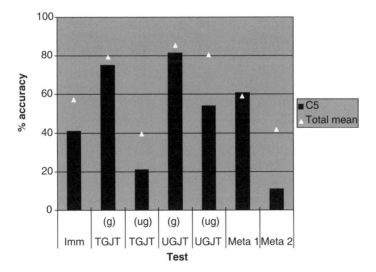

Figure 8.7 Cluster 5: Comparison of percentage accuracy on all subtests

Knowledge Test (identification of rules matching errors). They were particularly low on measures of implicit knowledge, and on Part 2 of the Metalinguistic Knowledge Test (parsing), as seen by their scores in Table 8.3. This group was made up of 10 participants from China and 3 others from Taiwan, Hong Kong and Israel. The mean starting age of instruction was 11.46 years. All had begun learning English at school, 10 of the 13 had begun in high school and reported having studied English for between 5 (50%) and 14 years. All reported instruction as being either formal or a mixture of formal and informal techniques. They had spent from 0 to 6 years in an English-speaking context, two thirds (69%) having been in New Zealand for 0–3 years. Only 3 of the 13 participants in this group (23%) reported using English as their most spoken language.

The following section provides a discussion of these results, including further analysis of the results relating to learning experiences with English.

Discussion

The results of the cluster analysis provide further support for a distinction between two types of knowledge, which are separably measurable. Participants tended to cluster according to performance on best measures of implicit knowledge on the one hand, and best measures of explicit knowledge on the other. That is, if they tended to perform well on one measure of implicit knowledge, their performance on other measures of implicit knowledge was comparable; performance on the ungrammatical items on the TGJT by each cluster tended to mirror performance on the EIT. For these two tests, the difference between the groups was most clearly marked. Similarly, performance on explicit measures tended to be comparable within clusters.

Other measures used that were not identified as 'best' measures, elicited variable performance that did not necessarily match performance on best measures. For example, performance on the Metalinguistic Knowledge Test, Part 2, varied markedly between groups, yet not necessarily in concord with group performance on other measures of explicit knowledge (UGJT and Metalinguistic Knowledge Test, Part 1). This suggests that this test elicits use of related knowledge that was not necessarily tapped by the other measures of explicit knowledge, namely formal knowledge of metalanguage (see Chapter 9). In general then, the results of the cluster analysis concur with the findings described in Chapter 2 concerning what constituted the best measures of implicit and explicit knowledge.

In terms of the second research question, concerning the relationship between type of knowledge and language learning experiences, some patterns arise from the data.

Starting age of instruction

Firstly, the results provide further support for an effect for starting age of instruction or L2 exposure, on L2 acquisition, as seen in Figure 8.8. Remembering that the clusters from 1 to 5 steadily decrease in performance on implicit measures, we see an association between cluster and age when instruction started; the earlier the age of instruction, the better their performance on measures of implicit knowledge. This

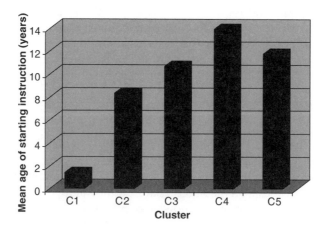

Figure 8.8 Age of starting instruction in English by cluster

supports the findings described in Chapter 2, which were based on a subset of roughly half the current population.

Length of instruction

Comparing the reported length of time learning English according to cluster, a pattern emerges in which better test performance is associated with greater length of instruction. Figure 8.9 shows this pattern, comparing Clusters 2–5 (native speakers were excluded from this analysis so Cluster 1 is not included here as the *n*-size was too small). Previous studies have focused on length of education in mainstream classes (Flege *et al.*, 1999) and have found correlations between length and performance on rule-based items on GJT tests. Further research needs to probe more carefully into type (e.g. mainstream education versus language specific classes) and nature of instruction (e.g. grammar-oriented or communicative-oriented). Additionally, as seen in Flege *et al.* (1999), in order to demonstrate a relationship between length of instruction and L2 knowledge, age, clearly a related variable, needs to be controlled for.

Length of years in an English-speaking country

As Flege and Liu (2001) point out, LOR is not necessarily an indication of quality or quantity of L2 input (see also Jia & Aaronson, 2003). As seen in Figure 8.10, there is no clear relationship between length of time in an English-speaking country and implicit knowledge. While Cluster 3 emerges as the group with the highest reported mean length of time in an English-speaking country, their performance on tests is in the mid

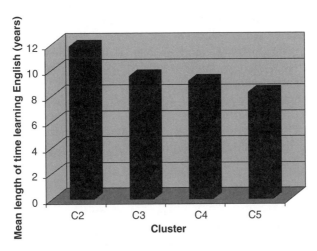

Figure 8.9 Mean length of time spent learning English by cluster

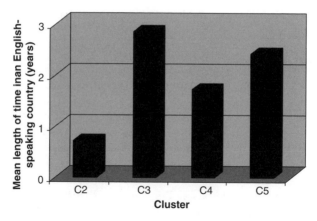

Figure 8.10 Mean length of time spent in an English-speaking country by cluster

range for both explicit and implicit measures. Conversely, Cluster 2 is superior in performance, yet this is the group with the lowest mean LOR. It should be noted that in Flege and Liu's study, effects for LOR on students in terms of increases in knowledge of morphosyntax were only apparent after several years of study. In the current study, the majority of those students living in New Zealand had been there fewer than three years.

Type of instruction

While the results summarized in Figure 8.11 suggest that type of instruction may be associated with type of knowledge, further research is needed. There is some indication, for example, that the relatively poor performance of Cluster 5 could be related to a lack of input in their instruction. This group alone reported no experience of informal instruction, and greatest formal instruction. However, the questionnaire data were not specific enough for a clear identification of learning experiences. Most participants reported a combination of types of instruction. Qualitative interview data may be necessary here in order to probe the relationship between instruction and implicit knowledge.

L2 use

Similarly, the relationship between L2 use and implicit knowledge is unclear. A pattern emerges between performance on the tests and reported L2 use, with greatest use of English by those who perform best (Cluster 1) and conversely, limited L2 use by those who whose

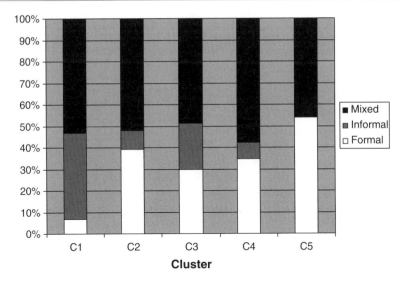

Figure 8.11 Type of instruction by cluster

performance is poorest (Cluster 5). It is most likely that L2 use in this case reflects both opportunity and ability.

The above findings concerning experiences of L2 users are indicative of relationships between implicit knowledge and onset of learning, length and type of instruction as well as opportunity for L2 use. Clearly, these factors are all related and require further research. One difficulty in investigating aspects of language learning experience is the many associated factors, particularly regarding L2 context and the quality and quantity of L2 input. Of great interest too is the role of the L1 (McDonald, 2000) on acquisition of morphosyntactic features.

Conclusions

The results of this study provide further evidence that the tests used do indeed provide relatively separate measures of different kinds of language knowledge. The clusters revealed differences between performance on implicit measures on the one hand, and explicit measures on the other. The clusters were not characterized by high performance on some explicit and implicit measures and low performance on other implicit and explicit measures.

Secondly, the results are indicative of associations between language learning experiences and L2 knowledge. In particular, the study supports the relationship between age of learning and type of knowledge. Those who had begun learning English at an early age (including as an L1) appear to have greater implicit knowledge than their counterparts who began later. The results of the cluster analysis were also indicative of associations between implicit knowledge and (1) type of instruction and (2) other age-related factors, including length of instruction. Time spent in an English-speaking country was not seen to be associated with performance on the tests.

The fact that the majority of L2 users in this study scored lower on implicit measures than on explicit measures suggests that most learners, educated in countries characterized as offering limited or no L2 use, are unlikely to achieve high levels of implicit knowledge. However, the difference in scores may simply reflect a test method factor. Interestingly, it was the Malaysian students who scored highest on implicit knowledge tests, after the native and near-native speakers. Many of these students lived in a multilingual environment in which English played a strong role in education and business contexts, in other words, in contexts that afforded opportunities for L2 use.

Limitations and Future Research

As explained in Chapter 2, previous analyses of the Marsden Project data used factor analyses to explore relationships between test performance and the constructs of explicit and implicit knowledge. This study has expanded this work by using a larger data set and, through the use of a cluster analysis, by exploring relationships between aspects of learning experience and L2 knowledge. The inclusion of the large group of students from Malaysia, allowed fruitful comparisons between participants who were currently studying in an English-speaking context and those studying in a FL context. However, all participants were students with a high level of education, studying English in a formal environment, i.e. in a university environment or in private language schools. Future research among L2 users with little formal education (e.g. Bigelow & Tarone, 2004) would be desirable. Furthermore, the questionnaire used was very limited in scope.[5] In order to investigate the research questions in greater depth, the use of a more detailed questionnaire, together with follow-up interviews is needed in order to elicit richer data for more qualitative analysis. The findings of the current study suggest such an exploration to be worthwhile, particularly using measures of explicit and implicit knowledge as a means of characterizing the learners' L2 proficiency.

Notes

1. DELNA is a test designed for use at The University of Auckland to identify students' language support needs in reading, listening and writing.
2. Some participants reported their L1 as 'Chinese', while others reported Cantonese or Mandarin. These have been recorded separately. Some participants ($n = 8$) did not report L1.

3. The reader is referred to Csizér and Dörnyei (2005) and Kojic-Sabo and Lightbown (1999) for examples of other studies using cluster analysis. These two studies each provide a detailed explanation of cluster analysis.
4. Excludes native speakers and students in Malaysia, as these two groups did not complete this information in the questionnaire.
5. As the questionnaire was attached to a lengthy test battery, time constraints precluded the use of a detailed instrument or the use of open-ended questions.

Chapter 9

Exploring the Explicit Knowledge of TESOL Teacher Trainees: Implications for Focus on Form in the Classroom[1]

ROSEMARY ERLAM, JENEFER PHILP AND CATHERINE ELDER

Introduction

Research on form-focused instruction (FFI) suggests a key role for grammar instruction within a communicative approach (Doughty & Williams, 1998; Ellis, 1994, 1995, 1997, 1998; Long, 1996, 2000; Long & Robinson, 1998; Nassaji & Fotos, 2004; Norris & Ortega, 2000; Spada, 1997). There are different ways in which FFI is realized in second language (L2) classrooms. These range from more explicit instruction to implicit feedback, and incorporate varying degrees of elaboration (Doughty & Williams, 1998; Sharwood Smith, 1991). Thus, the L2 teacher has many different options for rendering form-meaning connections more transparent for the learner. However, as this paper suggests, limitations in L2 proficiency and in metalinguistic knowledge may mean teachers do not use all FFI options effectively.

While metalinguistic knowledge is clearly not the same as language proficiency, and a number of studies have shown only moderate positive correlations between the two (Alderson *et al.*, 1997; Elder *et al.*, 1999; Renou, 2000), both are now regarded as critical for effective language teaching. Andrews (2003), citing Wright and Bolitho's (1997) model of classroom language content and use, emphasizes the interconnection between proficiency and language awareness and argues that a teacher's language awareness (TLA) incorporates both knowledge *about* the language and knowledge *of* the language. Particular to TLA is a metacognitive aspect, drawing from both types of knowledge, which enables the teacher to plan learning activities, modify and mediate input from other sources and respond to learner production and questions in the context of such activities. As Wright (2002: 115) notes, 'a linguistically aware teacher not only understands how language works, but understands the student's struggle with language and is sensitive to errors and other interlanguage features'. Research conducted with ESL practicum supervisors by Derwing and Munrow (2005) and Llurda (2005) confirms the importance of metalinguistic knowledge (along with language proficiency and pedagogical skills) for effective language teaching.

Elder (1994, 2000), exploring the construct of teacher language proficiency for testing purposes, proposes that language teachers need to (a) be proficient enough in the target language (TL) to provide rich and well-formed models for their learners; (b) tailor their input to make it comprehensible to learners, and, most importantly for the current study; (c) have sufficient metalinguistic knowledge both to explain grammatical rules and to respond to learner errors (using whatever strategies are appropriate to the particular learning context). The Italian teacher proficiency test that Elder refers to includes a task that requires candidates to explain TL errors in terms that would be intelligible to an L2 learner. A similar error correction and explanation task has been used in the Hong Kong language proficiency Assessment for Teachers of English (Coniam & Falvey, 2002).

Work on TLA, however, suggests that not all teachers are well equipped to offer such explanations or to exploit the potential of different options within FFI (Andrews, 1999, 2003; Bolitho, 1988; Mitchell, 2000; Wright, 1991; Wright & Bolitho, 1997). Bolitho (1988) and Andrews (1994, 2003) report a perceived inadequate grammatical knowledge or awareness among teacher trainees in the English-speaking West, where grammar is seldom taught in mother tongue classrooms. However, Andrews (2003), citing Wright (1991), suggests this may be less true of 'non-native' L2 teacher trainees from outer circle and peripheral contexts (Kachru, 1985) because of the inclusion of explicit grammar pedagogy in their prior education, and as part of teacher training programmes. Nemtchinova (2005) and Liu (2005) are in agreement, listing superior knowledge of grammar among the positive aspects that non-native teachers of English bring to their teaching. These claims are not often tested, however, and even if they are true, it cannot be assumed that knowing the explicit rules of TL grammar will result in the ability to produce acceptable TL explanations for L2 learners. Grammar instruction in foreign language teaching contexts (even those espousing the communicative approach) is, after all, typically delivered to L2 learners in their mother tongue rather than through the medium of the TL (Duff & Polio, 1990; Kim & Elder, 2005, 2008; Mitchell, 1988; Polio & Duff, 1994). Also worth noting are the results of previous research assessing learners' levels of metalinguistic knowledge (Alderson *et al.*, 1997; Elder *et al.*, 1999; Elder & Manwaring, 2004; Green & Hecht, 1992; Renou, 2000). These show that the ability to verbalize grammatical rules in the TL is often quite limited, even among advanced undergraduate learners of a foreign language with many years of prior formal instruction. Whether this is due to conceptual confusion about the workings of the language, limited language proficiency, a lack of appropriate metalanguage or a combination of these is not entirely clear, but it is a matter for concern given that university language departments are usually the recruiting ground for foreign language teachers.

Research Questions

In the present study, a Metalinguistic Knowledge Test (MKT; adapted from Alderson *et al.* 1997) was used to test the explicit language knowledge and understanding of grammatical rules of two groups of students. The first ($n = 61$) was a group of non-native speakers (NNS) with high proficiency in English. All were trainee English language teachers from Malaysia. (This study is an extension of an earlier one conducted with this group of students and reported in Elder *et al.*, 2007.) The second ($n = 33$) was a group of native speakers (NS), also trainee teachers of English as a second language. Seven were students at a teacher training institution in New Zealand and the remaining 26 were students at a Canadian University. The research questions that the study addressed are as follows:

(1) What level of metalinguistic knowledge do
     (a) the NNS teacher trainees have?
     (b) the NS teacher trainees have?
(2) Is there a significant difference between the levels of metalinguistic knowledge of the two groups of teacher trainees (NNS and NS)?
(3) What kinds of rules/metalinguistic terms present particular difficulties for
     (a) NNS teacher trainees?
     (b) NS teacher trainees?
(4) For NNS teacher trainees, is metalinguistic knowledge associated with the ability to recognize error?
(5) What are the implications of these findings for the teaching of Focus on Form (FoF) in second language classrooms?

Method

A total of 94 students participated in the study. These students formed two separate groups, as described above.

Non-native speaker participants

There were 61 students in this group, all enrolled in a 18 months of foundation programme at an international languages teacher training institute in Malaysia. At the time of the study, the students were nearing completion of their foundation programme and preparing to embark on a four-year BEd degree, the middle two years of which were to be completed at Universities in New Zealand, Australia or the UK. On completion of this 'sandwich' degree, students would be expected to take up positions as English language teachers in primary or secondary schools in Malaysia.

All students had studied English as a second language from the age of seven, at primary and secondary school in Malaysia. They had been selected for admission to the institute on the basis of their high school grades, in particular their English language marks. Their results on the Diagnostic English Language Needs Assessment (DELNA), a test used to identify their language support needs in reading, listening and writing, confirmed that the vast majority of them performed above the threshold deemed necessary to cope with the academic language demands of an English-medium university. All students were between 19 and 21 years of age. During the 18 months of foundation studies, students attended a variety of English classes, namely English studies (literature), Language description (grammar) and Language development (proficiency). A social studies class was also conducted in English. The Language description classes were of approximately three hours duration per week and were taught over a period of 18 months (120 contact hours in total). The content of the course dealt with such areas as word classes, phrases and clauses, sentences patterns, sentence types, cohesive devices, words and meanings and lexical relationships.

Native speaker participants

As described above, the 33 NS participants were training to be teachers of English for speakers of other languages (ESOL) at two different institutions. Seven were students at a teacher training institution in New Zealand and 26 were students at a Canadian University.

The teacher trainees in New Zealand were enrolled in a graduate teaching diploma, having previously completed an undergraduate degree. They had elected to specialize in the teaching of ESOL. Prior to completing the MKT (described below), they filled out a brief background questionnaire, from which the following information was elicited. Students were all aged between 21 and 31, the mean age being 26 years. Four students had no prior experience of teaching ESOL, one had three year's experience and two had less than a year's experience. Three students indicated that they had studied a language other than English, one student had studied two. Four students indicated that they had studied English grammar at some time and three students did not specify any study of English grammar.

The 26 students studying at the Canadian University were enrolled in a Linguistics and Language Studies Masters level course in the teaching of English grammar. These students also wrote answers to questions asking them about their personal background. Thirteen of the 26 students were bilingual in that they listed another language along with English as their first language; for the majority, this was French. To a question asking whether they had studied grammar previously, four students indicated that they had studied English grammar and eight that they had studied the grammar of another language. Eleven students indicated that they had some experience of teaching ESOL.

Metalinguistic Knowledge Test

The MKT used in this study was an adaptation of an earlier test of metalanguage devised by Alderson et al. (1997). An earlier version of this test is described in Chapter 2 and evidence for its validity is presented in Chapter 5. In this earlier version, students were presented with ungrammatical sentences, each of which contained a typical learner error in relation to a specific language structure, and were asked to choose from a list of four statements the one which best explained the error. The rationale for the choice of these structures has already been presented (see Chapter 2). In this study, this earlier multichoice version was replaced with a version with an open-ended response format that would enable the researchers to ascertain whether teacher trainees could give adequate explanations for common errors. The first part of the test (Part 1), therefore, presented students with 15 ungrammatical sentences, each containing an error that was underlined. (In the original version of the test, there was a total of 17 structures.) In this version, the structure third person -s was unintentionally omitted and the item testing for dative alternation had to be eliminated from the data set because there were difficulties in deciding on appropriate criteria for scoring it. Test-takers were asked to write in English a rule 'which explains why the sentence is ungrammatical'. The second part of the test (Part 2) was identical to the version described in previous chapters. It consisted of two sections (a and b). In the first, participants were asked to read a short text and find examples in it of 19 specific grammatical features (e.g. preposition, finite verb). In section (b), they were asked to identify the named grammatical parts in a set of four sentences. (The entire test can be found in the Appendix.)

The NNS participants also completed the Untimed Grammaticality Judgment Test (UGJT), described in Chapter 2 and discussed in more detail in Chapter 4. It consisted of 68 sentences, evenly divided between grammatical and ungrammatical. There were four sentences to be judged for each of 17 grammatical structures, the 15 that were targeted in the MKT, plus the two that had been omitted (third person 's', dative alternation). For each item, participants were required to indicate whether the sentence was (a) grammatical or (b) ungrammatical.

Test administration

The NNS participants completed both tests during a period in which one of the researchers was visiting Malaysia along with another colleague to administer DELNA to these and other students from the institute. Both were administered as pen-and-paper tests with no time limit. The MKT was completed first, followed by the GJT.

The NS participants in New Zealand also completed the MKT test as a pen-and-paper test, under the supervision of one of the researchers. The students at the Canadian University completed the MKT under the supervision of their lecturer and course convener. The latter, who was known to the researchers, had shown interest in the study and agreed to participate in data collection.

Scoring

Responses to Part 1 of the MKT were scored according to two criteria. The first was the formulation of a rule to account for the underlined error (rule score). For each item, criteria were established that would determine whether a given explanation was an *adequate* formulation of the appropriate rule or not. It is important to note here that the criteria for adequate formulation of a rule did not require the use of metalinguistic terminology, but simply the ability to articulate the concept/s deemed to be central in each case. We were, in other words, attempting to avoid, as far as possible, any confusion between the knowledge that was being assessed (knowledge of language) and the means used to express it (metalanguage) (Andrews, 2005: 13). The judgments of two expert applied linguists were used as a basis for deciding the criteria for each item, with reference to relevant pedagogic or descriptive grammar texts as required. Participants scored 1 mark for an adequately formulated rule and a maximum of 15 for this part of the text. Criteria were initially established for the formulation of a rule that completely explained the underlined error. However, given the small number of instances of such completeness and the difficulty of supplying a complete rule without also using metalingual terminology, this criteria was later abandoned.

For each item, participants were also given a score for their use of metalingual terminology (metalang. score). While, as already noted, the test rubric did not require them to use metalanguage, the two examples provided before starting the test (see Appendix) did demonstrate the use of metalingual terminology (which is extremely hard to avoid in some cases). For each item, a list of acceptable metalingual terms was generated. Participants had only to use one of the specified terms to score 1 mark for each item in this category. The maximum score possible in this section was 15.

For each item, the scoring criteria (see Appendix for examples) were first 'trialled' with a selection of 'sample' answers taken from participants' scripts. Two of the researchers applied the scoring criteria to rate this selection of items. This, at times, necessitated the reformulation and reworking of criteria. Subsequent to this trialling and refinement (if necessary) of criteria, a rater was 'trained' with respect to the criteria and given the sample items to rate. She then compared her ratings with those of one of the researchers and reasons for any disparity were discussed and resolved. She and the researcher then rated the remaining scripts independently and later compared their ratings. Any differences were discussed and agreement was usually reached. In those few cases where discussion did not resolve differences, the ratings of the researcher were taken as the final scores.

In Part 2 of the test, the acceptable answer/answers to each question was previously determined by the rater and the researcher, and a marking key was developed. The rater then scored each section, giving 1 mark for each acceptable answer. Any item, in this or the previous section, for which an answer was not provided, was scored as incorrect. The total maximum score for Part 2 of the test was 23.

The UGJT was scored dichotomously. The maximum score for this test was 68.

Test reliability

Given that the results from Part 1 of the test are used independently from those of Part 2 as an indication of participants' knowledge of the targeted grammatical structures, reliability of this section was estimated separately. Internal consistency was calculated using Cronbach's alpha, yielding, for the NNS group, $\alpha = 0.81$. Inter-rater reliability was also established for Part 1 (rule score) of the test, given that scoring required making subjective judgments about the acceptability of participants' attempts to formulate rules. Correlations between initial scores (i.e. before joint discussion of differences in ratings) given by the two raters for participants' attempts at rule formulation were: $r = 0.96$. Reliability of Part 2 of this test was also estimated using Cronbach's alpha, yielding $\alpha = 0.85$. Reliability of the total test (i.e. Parts 1 and 2 combined) was $\alpha = 0.88$.

For the NS group, internal consistency for Part 1 of the test was calculated using Cronbach's alpha, $\alpha = 0.87$. Reliability of Part 2 of this test was also estimated using Cronbach's alpha, yielding $\alpha = 0.90$. Reliability of the total test (i.e. Parts 1 and 2 combined) was $\alpha = 0.92$.

For the UGJT, internal consistency of the judgment accuracy scores was calculated using Cronbach's alpha, yielding $\alpha = 0.66$.

Results

Descriptive statistics for participants' performance on Parts 1 and 2 of the MKT are presented in Table 9.1.

Results for Part 1 show that NNS participants scored a mean of 7.41 (out of a maximum total score of 15) for their ability to formulate an acceptable rule in relation to the 15 targeted grammatical structures. They scored a mean of 5.07 (out of a maximum total score of 15) for their ability to use appropriate metalingual terminology in their rule explanations. Performance ranged widely on both parts of the test as evidenced by the relatively large standard deviations. However, no candidate achieved a perfect score.

NS participants scored lower than NNS participants ($M = 4.36$) for their ability to formulate an acceptable rule. On the other hand, the two groups' performance in terms of ability to use appropriate metalingual terminology in their rule explanations was very similar ($M = 5.07$, $M = 5.06$). Once again, standard deviations attest to a wide range of performance and no candidate achieved a perfect score.

Correlations were carried out between the two sets of scores on Part 1 of the test to see to what extent participants' ability to formulate a rule was related to their ability to use metalingual terms. For NNS there was a significant correlation, $r = 0.664$, $p = 0.01$. The correlation for NS was higher, $r = 0.764$, $p = 0.000$.

Students performed somewhat better on Part 2 of the test, which required them to identify specific grammatical features from a text or sentences, although again the score range was wide and no candidate attained the maximum score. For NNS, the mean score was 13.97 out of a maximum total score of 23. For NS, the mean score was 12.61. A correlation was carried out between scores for formulating rules on Part 1 of the test and scores on Part 2 of the test to see to what extent participants' ability to formulate rules was related to their ability to identify grammatical features from a text or sentences. There was a

Table 9.1 Descriptive statistics for Metalinguistic Knowledge Test

Metalinguistic knowledge test		*NNS (n = 61)*			*NS (n = 33)*		
		M	*SD*	*Range*	*M*	*SD*	*Range*
Part 1	Rule (/15)	7.41	2.91	1–14	4.36	3.28	0–13
	Meta (/15)	5.07	2.93	0–14	5.06	3.02	0–12
Total		12.48	5.33	3–28	9.42	5.92	0–25
Part 2	(/23)	13.97	4.76	1–22	12.61	5.92	1–21

modest but statistically significant correlation for NNS, $r = 0.390$, $p = 0.002$. For NS, the correlation was again higher, $r = 0.500$, $p = 0.003$.

To ascertain whether there was a significant difference between NS and NNS performance on the different parts of the test, t-tests were conducted. The first t-test compared performance on total scores of Part 1 of the MKT, examining rule formulation and use of metalingual terminology. NNS outperformed NS, t (92) $= 2.70$, $p = 0.008$. The second and third t-tests compared performance on each of these two skills of Part 1 of the test. NNS outperformed NS in terms of ability to formulate an acceptable rule (t (92) $= 4.837$, $p = 0.000$), but not in terms of ability to use metalingual terminology (t (92) $= 0.008$, $p = 0.994$). There was no significant difference between the two participant groups in terms of performance on Part 2 of the MKT, testing the ability to identify grammatical features from a text or sentences ($t(92) = 1.20$, $p = 0.231$).

Table 9.2 presents, for each participant group, the percentage correct of rule formulation scores for each of the 15 items of Part 1 of the MKT, in order of increasing difficulty.

The structures for which the NNS participants performed best in terms of formulating an adequate rule were (in order of increasing difficulty) regular past tense, plural -s, possessive -s and comparatives. The structures that were most difficult (from most to least difficult) were ergatives, verb complements and unreal conditional. NS performed best on (in order of increasing difficulty) plural -s, comparatives, possessive -s and relative clauses. The most difficult structures for them (from most to least difficult) were yes/no questions, ergatives and *since* and *for*.

Table 9.3 presents the percentage correct for items in Part 2 of the MKT. Items are again presented in terms of increasing difficulty. In this part of the test, participants were asked to identify exemplars of named grammatical features in a text or sentences.

The grammatical features correctly identified by the greatest number of NNS students were (in increasing order of difficulty): subject, verb, countable noun and noun/pronoun. The features that were identified by the least number of NNS students were (from most to least difficult): conditional verb (only 5% of students correctly identified this feature), agent and finite verb. For NS participants, the grammatical features that were easiest to identify correctly (in increasing order of difficulty) were subject, noun, verb and adjective. Those that were least easy to identify were (in increasing order of difficulty) agent, finite verb and modal verb.

Descriptive statistics for NNS participants' performance on the UGJT are presented in Table 9.4. The NS group did not complete this test due to time constraints, but previous research (see Chapters 2 and 4) suggests that a high rate of correct responses would be likely.

Participants scored highly on this test, $M = 60.21$ out of a possible maximum score of 68, showing that they were able to perform to a high

Table 9.2 Percentage correct for rule formulation scores, Part 1 Metalinguistic Knowledge Test

NNS			NS		
Item	*Grammatical structure*	*Percentage correct*	*Item*	*Grammatical structure*	*Percentage correct*
8.	Regular past tense	78.69	5.	Plural -s	57.58
5.	Plural -s	73.77	4.	Comparatives	39.39
7.	Possessive -s	73.77	7.	Possessive 's'	39.39
4.	Comparatives	70.49	15.	Relative clauses	39.39
9.	Indefinite article	63.93	13.	Question tags	36.36
13.	Question tags	63.93	9.	Indefinite article	33.33
12.	Adverb placement	60.66	12.	Adverb placement	30.30
15.	Relative clauses	45.90	1.	Modal verbs	27.27
11.	Yes/no questions	42.62	3.	Unreal conditional	24.24
14.	Since and for	42.62	8.	Regular past tense	21.21
1.	Modal verbs	37.70	10.	Embedded questions	21.21
10.	Embedded questions	29.51	2.	Verb complements	18.18
3.	Unreal conditional	21.31	14.	Since and for	18.18
2.	Verb complements	19.67	6.	Ergatives	15.15
6.	Ergatives	16.39	11.	Yes/no questions	15.15

level when required to judge the grammatical acceptability of sentences containing the targeted structures. In fact, there was a ceiling effect on this test, with a number of participants obtaining perfect or near perfect scores (this lack of variability in scores may explain the low reliability rating on this test, $\alpha = 0.66$). It is interesting to note that they performed at a similar level when judging both the grammatical ($M = 29.66$) and ungrammatical

Table 9.3 Percentage correct for items in Part 2 of the Metalinguistic Knowledge Test

	NNS			NS	
Item	*Grammatical structure*	*Percentage correct*	*Item*	*Grammatical structure*	*Percentage correct*
20	Subject	91.80	20	Subject	96.97
1	Verb	90.16	2	Noun	93.94
8	Countable noun	88.52	1	Verb	87.88
2	Noun	86.89	6	Adjective	66.67
19	Pronoun	86.89	22	Direct object	63.64
3	Preposition	85.25	3	Preposition	63.64
12	Modal verb	73.77	9	Indefinite article	63.64
22	Direct object	73.77	19	Pronoun	63.64
7	Adverb	72.13	14	Conjunction	60.61
13	Past participle	70.49	16	Infinitive verb	60.61
14	Conjunction	65.57	11	Auxiliary verb	57.58
6	Adjective	60.66	21	Infinitive	57.58
16	Infinitive verb	57.38	4	Passive verb	54.55
18	Comparative form	57.38	7	Adverb	54.55
10	Relative pronoun	54.10	8	Countable noun	51.52
11	Auxiliary verb	49.18	5	Conditional verb	42.42
4	Passive verb	47.54	13	Past participle	42.42
21	Infinitive	47.54	18	Comparative form	39.39
23	Indirect object	44.26	10	Relative pronoun	33.33
9	Indefinite article	42.62	23	Indirect object	30.30
15	Finite verb	34.43	12	Modal verb	27.27
17	Agent	11.48	15	Finite verb	27.27
5	Conditional verb	4.92	17	Agent	21.21

Table 9.4 Descriptive statistics for Grammaticality Judgment Test

Grammaticality Judgment Test	M	SD	N	Max score	Range	Percentage mean
Ungrammatical sentences	30.56	2.89	61	34	22–34	89.88
Grammatical sentences	29.66	2.72	61	34	23–34	87.24
Total	60.21	4.24	61	68	51–68	88.54

Table 9.5 Percentage correct for items in Grammaticality Judgment Test

Grammatical structure	Percentage correct
Modal verbs	95.49
Indefinite article	95.08
Adverb placement	95.08
Indefinite article	95.08
Possessive -s	93.85
Verb complements	93.44
Question tags	93.44
Regular past tense	89.34
Since and for	88.52
Dative alternation	88.52
Yes/no questions	86.48
Ergatives	84.84
Relative clauses	83.61
Embedded questions	82.38
Plural −s	81.97
Unreal conditional	80.74
Comparatives	77.46

sentences ($M = 30.56$) given that results on the GJT have already suggested that the two types of item are tapping different types of knowledge – implicit knowledge in the case of the grammatical items and explicit knowledge in the case of the ungrammatical items (see Chapter 2).

Table 9.5 presents the facility value (i.e. percentage correct) for items in the UGJT according to each grammatical structure tested (there were four

Table 9.6 Correlational matrix for performance on Part 1 of Metalinguistic Knowledge Test and performance on UGJT

Test	UGJT total	UGJT–gram.	UGJT–ungram.
Part 1 rule score	0.300*	0.111	0.337**
Part 1 metalang score	0.349**	0.070	0.447**
Part 1 total	0.356**	0.099	0.430**
Part 2 total	0.279*	0.192	0.228

*$p < 0.05$.
**$p < 0.01$.

items testing for participants' ability to judge the grammaticality of sentences in relation to each target structure).

It is interesting to note that the three structures for which participants scored highly when required to formulate a rule, that is, regular past tense, plural -s and possessive -s, were not among the three structures that they found easiest in terms of making a grammaticality judgment. Accuracy rates were nevertheless high on these items (89, 81 and 94%, respectively), far higher than for the corresponding items on the rule explanation section of the MKT.

Table 9.6 presents correlations between performances on all parts of the MKT and performances on the UGJT (grammatical items, ungrammatical items, total score).

Results show that there were significant correlations between scores on all parts of the MKT and both total scores and scores for ungrammatical items on the UGJT (the correlation between Part 2 total and GJT – ungrammatical scores was the only exception). Interestingly, correlations between Part 1 metalanguage scores (based on use of relevant terminology) and the ungrammatical items on the GJT were higher than those for Part 1 rule scores (indicating the appropriateness of the explanations provided). Correlations for Part 2 of the test, which tested participants' ability to match specific grammatical terms to their linguistic exemplars in a text/sentence, were weaker.

Discussion

The discussion will be organized around the research questions set out above.

(1) What level of metalinguistic knowledge do (a) the NNS teacher trainees and (b) the NS teacher trainees have?

The results of the MKT show that, in spite of their extensive English training which includes an explicit focus on the formal features of English, NNS trainee teachers vary widely in their level of metalinguistic knowledge and, as a group, perform rather poorly on all parts of the test and on Part 1 (rule formulation) in particular. Even with a scoring system that accepts approximate explanations of errors, the participants achieve less than 50% of acceptable responses on the rule explanation task. Their command of metalinguistic terminology (which correlates moderately with the ability to verbalize rules, $r = 0.664$, $p = 0.01$) is even weaker, although we must concede that participants may have deliberately chosen *not* to use technical language in this section of the test. Their performance on Part 2 of the test, which required them to identify grammatical forms, is somewhat stronger in that they achieved a mean score of over 50% ($M = 13.97$, max score $= 23$).

NS teacher trainees perform at an even lower level than the NNS in terms of ability to give an acceptable rule explanation for errors. Their mean score for this section of the test is only 4.36 out of a maximum score of 15. Their use of metalinguistic terminology is on a par with NNS (NNS, $M = 5.07$; NS, $M = 5.06$). They also achieve a mean score of just over 50% on Part 2 of the test measuring the ability to identify grammatical forms ($M = 12.61$, max score $= 23$). These results suggest that the grammatical knowledge that NS teacher trainees do have is largely confined to the ability to recognize parts of speech. This is knowledge that they may have picked up from either studying a second or foreign language (the majority of students either spoke or had studied another language) or from a study of English grammar (12 of the 33 students indicated they had studied some English grammar). It is perhaps not surprising that their ability to identify rules that explain errors is less developed, especially given that the majority (14/33) had no experience of teaching ESOL.

(2) Is there a significant difference between the levels of metalinguistic knowledge of the two groups of teacher trainees (NNS and NS)?

Results show that there is a significant difference between NNS and NS ability on Part 1 of the test ($t(92) = 2.70$, $p = 0.008$) and that this difference is due to the NNS outperforming the NS in terms of ability to formulate a correct rule to explain errors ($t(92) = 4.837$, $p = 0.000$). It is perhaps surprising that the difference is so much in favor of the NNS (NNS, $M = 7.41$; NS, $M = 4.36$) when one considers that, in having to formulate a rule in English, they are using a language in which they may not be as proficient as NS. We may speculate that exposure to grammatical rules may be much greater in L2 than in L1 classrooms, with the result that NNS are more knowledgeable in this area.

There is, on the other hand, no significant difference between NNS and NS performance in terms of ability to use metalingual terminology ($t(92) = 0.008$, $p = 0.994$) or ability to identify grammatical features from a text or sentences ($t(92) = 1.20$, $p = 0.231$). This may be because metalanguage is a feature of both L1 and L2 classrooms.

It is interesting to compare the above findings with those reported in Chapter 5. Scrutiny of means for Part 2 of the MKT (which contained identical items to those used in this study) suggests that the participants in this study, regardless of their language background were considerably more metalinguistically competent, either because of the nature of their prior schooling, or because they were motivated enough to train as language teachers, and therefore had a greater interest in language analysis. While in both studies there was a NNS advantage with respect to the total metalinguistic knowledge score, performance on the two tests' components varied across studies. The NNS advantage manifested only on Part 1 of the test in the current study and only on Part 2 of the test in the previous one. These conflicting findings suggest the need for caution in generalizing findings from this study to other populations.

Evidence for the fact that Part 1 (rule formulation) and Part 2 (identifying forms) of the test seem to be measuring rather different constructs comes from the fairly weak correlation between subtotals on each part (NNS, $r = 0.390$, $p = 0.002$; NS, $r = 0.500$, $p = 0.003$). This correlation is considerably lower than that reported between Parts One and Two of the multichoice version of the MKT described in Chapter 5 ($r = 0.553$). Thus, although the two parts of the test draw on a common knowledge base, we may posit that the receptive knowledge required to parse a sentence differs psycholinguistically from the ability to actively verbalize grammatical rules. The mean scores for each part also indicate that all participants were somewhat better equipped to do the former than the latter. This may be partly a function of their traditional education, where parsing may have been a regular classroom activity. The poor results on the rule formulation task correspond to the findings of previous research (Green & Hecht, 1992; Sorace, 1985), which indicate that learners, even those with considerable experience of traditional instruction with a FoF orientation, do not necessarily learn the rules about language that they have been taught. However, as Bialystok (1979), Green and Hecht (1992) and Renou (2000) also found, the participants in the current study appear to have understood some grammatical rules better than others. We will speculate further about the reasons for this in (3).

(3) What kinds of rules/metalinguistic terms present particular difficulties for (a) NNS teacher trainees and (b) NS teacher trainees?

For rule formulation, it is interesting to note that there is perhaps more similarity than difference between NNS and NS in terms of what they each found easy and difficult. For each, the same three structures (plural -s, possessive -s and comparatives) featured among the four that they found easiest. For each group, verb complementation and ergative verbs were among the hardest four structures in terms of explaining errors. There were, however, differences in terms of the structures that each group found difficult. For NNS, regular past tense was ranked 1st (i.e. the easiest structure), for NS this structure was ranked 10th. Similarly, NS found it more difficult to give a rule explanation for yes/ no questions than NNS. For NS, this structure was ranked last (15th), whereas for NNS it was ranked 9th. On the other hand, NNS found it more difficult to give a rule explanation for relative clauses and for unreal conditional (ranked 8th and 13th, respectively) than did NS (ranked 4th and 9th).

For identification of grammatical structures, again there were similarities in terms of those items that each group found easy and difficult. Both groups found the structures subject, noun and verb among the four easiest to identify and finite verb and agent among the three most difficult. The differences were interesting – for NNS, countable noun ranked third, while for NS this structure was considerably more difficult with a ranking of fifteenth. Other structures that NNS found considerably easier than NS were modal verb, and past participle (ranked 7th and 10th, respectively for NNS and 22nd and 17th for NS). On the other hand, NS found indefinite article (ranked 7th) considerably easier to identify than did NNS (ranked 20th).

It is interesting to see that the grammatical categories that the advanced Malaysian learners of English found easiest to identify (Subject, Verb and (Countable) Noun) were those which probably appear early in language text books and are likely to feature in any beginners ESL course. The more difficult items – Conditional, Agent and Finite Verb – tend to appear later in the pedagogical sequence. As for rule explanations, it is noteworthy that three of the easy items – Plural *s*, Possessive *s* and Comparative – all appear frequently in elementary English text books, whereas the more difficult ones – Ergatives, Verb complement and Unreal conditional – generally do not at this level. There may therefore be some relationship between pedagogical exposure (to English grammar) and item difficulty. Structures that are taught early are likely to be recycled and consolidated at later stages of learning with the result that learners achieve a stronger understanding of them.

For NS, it may be that the rules that are specific to English (e.g. regular past tense -ed, yes/no questions) are more difficult for them because they have automatized them early on, that is, developed implicit but not explicit knowledge of them. On the other hand, rules for forms that are also characteristic of other languages that they may have studied (e.g. relative clauses and conditionals) may present them with less difficulty. Similarly, those structures that are more specific to English and that cause NNS problems (e.g. countable noun, modal verb) may be easier for a NNS to identify than for a NS.

But, there are also likely to be other factors involved in determining difficulty as explicit knowledge. In Chapter 6, two general factors were considered – conceptual clarity and the metalanguage needed to verbalize a rule. In the case of Plural and Possessive -s, the relevant rules are relatively straightforward and are also verbalizable with minimal metalanguage (N. Ellis, 1996, 1999). Other forms do not regularly appear as a focus of instruction, such as the need to use the active verb form with ergative verbs like 'improve'. Rules for such forms are clearly more complex and hence less amenable to explanation. To explain why 'His grades *were improved* last year' is an erroneous sentence, candidates would require knowledge of the class of ergative verbs and its specific exemplars, as well as an understanding of the distinction between the active and passive mode, including the concept of (hidden) agency. N. Ellis (1999) argues that such structures are more likely to be learned implicitly on an item-by-item basis, initially as formulaic utterances. It is, therefore, feasible that the participants in this study may never have encountered or needed to articulate the relevant rule.

What is very clear from the difficulty order of items in the rule section is that the difficulty of metalinguistic items is not related to any acquisitional order. The comparative form, for example, is a relatively late acquired feature, but the rule about double marking in the sentence 'Languages are *more easier* to learn when you are young', appears to have been quite easy for test-takers to explain. Verb complements on the other hand have been shown to be acquired relatively early, but their wrong use in the sentence 'Hiroshi *wants visiting* the United States this year' was explained adequately by only 18% of NS respondents and 20% of NNS respondents.

As for metalinguistic terms, it is clear from some of the garbled explanations supplied by the participants that many are confused about both their meaning and application. Take the following example produced as an explanation of the wrong verb form in the question 'Does Liao *has* a Chinese wife?'

In this context, 'has' should be written in past 'had'. It is universally acknowledged that 'had' refers to possessive nouns, and referring to the sentence, which means Liao had a Chinese wife.

In the following example, the testee has confused metalinguistic terms in explaining the overuse of modals:

'I *must have to* wash my hands'

You do not have to put 'must' there because you cannot put a noun before a noun.

These examples, and there are many others besides, suggest that many of the participants, for a range of reasons, have poor understanding of both the explicit rules of English and the terms in which such rules are traditionally couched. Although space precludes an extensive discussion of the nature of learner misunderstandings, it is clear from the language of the examples presented above that they are, in many cases, attempting to mimic the discourse of pedagogical grammars, making reference to notions of generality (e.g. 'it is universally acknowledged') and constraint (e.g. 'you cannot put') or obligation (e.g. 'should be written'), which are characteristic of pedagogical rules, without having a clear conceptual understanding. However, some participants were less ambitious and confined themselves to correcting the targeted error with no attempt at generalization beyond the particular instance, for example:

#The cake *that you baked it* tastes very nice'.

You should omit 'it'.

Such a response, while it was not deemed acceptable on our test, is arguably more useful as feedback for a learner than the confused explanations exemplified above.

(4) Is metalinguistic knowledge associated with the ability to recognize error?

Results reported in Table 9.6 show a moderate (and statistically significant) correlation ($r = 0.40$) between scores on Part 1 of the MTK and those derived from the ungrammatical sentences in the UGJT, which measure different exemplars of the same set of structures. Both the rule and metalinguistic terminology sections contribute significantly to this relationship, suggesting that detection and explanation go hand in hand at least to some extent, probably because explicit knowledge contributes to the resolution of both types of item (N. Ellis, 2005). However, given the substantial difference in the difficulty of the two tests, as indicated by the difference in means (51% on MTK and 89% on the UGJT), we cannot take for granted that if a test-taker can recognize an error in a sentence, s/he will be able to explain why the item is wrong or invoke the relevant TL rule (see also Alderson *et al.*, 1997; Brumfit *et al.*, 1996; Elder *et al.*, 1999) for a similar conclusion.)

At the item level, there were also some notable differences in difficulty across the tests (see Clapham (2001) and Hu (2002) who report a similar variation in performance on particular items according to task demands). Whereas errors in the use of a Modal Verb, Adverb Placement and an Indefinite Article were the easiest to recognize, these were not, as we have seen above, the easiest items to explain. Conversely, there are some items, such as the Comparative, which were harder on the UGJT than the MKT. It seems then that an incorrect answer on an error detection item does not always imply absence of metalinguistic knowledge.

(5) What are the implications of these findings for the teaching of focus on form in second language classrooms?

Findings of the study suggest that these particular students, in spite of being admitted to TESOL programmes as teacher trainees, have a disturbing lack of knowledge about the rules of English grammar as well as, in many cases, a limited command of the technical terms required to explain these rules to L2 learners, if or when the need arises.

This conforms with the findings of other investigations of metalinguistic knowledge involving advanced foreign language learners (Alderson *et al.*, 1997; Elder *et al.*, 1999; Elder & Manwaring, 2004; Renou, 2000) and confirms what other researchers (Andrews, 1994, 2003; Bolitho, 1988) have suggested is likely to be the case for NS who have often not had any formal experience of language study. Regardless of whether the teacher is a NS or a NNS, a poor command of metalinguistic knowledge is likely to impact negatively on the quality of FFI, both in traditional grammar-based classrooms and in other meaning-focused teaching, where FoF instruction is incidental rather than systematic. Although reactive FoF feedback that is accompanied by some kind of metalinguistic explanation has been found to account for a proportion of teacher feedback moves (Havranek, 2002; Loewen & Philp, 2006; Lyster & Ranta, 1997), little attention has been paid in FoF studies to the quality of this feedback or, more precisely, to the accuracy and intelligibility of the metalinguistic information imparted to learners and its possible effect on learner uptake. This is clearly an area where further research is needed.

In the meantime, it seems reasonable to propose that where there are gaps in teachers' explicit knowledge, it may be better to adopt alternatives to FoF teaching strategies that draw less heavily on a command of technical terminology and the ability to verbalize grammatical rules. As far as pre-emptive focus on form is concerned, the generally poor explanations offered for certain structures (such as ergatives) by this group of participants suggests that such structures may be better avoided altogether as the target for explicit instruction and left for learners to acquire implicitly via positive evidence alone (N. Ellis, 1999). As for reactive strategies, because all participants in this study appear to have had little difficulty detecting grammatical errors (as indicated by their high level of performance on the UGJT and their tendency to correct errors rather than explain the relevant rules), teacher trainees might be advised to resort where possible to prompts and recasts, rather than metalinguistic explanations, as an alternative means of drawing learners' attention to errors in their production, although, as shown in Chapter 13, more explicit types of corrective feedback (including those involving metalinguistic explanation) have generally proved more effective.

Ideally, a teacher should have the necessary knowledge and skill to draw on the full range of FoF options, including the provision of explicit grammatical information when learners signal the need for it. As N. Ellis (1999: 30) maintains, 'Learning the patterns, regularities or underlying concepts in a complex domain with advance organizers and instruction is always better than learning without cues' and explicit language knowledge has a clear role to play in planning and implementing FFI, whether of the Focus on Form or Focus on Forms variety.

Conclusion

Based on the recognition of the importance of FFI in second language classrooms (Doughty & Williams, 1998; Ellis, 1994, 1995, 1997, 1998; Long, 1996, 2000; Long & Robinson, 1998; Nassaji & Fotos, 2004; Norris & Ortega, 2000; Spada, 1997), this paper has considered the kinds of knowledge and skill that teachers need to deliver such instruction effectively. We have argued that language teachers not only need high levels of language proficiency to be able to provide rich and well-formed input for learners, but also need sufficient explicit knowledge about language to be able to plan FFI and respond appropriately to learner needs through judicious use of a range of FoF options. Responding to claims that many language teachers are ill-equipped for this task, we have explored the levels of explicit language knowledge and language proficiency among two groups of TESOL teacher trainees: a group of Malaysian undergraduates especially selected to participate in an off-shore teacher education course, who had received explicit grammar instruction, and a group of NS from New Zealand and Canada with little prior English grammar instruction.

To do so, we have drawn on a range of custom-built instruments that allow us to explore performance across different task types, including grammaticality judgment and rule explanation tasks targeting parallel sets of structures. While the English language proficiency of these teacher trainees was found to be quite high, our investigation revealed significant lacunae in their knowledge about language and a highly uneven performance across the different task types. We believe that these lacunae need to be addressed in teacher education programmes to ensure that any FoF activity in which such teachers engage will be conducive to second language learning.

The findings of this study signal the need for diagnostic testing of trainee teachers' metalinguistic knowledge (not just their ability to use the TL, which, as noted above, may be an unreliable predictor of such knowledge), using an instrument similar to the MKT described in this paper. The advantage of both the MKT and the UGJT is their systematic sampling of a range of grammatical structures (although others could certainly be added) and, in the case of the MKT, the careful attention paid to establishing criteria that (a) identify critical 'bottom line' indicators of grammatical understanding rather than insisting on perfect rule for-mulations, and (b) attempt to assess grammatical understanding in-dependently of the use of metalingual terminology. Separating the two is clearly important given the debates about the utility (or otherwise) of such terminology for teaching purposes (Andrews, 2005).

Diagnostic testing could provide a basis for individualized strategic advice about alternatives to explicit FoF instruction in the communicative classroom and about the range of options available when teachers wish to draw their learners' attention to an error in learner production that they feel ill equipped to explain. Such testing could also identify priorities for formal teaching intervention or for self-instruction in relation to particular TL structures in order to strengthen L2 teachers' explicit knowledge base. While there may be constraints on the time available for formal grammatical instruction in a teacher education program, there is no reason why teachers cannot build their metalinguistic knowledge progressively throughout their careers, provided that they are aware of its importance. (For example, in a study of four experienced ESL grammar teachers, conducted by Johnston and Goettsch (2000) elicited reports that their knowledge of English grammar evolved progressively as they sourced course textbooks and grammar reference books (see also Berry, 2001).) Future research will, however, need to monitor the effectiveness of such knowledge building (whether via formal instruction or self-access), given the apparent failure of explicit instruction to produce high levels of understanding about the workings of English and other languages. There are also dangers in an undue focus on the testing and development of metalinguistic knowledge independent of pedagogical skill. The cognitive sophistication involved in the former may sometimes be in conflict with the simplification skills required for the latter, as Elder (2001) and others have pointed out. Teacher trainees need to be mindful of the distinction between displaying what they know for testing purposes and using what they know to plan and deliver FoF instruction in ways that will be sensitive to learner needs. Teacher education programs have an important role here (Fotos & Nassaji, 2007).

Acknowledgements

The authors wish to thank Ellen Cray for her generous provision of the NS data, and Susan McKenna and Yiqian Cao for assistance with the analysis of data for this paper.

Notes

1. Elder *et al.* (2007) reports on a subset of the data presented here, and some portions of the two chapters are repeated.

Form-focused Instruction and the Acquisition of Implicit and Explicit Knowledge

The chapters in Part 4 examine the effects of form-focused instruction (FFI) on the acquisition of both implicit and explicit second language (L2) knowledge. In the studies reported in these chapters, different types of FFI are investigated

In various publications, Ellis (1998, 2001, 2008) has described a set of methodological options for conducting FFI with a view to providing a basis for both the teaching of grammar and researching the effects of FFI on acquisition and learning. Ellis distinguishes four macro-options:

(1) Input-based options (i.e. instruction that involves the manipulation of the input that learners are exposed to or are required to process). They include enriched input (i.e. input that contains many examples of the target structure), enhanced input (i.e. input with the target feature made salient to the learners, for example, by means of emphatic stress, bolding or an instruction to attend to some specific feature), and structured input (i.e. input that has been contrived to induce processing of the target feature for meaning). These options are all comprehension-based and cater to either implicit learning (in the case of enriched and structured input) and to somewhat more explicit learning (in the case of enhanced input).

(2) Explicit options (i.e. instruction directed at helping learners develop explicit knowledge of the target structure). They include both direct explicit instruction (i.e. learners are provided with metalinguistic descriptions of the target feature) and indirect explicit instruction (i.e. learners are provided with data illustrating the target feature and are required to 'discover' the rule for themselves). Explicit options cater to explicit language learning.

(3) Production options (i.e. instruction directed at enabling/inducing learners to produce utterances containing the target structure). Production options can be distinguished in terms of whether they involve text-manipulation (e.g. fill-in-the-blank exercises) or text-creation (e.g. focused tasks – see Ellis, 2003). Text-manipulation options constitute a form of explicit instruction whereas text-creation options are more implicit.

(4) Corrective feedback options (i.e. instruction directed at providing learners with negative evidence regarding the linguistic accuracy of their own production). Corrective feedback can be implicit (e.g. recasts or requests for clarification) or explicit (e.g. metalinguistic explanation or elicitation).

The studies in Part 4 investigated these options (or combinations of options) in terms of what effect they have on learners' acquisition of implicit and explicit knowledge. As explained in Chapter 1, a clear distinction needs to be drawn between implicit/explicit instruction on the one hand and implicit/explicit knowledge on the other. Whether implicit instruction leads to implicit knowledge and explicit instruction to explicit knowledge remains an open question, which these studies attempted to answer.

In Chapter 10, Erlam, Loewen and Philp compare the effects of an input-based and output-based approach to teaching the indefinite article *a* to express generic meaning. The input-based instruction involved a combination of two of the macro-options – an input-based option (structured input) and direct explicit instruction. The output-based instruction involved three macro-options – direct explicit instruction, production practice (both text-manipulation and text-creation) and corrective feedback. The study is informed by previous research that has investigated the relative effects of input-based and output-based language instruction. While the results of this research are mixed, it has shown that input-based instruction can lead to acquisition and in some cases that it is more effective than instruction consisting of production practice. A weakness of previous studies, however, is that no convincing measure of implicit knowledge was included. Using measures of implicit and explicit knowledge based on the tests examined in Part 2 of this book, Erlam *et al.* were able to show that both input-based and output-based instruction benefited both types of knowledge. In contrast to some other studies, this study did not find input-based instruction more effective than instruction that provided opportunities for production. In fact, on balance, the output-based instruction was more effective. Erlam *et al.* suggest that the production practice may have been effective because it enabled learners to identify the meaning conveyed by the target form. This study, then, provides evidence in support of output-based instruction of the present-practice-produce (PPP) kind while at the same time supporting claims that input-based options can be effective.

Whereas Chapter 10 investigated intentional learning, the study reported in Chapter 11 (Loewen, Erlam and Ellis) examined incidental learning (i.e. whether learners were able to acquire a feature while the focus of their attention was directed elsewhere). The target structure was third person -s – a feature that previous research has shown to be late-acquired and, in the case of some learners, not acquired at all. This feature is difficult to learn because it lacks saliency and has no clear functional value. It also involves an advanced processing procedure (see Pienemann, 1998). A further reason for learners' failure to acquire it might be because exposure to it in input is only intermittent. The question asked, therefore, was whether intensive exposure to input containing this feature when learners' attention was focused elsewhere could overcome its lack of saliency at least for those learners who had begun to acquire it. The study found that such input had no effect on learners' implicit or explicit knowledge irrespective of their developmental level. This study, then, failed to demonstrate that incidental acquisition of grammar is possible, although this may simply reflect the special difficulty of third person -s.

The study reported in Chapter 12 (Reinders and Ellis) did not originate in the Marsden Project, but is included here because of its clear relevance to the theme of Part 4.[1]. It examines the effects of two types of instructional input on both intake and acquisition. The two types differ in terms of whether they cater to implicit or more explicit learning. Enriched input is input that has been seeded with the target structure (in this case subject-verb inversion following negative adverbs such as 'never' and 'rarely') in order to expose learners to multiple exemplars of the structure in meaning-focused tasks. In the enhanced input, enhancement took the form of an instruction to notice the target structure in the input. Both types of input resulted in intake and in acquisition, although only in the case of grammatical sentences of a timed grammaticality judgment test (considered a measure of implicit knowledge). There were no group differences where intake was concerned, but the enriched input group outperformed the enhanced input group on the grammatical items of the Timed Grammaticality Judgment Test. Where explicit knowledge was concerned, the input treatments were found to have a deleterious affect, possibly because the learners were unable to work out the rule for negative adverbs for themselves.

Chapter 13 (Ellis, Loewen and Erlam) reports a study of the effects of implicit and explicit corrective feedback on the acquisition of English past tense *-ed*. Low-intermediate learners, who already had explicit knowledge of this feature but only limited implicit knowledge, completed two communicative tasks during which they received either recasts (implicit feedback) or metalinguistic explanation (explicit feedback) in response to any utterance that contained an error in the target structure. Acquisition was measured by means of an Elicited Oral Imitation Test (designed to measure implicit knowledge) and both an Untimed Grammaticality Judgment Test and a Metalinguistic Knowledge Test (both designed to measure explicit knowledge). Statistical comparisons of the learners' performance on the post-tests showed an advantage for the explicit instruction (especially on the delayed post-test). The explicit feedback group outperformed both the control group and the recast group on the measures of implicit and explicit knowledge. In contrast, the implicit feedback group appeared to benefit little from the feedback.

These four chapters illustrate how the framework of instructional options developed by Ellis can be applied to the design of FFI studies. They also suggest the importance of ensuring that measures of both implicit and explicit knowledge are included in the design of such studies. Overall, they provide evidence that FFI (especially of the more explicit kind) can have an effect on implicit as well as explicit L2 knowledge. This constitutes an important finding for both second language acquisition (SLA) theory-building and pedagogical practice.

Note

1. Reinders and Ellis' study originated in Reinders' (2006) unpublished doctoral thesis 'The effects of different task types on L2 learners' intake and acquisition of two grammatical structures', University of Auckland.

Chapter 10

The Roles of Output-based and Input-based Instruction in the Acquisition of L2 Implicit and Explicit Knowledge

ROSEMARY ERLAM, SHAWN LOEWEN and JENEFER PHILP

Introduction

The crucial role that input plays in second language acquisition is widely attested; as VanPatten (2004) notes, any theory of acquisition is input-dependent in some way. There are, however, conflicting views of the role that output plays in the language acquisition process. One of the key questions is whether output is merely facilitative of acquisition or whether acquisition is output-dependent. The latter position allows a much stronger role for output. This chapter describes a study that aimed to investigate the relative roles of input and output in the language acquisition process and in particular to address the question of whether there is a role for output in the acquisition of implicit language knowledge.

No Specific Role for Output in Language Acquisition

Interest in the debate as to what role, if any, output plays in language acquisition was perhaps rekindled by findings from initial research on Processing Instruction, which did not specifically set out to ask such a question. However, a range of studies (Benati, 2001; Cadierno, 1995; Cheng, 1995; VanPatten & Cadierno, 1993; VanPatten & Sanz, 1995; VanPatten & Wong, 2004) raised the question as to whether output contributed in any way to acquisition. These studies demonstrated that students who had received instruction consisting of input only did better on interpretation tasks than students who had worked only at output activities. They also showed that these same students, who had received input only, performed as well on production tasks as the students who had worked only at output activities. The interest thus generated led to a number of studies looking at the relative effects of input and output (e.g. DeKeyser & Sokalski, 2003; Erlam, 2003; Salaberry, 1997).

According to VanPatten (2004), acquisition consists of three main processes:

(1) Input processing, by which process form-meaning connections (FMC) are made and parsing takes place.
(2) Accommodation, entailing partial or complete incorporation of a surface feature into the developing language system.
(3) Restructuring, i.e. changes in linguistic behavior as a result of accommodation.

A key aspect of this model is the crucial role that it allows for input as the primary component. Input, VanPatten (2004) claims, is sufficient to cause change in learner competence. VanPatten is, of course, not alone – Krashen (1989) and Schwartz (1993) were both early proponents of the idea that input alone can directly affect acquisition. More recently, N. Ellis's (2004) connectionist accounts of language learning have also stressed the importance of input in driving acquisition.

In such a model, one may wonder what role, if any, there is for output. VanPatten (2004) claims that output can promote acquisition but that it does not appear to be necessary. Similar to any other focus-on-form technique, output speeds up acquisition. Its role is one that is limited to 'access' – that is, through engaging in language output the learner is required to access a FMC that has been incorporated into the learner's developing system. This process of access serves to strengthen the FMC and to thus develop fluency and accuracy. This ancillary role for output is evident in the following statements with which Van Patten (2004: 43) concludes his discussion of this issue:

> We are currently unable to support any specific role for output in the creation of an underlying competence that contains form-meaning connections. At best we can say that input is necessary for acquisition, but input and output may be better – we just don't know how or under what circumstances.

Evidence in support of a position that claims that input drives acquisition and output has no specific role has already been referred to above. A number of Processing Instruction studies have had learners work with structured input tasks (or 'pushed input'; Izumi, 2003) and produced evidence to show that these students perform better on interpretation tasks and as well as on production tasks as students who have worked solely on output tasks (Benati, 2001; Cadierno, 1995; Cheng, 1995; VanPatten & Cadierno, 1993; VanPatten & Sanz, 1995; VanPatten & Wong, 2004).

However, this research tends to compare Processing Instruction with Traditional Instruction, a form of output-based instruction (OI), which has students work at mechanical drills and where there is not a consistent focus on meaning. Studies that have compared Processing Instruction with meaning-based Output Instruction have produced conflicting results (Allen, 2000; Collentine, 1998; DeKeyser & Sokalski, 1996; Erlam, 2003; Salaberry, 1997), demonstrating that students who engaged in language output made greater gains in language production tasks following treatment than students who worked with language input. In studies conducted by Farley (2001, 2004), students who had worked at meaning-oriented output instruction (MOI) performed as well on both interpretation tasks and production tasks as students who had engaged with language input only through structured input tasks. VanPatten's interpretation of results in the first case (Allen, 2000; Collentine, 1998; DeKeyser & Sokalski, 1996; Erlam, 2003; Salaberry, 1997) is that Processing Instruction was not administered correctly and in the second case (Farley, 2001, 2004), that gains made by the groups who worked at output tasks were due to the fact that the output served as input for their learning, a conclusion with which Farley, himself, concurs.

To conclude, proponents of this position claim that output benefits acquisition only at the end of the language acquisition process (i.e. once a FMC has been established in interlanguage). In other words, output only has a subsidiary role in strengthening FMC through 'access', of which a byproduct is improved fluency and accuracy. Output can also serve to generate input (one learner's output can be another's input), which, of course, proponents of this position claim is the real driving force behind acquisition.

A Greater Role for Output in the Language Acquisition Process

More recently, the question has arisen as to whether learners are quite as reliant on input as has been generally claimed in second language acquisition theory and research (DeKeyser, 2007). This has led to increased interest in a possible role for production.

Levelt's speech production model (Levelt, 1989) does not explain the language acquisition process, but it does help us hypothesize how engaging in language production may give learners opportunities to engage with the cognitive processes, such as hypothesis testing (Muranoi, 2007), which are crucial for acquisition. According to Levelt's model, a feedback system allows for both internal and overt speech to be fed back to a conceptualizer where it may be monitored. Attention can be given here as to whether the speech is well-formed and appropriate – processes which, as Izumi (2003: 184) explains, can serve 'as an internal priming device for grammatical consciousness-raising' for language learners. In a similar vein, Swain's Output Hypothesis (Swain, 1985) suggests that output practice can facilitate acquisition if it allows for cognitive processes such as noticing, hypothesis testing, syntactic processing and metalinguistic reflection. As Larsen-Freeman (2003: 115) states, 'output practice, then, does not simply serve to increase access to previously acquired knowledge. Doing and learning are synchronous'. In his award-winning paper, Toth (2006) suggests that output may 'grow' the L2 linguistic system. The act of producing language may force cognitive processes that lead to restructuring of the developing system, as hypothesized by Swain (1985).

Perhaps the most convincing evidence in support of a greater role for output in the language acquisition process comes from contexts where students have had reduced opportunities to engage in language output. There has been widespread interest in the research literature in students in immersion contexts who have had massive amounts of exposure to the target language but whose spoken and written language falls far short of their native-speaker peers (Lightbown & Spada 1990, 1994). Swain (1985) concluded that these students are not pushed enough to produce output, that there is little social or cognitive pressure to produce more target-like language because their peers already understand them.

More recently there has been interest in experimental research that supports a positive role for output practice in conjunction with input (Izumi, 2002; Izumi & Bigelow, 2000; Izumi *et al.*, 1999; Morgan-Short & Bowden, 2006; Swain, 1995; Swain & Lapkin, 1995). In Izumi's (2002) study, students who experienced a treatment that included opportunities to engage in language output as well as exposure to input, outperformed those exposed to input only in learning English relativization. In explaining his results, Izumi (2002) concludes that pushed output is an 'internal attention-drawing technique' and that it may have resulted in three related processes:

(1) The detection of formal elements in the input through priming induced by internal feedback.
(2) Integrative processing of the target structure.
(3) The noticing of mismatches between one's interlanguage and the target language.

Nevertheless, while providing a plausible role for output, Izumi's study stops short of providing clear evidence for these processes.

A more recent computer-based experimental study conducted by Morgan-Short and Bowden (2006) and investigating Spanish preverbal direct object pronouns (a replication of VanPatten & Cadierno, 1993) found that OI that included some input led to at least as much linguistic development as input-based instruction (InI) that did not include output. This study is another contribution to an increasing body of literature that suggests that output, when it is meaningful and leads learners to make FMC, can directly promote linguistic development. It is also interesting to note that this may be possible not only in the later stages of instruction, but also during the early stages of learning of new language forms.

Toth's innovative study (2006), which analyzed transcript data of students working with language output in a classroom setting, provided evidence that he claimed demonstrated that a learner's push to syntactically encode what she meant to say, in combination with input from others and her own conscious reflection about how the target language 'worked', drove grammatical development. He maintains that it would be an overstatement to claim that input alone was the singular force behind her correct formulation of the target structure. In both Izumi (2003) and Toth (2006), learners engaged in output were required to process FMC at a deeper level than learners who were working at structured input tasks only.

The Contribution of the Present Study to this Debate

One step in helping resolve the conflict as to what role, if any, there may be for output in the second language acquisition process, is to examine the relative impact of InI and OI on the developing language system through the use of measures of implicit and explicit language knowledge. A number of researchers have been unanimous in specifying the contribution that a more precise assessment of explicit and implicit knowledge could make to this debate. DeKeyser (2007) underlines the limitation of current research in its use of controlled or nonspontaneous assessment tasks to measure second language development, and Toth (2006) states that assessment of implicit knowledge could help us know whether the L2 system is susceptible to restructuring through input- or output-based language processing. Muronoi (2007: 76) calls for 'more extensive elicitation tasks that characterize overall language abilities'. Another way of contributing to our understanding of whether OI enables learners to internalize new language is to investigate whether there is a transfer of knowledge from the language used in treatment sessions to novel test items. No research has looked at this question with regard to OI and only one input-based study has addressed the issue (Farley, 2004). Farley investigated whether Processing Instruction and Meaning-based Output Instruction would bring about improved performance on sentence level tasks involving the interpretation and production of novel subjunctive forms. He found that both types of instruction led to significant gains for the interpretation and production of forms to which students had not been introduced during instruction. However, it is important to note that although transfer of learning was evident with respect to regular subjunctive forms, there was no evidence of general-ization of learning to irregular subjunctive forms.

This study aims to address the questions of, firstly, whether giving students the opportunity to engage in language output leads to acquisition, and secondly, whether this is of greater benefit than input alone. It will use tests of implicit and explicit language knowledge as measures of student learning and it will also look at whether there is any transfer of learning to new language forms.

The research questions for the present study were as follows:

(1) Does OI lead to gains on
   (a) a measure of implicit language knowledge?
   (b) a measure of explicit language knowledge?
(2) Which type of instruction – OI or InI – is more effective when the effects of instruction are assessed in terms of
   (a) a measure of implicit language knowledge?
   (b) a measure of explicit language knowledge?
(3) Does either OI or InI bring about improved performance on novel test items when the effects of treatment are assessed in terms of measures of implicit and explicit language knowledge?

Method

Participants

The study was conducted in two private language schools in Auckland. Students in each school were enrolled in short courses in 'general English' of between four and six weeks' duration. In each school, two intact classes of intermediate-level students were randomly allocated to one of two treatment options (OI or InI). Students receiving OI ($n = 8$, $n = 10$) totaled 18, while students receiving InI ($n = 9$, $n = 11$) totaled 20. A third group of students, at one of the language schools, received no instruction, but took part in all testing episodes. This group, the Control, totaled 12. A total of 51 students took part in the study.

Students were asked to complete a background information questionnaire that required them to give information about their first language and length of exposure to English. Most students came from an Asian language speaking background (Japanese, Chinese, Korean, Taiwanese), the remainder came from a variety of language backgrounds (Spanish, Arabic, German, Russian, Portuguese). Table 10.1 provides more information about the background of the students.

Design

All students were pre-tested three days before they received treatment (i.e. at the end of a teaching week). Instruction took place over two consecutive days in each language school. Each class received two lessons, each of one-hour duration. All lessons were taught by the same

Table 10.1 Background information of participants

	OI group (n =18)	InI group (n =20)	Control (n =12)
Asian language background	14	13	6
Time spent learning English (years)	8	6.9	5.9
Time spent in an English-speaking country (months)	3	9	3

researcher. Post-testing was completed the day following the second lesson and delayed post-testing two weeks later. The Control group received no instruction, but completed all testing episodes over the same time scale as the treatment groups.

Target structure

The target structure was the use of the indefinite article to mark generic reference. Generic reference can be marked in a number of ways for count nouns, for example, zero article with plural noun, indefinite article with singular noun and definite article with singular noun. Examples are given below.

Cheetahs run fast.
A cheetah runs fast.
The cheetah runs fast.

Celce-Murcia and Larsen-Freeman (1999) point out that the indefinite article is the most concrete and colloquial way of expressing a generality. It is used most appropriately when the context is specific. They also describe it as being commonly used for countable inanimate objects that gradually developed over time and are not thought of as being invented, for example, book, window, table, chair and so on.

e.g. *A book fills leisure time for many people.*

When noncount nouns are used generically, the indefinite article is omitted.

e.g. *Water is essential for life.*

In this study, the focus was the use of the indefinite article with count nouns, as well as the omission of the article with noncount nouns, to convey generic reference.

The reasons for choosing generic articles as the target structure were twofold. Firstly, it is a structure that occurs with reasonable frequency in language input, but also one that causes difficulty even for advanced learners. There are a number of reasons why learners may have difficulty establishing that the meaning conveyed by the indefinite article 'a/an' is generic. Firstly, it is a structure that is not salient to learners. According to VanPatten's model of input processing, learners may or may not make connections between a form in the input and its meaning. One of VanPatten's input processing principles states:

P1a. Learners process content words in the input before anything else.

If a content word and a grammatical form both encode the same meaning, the learner's processing mechanisms need only rely on the lexical form and not the grammatical form to get semantic meaning. As Harrington (2004) also points out, learners often have difficulty with 'little' words conveying grammatical information. The generic indefinite article fits all these criteria. It is a 'little' word conveying no more information than the lexical form it precedes. It is, furthermore, omitted when noncount nouns are used generically, so that learners have the added confusion of receiving input that does not include the indefinite article. There are thus strong reasons why generic indefinite articles would not be noticed and therefore not processed by learners.

A second reason why generic 'a/an' is difficult for learners is that it is complex. Young (1996) outlines the complexity with which meaning is mapped onto form in the article system in English. As we have already seen above, the definite article 'the' and the indefinite article 'a/an' function in ways that overlap with each other and with other linguistic forms. They each can be used to convey generic reference, along with zero article, and furthermore 'a/an' can convey a variety of other meanings. It can be used to convey nonspecific meaning and to represent a particular type of class (i.e. to classify). The indefinite article (and indeed the definite article) violates what Andersen (1984) describes as the One-to-One Principle, which states that acquisition of a form is facilitated when there is a clear and unique correspondence between the form and its meaning.

Thirdly, the generic use of the indefinite article is also a feature that is not commonly taught. The use of zero article with a plural noun is most commonly taught to convey generic reference (Parrott, 2000).

Evidence that students in this study had only limited implicit or explicit knowledge of the target structure comes from their performance on the pre-tests of the measures used to assess learning. Students scored an average of 43% on the Oral Elicited Imitation Test (EI) and 62% on the Untimed Grammaticality Judgment Test (UGJT).

Instructional treatments

There were two instructional packets for the treatment. The OI packet consisted of eight meaning-based output activities and the InI packet consisted of eight structured input activities. The activities were matched for subject matter and vocabulary. Both groups received the same explicit instruction at the beginning of Days 1 and 2 of instruction. This explicit instruction covered the following points:

Day 1: Indefinite use of article 'a' with the meaning of ONE

Use of indefinite article to make a generalization, not referring to just one person/thing

Use of plural noun as another possible way of making a generalization

Day 2: Revision of explicit information given on Day 1

Expressing generalization with an uncountable noun

Instruction for the OI group followed a PPP (presentation/practice/production) format (Gower & Walters, 1983). There was, however, a focus on meaning at all times, in order to maximize the possibility that learners could acquire proper FMC (Izumi, 2003). The explicit instruction, as described above, was given during the presentation phase. During the practice phase, students were encouraged to use the target language structure in a linguistically controlled context. In one activity, the students were told that they would take part in an animal quiz (they were divided into groups who competed against each other to be the first with an acceptable response). The students were given descriptions, for example, 'This animal is a very dangerous animal' – and asked to specify an animal that fitted with each description. (In this case, the answer was 'a lion' – although a number of other responses would have been acceptable.) As a prompt or as confirmation of an answer, they were shown pictures of animals on overheads, for example, for the description given above they were shown a picture of three lions advancing towards a very frightened man. Students were given feedback in relation to the answers they supplied, that is, a response that omitted the generic article, for example, was recast so that they heard the correct form. Another activity that students in this group also worked at was one where they had to decide in pairs what sort of behaviors characterized 'a good teacher/student' etc. and then say whether they agreed or not. This, and other activities that this group completed (see below and examples given in the Appendix), encouraged students to engage in meaningful interaction with each other.

During the production phase of the treatment, students were given free practice in using the target structure, that is, they were not given linguistic resources to help them complete the activity. They were told, for example, that they had to make up, as a group, dictionary definitions for a number of words associated with personality types, e.g. introvert/introversion etc. An example was given to all students on an overhead projector. For each word group, one group was given a clue to help them understand the target words, the rest of the class were not. When all groups had written definitions, these were read out and students had to vote for the one that they thought was correct. Examples of student answers for this activity are:

> Introvert: An introvert mean is person who don't like to introduce himself to other people.
> Kleptomania: Kleptomania makes someone angry.

The InI group, based on VanPatten's model of Processing Instruction, received additional explicit instruction in which the strategy that did not help them learn language effectively, in this case the One-to-One Principle, was described to them. They were told that they had to learn that 'a/an' could have a different meaning from that with which they were already familiar. They then worked at structured input activities that aimed to train them to distinguish generic from particular meaning. These activities were modeled closely on those that the OI group worked at, but were designed to encourage them to process both written and oral input, and did not require them at any time to engage in producing language output. In one activity, students were shown a series of pictures on overheads. They were shown, for example, two pictures, one of a lion sleeping under a tree and a second of three lions advancing on a very frightened man (as described above). The sentence: 'A lion is a very dangerous animal' – was presented orally and they were asked to choose the picture that best matched the sentence. The correct choice (i.e. the second picture) encouraged them to make the connection between indefinite article 'a' and generic reference (in contrast to denoting a single animal). Students were given feedback in relation to answers they supplied in class. (See the Appendix for examples of activities used in instructional treatments).

Testing

Participants completed an Oral Elicited Imitation Test, designed as a measure of primarily implicit knowledge, and a UGJT, designed as a measure of primarily explicit knowledge. The two tests, described in greater detail below, were adaptations of those described elsewhere in this volume (see Chapters 2–4) and consisted of items that were specifically developed to measure learning of the target structure used in this study.

The Oral Elicited Imitation Test consisted of 32 statements, 17 of which contained generic 'a' in a grammatically correct context and seven of which contained generic 'a' in a grammatically incorrect context. A further eight statements contained examples of noncount nouns used generically, in both grammatically correct and incorrect contexts. In 17 statements, the target items assessed had not been presented to participants during the instructional treatments, that is, they were 'novel' test items. In the remaining 15 statements, the target items were forms that had been introduced in the treatment sessions, that is, 'old' test items. As far as possible, statements were designed so that the target structure was not placed initially in the sentence to prevent it becoming more salient to participants. Examples of test items are:

In general, a good teacher knows her students' name.
[grammatical/old item]
During games, soccer player runs a lot.
[ungrammatical/novel item]
Information travels around the world on the internet.
[grammatical/old item]

The statements were presented on audiotape to participants by an interviewer. Participants were told that they were to complete a Beliefs Questionnaire and were asked to indicate on paper by checking one of three boxes whether each statement was true, not true or whether they were not sure (thus ensuring a primary focus on meaning). Participants were then told to repeat the statement in *correct* English. Pre-test training gave participants practice in responding to both grammatical and ungrammatical test items. During this training, participants were told what their responses should have been. It should be noted that participants heard each statement only once and in real time.

Grammatical items were scored as correct if the target structure was correctly repeated and ungrammatical items were scored as correct if the target structure (presented in a grammatically incorrect context) was spontaneously corrected. Incorrect suppliance or avoidance of the target structure was scored as 0. Participants' total scores were averaged, that is, divided by the total number of items. The decision to report scores as percentage data was made because the sound quality of the recording at times meant that a decision about some responses could not be made. These were thus scored as missing data. Therefore, this meant that participants' total scores had to be averaged over the items for which there was data, so they were not penalized for those responses that could not be coded. Over the course of the three imitation tests (i.e. pre-test, post-test 1 and post-test 2), the number of such missing items ranged from 0 to 11, with an average of 1.3 (SD = 2.4). One version of the test was used over all three testing sessions. However, the order of presentation of the testing items was different for each test administration. Reliability, using internal consistency, was estimated on all versions of the test, giving Cronbach's alpha as follows: pre-test, $\alpha = 0.809$; post-test, $\alpha = 0.816$; delayed post-test, $\alpha = 0.869$.

The UGJT consisted of 24 sentences, 8 of which contained generic 'a' in a grammatically correct context and 8 of which contained generic 'a' in a grammatically incorrect context. A further eight sentences contained examples of noncount nouns used generically, in both grammatically correct and incorrect contexts. In 12 sentences, the test items were novel test items. In 12 sentences, test items were forms that had been introduced in treatment sessions (i.e. old test items). Again, wherever possible, the target structure was not placed initially in the sentence. Examples of test items are:

> *To avoid accidents, a bus driver always pays attention.*
> [grammatical/new item]
> *In class, good student listens to the teacher.*
> [ungrammatical/old item]
> *Often, an information helps people make good decisions.*
> [ungrammatical/old item]

The test was a pen-and-paper test with each sentence presented on a new page. Participants were given as long as they liked to complete the test, but were told that they must not turn back to look at previous test items. Test-takers were asked to indicate by ticking the relevant box whether each sentence was correct or incorrect. Once again, one version of the test was used over all three testing sessions, however the order of presentation of items was different for each test administration. Reliability, using internal consistency, was estimated on all versions of the test, giving Cronbach's alphas as follows: pre-test, $\alpha = 0.322$; post-test, $\alpha = 0.792$; delayed post-test, $\alpha = 0.730$. It is suggested that the poor reliability estimate for the pre-test may be due to the fact that students had little prior knowledge of the target structure and were mainly guessing on this test. Average scores on the pre-test (i.e. 62%) are not much greater than would be expected were students to guess.

Descriptive statistics were calculated for each test. In order to determine if there were any statistically significant differences among the pre-test scores, one-way ANOVAs compared the five groups (as described above, each treatment group was made up of two groups from different institutions; the Control group was an intact class) on both the Elicited Imitation and Grammaticality Judgment tests. No significant differences were found among the groups on the Oral Elicited Imitation Test, $F(4, 46) = 1.240$, $p = 0.307$ or on the UGJT, $F(4,46) = 0.455$, $p = 0.768$. Therefore, the results for the individual groups were combined according to the instructional treatment received.

In order to investigate the effects of the treatment, mixed-design ANOVAs were performed. The assumption regarding sphericity was checked using Mauchly's test, and if the condition of sphericity was not met, the Greenhouse-Geisser correction was reported (Field, 2005). The assumption regarding normal distribution was checked using the Kolmogorv-Smirnov test of normality, which showed a normal distribution on the EI test for all groups. For the UGJT, the OI and the Control groups violated the assumption of normality on post-test 1, $D(18) = 0.220$, $p = 0.022$ and $D(12) = 0.286$, $p = 0.007$, respectively. In addition, an investigation of the skewness and kurtosis coefficients revealed that only the skewness coefficient for the OI group on the UGJT post-test 1 was significant at the $p < 0.05$ level. Finally, Levene's test of homogeneity of variance did not reveal any violations of this assumption for any of the groups on any of the tests. Given that ANOVA is fairly robust to violations of assumptions (Field, 2005), a mixed-design ANOVA was used; however, in the case of significant interaction effects, the more conservative Bonferonni *post-hoc* test was used to investigate group differences. The significance level was set at 0.05 for all statistical tests.

Effect sizes for the two experimental groups were calculated using Cohen's *d*-index. As described by Norris and Ortega (2000), *d* was calculated by contrasting each experimental group with the Control group on the post-tests.

Results

Descriptive statistics for the Oral Elicited Imitation Tests are presented in Table 10.2. A repeated measures ANOVA on the Oral Elicited Imitation Test found a statistically significant main effect for both test time, $F(1.7, 78.6) = 26.719$, $p < 0.001$, and group, $F(2, 47) = 3.933$, $p = 0.026$. There was also a significant interaction effect for test time and group, $F(3.3, 78.6) = 2.692$, $p = 0.046$. A *post hoc* analysis revealed that the OI group differed significantly from the Control group on both post-test 1 and 2; however, the InI group did not differ from either the OI or Control groups on either of the tests.

The results of the Grammaticality judgment test are presented in Table 10.3. For each test, two scores are given, the total score and the score for the ungrammatical items only. This is because previous research (see Chapters 2 and 4) suggests that ungrammatical items are a purer measure of explicit language knowledge.

Table 10.2 Descriptive statistics for Oral Elicited Imitation Test

	OI group (n =18)		*InI group* (n =20)		*Control* (n =12)	
Test	*M*	*SD*	*M*	*SD*	*M*	*SD*
Pre-test	0.41	0.17	0.45	0.16	0.38	0.17
Post-test 1	0.62	0.18	0.59	0.18	0.45	0.16
Post-test 2	0.69	0.20	0.62	0.20	0.43	0.18

Effect sizes for post-test 1: OI, $d = 0.99$ and for InI, $d = 0.79$.
Effect sizes for post-test 2: OI, $d = 1.35$ and for InI, $d = 0.98$.

Table 10.3 Descriptive statistics for Grammaticality Judgment Test

Test	OI group (n =18)		InI group (n =20)		Control (n =12)	
	M	M	M	SD	M	SD
Pre-test – total	0.63	0.63	0.58	0.14	0.61	0.09
Pre-test – ungramm.	0.68	0.68	0.58	0.25	0.58	0.17
Post-test 1 – total	0.82	0.82	0.76	0.16	0.60	0.14
Post-test 1 – ungramm.	0.80	0.80	0.71	0.24	0.53	0.30
Post-test 2 – total	0.86	0.86	0.79	0.14	0.67	0.12
Post-test 2 – ungramm.	0.83	0.83	0.79	0.21	0.57	0.22

Effect sizes for post-test 1 total scores: OI, $d = 1.70$ and for InI, $d = 1.05$.
Effect sizes for post-test 2 total scores: OI, $d = 1.70$ and for InI, $d = 0.90$.
Effect sizes for post-test 1 ungrammatical scores: OI, $d = 1.30$ and for InI, $d = 0.69$.
Effect sizes for post-test 2 ungrammatical scores: OI, $d = 1.70$ and for InI, $d = 1.0$.

A repeated measures ANOVA found a statistically significant effect for test time, $F(1.5, 71.2) = 37.511$, $p < 0.001$, and group, $F(2, 47) = 8.405$, $p = 0.001$ on the total scores on the UGJT. There was also a significant interaction effect between test time and group, $F(3.0, 71.2) = 5.218$, $p = 0.003$. A *post hoc* analysis revealed that both the OI and InI groups differed significantly from the Control group on both post-test 1 and 2; however, the OI and PI groups did not differ significantly from each other.

For the ungrammatical items, the repeated measures ANOVA found significant effects for both test time $F(1.6, 74.1) = 7.789$, $p = 0.002$ and group, $F(2, 47) = 5.626$, $p = 0.006$, as well as an interaction effect between test time and group, $F(3.2, 74.1) = 2.672$, $p = 0.05$. A *post hoc* analysis revealed that the OI group differed significantly from the Control Group on post-test 1 and 2; however, the InI group differed significantly from the Control group only on post-test 2 and not on post-test 1. Again, the OI and InI groups did not differ significantly from each other on either of the tests.

In each test, as explained above, there were forms to which participants had been introduced in treatment sessions, that is, 'old' test items as well as 'novel' test items (i.e. forms that had not been introduced during instructional treatments). Descriptive statistics for performance of all groups on novel and old items in the Oral Elicited Imitation Tests are presented in Table 10.4.

A repeated measures ANOVA on the 'old' items on the Oral Elicited Imitation Test found statistically significant main effects for test time, $F(2, 94) = 27.257$, $p < 0.001$ and group, $F(2, 47) = 4.798$, $p = 0.013$. There was

Table 10.4 Descriptive statistics for the old and novel items of the Oral Elicited Imitation Test

	OI group (n =18)		InI group (n =20)		Control (n =12)	
	M	M	M	SD	M	SD
Old items						
Pre-test	0.38	0.20	0.35	0.19	0.32	0.18
Post-test 1	0.58	0.20	0.57	0.22	0.40	0.20
Post-test 2	0.69	0.17	0.58	0.20	0.38	0.21
Novel items						
Pre-test	0.43	0.17	0.52	0.18	0.42	0.19
Post-test 1	0.66	0.18	0.62	0.18	0.50	0.16
Post-test 2	0.68	0.23	0.65	0.23	0.48	0.18

Effect sizes for post-test 1 old items: OI, $d = 0.90$ and for InI, $d = 0.80$.
Effect sizes for post-test 2 old items: OI, $d = 1.70$ and for InI, $d = 0.98$.
Effect sizes for post-test 1 novel items: OI, $d = 0.93$ and for InI, $d = 0.69$.
Effect sizes for post-test 2 novel items: OI, $d = 0.95$ and for InI, $d = 0.80$.

also a significant interaction effect between test time and group, $F(4, 94) = 3.118$, $p = 0.019$. A *post hoc* analysis revealed no significant differences among the groups on post-test 1; however, on post-test 2 both the OI and InI groups differed significantly from the Control group, but not from each other.

A repeated measures ANOVA on the 'novel' items on the Oral Elicited Imitation Test found a statistically significant main effect for test time, $F(2, 94) = 20.302$, $p < 0.001$ but not for group, $F(2, 47) = 2.677$, $p = 0.079$. There was a significant interaction effect between test time and group, $F(4, 94) = 2.970$, $p = 0.023$. A *post hoc* analysis revealed no significant differences among the groups on post-test 1; however, on post-test 2 the OI group differed significantly from the Control group, but the InI group did not differ significantly from the other two groups.

Descriptive statistics for performance of all groups on novel and old items in the UGJT are presented in Table 10.5.

A repeated measures ANOVA on the 'old' items on the UGJT found statistically significant main effects for test time, $F(2, 96) = 32.955$, $p < 0.001$ and group, $F(2, 47) = 7.061$, $p = 0.002$. There was also a significant interaction effect between test time and group, $F(4, 96) = 5.901$, $p < 0.001$. A *post hoc* analysis revealed that both the OI and InI groups differed significantly from the Control group on post-tests 1 and 2; however, the OI and InI groups did not differ significantly from each other.

Table 10.5 Descriptive statistics for old and novel items of the Untimed Grammaticality Judgment Test

	OI group (n = 18)		InI group (n = 20)		Control (n = 12)	
	M	M	M	SD	M	SD
Old items						
Pre-test	0.57	0.15	0.57	0.17	0.60	0.09
Post-test 1	0.83	0.15	0.78	0.17	0.61	0.16
Post-test 2	0.88	0.12	0.82	0.15	0.62	0.18
Novel items						
Pre-test	0.69	0.12	0.58	0.15	0.61	0.13
Post-test 1	0.82	0.13	0.74	0.18	0.58	0.21
Post-test 2	0.83	0.11	0.76	0.16	0.72	0.13

Effect sizes for post-test 1 old items: OI, $d = 1.40$ and for InI, $d = 1.00$.
Effect sizes for post-test 2 old items: OI, $d = 1.80$ and for InI, $d = 1.20$.
Effect sizes for post-test 1 novel items: OI, $d = 1.50$ and for InI, $d = 0.84$.
Effect sizes for post-test 2 novel items: OI, $d = 0.93$ and for InI, $d = 0.27$.

A repeated measures ANOVA on the 'novel' items on the UGJT found a statistically significant main effect for test time, $F(1.7, 79.3) = 14.491$, $p < 0.001$ and for group, $F(2, 47) = 7.053$, $p = 0.002$. There was, however, no significant interaction effect between test time and group, $F(3.4, 19.3) = 2.193$, $p = 0.088$. As there was no interaction effect, no *post hoc* analysis was conducted.

A summary of the results is presented in Table 10.6. In general, the OI group performed consistently better than the Control group, with significant differences between the two groups on most measures. In addition, the InI group outperformed the Control group on many measures, particularly in the delayed post-test conditions. The OI and InI groups never differed significantly from each other.

Discussion

Research question 1 asked whether there were gains for OI on measures of implicit and explicit language knowledge. The answer to this question is yes. The OI group made significant gains from pre-test to both post-tests on the Oral Elicited Imitation Test, a measure of primarily implicit knowledge. This group also made significant gains from pre-test to both post-tests on total scores of the UGJT, a measure of primarily explicit knowledge. From the pre-test to post-test 2, there were also

Table 10.6 Results summary

Test	Post-test 1	Post-test 2
Oral Elicited Imitation		
Overall	OI > Control	OI > Control
Old items	No significant differences	OI, InI > Control
Novel items	No significant differences	OI > Control
Grammaticality Judgment Test		
Overall	OI, InI > Control	OI, InI > Control
Ungrammatical items	OI > Control	OI, InI > Control
Old items	OI, InI > Control	OI, InI > Control
Novel items	No significant differences	No significant differences

statistically significant gains for ungrammatical scores, arguably a purer measure of explicit knowledge (see Chapters 2 and 4). Additional evidence for the gains that the OI group made on all measures is the effect sizes, which can be classified as large ($d > 0.80$), according to Cohen (1988). The results showed no gains for the Control group over time on these tests, indicating that the gains for the OI group cannot be attributed to test familiarity.

Previous research has shown gains for OI on measures of explicit language knowledge, but the evidence that OI has had any impact on learners' underlying language systems has been inconclusive, at best. This study shows positive gains for OI on a test that minimizes the possibility of students monitoring their language output, by requiring them to focus on meaning rather than linguistic form and by requiring them to process and produce language in real time. This result lends credence to claims that giving students the opportunity to produce language output does impact significantly on their developing language system.

Research question 2 asked whether OI or InI was more effective when learning was measured on tests of implicit and explicit language knowledge. The answer to this question is perhaps a qualified 'no'. First of all, it is 'no' because the mixed design ANOVAs revealed no statistically significant differences between the performance of either group on either the Oral Elicited Imitation Test or the UGJT post-tests. However, we need to qualify this 'no' by recognizing that there were, overall, greater gains for the OI group than for the InI group. Firstly, in all cases, effect sizes were larger for the OI group (e.g. $d = 0.99$, $d = 1.35$, $d = 1.70$, $d = 1.70$) than for the InI group (e.g. $d = 0.79$, $d = 0.98$, $d = 1.05$,

$d = 0.90$). Secondly, gains for the OI group were statistically greater than those for the Control group on both Oral Elicited Imitation post-tests (the InI group did not make gains that were statistically greater than the Control group on either test). This constitutes a challenge to researchers who claim that output plays only an accessory role in the language acquisition process.

Critics may suggest that the lack of statistically significant differences between the two groups in terms of learning outcomes may simply reflect a lack of difference in the treatments that each group received. Certainly, each instructional treatment was meaning-based and each required students to make FMC. For example, in Activity 4 (see Appendix) the role play of the alien from outer space asking about 'humans' established a context that would enable students in the OI group to understand that the indefinite article conveyed generic reference. Activity 7 (see Appendix) enabled students in the InI group to establish FMC. It is also possible that the output that students in the output group produced may have constituted meaningful input for other learners, thereby affording more opportunity for learning. According to VanPatten, this is a crucial reason for any learning gains that students make as a result of engaging in producing output. Another component of instruction that was consistent for each group and thus may also have accounted for learning (especially as measured by the UGJT) was the explicit instruction that focused learner attention on the target structure and made it salient, as indeed, did the corrective feedback that each group received.

However, there are three main reasons as to why the lack of significant differences between the two groups cannot be explained by postulating that the treatments were not differentiated enough. Firstly, the key difference between the two groups is one that proponents of input-based methods of instruction, including Processing Instruction, claim are crucial to acquisition. Students in the Input group *never* engaged in language output, whereas students in the Output group were given opportunities to produce the target structure in both lessons. The opportunity for students in the Input group to work with structured input is hypothesized by VanPatten (2004) to provide opportunities to make form-meaning mappings and to allow for attention to be fully focused, rather than diverted by the pressure to produce. In this way, the process of internalizing new forms into the developing system is able to take place. In addition, the instruction that students in the Input group received included information about how an unhelpful processing strategy (in this case the One-to-One Principle) may work to their disadvantage. In considering the question of the difference between the two groups, it is perhaps salutary to remember that a criticism that has often been made of Processing Instruction is that it has contrasted an InI with an OI that is *too* mechanical and thus disadvantages learners too obviously (DeKeyser *et al.*, 2002). The production practice in many of the Input Processing studies (e.g. VanPattern & Cadierno, 1993) has been very mechanical with no opportunity for students to engage in meaningful interaction (Farley, 2001).

Secondly, the lack of any significant difference in gains may be due to another variable, that is, the different measures of learning that were used in this study. We cannot be sure what the results would have been had the measures been more in line with those used in previous research. Researchers in Processing Instruction tend to use interpretation tests and controlled production tests. Izumi (2002) used an interpretation test, sentence combination test, picture-cued sentence completion test and grammaticality judgment test. Toth (2006) used a written production test and a grammaticality judgment test. As Norris and Ortega (2000) point out, the results of experimental research depend on the measures of language acquisition used. One of the strengths of this study is that the measures used are designed to give us information about the relative impact of the instruction on both implicit and explicit language knowledge. It is interesting to note that despite the difference in measures used, this study has produced results that are in line with other research, that is, students who had not produced the target structure at all in the experimental treatments were able to produce it in the Oral Elicited Imitation Test just as well as those students who had engaged in meaningful production during the treatment sessions (note that for 'old items' students in the Input group outperformed the Control group on post-test 2). The results from the Oral Elicited Imitation Test demonstrate that input does impact on the developing language system.

The lack of statistically significant differences between the two groups is all the more surprising given the fact that the learners had, prior to the study, only poorly acquired the target structure. While students were familiar with the indefinite article itself, they had clearly not acquired its use to express generic reference, as shown by low scores on the pre-test of the Elicited Oral Imitation Test (only 43%). If, as VanPatten (2004) claims, the pressure to produce output diverts attention away from processing the structure adequately at earlier stages of learning, one can wonder how, in this study, students in the Output group could have performed better than students in the Input group. As Toth (2006) concludes in his study, one would expect that, if there was no role for output in the acquisition process, spending so much time accessing the target structure, rather than purely processing it, would impact negatively on the learning of students in the Output group. Clearly, the results in this study, demonstrate otherwise. They provide evidence to suggest that output may, of itself, promote the establishment of FMC and lead to growth in the L2 linguistic system.

Research question 3 asked whether either OI or InI would bring about improved learning on novel test items when learning was measured on tests of implicit and explicit language knowledge. The answer to this question is both yes and no. On the Oral Elicited Imitation Test, there were statistically significant gains for novel items by the Output group on the delayed post-test, but none by the Input group. On the UGJT, there were no statistically significant gains across testing episodes for novel test items for either group. On the other hand, there were gains for both groups on the UGJT and on the delayed post-test of the Oral Elicited Imitation Test for old items. Results that show gains for the Output group on the delayed post-test of the Oral Elicited Imitation Test provide additional evidence that output may impact on the development of implicit knowledge. It is also interesting to note that this learning was evident over time and not immediately; in other words, it seems that time was needed in order for the developing system to be impacted significantly and for learning to be evidenced.

One of the limitations of the present study is that we are unable to specify what exactly accounted for the gains in learning that participants in the OI group made. Unfortunately, unlike Toth (2006), we do not have recordings of classroom interaction that are sufficiently clear and that allow for the careful examination of the cognitive processes that learners were engaged in. We can surmise that learners who engaged in output may have been required to process FMC at a deeper level than those who worked with structured input only (Izumi, 2003; Toth, 2006). Or we can suggest, as Izumi (2003) does, that the requirement that students produce output necessitated the processing of language that may not have been necessary for comprehension and that there was a shift from purely meaning-oriented processing strategies towards more syntactically sensitive ones. We can also suggest that the corrective feedback that learners received in relation to errors they made when producing the target structure forced them to notice the mismatch between their own output and the target structure (Izumi, 2002), a cognitive process that may have led to the restructuring of the developing system (Toth, 2006). As Swain (1985) suggests, one of the functions of output is to allow students the opportunity to receive feedback on their trials with new language. The type of feedback that students in the Output group received in this study was qualitatively different to that which students in the Input group received. The feedback available to the Input group alerted them only to the accuracy of choices they made when responding to language input. Obviously, more observation and analysis of the processes students are engaged in when producing output in the language classroom is necessary. However, what we do know is that OI that included some input led to at least as much linguistic development (more in terms of generalization of learning to new linguistic items) than InI that included no output. In this respect, our study replicates the results of Morgan-Short and Bowden (2006).

Conclusion

The study reported in this chapter provides evidence to show that a method of instruction that gives learners the opportunity to engage in producing language output leads to the acquisition of implicit language knowledge. In this study, the fact that the learners performed so poorly on the Oral Elicited Imitation pre-test demonstrated that they had not fully incorporated the target feature into their developing language system. The learning gains the Output group manifested are all the more interesting because they challenge claims that there is no specific role for output in the creating of an underlying competence (VanPatten, 2004). Indeed, they suggest that output formulation may lead to the processing of form-meaning mappings and impact on the L2 developing system.

The results of this study also suggest that OI is as effective as InI when it allows learners to take part in meaningful interaction and when the learning outcomes are measured on tests of implicit and explicit language knowledge. The fact that in this study, students in both instructional groups showed gains in implicit language knowledge, demonstrates that output and input both impact on the developing language system. This may suggest that there are different routes to L2 development and future research may do well to investigate whether particular structures are more amenable to one type of instruction than the other.

In this study, it is important to acknowledge some evidence of greater gains for output instruction, especially in terms of generalization of learning to linguistic items that are not targeted during treatment. More research is needed, in particular, studies that examine the processes that learners engage with when producing output in the language classroom, so that we can increase our understanding of what exactly accounts for learning gains made.

Chapter 11

The Incidental Acquisition of Third Person -s as Implicit and Explicit Knowledge

SHAWN LOEWEN, ROSEMARY ERLAM and ROD ELLIS

Introduction

The study reported in this chapter was motivated by an observation made by Hulstijn (2003: 357):

> (The study of) incidental and intentional learning appears prominently in one domain but not at all in another. Incidental and intentional learning mainly figure in the area of vocabulary (including spelling). They do not appear at all in the areas of phonetics and phonology, however, and *only exceptionally in the area of grammar.* (italics added)

The fact that there have been so few studies of the incidental acquisition of grammar is surprising given the importance of this type of acquisition for the general claim that learners are able to learn the grammar of a second language (L2) naturalistically through exposure to comprehensible input or interaction (Krashen, 1981; Long, 1996). Also, one of the central claims of those researchers who adhere to the view that L2 learners have continued access to Universal Grammar is that learning requires only positive evidence and will take place naturally as long as this is available (Schwartz, 1993) – a position that also implies that incidental acquisition of grammar is possible. However, other researchers (such as those associated with the evaluation of immersion programmes in Canada – e.g. Genesee, 1987) have noted that learners who have had ample opportunity to acquire grammar incidentally, often fail to acquire more marked grammatical features (e.g. the distinction between passé composé and imparfait in L2 French – Harley, 1989). The question arises, then, as to whether incidental acquisition of grammar (especially of marked or redundant features) is in fact possible. The more or less complete absence of studies that have addressed this question is puzzling. This chapter reports such a study, drawing once again on the instruments designed to measure implicit and explicit knowledge discussed in Part 2 of this book.

The chapter begins by defining 'incidental acquisition' (not an easy task!). It then examines the few previous studies of the incidental acquisition of grammar. There follows a brief review of research that has addressed the target structure of our study (subject-verb agreement in third person -s of the present simple tense). The rest of the chapter reports the study.

Intentional versus Incidental Learning

Drawing on cognitive psychology, second language acquisition (SLA) researchers have distinguished intentional and incidental language learning. The essence of intentional learning is that it involves a deliberate attempt to learn; this is likely to involve awareness. For example, a learner may set out to read a book with the express purpose of increasing his/her vocabulary and is therefore likely to consciously attend to new words in the text and be aware of his/her attempt to learn them. In contrast, incidental learning is characterized by an absence of intentionality to learn, but may still involve impromptu conscious attention to some features of the L2.

Distinguishing intentional/incidental learning on the one hand from explicit/implicit learning on the other is not easy. In fact, it is doubtful whether a clear conceptual distinction can be made. Intentional learning of grammar cannot be distinguished easily from explicit learning, as the former is very likely to involve some attempt to 'understand' the underlying principle of what is to be learned, while the latter pre-supposes intentionality. Nor can incidental and implicit learning be clearly separated. Obviously, both involve an absence of intentionality. Nor can they be distinguished in terms of awareness. It would not be possible, for example, to claim that incidental acquisition may involve awareness whereas implicit learning definitely does not, as even implicit learning may involve awareness at the level of noticing. The two pairs of terms have been distinguished methodologically, however. It is possible, for example, to identify prototypical tasks for investigating the four types of learning, as shown in Table 11.1 (taken from Chapter 9 in Ellis, 2008).

As illustrated in row one of Table 11.1, the methodology for investigating incidental learning involves three essential characteristics: (1) learners are not told what the focus of the study is, (2) the instructional materials contain copious examples of the target of the study (i.e. there is 'input-flooding') and (3) either they are not told they will be tested or their attention is focused on some other aspect than the target that is to be tested.[1] Thus, incidental learning involves the 'learning of one thing (e.g. grammar) while the learner's primary objective is to do something else' (Schmidt, 1994: 16). Of course, there can be differences in what the 'something else' is. In previous studies

Table 11.1 Typical tasks for investigating four types of learning

Approach	Typical task
(1) Incidental learning	Either (1) learners are given a task but not told they will be tested or (2) they are given a task that focuses their attention on one aspect of the L2 and, without being prewarned, tested on some other aspect of the task (e.g. they are taught a specific grammatical feature and then tested on whether they have learned a different grammatical feature which they were exposed to but not taught).
(2) Intentional learning	Learners are given a task (e.g. they are taught and given practice in using a specific grammatical feature), told they will be tested afterwards and then tested on the task as set.
(3) Implicit learning	Learners are simply exposed to input data, asked to process it for meaning and then tested (without warning) to see what they have learned (e.g. they are exposed to input that contains plentiful exemplars of a specific grammatical feature but do not have their attention focused on this feature).
(4) Explicit learning	Learners are either given an explicit rule relating to a specific feature which they then apply to data in practice activities (deductive explicit learning) or they are asked to discover an explicit rule from an array of data provided (i.e. inductive explicit learning).

Source: Ellis (2008)

(see below), it has involved attention to meaning (as opposed to form), as suggested by Schmidt's definition. An alternative, however, might be to focus learners' attention on one grammatical feature (the supposed target feature) but test them on a different feature (the actual target feature of the study). This latter approach is the one adopted in the study reported in this chapter.

Studies of Incidental Learning of L2 Grammar[2]

There have been a number of studies that have investigated the effects of input-flooding on L2 acquisition (see Ellis (1999) for a review of these). However, these studies investigated enhanced input (i.e. input where the target feature was highlighted in some way) in order to draw attention to it. Thus, they cannot be considered to have investigated incidental acquisition, as the effect of the enhancement may have been to encourage learners to intentionally learn the target feature. Hulstijn (2003) identified only three studies of incidental learning (Hulstijn, 1989; Robinson, 1996,

1997) that have explicitly used the term 'incidental'. One further study by Robinson (2005b) will also be considered.

Hulstijn (1989) conducted two studies involving a natural language (L2 Dutch) and an artificial language. Learners were presented with word order structures implicitly (i.e. the structures were not explained to them) and incidentally (i.e. they did not know they would be tested for recall of the structures). They were assigned to one of three treatments involving exposure to sentences containing the target structures. One group (the form-focused group) had to perform an anagram task that directed their attention to the structure without any need to consider its meaning. The second group (the meaning-focused group) were shown the same sentences on a screen and asked to respond meaningfully to them by saying 'yes', 'perhaps' or 'I don't know'. The third group (the form- and meaning-focused group) was simply told to pay attention to both form and meaning, but was given no special task to perform. The results showed that the form-focused group outperformed the other two groups in terms of gains in scores on a sentence-copying task and a task requiring cued recall of the sentences used in the learning tasks. Hulstijn interpreted the results as showing that attention to form when encoding input is a 'sufficient condition' for implicit and incidental learning. However, as the meaning-focused group also produced significant gains, the hypothesis that exclusive attention to meaning will inhibit acquisition was not supported. It is possible, though, that the learners in this group engaged in some degree of 'noticing' of the target structures. As Hulstijn pointed out, meaning may be the learner's first priority, but attention to form occurs as a 'backup procedure' in case meaning fails to provide an adequate interpretation.

Robinson (1996) investigated 104 predominantly intermediate-level Japanese English as a second language (ESL) learners' acquisition of two grammatical features; pseudo-clefts of location (which Robinson considered a 'hard rule') and subject-verb inversion following an adverbial fronting (considered an easy rule). There were four instructional conditions in this study: (1) implicit condition (remembering sentences), (2) incidental condition (the learners were asked to read the sentences containing the target structure in order to understand their meaning), (3) rule-search condition (identifying rules) and (4) instructed condition (written explanations of rules). Learning was measured by means of a grammaticality judgment test measuring correctness of judgments and response times. There was also a debriefing questionnaire to measure learners' awareness of the target structures. Robinson found no significant differences in either accuracy or speed of response in judging sentences between the implicit and incidental conditions, suggesting that they functioned similarly. The instructed learners, however, were significantly more accurate than the incidental learners on the easy rule but not on the difficult rule. The learners in the incidental (and the implicit) condition were more likely to report awareness of the hard feature than the easy feature.

Robinson's (2005b) study was a replication of Knowlton and Squire (1996). The latter study involved an artificial language, but Robinson investigated a natural language – Samoan. Another interesting feature of Robinson's study was that it involved complete beginners. The learners (Japanese university students) were first asked to memorize the meanings of a number of Samoan words. They were then exposed to 150 tokens each of three Samoan grammatical rules, two of which involved the use of particles and the other the incorporation of the direct object into verbs. The participants were asked to try as hard as possible to understand the meaning of each sentence. They were asked to respond to yes/no comprehension questions and received feedback on the correctness of their responses. Results showed clear evidence of learning of all three target structures on old items in a grammaticality judgment test (i.e. the same sentences as in the training materials) but only for one of the structures (the locative particle) on new items.

Two other studies, although not technically studies of incidental learning, will be considered because they address a key issue. VanPatten (1990) asked learners to listen to a text in Spanish under four conditions. In one task, the learners were instructed to listen for content only. In a second task, they listened for content and the word *inflacion*, making a check mark each time it occurred. In the third task, they listened for content and checked each time they heard the definite article *la*. In the fourth task, they listened for content and checked each time they heard the verb morpheme *-n*. VanPatten reported a significant difference on the comprehension scores (derived from asking students to recall the text) for tasks one and two on the one hand and tasks three and four on the other. There was no difference between the scores for tasks one and two or between those for tasks three and four. In other words, when the learners attended to form, their comprehension suffered. VanPatten's results were replicated in a study based on a reading text by Wong (2001). The significance of these studies is that learners (especially low proficiency ones) have difficulty attending to two aspects (form and meaning) of the input at the same time due to limited processing capacity.

What do these studies suggest about the incidental language learning of grammar? First, they show that incidental learning can take place, even with difficult rules. However, second, this may simply involve 'item learning' (i.e. learners remember the specific items they have been exposed to) and not 'system-learning' (i.e. the internalization of a 'rule' that can be successfully applied to new exemplars of the target feature). Third, attention is involved. Learners' capacity to learn grammatical features incidentally may depend on whether they are able to 'dual task' successfully. That is, if they are able to attend to both meaning and form then incidental learning is possible. However, if they experience difficulty in doing so, incidental learning may be impossible or very limited.

No study to the best of our knowledge has investigated incidental learning in a design that focuses attention on one grammatical feature but tests acquisition of a different feature. Incidental learning in this condition also requires dual tasking, but in this case it involves two tasks of the same kind (i.e. both involve form). Such a study is of obvious pedagogical value; teachers are likely to be interested in the possibility that even though they may be focusing their teaching on grammatical feature *x*, learners may also (or even instead) be acquiring features *y, z . . . n*. Ellis (1984) provided an example of this. He noted that as a result of a lesson consisting of the drilling of teaching plural forms (e.g. 'These are pens'), the two learners he studied demonstrated learning of copula *be* but not of plural forms. Ellis suggested that this was because they had been massively exposed to this feature during the lesson.

The Acquisition of Third Person -s

There is plenty of evidence in the L2 acquisition literature that third person -s is late acquired. The early morpheme studies (e.g. Dulay & Burt, 1973), placed this morphological feature low down on the 'natural order of acquisition'. In their meta-analysis of 12 of these studies, Goldschneider and DeKeyser (2001) found that third person -s achieved the lowest score out of six morphological features in 11 of the morpheme studies included in the meta-analysis. The mean accuracy score for third person -s in these 12 studies was only 37.55%.

The morpheme studies examined accuracy of suppliance of third person -s in data collected cross-sectionally from large groups of learners. Similar results have been obtained from in-depth studies of smaller groups of learners and in longitudinal studies. Stauble (1984), for example, examined six Spanish and Japanese learners' suppliance of third person -s in conversational data. She reported that whereas *is*-copula was fairly well established in the production of the learners, in the eight learners Stauble classified as basilang speakers, subject-verb agreement was only minimally expressed (varying between 0 and 23%). The two Spanish mesolang learners did better, both achieving 56% target-like use, but the two mesolang Japanese learners could only achieve 10 and 19%. Accuracy in the use of third person -s was notably lower than for other grammatical morphemes (e.g. past irregular) investigated in this study. Stauble's study also indicates that the acquisition of third person -s may be influenced by the learners' L1.

Lardiere (1998) investigated suppliance of third person -s in different linguistic contexts by one Chinese learner of L2 English (Patty). She collected three sets of data, one after Patty had been in the USA for about 10 years and two some eight years later. The results are shown in Table 11.2. Whereas Patty did demonstrate acquisition of agreement marking in copula *be*, she displayed very little ability to mark either auxiliary verbs or main verbs for third person -s. This led Lardiere (1998: 367) to claim that 'this particular aspect of her English has most likely fossilized'.

Why do learners experience such difficulty in achieving high levels of accuracy with third person -s? Depending on one's theoretical orientation different explanations are available. Two explanations will be considered here; Pienemann's (1998, 2005) Processability Theory and N. Ellis' (2006) account of associative language learning.[3]

Pienemann's Processability Theory seeks to explain acquisitional sequences in terms of a set of processing procedures (see Chapter 6). As Pienemann (2005: 2) put it 'once we can spell out the sequence in which language processing routines develop we can delineate those grammars that are processable at different points of development'. The Processability Theory views acquisition in relation to L2 production. Pienemann (2005: 13) hypothesized that 'processing devices will be acquired in their sequence of activation in the production process'. Thus, the failure to master a low-level procedure blocks access to higher-level procedures and makes it impossible for the learner to acquire those grammatical features that depend on them. Pienemann identified a hierarchy of procedures, which are distinguished by the nature of the grammatical information that the learner needs to deposit and exchange in what Pienemann called 'feature unification'. The procedure governing the acquisition of third person -s is the S-procedure – the penultimate language generation process in the hierarchy. The S-procedure involves exchange of information between heads of different phrases. The features of one constituent (the subject-noun phrase) are deposited in the S-procedure and subsequently placed in another constituent (the verb phrase). When this becomes possible, learners are able to mark the third

Table 11.2 Third person -s marking in obligatory contexts by one L2 learner

Recording	Overall% accuracy	% Accuracy on copula be	% Accuracy in aux do and have	% Accuracy in main verbs
1	48.8	39.37	4.67	4.76
2	86.44	69.78	16.66	0.00
3	71.26	59.26	7.46	4.54

Source: Lardiere (1998)

person of the present simple tense with the -s morpheme. Thus, according to this account, third person -s is late acquired because learners do not master the production process involved until late on.

N. Ellis (2006) draws on various constructs from associative learning theory to identify the factors that contribute to the learning difficulty of morphemes like third person -s; the multifunctionality of the -s morpheme (it signals plurality, possession as well as occurring in contracted form in copula and auxiliary *be*), its redundancy (person is signaled by the pronoun/noun in English) and hence its low functional value, and the difficulty of perceiving it in oral input. Together these factors jointly contribute to its low salience. As N. Ellis (2006: 170) notes:

> Many grammatical meaning-form relationships, particularly those that are notoriously difficult for second language learners like grammatical particles and inflections such as 3rd person '-s' of English, are of low salience in the language stream.

Ellis goes on to explain that the sheer frequency and predictability of bound morphemes such as third person -s leads to the deformation of their phonetic structure, blurring the boundaries between them and the surrounding words. Such a morpheme cannot be easily pronounced in isolation. Furthermore, it is low in stress and so cannot be readily perceived even in input that has been simplified through foreigner or teacher talk. Thus, if such a feature cannot be easily perceived 'bottom-up', learners must rely on 'top-down' processing. Ellis proposes that this requires support from their overall knowledge of the language – e.g. knowledge of a critical mass of content words.

N. Ellis (2006: 178) discusses another cognitive process that is linked to the problem of perception and can account for why the problem in acquiring third person -s is so persistent – 'blocking'. He explains this as follows:

> Blocking is a result of an automatically learned inattention. But this learned inattention can be pervasive and long standing: once a cue has been blocked, further learning about the cue is attenuated.

Blocking arises when there are two linguistic cues that realize a meaning and the more salient of these is learned, thereby overshadowing the other. Such is the case with third person -s. The meaning signaled by this feature is 'person', but this meaning is also signaled by the preceding subject of the verb (whether noun or pronoun), which is perceptually more salient. Blocking may become stronger if the learner's L1 contains no equivalent morphological marker on the verb. Once inattention to the -s morpheme becomes normal for the learner, it is difficult to reverse this process.

Low saliency and blocking together provide an explanation for why learners experience such difficulty with acquiring third person -s and why this problem persists. The question arises as to whether, with sufficient input, frequency and intensity of exposure can overcome the obstacles to learning. N. Ellis (2006: 180) is pessimistic:

> under these circumstances of low salience and blocking, all the extra input in the world might sum to naught, and we describe the learner as having "fossilized" with an IL reminiscent of the Basic Variety.

This would appear to be a rejection of the possibility that incidental acquisition of third person -s can take place even under conditions of input flooding. However, some L2 learners (even those learning naturalistically) do succeed in acquiring third person -s, so it might be premature to rule out the possibility that under certain conditions, this recalcitrant feature can be mastered.

It should be noted, however, that the research that both Pienemann and Ellis draw on to provide evidence for their theoretical positions is based on the analysis of more or less spontaneous production data, such as that collected in Stauble and Lardiere's studies. That is, learners are said to have difficulty in acquiring third person -s because they are unable to produce it accurately when communicating. It does not follow that learners lack declarative knowledge of this feature. They may well have received instruction in third person -s and be able to articulate the rule, which as Krashen (1982) has pointed out is functionally and formally 'simple'. In other words, whereas learners may fail to acquire third person -s as implicit knowledge, they may well learn it as explicit knowledge. Evidence for this claim can be found in the study of learning difficulty reported in Chapter 6. In this chapter, the accuracy scores obtained from measures of implicit and explicit knowledge for a variety of grammatical features, including third person -s, were compared. In a sample of 224 mainly Chinese learners of English, whose experience of learning English was primarily in an instructed context, the mean implicit knowledge score for third person -s was 46%, whereas the mean explicit knowledge score was 64%. Out of the 17 grammatical structures investigated, this difference between the implicit and explicit scores was one of the highest.

The study that we will now report examines the incidental acquisition of third person -s. Classroom learners were exposed to input that contained numerous exemplars of third person -s (i.e. an input flood) in a context where their attention was directed at another grammatical feature. In line with N. Ellis' theory of associative language learning, we hypothesized that the learners would be unable to develop implicit knowledge of third person -s under such conditions. We also hypothesized that the incidental nature of the instruction they were exposed to would not contribute to their explicit knowledge. However, in line with both Pienemann's Processability Theory and N. Ellis' view about the need for a sufficient knowledge base, we also wished to explore whether learners who had demonstrated that they were 'ready' to acquire third person -s were able to benefit from the input flood. Thus, the research questions were:

(1) Does extensive exposure to English third person -s during lessons targeting another linguistic structure lead to acquisition of
   (a) implicit language knowledge of this feature?
   (b) explicit language knowledge of this feature?
(2) Does learners' readiness to acquire third person -s mediate the effect of the extensive exposure on their acquisition of implicit knowledge of this feature?

Method

Participants

The study was conducted in two private language schools in Auckland. Students in each school were enrolled in short courses in 'general English' of between four and six weeks' duration. The treatment group, subsequently referred to as the Input Flood Group, was made up of two intact classes of intermediate-level students ($n = 9$, $n = 11$) in each school. A second group of students, at one of the language schools, received no instruction but took part in all testing episodes. This group, the Control Group, totalled 12. A total of 32 students took part in the study.

Students were asked to complete a background questionnaire, which required them to give information about their first language and length of exposure to English. Thirteen students in the treatment group had an Asian language-speaking background (Japanese, Chinese, Korean, Taiwanese). The remainder came from a variety of other language backgrounds. They indicated that they had on average spent 6.9 years learning English and spent an average of nine months in an English-speaking country. The Control Group had a similar profile: six out of the 12 students were Asian language speakers. They had on average spent 5.9 years learning English and three months in an English-speaking country.

Design

All students were pre-tested three days before they received instruction (i.e. at the end of a teaching week). Instruction took place over two consecutive days in each language school. Each class received two lessons, each of one hour duration. One of the researchers taught all lessons. Post-testing was completed the day following the second lesson and delayed post-testing two weeks later. The Control Group continued their regular classes but received no instruction on the targeted structure. They completed all testing episodes over the same time scale as the treatment group.

Instructional treatment

The treatment group received extensive incidental exposure to third person -s (the actual target structure of this study) while the learners' attention was directed to another linguistic feature, that is, the indefinite article *a* to express generic meaning (the apparent target structure). This structure was taught by means of input-based instruction involving structured input. The effectiveness of this instructional treatment with the indefinite article *a* was the subject of the study reported in the previous chapter.

The input materials used for the instruction directed at indefinite article *a* also exposed the participants to third person -s. Thus, while focused on indefinite article *a* there was opportunity for the participants to gain extensive input containing third person -s. The underlined words in the examples below indicate the focus of the instruction (the apparent target structure) while the italicized words show the incidental exposure to third person -s (the actual target structure of this study).

e.g. **A cheetah** *runs* fast

Cheap **transport** *makes* life easy.

The input-based instruction proceeded as follows. Students were given explicit instruction at the beginning of each of the two treatment sessions by explaining that the indefinite article can be used to make a generalization and that it is omitted with noncount nouns. Students then worked at structured input activities that aimed to train them to distinguish generic from particular meaning. These activities were designed to encourage them to process both written and oral input, but did not require them at any time to engage in producing language output. For example, in one activity they were given some general-izations about student life and were asked to indicate whether they agreed with each one or not.

e.g.

	Agree	Disagree
A good teacher makes students laugh.	☐	☐

Students thus obtained extensive oral and written input of third person -s but with no opportunity to produce sentences containing third person -s. In this way, it was possible to investigate whether and to what extent acquisition is driven by language input only. An analysis of lesson materials indicates that they were exposed to 51 examples of third person -s in written form. (This total includes exposure to regular verb forms only, it does not include exposure to irregular verb forms used in third person -s form). They were also exposed to 23 examples of regular third person -s verb forms in aural input while completing listening activities. However, the total of 74 examples of written and aural input probably under-represents the amount of exposure that students received to this structure, as it does not include the numerous examples of the structure that arose as students listened to the teacher explaining, introducing and correcting during the activities completed in class. In short, although the total exposure time was relatively short (two hours), the exposure to exemplars of the target structure (third person -s) was very intensive.

Measures of instructional outcomes

Participants completed two tests during each of the three testing episodes (pre-test, post-test, delayed post-test) – an Untimed Grammaticality Judgment Test and an Oral Elicited Imitation Test. Both these tests and the theoretical rationale that has informed their design have been described in the chapters in Part 2 of this book.

The Elicited Oral Imitation Test consisted of 32 statements, each of which created an obligatory context for use of a regular third person -s verb form. In 25 statements, participants heard a grammatically correct regular third person -s verb form. The remaining seven sentences were ungrammatical with respect to the verb form, that is, the -s inflection was missing. As much as possible, statements were designed so that the verb form was not placed initially in the sentence to avoid drawing the participants' attention to it. Examples of test items are given below:

In general, a good teacher knows her students' names [grammatical]
In today's world a woman work very hard [ungrammatical]

The statements were presented on audiotape to participants by an interviewer. The participants heard each statement only once and in real time. They were told that they were to complete a Beliefs Questionnaire and were asked to indicate on paper by checking one of three boxes whether each statement was true, not true or whether they were not sure (thus ensuring a primary focus on meaning). They were then told to repeat the statement in *correct* English. Pre-test training gave participants practice in responding to both grammatical and ungrammatical test items. However, the participants received no feedback on their responses to the actual test items. The same version of the test was used over all three testing sessions. However, the order of presentation of items was different for each test administration.

Grammatical items were scored correct if the regular third person verb form was correctly repeated and ungrammatical items were scored correct if the incorrect verb form was spontaneously corrected. Incorrect suppliance or avoidance of the target structure was scored as 0. Participants' total scores were averaged, that is, divided by the total number of items and expressed as a percentage. The decision to report scores as percentages was made because on the Elicited Imitation Test, the sound quality of the recording at times meant that a decision about some responses could not be made. These were thus scored as missing data. Therefore, this meant that participants' total scores had to be averaged over the items for which there was data, so they were not penalized for those responses that could not be coded. Reliability, using internal consistency, was estimated on all versions of the complete test, giving Cronbach's alphas as follows: Pre-test = .891, post-test 1 = .894, and post-test 2 = .894.

The Untimed Grammaticality Judgment Test consisted of 32 sentences. All sentences created an obligatory context for use of a regular third person -s verb form. In 24 sentences, the third person -s verb form was grammatically correct. The remaining eight sentences were ungrammatical with respect to the verb form, that is, the -s inflection was missing. Again, wherever possible, the target structure was not placed initially in the sentence. Examples of test items are given below:

At school, a student learns many different skills [grammatical]
Usually, a doctor listen to his patients [ungrammatical]

The test was a pen-and-paper test and each sentence was presented on a new page. Participants were given as long as they liked to complete the test, but were told that they must not turn back to look at previous test items. Test-takers were asked to indicate by ticking the relevant box whether each sentence was correct or incorrect. Once again, one version of the test was used over all three testing sessions but with the order of presentation of items different for each test administration.

Scores for all the sentences in the test and for the ungrammatical items alone were calculated and presented as percentages. Reliability, using internal consistency, was estimated on all versions of the complete test, giving Cronbach's alphas as follows: pre-test = .411, post-test 1 = 0.821 and post-test 2 = 0.799.

Mixed model ANOVAs were performed, with the scores of the Oral Imitation Test and the Grammaticality Judgment Test as dependent variables. Test time (pre-test, post-test 1 and post-test 2) was a within-subjects independent variable and group (Input Flood Group or Control Group) was a between-subjects independent variable. An alpha level of 0.05 was used. SPSS 12.0 was used to perform all statistics.

Results

Descriptive statistics for the Elicited Oral Imitation Test are presented in Table 11.3. A mixed model ANOVA on the Oral Elicited Imitation Test found a statistically significant main effect for test time, $F(2, 60) = 16.757$, $p < .001$, but not for group, $F(1, 30) = 0.088$, $p = 0.769$. There was also no significant interaction effect for test time and group, $F(2, 60) = 1.079$, $p = .346$.

The results of the Untimed Grammaticality Judgment Test are presented in Table 11.4. For each test, two scores are given, the total score and the score for the ungrammatical items only. This is because previous research (see Chapters 2 and 3) suggests that ungrammatical items are a purer measure of explicit language knowledge. A repeated measures ANOVA found no statistically significant effect for test time, $F(1.2, 34.5) = 2.381$, $p = .101$ or group, $F(1, 30) = .012$, $p = .913$ on the total scores on the Untimed Grammaticality Judgment Test. There was also no significant interaction effect between test time and group, $F(1.2, 34.5) = .014$, $p = .252$.

Table 11.3 Descriptive statistics for Elicited Oral Imitation Test

	Input-flood (n =20)		*Control* (n =12)	
Test	*M*	*SD*	*M*	*SD*
Pre-test	.40	.20	.40	.22
Post-test 1	.52	.25	.46	.20
Post-test 2	.54	.23	.53	.16

Effect sizes for post-test 1: PI, $d = 0$, and for post-test 2: PI, $d = 0$.

Table 11.4 Descriptive statistics for Untimed Grammaticality Judgment Test

	Input flood (n =20)		*Control* (n =12)	
Test	*M*	*SD*	*M*	*SD*
Pre-test – total	.67	.19	.64	.18
Pre-test – ungramm.	.76	.25	.65	.27
Post-test 1 – total	.75	.28	.73	.21
Post-test 1 – ungramm.	.64	.35	.77	.24
Post-test 2 – total	.73	.26	.76	.22
Post-test 2 – ungramm.	.59	.36	.73	.33

For the ungrammatical items, the repeated measures ANOVA also found no significant effects for test time, $F(1.5, 45.2) = 0.421$, $p = .602$ or group, $F(1, 30) = .320$, $p = .576$, but there was a significant interaction between test time and group, $F(1.5, 45.2) = 3.520$, $p = .05$. Figure 11.1 shows that while the Control Group improved somewhat from pre-test to post-tests, the Input Flood Group showed a decrease in the number of accurate judgments from pre-test to post-tests.

In summary, there was no effect for exposure to the linguistic structure, as measured by the two tests. There was a test effect on the imitation test, with all groups improving; however, the groups did so equally.

Finally, the effect of the learners' initial implicit knowledge of third person -s (as evidenced by the Elicited Oral Imitation Test)[4] was investigated as it was possible that this may have mediated the effect of the incidental exposure. The participants in the Input Flood and Control Groups were divided into three proficiency bands according to their scores in the pre-test, as shown in Table 11.5. The mean gain scores from pre-test to post-test 1 and from pre-test to post-test 2 for each of these subgroups are shown in Table 11.6. As some of the subgroups were very small, no ANOVA was run. However, it is clear from an inspection of the descriptive statistics that there was marked variation in the gain scores within each subgroup and that overall the Input Flood subgroups did not differ markedly from each other or from the subgroups of the Control Group. In other words, there was no evidence that the learners' existing knowledge of third person -s influenced their ability to benefit from the incidental exposure.

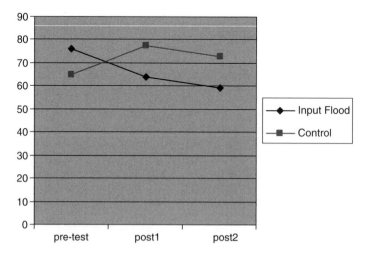

Figure 11.1 Ungrammatical GJT scores

Table 11.5 Number of participants in each band

Class	Accuracy band			Total
	<25%	26–50%	>50%	
Input flood	4	10	6	20
Control	3	6	3	12

Table 11.6 Proficiency level and Oral Elicited Imitation Pre-test scores

	Input Flood		Control	
Level	M	SD	M	SD
< 25%	.15	.06	.14	.05
26–50%	.33	.06	.40	.10
> 50%	.66	.06	.68	.06
Pre-test to Post-test 1 Gain Scores				
< 25%	.05	.13	.12	.17
26–50%	.17	.14	.06	.12
> 50%	.08	.17	− .03	.05
Pre-test to Post-test 2 Gain Scores				
< 25%	.12	.16	.30	.18
26–50%	.17	.11	.11	.13
> 50%	.12	.13	− .03	.05

Discussion

The first research question asked whether extensive incidental exposure led to acquisition of third person -s as either implicit or explicit knowledge. In accordance with the general aims of this book, the results for the effects on implicit and explicit knowledge will be considered separately.

Implicit knowledge was measured by means of the Elicited Oral Imitation Test. Pre-test scores showed that the learners in both the treatment and control groups possessed some ability to supply third person -s in sentences produced in real time while they were focused on meaning. However, the mean accuracy score for both groups was below 50%, with only nine out of the 32 learners scoring above 50%. In other words, these learners demonstrated poor control of this morphological feature, reflecting similar results obtained in other studies (e.g. Lardiere, 1998; Stauble, 1984) and in Chapter 6. Post-test Elicited Oral Imitation Test scores showed an improvement for both groups. However, the Input Flood Group did not improve any more than the Control Group. This suggests that the improvement was due to a test-practice effect and that the treatment had no effect on performance.

The failure of the learners' implicit knowledge to improve from the intensive exposure to third person -s can be explained by the fact that they were unable to dual-task (i.e. attend to third person -s as well as the indefinite article – the explicit focus of the instruction) and also by the low saliency of third person -s and possible blocking (i.e. automatically learned inattention). The results of this study are similar to those of Robinson (1996) but contrast with those of Hulstijn (1989) and Robinson (2006), both of whom reported results demonstrating that incidental acquisition had occurred. The results of this study also contrast with a number of other studies that have found a positive effect for input-flooding (e.g. Leeman *et al.*, 1995; Trahey & White, 1993) but, as noted in the introduction, the input in these studies was enriched, encouraging learners to attend deliberately to them and thus fostering intentional rather than incidental acquisition. The key to explaining the differences in the results of these studies probably lies in two related factors: (1) the intrinsic saliency of the target structure and (2) the extent to which the treatment encourages noticing of the structure. In the case of the present study, third person -s is clearly a nonsalient feature, while the learners' attention was actively directed at another structure (rather than just directed at processing for meaning).

Explicit knowledge was measured by means of the ungrammatical items on the Untimed Grammaticality Judgment Test, in accordance with the results reported in Chapters 2 and 3, which indicated that these provide the best measure of explicit knowledge. Pre-test scores showed that the learners in both the treatment and control groups already possessed substantial explicit knowledge of third person -s. Post-test scores showed that while the Control Group improved (presumably as a result of practice), the scores of the Input Flood Group declined (e.g. the scores in post-test 2 were 17% lower than those in the pre-test). The explanation for this almost certainly lies in the fact that the instruction directed at the indefinite article caused the learners to focus their attention on this structure and distracted them from attending consciously to third person -s errors in the ungrammatical sentences. For example, they may have judged a sentence such as:

Usually, a doctor listen to his patients.

as grammatical because they were focusing their attention on 'a doctor', which is in fact correct in this sentence. If this explanation is correct, it cannot be said that the learners' explicit knowledge deteriorated as a result of the treatment, but merely that they were distracted from accessing it. Clearly, though, the input flood did not lead to any incidental acquisition of explicit knowledge.

The second research question asked whether the learners' readiness to acquire third person -s mediated the effect of the input flood. To address this, we divided the Input Flood Group into three subgroups in order to investigate whether those learners with higher initial levels of control of this feature were better able to benefit from exposure to it than those learners with lower levels. The Elicited Oral Imitation Test scores were used for this analysis as the issue of control is more relevant to implicit than to explicit knowledge. There was no evidence that the treatment benefited the more advanced learners to a greater extent than the less advanced. In fact, the subgroups who received the input flood did not perform notably differently on the Elicited Oral Imitation Test from the subgroups who did not. Thus, initial proficiency did not affect learners' ability to acquire implicit knowledge incidentally when exposed to multiple examples of third person -s. This result suggests that, for difficult-to-acquire features, incidental acquisition does not become easier once a feature has become partially established in a learner's interlanguage.[5]

Conclusion

This study has demonstrated that incidental acquisition of third person -s as either implicit or explicit knowledge did not take place despite the fact that learners were exposed to multiple examples of it during instruction. The explanation offered was that because of the nonsaliency of the feature, blocking, and the powerful distracting effect of the instruction, the learners did not dual-task and thus did not notice the structure in the input.

It might be argued that the treatment lacked ecological validity (i.e. learners cannot be expected to learn one structure incidentally while their attention is being focused on another), but we would argue differently. In classroom settings, this is exactly what one might expect. Of course, teachers anticipate that learners will learn what they have been explicitly taught – and there is growing evidence that they do (Norris & Ortega, 2000) – but teachers also hope that learners will benefit more broadly from the focused instruction they provide, for, as Allwright (1984) has argued, instruction of any kind involves interaction and 'everything that happens in the classroom happens through a process of live person-to-person interaction'. Instruction focused on a specific grammatical structure affords opportunities for learning in general as well the target structure. Thus, it is important to investigate if this is the case.

Of course, this study does not demonstrate that incidental acquisition cannot take place in the classroom. It shows only that incidental acquisition of third person -s is difficult when the focus is another grammatical structure. It remains to be shown whether easier-to-acquire structures can or cannot be acquired under the same conditions. It also remains to be shown whether difficult structures like third person -s are acquirable incidentally when the dual tasking involves a focus on meaning rather than a focus on another structure.

Notes

1. Hulstijn (2003) distinguished two types of incidental learning studies in psychology. Type 1 studies ask learners to learn a set of stimuli (e.g. a list of words) with orienting instructions that did not inform them that they would be tested on completion of a task. In Type 2 studies, additional stimuli (e.g. specific morphological features in the list of words) that the participants were not told about were included in the task and subsequently tested. The study we conducted was an example of Type 2.
2. There are a large number of studies that have investigated the acquisition of L2 vocabulary. See Hulstijn (2003) for a review.
3. A further account of the learning difficulty of third person -s can be found in explanations based on Universal Grammar. However, as Lardiere (1998) pointed out, the theory affords a number of competing hypotheses, depending on the version of the linguistic model, which L2 studies have failed to resolve.
4. This analysis was not carried out on the Untimed Grammaticality Judgment scores as these were much higher than the Elicited Oral Imitation Test and did not permit dividing the groups into subgroups according to their pre-test scores.
5. We were not able to test Pienemann's (2005) claim that third person -s can only be acquired if learners have achieved the requisite prior processing device, for a number of reasons. First, we possessed no data relating to structures governed by prior processing devices. Second, Pienemann's theory of processability relates to 'onset' (i.e. the ability to produce at least two exemplars of a feature in free production) rather than to 'control' and our measures only provided information about 'control'. However, there are other grounds for believing that the learner's level of proficiency will affect processability. Learners with high proficiency will be better equipped to engage in dual tasking, as suggested by VanPatten's (1990) study.

Chapter 12

The Effects of Two Types of Input on Intake and the Acquisition of Implicit and Explicit Knowledge

HAYO REINDERS and ROD ELLIS

Introduction

The importance of ample input for second language (L2) acquisition is uncontroversial. At the same time, evidence exists (e.g. from studies in immersion settings) to show that even with massive exposure, certain aspects of the language develop slowly or not at all (Swain, 1988). This appears to apply especially to formal features that are semantically redundant and/or that are difficult to notice. The study of the incidental acquisition of third person -s reported in the preceding chapter provided clear evidence of this, as the learners failed to improve their accuracy of this feature despite intensive exposure to it. It appears that such features require some form of instructional intervention, although it remains unclear what type of intervention is most effective. One instructional possibility is 'input enhancement'.

The term input enhancement was used by Sharwood-Smith (1991, 1993) to refer to attempts to direct the learner's attention to a specific linguistic form in the input. Sharwood-Smith argued that this term is to be preferred to the earlier term he used to refer to the same idea ('consciousness-raising') because it makes no assumption as to whether the input alters the learner's mental state. 'Input enhancement implies only that we can manipulate aspects of the input but makes no further assumptions about the consequences of that input for the learner' (Sharwood-Smith, 1993: 176). Sharwood-Smith includes a number of techniques under the umbrella term of 'input enhancement' and makes a distinction between positive and negative input enhancement. The former refers to the manipulation of the input that learners are exposed to. The latter refers to input that is enhanced by means of explicit instruction and/or corrective feedback. In this chapter, we are concerned only with positive input enhancement. We will also make a distinction between 'input enrichment' (such as in the treatment in the preceding chapter) and 'input enhancement'.

This chapter reports a study that investigated the effect of two different types of input on both the intake and acquisition of a difficult grammatical structure (negative adverbs). The first of these (input enrichment) constitutes a form of implicit instruction, whereas the second (input enhancement) is more explicit in nature. As in the previous studies in this part of the book, the effect of the instruction will be measured in terms of both implicit and explicit L2 knowledge. First, the key constructs that inform the study will be defined. Then, a number of studies that have examined the types of input we are interested in will be examined.

Definition of the Key Constructs

The specific types of input we are interested in are (1) 'enriched input' (i.e. input that has been seeded with the target structure so that learners are exposed to a high frequency over a period of time) and (2) 'enhanced input' (i.e. enriched input combined with an explicit instruction to the learners to pay attention to the target structure – i.e. 'noticing instruction'). Both constitute *focus on form* techniques, as this construct was defined by Doughty and Williams (1998a). That is, focus-on-form instruction is an attempt to focus learners' attention on form in the context of an activity where their primary attention is on meaning. The particular feature of focus-on-form instruction that the two types of input address is what Doughty and Williams (1998b) refer to as 'learner attention', which they differentiate in terms of whether the technique involves 'attracted' attention or 'directed' attention. Enriched input, we would argue, constitutes an example of attracted attention, as the high density of sentences containing the target structure is predicted to cause the learners to notice it. In contrast, enhanced input (i.e. enriched input combined with an explicit instruction to pay attention to the target structure) constitutes 'directed attention'. Both types can be considered examples of unobtrusive focus-on-form in Doughty and Williams' taxonomy. In this respect, they contrast with obtrusive techniques such as input-processing instruction (VanPatten, 1996) and consciousness-raising tasks (Fotos & Ellis, 1991).

Enriched input is input where a specific L2 feature occurs with high frequency (sometimes referred to as 'input flooding'). Studies that have investigated enriched input draw on Schmidt's Noticing Hypothesis (1990, 1994), which states that, in order for learners to acquire from input, they must first pay conscious attention to exemplars of particular forms. By artificially increasing the saliency of the target structure, it is thought that learners will notice and thus acquire the structure more easily.

Enriched input in the context of a meaning-focused activity caters to *incidental learning*. This is defined operationally by Hulstijn (2003) as the learning that results when learners are provided with L2 input without telling them that they will be tested afterwards. One way in which this can be achieved is by engaging learners in a communicative activity where their attention is focused on extracting meaning from input and then testing whether they have learned a specific linguistic feature in the input. As Hulstijn points out (and as noted in Chapter 11) most of the studies of incidental acquisition have examined vocabulary and there are very few studies that have investigated grammar learning. In the study reported in this chapter, participants in the enriched input condition were asked to complete meaning-focused tasks, but were not told they would be tested on the target structure (or tested at all). It should be noted, however, that this condition differs from that in the preceding chapter in that here no attempt was made to distract the learners' attention by focusing on a different grammatical structure. Learners were free to attend to the target structure (negative adverbials) as they processed the input for meaning.

Enhanced input is input where the target feature has been emphasized in some way – glossing, bolding or underlining. In the present study, the input was enhanced by directing students' attention explicitly to the target structure. As such, it encouraged intentional learning. However, in a context where the learners' attention was primarily focused on the meaning of the input and where they were simply asked to look out for the target structure and were not forewarned they would be tested on the structure, it is less clear that they would engage in intentional learning.

Noticing refers to the cognitive activity that learners engage in when they consciously attend to some linguistic feature in the input. Once learners have noticed a feature, they are able to rehearse it in short-term memory and thus increase the likelihood of acquiring it (i.e. integrating it into their interlanguage). Input can be enhanced by means of an instruction to the learners to pay attention to a specific feature. The instruction might simply ask the learners to look out for exemplars of the target feature or it might ask them to try to work out the rule to explain how the target feature works. Both types of instruction are likely to encourage *intentional learning*, but the former (the type investigated in this study) probably less than the latter.

The study also draws on two other constructs: intake and acquisition. As McLaughlin (1987: 13) pointed out, the term *intake* 'has taken on a number of different meanings, and it is not always clear what a particular investigator means in using it'. Some theorists view intake as an initial stage of learning, intermediate between input and acquisition. Gass (1997), for example, distinguishes a number of stages starting from raw input. She suggests that several factors (including time pressure, frequency, affect, salience, associations and prior knowledge) influence whether input gets noticed, or apperceived. Apperception is conceptualized as a priming device that prepares the learner for the possibility of subsequent analysis and intake, which Gass (1997: 5) defines as the 'process of assimilating linguistic material'. Intake can thus be conceptualized as apperceived input that has been further processed. Other theorists, however, use the term to refer to the entire process of acquisition. Chaudron (1985: 1), for example, defines it as 'the mediating process between the target language available to learners as input and the learners' internalized set of L2 rules and strategies for second language development'. Kumaravadivelu (1994) likewise defines intake as a complex process starting with detection and ending with acquisition. It is difficult to see how intake can be distinguished from learning in such definitions. In this study, we adopt Gass' position and seek to distinguish intake from acquisition. We define intake as a subset of the detected input (comprehended or not) that is held in short-term memory and from which connections with long-term memory may be created or strengthened.

Not surprisingly given the differences in the definition of intake, a range of operationalizations of this construct exists. Rosa and O'Neill (1999) recommend using performance measures such as recall protocols, cloze tests, grammaticality judgments and rule formation, all to be administered soon after the treatment or exposure to the target input. Leow (1993, 1995) also used multiple-choice recognition tasks and gave participants very limited time to complete the tasks, which were administered immediately after exposure. Shook (1994) made use of both production tests (a cloze test and a sentence completion) and a recognition test (a multiple-choice sentence completion), all of which were administered immediately following the exposure. Shook (1994: 85) claims that 'it is most improbable that the data collection procedures used could reflect anything except the immediacy of Process I (the input-to-intake stage), and thus this study does not reflect any acquisition of the grammatical input'. What is common to all these methods is the attempt to probe what is held beyond short-term memory and to avoid measuring existing knowledge. The key lies in assessing what learners have noticed immediately after (but not during) exposure to input. In this study, we used a production measure; we took correct use of the target structures in written output produced shortly after exposure to the enhanced input as evidence of intake.

The final construct we will consider is *L2 knowledge*. As in the rest of this book, two types of knowledge are distinguished – *implicit knowledge* and *explicit knowledge*. These two types of knowledge were defined in Chapter 1. The acquisition of these two types of knowledge can be measured using grammaticality judgment tests (GJT). In Chapters 2 and 4, it was shown that a GJT with limited response times predisposes learners to draw more on implicit knowledge, while a test with unlimited response times can allow learners to access more explicit knowledge, especially in the case of the ungrammatical sentences in the test. This is the approach to measuring acquisition that was followed in this study.

Previous Studies of Enriched and Enhanced Input

The following review will only consider studies where the target feature was a grammatical one. It will include studies where learners were simply exposed to enriched input and studies where learners' attention was directed towards the target structure (i.e. an attempt was made to induce noticing of the target structure).

A key question regarding the efficacy of enriched and enhanced input is whether learners actually notice the target structure. This was investigated in a study by Jourdenais *et al.* (1995). They found that English-speaking learners of L2 Spanish were more likely to make explicit reference to preterit and imperfect verb forms when thinking aloud during a narrative writing task if they had previously read texts where the forms were graphologically highlighted. They also found that the learners exposed to the enhanced text were more likely to use past tense forms than the learners who just read an enriched text (i.e. a text with the same number of target items but with no enhancement).

A number of studies have investigated whether enriched input results in acquisition. Trahey and White (1993) examined whether an 'input flood' (viewed as 'positive input') was sufficient to enable francophone learners of L2 English to learn that English permits adverb placement between the subject and the verb (French does not), but does not permit placement between the verb and object (French does). Exposure occurred one hour a day for 10 days. The target structure was not highlighted in any way. The learners succeeded in learning the subject-adverb-verb (SAV) position, but failed to 'unlearn' the ungrammatical subject-verb-adverb-object (SVAO) position. In a follow-up test administered one year after the treatment, however, Trahey (1996) found that the beneficial effects of the input flood on the acquisition of SAV had disappeared.

J. White (1998) compared the effects of three types of input: (1) typographically enhanced input flood plus extensive listening and reading, (2) typographically enhanced input by itself, and (3) a typically unenhanced input flood (i.e. what we have called 'enriched input'). This study found that the three types of input worked equally effectively in assisting Francophone learners to acquire the possessive pronouns *his* and *her*, leading White to conclude that the target structure was equally salient in all three.

Very few studies have investigated the effect of input that has been enhanced by means of noticing instructions. Leeman *et al.* (1995) examined the effects of input enhancement on the acquisition of preterit and imperfect Spanish verb forms that were highlighted in written input.

The learners were told to pay special attention to how temporal relations were expressed in Spanish and also received corrective feedback from the teacher. Post-tests showed that the learners outperformed a comparison group that did not receive the enhanced input. However, because they received instruction involving several options, it is not possible to claim that the benefits were solely due to the enhanced input.

Leow's (1998) study also investigated the effects of a noticing instruction. Following Tomlin and Villa (1994), Leow distinguished three levels of noticing (alertness, orientation and detection) and set out to investigate these by asking learners of L2 Spanish to complete a crossword that required attention to the irregular third-person singular and plural preterit forms of stem changing -*ir* verbs. Orientation was operationalized through a noticing instruction: 'Please note that some of the forms of the verbs are irregular'. The opportunity for detection was provided by ensuring that the irregular forms needed to complete some of the clues were available in a number of other clues. While all four groups were designated as + alertness, they differed in terms of whether they were -orientation/-detection (Group 1 – the control group), + orientation/-detection (Group 2), + orientation/ + detection (Group 3) or -orientation/ + detection (Group 4). The results showed that Groups 3 and 4 outperformed both the control group and Group 2 on all the post-tests, but did not differ significantly themselves. In other words, the groups that had the opportunity to detect the target forms in the input outperformed those that did not, and simply orientating the learners to the existence of the form without the opportunity for detection had no effect.

A number of studies have investigated the effects of instruction that involved simple exposure to the target structure through enriched/ enhanced input together with instruction that included explicit reference to the target structure (often in the form of rule presentation).

Alanen (1995) conducted a study with four groups; (1) a control group, (2) an 'enhancement group' that received input in two 15-minute instructional periods, (3) a 'rule group' that received just explicit instruction and (4) a 'rule + enhanced group' that received both enriched input and explicit instruction. The enhanced input took the form of two short texts in which the target features had been italicized. Learning was measured by means of a sentence completion task, a grammaticality judgment task and a rule statement task. The learners were also asked to think aloud during the treatment. The main finding was that Groups (3) and (4) outperformed Groups (1) and (2). Also, there was no difference between Groups (1) and (2) or between Groups (3) and (4). One reason why the enhanced input in (2) had no clear effect on acquisition in this study might have been that the period of instruction was too short.

Rosa and O'Neill (1999) compared the effects of instruction directed at learning the Spanish contrary to fact conditional (a complex structure) by university-level learners of L2 Spanish. Four types of instruction were included in this study; (1) rule explanation + rule search, (2) rule explanation + no rule search, (3) no rule explanation + rule search, (4) no rule explanation + no rule search; (3) corresponds to what we have called 'enhanced input' and (4) to 'enriched input'. Acquisition was measured by means of a time-pressured multiple-choice recognition task, while think-aloud protocols were used to measure awareness of the rule. Awareness was operationalized as a verbal reference to the target feature during task execution and thus might be considered a measure of intake. Two types of awareness were distinguished – 'noticing' if no reference was made to the underlying rules and 'understanding' if there was. All the groups improved from pre- to post-test. The instructed condition (i.e. (1)) proved superior to the enriched input-only condition (i.e. (4)). Also, more aware participants, both those showing greater 'noticing' and those showing greater 'understanding', performed better on the multiple-choice recognition task.

Radwan (2005) also investigated the effects of instruction involving a focus on meaning-only compared with input enhancement and rule provision on learning and awareness of English dative alternation. He also investigated if differences in awareness affected learning. Forty-two lower-intermediate participants were pre-tested for prior knowledge of the target structure, and one day later given a short story to read which contained a high number of datives. Reading of the short story was followed by comprehension questions. The next day, a similar treatment was administered, but in addition, participants were given a narration task that involved describing a set of pictures. Participants were asked to think aloud while completing the task in order for the researcher to gauge their awareness. The treatments were followed by a post-test (one day later) and a delayed post-test (one month later). A control group only completed the tests. Radwan found a significant advantage for the rule-group over the other groups, which failed to make significant progress. This advantage was maintained on the delayed post-test. He also found that participants showing a greater degree of awareness during the narration task did better on the tests. However, awareness at the level of noticing was not as good a predictor of learning as awareness at the level of understanding.

It is not easy to draw clear conclusions from these studies. Although they have investigated what appear to be similar constructs (e.g. enhanced/enriched input, noticing, intake, directed learning), they have operationalized these in very different ways, drawing on very different disciplines in doing so (i.e. different schools of psychology and language pedagogy). As a result, it is difficult to compare results. The following conclusions, therefore, must be viewed as tentative:

(1)   There is some evidence that enriched and enhanced input can help L2 learners acquire some new grammatical features and use partially learned features more consistently, although it may not enable learners to eradicate erroneous rules from their interlanguage. Enriched input appears to work best if the instructional treatment provided learners with extensive exposure to the target features and was relatively prolonged (i.e. 'input flooding'). Enhanced input generally is more effective, especially if it includes a noticing instruction to assist noticing.
(2)   Noticing appears to be related to learning, especially if it involves 'detection' and 'awareness'.
(3)   Simple exposure to enriched input typically results in low levels of awareness of the target structure.
(4)   Exposure to enriched input has been consistently shown to be less effective than instruction that is more explicit (e.g. a rule-search or an explicit instruction condition).

Finally, it is worth noting that none of the studies reviewed above attempted to distinguish the effects of enriched/enhanced input on the acquisition of implicit and explicit L2 knowledge. It should also be noted that many of the studies used GJTs to measure acquisition, but invariably these were of the untimed type.

The study reported below builds on the previous research by examining the effects of enriched and enhanced input. There were two conditions: (1) enriched input (i.e. input that has been seeded with the target structure) and (2) enhanced input (i.e. enriched input combined with a noticing instruction). A unique feature of the study is that it will examine the effects of these two types of input on both intake and acquisition. A further feature is that we will attempt to distinguish what has been acquired in terms of implicit and explicit knowledge.

Method

The research questions this study addressed were:

(1)   What are the effects of enriched/enhanced input on (a) *intake* and (b) *acquisition* of English negative adverbs?
(2)   What difference is there in the effects of two types of input (i.e. enriched input and enhanced input) on (a) *intake* and (b) *acquisition* of English negative adverbs?

The input conditions were operationalized by means of three reproduction tasks. In the case of the enriched input condition, learners completed meaning-focused tasks that had been seeded with several examples of negative adverbs. In the case of the enhanced output condition, learners completed the same tasks but were also instructed to pay attention to the position of the auxiliary verb in the sentences in the input. Measures of intake were obtained from the participants' performance of the treatment tasks. Acquisition was measured by means of a timed and an untimed GJT.

Design

Participants completed the pre-tests and were then randomly assigned to one of the two treatment conditions (enriched input versus enhanced input). Participants completed a treatment task in their selected condition on three separate occasions. Immediately following the third occasion, the post-tests (a timed and an untimed GJT) were administered. The delayed post-tests were administered one week later. There was no separate control group in the study. However, as an alternative to a control group, the participants' performance on the items measuring knowledge of negative adverbs (the target structure) was compared with their performance on distractor items in the tests. Table 12.1 summarizes the design of the study.

Participants

The participants were 28 students from an upper-intermediate proficiency level in a New Zealand private English language school. They volunteered to join the study in exchange for financial compensation of approximately NZD$10 per hour. Sixteen of the participants were female and 12 male. Fifteen participants came from East Asia (Japan, Korea, China) and four came from Switzerland. Altogether, the participants came from a total of 11 different countries and had 10 different first

Table 12.1 Design of the study

Week 1 – Pre-test (all participants)	
Week 2-3-4 – Treatments	
	Negative adverbs
Enriched input	$n = 17$
Enhanced input	$n = 11$
Week 4	Immediate post-test
Week 5	Delayed post-test

languages. Most of the participants had lived in an English-speaking country for less than six months.

The participants had been given an in-house placement test earlier in the year to determine their class level. After one week, consultation between the student and the classroom teacher, and where necessary the Director of Studies, took place. The school considered upper-intermediate level students to be the equivalent of level B2 of the European Framework. That is, it was expected that students

> Can understand the main ideas of complex text on both concrete and abstract topics, including technical discussions in his/her own field of specialization. Can interact with a degree of fluency and spontaneity that makes regular interaction with native speakers quite possible without strain for either party. Can produce clear detailed text on a wide range of subjects and explain a viewpoint on a topical issue giving the advantages and disadvantages of various options. (Council of Europe, 1996)

Learners at the upper-intermediate level were used in this study in an attempt to ensure that they had not yet acquired the target structure (negative adverbs) but were developmentally ready to do so.

Target structure

The target structure was negative adverbs with inversion of subject and auxiliary, as in the example:

Seldom **had he** seen such a beautiful woman.

Other negative adverbs requiring subject-verb inversion are 'never', 'rarely', 'seldom' and 'hardly'.

R. Ellis (2006; Chapter 6) proposed a number of criteria for determining the level of difficulty of grammatical structures as implicit and explicit knowledge. The difficulty of negative adverbs is now considered in the light of these criteria.

(1) Difficulty of negative adverbs as implicit knowledge
    Input frequency; negative adverbs are relatively rare as confirmed by an analysis of the British National Corpus (frequency ranged from 276 occurrences for 'not only was' to 3 for 'seldom do' and fewer for a range of other adverb/auxiliary combinations).
    Saliency; negative adverbs can be considered salient in that they are sentence-initial, but the inversion of subject and verb, which involves the use of an auxiliary, is probably less salient as the auxiliary is typically unstressed.
    Functional value; the 'function' of this structure (the negative meaning associated with the adverb) is conveyed lexically and thus the subject-verb inversion is redundant.

Regularity; only negative adverbs require subject-verb inversion – other adverbs of time, place and manner (e.g. 'yesterday', 'there' and 'rapidly') take normal subject-verb word order.

Processability; in terms of Pienemann's (1998, 2005) hierarchical processing operations, negative adverbs with subject-verb inversion will be late acquired (i.e. they involve what Pienemann refers to as S-procedure).

(2) Difficulty of negative adverbs as explicit knowledge

Conceptual clarity; negative adverbs with subject-verb inversion are functionally relatively simple but formally complex as they involve a variety of auxiliary forms; the declarative rule required to explain them is also not easily extractible from data.

Metalanguage; it will be difficult to avoid the use of metalanguage in articulating the declarative rule for negative adverbs (e.g. 'adverb', 'negative', 'auxiliary', 'subject', 'main verb').

In short, Ellis' criteria indicate that negative adverbs with subject-verb inversion constitute a difficult structure for both implicit and explicit knowledge. It should be noted, however, that Robinson (1996) used negative adverbs as his 'easy rule'. Perhaps it can be considered 'easy' in comparison with the other structure Robinson investigated (pseudo-clefts of location), but it is likely that many learners will fail to acquire negative adverb structures without some form of instructional intervention. The purpose of the study was to examine whether intervention in the form of enriched/enhanced input could assist them to acquire it.

Treatment

This study used three types of treatment tasks (described below). Each treatment task consisted of oral or written input in the form of a text about a range of general interest topics that had been seeded with several instances of the target structure (i.e. the texts were enriched in terms of the frequency of the target structure). In total, each student was exposed to 36 sentences with negative adverbs. The nature of the exposure differed. In the case of the *enriched input condition*, the learners were simply instructed to complete the tasks. That is, they were given no indication of what to look out for. In the case of the *enhanced input condition*, the learners were given the following instruction:

Listen carefully and pay attention to where the auxiliary verb comes in each sentence. For example in the sentence "Rarely has so much rain fallen in such a short time" the auxiliary is "has" and it comes before the subject of the sentence "so much rain".

That is, in the enhanced condition their attention was specifically and explicitly drawn to the target structure.

Each student completed one of the three types of tasks described below. Each student took part in three treatment sessions involving the same type of task. It should be noted that although different students completed different tasks, all three types of tasks figured equally in both the enriched input and the enhanced input conditions. In the case of the former, five students completed the dictation task, five completed the individual reconstruction task and seven completed the collaborative reconstruction task. In the case of the latter, four students completed the dictation task, three completed the individual reconstruction task and four completed the collaborative reconstruction task. The treatment tasks were:

(1) *Dictation.* Participants were asked to listen to a passage of about 60–70 words on a computer and write it out section by section as in a standard dictation. Before the actual treatment, they completed three practice passages. Participants first listened to the entire passage and then again section by section while writing out each section as they heard it. Each section contained no more than 10 words and mostly around seven or eight. The treatment thus involved immediate recall. There were four passages containing three target sentences in each treatment session.

(2) *Individual reconstruction.* The individual reconstruction treatment involved delayed rather than immediate recall of the texts. Participants were asked to listen twice to a passage of about 60–70 words. Participants were allowed to take notes. They then attempted to reconstruct it by writing it out. While they were doing this, they were asked to talk-aloud (Ericsson & Simon, 1993). Instructions for this treatment were in the form of a video demonstrating talk-aloud.

(3) *Collaborative reconstruction.* The collaborative reconstruction treatment was similar to the individual reconstruction treatment except that two participants were paired and were asked to reconstruct the text together. It therefore also involved delayed recall.

It should be noted that differences in performance of these three tasks was not the focus of the study reported in this chapter, as both the enriched input and enhanced input conditions involved all three tasks.

Tests

The same tests were administered on three occasions – as a pre-test, an immediate post-test and a delayed post-test (see Table 12.1). There were two tests: a timed GJT and an untimed GJT. A description of these follows.

Timed GJT

This test consisted of 50 sentences, 20 of which contained negative adverbs. Of these, 10 were grammatical and 10 ungrammatical sentences. The other 30 items consisted of sentences with other adverbial structures relating to adverb position and to the difference in form between adverbs and adjectives. In this test, sentences were shown on screen and participants had to press the 'enter' key if they thought the sentence on the screen was correct and the left-hand 'shift' key if they thought it was not correct. The keys were labeled with stickers indicating 'correct' and 'incorrect'. There were eight practice sentences during which the researcher was present to give clarification where needed. The test was developed in the same way as the timed GJT in Chapters 2 and 4. That is, it was first trialled on native speakers and similar learners in order to establish a time limit for each sentence. The time limit for each sentence was longer than the mean time taken by the native speakers on that sentence, but shorter than that of the non-native speakers. The learners were given relatively more time on the earlier than the later items in the test. They were told that they might not be able to respond to all the items in time, but that they should try to answer as many as they could.

Untimed GJT

The untimed test contained the same sentences (but in a different order) as the timed test. There was no time limit for judging each sentence. Students entered their responses on the computer as for the timed GJT.

Previous research (see Chapters 2 and 4) has shown that timed and untimed GJTs measure separate constructs. In line with the findings of these studies, we propose that the timed GJT (especially the grammatical sentences) provides a measure of the learners' implicit knowledge and the untimed GLT (ungrammatical sentences) provides a measure of their explicit knowledge.

The reliabilities of negative adverb items and the control items were assessed by means of Cronbach's alpha and are shown in Table 12.2. The alphas ranged from a high of 0.928 to a low of 0.605.

Table 12.2 Reliability alphas for the grammaticality judgment tests

	Pre Tim	*Pre Unt*	*Post Tim*	*Post Unt*	*Dpt Tim*	*Dpt Unt*
Control	0.841	0.725	0.928	0.789	0.84	0.852
Negative adverb	0.605	0.770	0.779	0.882	0.732	0.857

Pre = pre-test, Post = post-test, Dpt = delayed post-test, Tim = timed, Unt = untimed.

Analysis

The tasks and tests completed by the learners were used to obtain the following measures: (1) intake of the target structure, (2) acquisition of L2 implicit knowledge of the target structure, and (3) acquisition of L2 explicit knowledge of the target structure. The measures are described below.

Intake

As discussed in the introduction, intake can be operationalized as information held in short-term memory after exposure to the target language. Intake then, needs to be determined immediately after exposure to the target feature. In the present study, correct suppliance of the target items *during* the treatments was taken as a measure of intake. The time between hearing the input and reproducing it was sufficiently long to prohibit mimicking, but sufficiently short for it to remain in short-term memory. This is self-evidently the case for the individual and collaborative reconstruction tasks, as the learners could not have memorized the whole texts they had heard. It was also likely in the dictation task as the chunks the learners were asked to reproduce were too long for easy memorization. The reproductions of the learners were inspected and occasions where they attempted to reproduce a sentence with a negative adverb identified. Responses were judged as correct as long as the participants inverted subject and auxiliary. Spelling and other errors not relating to the target structures were discounted (e.g. one learner spelt 'do' as 'to'). Also, there was no expectancy that learners would reproduce the exact words of an input sentence. For example, for the sentence 'No sooner does there seem to be a solution then another problem arises', one learner responded:

No sooner is it solution ... and the other problem is the ice

Here, the wrong auxiliary was chosen but the word order was correct so the sentence was scored as correct. However, any sentence starting with an adverb and followed by a subject were scored as 'incorrect'. Sentences with no auxiliary (e.g. *No sooner that I arrived...*) or without a subject (e.g. *No sooner had arrive*) were also scored as incorrect.

Implicit L2 knowledge

The implicit knowledge scores were arrived at by totaling the number of correct judgments that the learners made in the timed GJT. Total scores and also separate scores for the 10 grammatical and the 10 ungrammatical sentences were calculated as previous research has indicated that these measure separate constructs (R. Ellis, 2005; Hedgcock, 1993). To measure acquisition of implicit L2 knowledge, gain scores from pre- to immediate post-test, from pre- to delayed post-test and from immediate to delayed post-test were calculated.

Explicit L2 knowledge

A similar scoring procedure was followed for measuring explicit L2 knowledge, but this time the responses to the untimed GJT were used. Again, total scores and separate scores for the grammatical and ungrammatical sentences were calculated. To measure acquisition of explicit L2 knowledge, gain scores from pre- to immediate post-test, from pre- to delayed post-test and from immediate to delayed post-test were calculated.

Control items

Learners' responses to the 30 items in the GJTs that did not contain the target structure were used as the control items in this study. Total scores on these items together with scores for the grammatical and ungrammatical items separately were calculated. Gain scores were then computed.

As participants in the study completed multiple treatments and tests, repeated measures analysis of variance models (ANOVAs) were used to investigate group differences. For *post-hoc* analyses the Least Significant Differences (LSD) method was used. This method is considered liberal in that it compares means for all possible data sources separately, rather than combined. Considering the fairly small number of data sources, and considering that the present study was exploratory, the use of LSD was deemed acceptable. For all statistical analyses the alpha level was set at 0.05.

Results

First, the results for intake will be presented followed by those for acquisition.

Intake

Table 12.3 shows the enriched input and enhanced input groups' scores for intake of negative adverbs. The results show a clear improvement for scores obtained by both groups from Time 1 to Time 2 and from Time 2 to Time 3. The time difference was statistically significant ($F(1,81) = 28.82$, $p < 0.001$). Scores for the enhanced input group are higher at treatment Time 2 and Time 3 than those for the enriched input group. However, a one-way ANOVA did not show a significant effect for

Table 12.3 Intake scores for negative adverbs

	Time 1		*Time 2*		*Time 3*	
	Mean	*SD*	*Mean*	*SD*	*Mean*	*SD*
Enriched input ($n = 17$)	0.155	0.152	0.328	0.236	0.441	0.276
Enhanced input ($n = 11$)	0.126	0.113	0.454	0.356	0.606	0.327

treatment condition $(F(1,81) = 2.41, p = 0.124)$. A t-test for two independent groups also failed to show a significant difference for the Time 3 scores $(t = 1.436;$ df 26; $p = 0.348)$.

Acquisition

Gain scores for the timed and untimed GJTs were calculated separately. Table 12.4 shows the mean gain scores (1) from pre-test to post-test, (2) from pre-test to delayed post-test, and (3) from post-test to delayed post-test for the timed GJTs. Gain scores from pre- to post-tests were higher for the enriched input than the enhanced input group. They were also higher for the grammatical than the ungrammatical items.

First, the differences between total gain scores on target and control items were compared by means of a 2 (negative adverbs/control) × 3 (gain scores) repeated measures ANOVA. This showed no statistically significant difference $(F(1,333) = 1.16, p = 0.283)$. In other words, the instruction had no effect on acquisition of negative adverbs as measured by total scores of the timed tests. However, for the grammatical items in the timed tests, the gain scores for the negative adverbs were significantly greater than for the control items $(F(1,165) = 9.71, p = 0.002)$ with a medium effect size $(d = 0.48)$. There was also a significant difference on the ungrammatical items $(F(1,165) = 4.49, p = 0.035)$, but this was to the advantage of the control items.

Next, an ANOVA was performed to establish if there was an effect for instructional condition. This was not the case for gain scores on the grammatical items from pre-test to post-test $(F(1,54) = 0.31, p = 0.581)$. However, from pre-test to delayed post-test there was a difference $(F(1,54) = 4.95, p = 0.03)$, to the advantage of the enriched input condition. The effect size was $(d = 0.62)$.

Descriptive statistics for the untimed GJT are shown in Table 12.5. The gain scores for the negative adverb grammatical (but not ungrammatical) items are generally larger than those for the control items. Both the enriched input and the enhanced input groups manifested gains on the grammatical but not the ungrammatical items.

A 2 (target/control) × 3 (gain scores) repeated measures ANOVA using total scores showed no significant difference between negative adverb and control items $(F(1,333) = 0.147, p = 0.225)$, indicating that instruction had no overall effect on participants' acquisition of negative adverbs as measured by the untimed tests. However, in the case of the grammatical items, a significant difference was found $(F(1,165) = 15.75, p < 0.001)$ with a medium effect size $(d = 0.611)$. Gains were greater for the negative adverb items. For ungrammatical items there was a significant difference between gain scores on negative adverb and control items $(F(1,165) = 5.37, p = 0.021)$; however, this was to the advantage of the control items.

Table 12.4 Gain scores negative adverbs and controls on the timed GJTs

NA Timed tests	Negative adverbs				Controls			
	Grammatical		*Ungrammatical*		*Grammatical*		*Ungrammatical*	
	Gain	*SD*	*Gain*	*SD*	*Gain*	*SD*	*Gain*	*SD*
Pre-test to post-test								
Enriched input (*n* = 17)	0.241	0.245	0.058	0.2	− 0.041	0.197	0.15	0.213
Enhanced input (*n* = 11)	0.118	0.357	0.072	0.241	− 0.009	0.347	0.127	0.2
Pre-test to delayed post-test								
Enriched input (*n* = 17)	0.311	0.228	0.076	0.301	0.052	0.18	0.12	0.141
Enhanced input (*n* = 11)	0.081	0.354	− 0.027	0.296	− 0.081	0.389	0.213	0.23
Post-test to delayed post-test								
Enriched input (*n* = 17)	0.07	0.323	0.017	0.283	0.094	0.265	− 0.029	0.261
Enhanced input (*n* = 11)	− 0.036	0.456	− 0.1	0.322	− 0.072	0.337	0.086	0.282

Table 12.5 Gain scores for negative adverbs and controls on the untimed GJTs

NA Untimed tests	Negative adverbs				Control			
	Grammatical		Ungrammatical		Grammatical		Ungrammatical	
	Gain	SD	Gain	SD	Gain	SD	Gain	SD
Pre-test to post-test								
Enriched input (n = 17)	0.229	0.271	−0.058	0.19	−0.035	0.176	0	0.269
Enhanced input (n = 11)	0.218	0.292	−0.1	0.282	0.054	0.211	0.04	0.204
Pre-test to delayed post-test								
Enriched input (n = 17)	0.252	0.316	−0.041	0.308	−0.011	0.226	0.05	0.22
Enhanced input (n = 11)	0.254	0.5	−0.236	0.372	0.09	0.344	−0.004	0.328
Post-test to delayed post-test								
Enriched input (n = 17)	0.023	0.185	0.017	0.255	0.023	0.204	0.05	0.235
Enhanced input (n = 11)	0.136	0.441	−0.136	0.297	0.036	0.254	−0.045	0.342

Next, ANOVAs were performed to establish if there was an effect for instructional condition. No statistically significant differences were found on the gain scores for the grammatical items (pre-test to post-test ($F(1,54) = 0.3$, $p = 0.586$); pre-test to delayed post-test ($F(1,54) = 1.06$, $p = 0.307$); post-test to delayed post-test ($F(1,54) = 0.74$, $p = 0.394$)).

Summary

The following is a summary of the main results:

(1) Intake scores as a whole rose over the period of instruction, but there was no difference between the enriched input and enhanced input groups.
(2) Overall, the instruction had no effect on the acquisition of implicit knowledge as measured by the total scores of the timed GJTs. However, effects were evident when the grammatical and ungrammatical sentences were examined separately. The instruction resulted in higher scores for negative adverb items in the case of the grammatical sentences, but in lower scores than the control items for the ungrammatical sentences. The enriched input group outperformed the enhanced input group in the long term (i.e. in gain scores between pre- and delayed post-test) on the grammatical sentences in the timed GJTs.
(3) Overall, the instruction had no effect on the acquisition of explicit knowledge as measured by total scores on the untimed GJTs. However, again, effects were evident when the grammatical and ungrammatical sentences were examined separately with the same pattern of results as for the timed GJTs. However, there was no statistically significant difference in any of the untimed GJT gain scores between the enriched input and enhanced input groups.

Discussion

The first research question asked what effects enriched/enhanced input had on intake. Intake was measured in terms of the learners' use of the target structure (negative adverbs with subject-verb inversion) in three different reproduction tasks (dictation, individual reconstruction and collaborative reconstruction), which were completed on three different occasions.

An inspection of the means in Table 12.3 shows that on the first occasion intake was negligible (only 16% for the enriched input group and 13% for the enhanced input group). Over time, however, intake increases steadily so that by the third occasion intake scores have reached 44% for the enriched input condition and 61% for the enhanced input group. The time difference was statistically significant. Thus, it would seem that intake increases along with exposure to the target form.

However, there was no statistically significant difference in the intake scores of the enriched input group (which only received exposure to sentences containing negative adverbs) and the enhanced input group (which received the same exposure but was also directed to pay attention to the sentences with negative adverbs). In other words, the noticing instruction did not lead to significantly greater intake. This indicates that it was the repeated exposure to the target structure that enabled the learners to notice the target structure and rehearse it in short-term memory sufficiently to reproduce it. Leow (1998) also found that an orienting instruction had no effect on learners' acquisition of irregular Spanish verb forms. This study reports that a very similar orienting instruction had no effect on learners' intake of a difficult syntactic feature. Clearly, it would be premature to conclude that a noticing instruction is ineffective in assisting acquisition but, to date, there is no evidence that it can be effective.

The second research question concerned whether the enhanced input treatments resulted in acquisition. Acquisition was measured by means of timed and untimed GJTs with a view to providing relatively separate measures of implicit and explicit knowledge.

The intake scores suggest that the learners obtained sufficient information from the tasks to make acquisition of the target structure possible. However, intake does not guarantee acquisition. It is possible that learners are able to notice and rehearse a grammatical form in their short-term memories and therefore reproduce it, yet be unable to integrate it into their interlanguage systems. This is the very point of the theoretical distinction between 'intake' and 'acquisition', as in Gass' (1997) model. The results in Table 12.4 show that, overall, the learners did not perform better on the target items than on the control items in the timed GJT. In other words, there was no evidence that the instruction led to acquisition. However, when the grammatical and ungrammatical items were examined separately, it emerged that the learners performed better on the target items in the case of the former and worse in the case of the latter. Similar results were obtained for the untimed GJT. This asymmetry in performance on grammatical and ungrammatical items has been observed in other studies (e.g. R. Ellis, 2005; Hedgcock, 1993). One interpretation of these results is that the input assisted the acquisition of implicit knowledge, but not explicit knowledge. Such an interpretation makes sense given that the input treatment of both groups in this study favored the development of implicit rather than explicit knowledge. There was no deductive or inductive explicit instruction that might have assisted the development of explicit knowledge. In fact, the noticing instruction seems to have had a deleterious effect on the learners' explicit knowledge of negative adverbs, as the gain scores on the ungrammatical items in both the timed and untimed GJTs were very small and frequently negative. Indeed, in the case of the ungrammatical items of the untimed GJT (arguably the best measure of explicit knowledge), the gain scores of the enhanced input group were all negative. The likely explanation for this is the cognitive difficulty of understanding how this particular structure works without the assistance of detailed explicit instruction.

Given that there was no difference in the intake levels of the two treatment groups, it might be predicted that there should be no difference in their levels of acquisition. This proved to be the case for the gain scores from pre- to immediate post-test on the grammatical items of the timed GJT, but not for the gain scores from pre- to delayed post-test. That is, in the long term, the incidental exposure to enriched input worked better than the exposure to enhanced input. No group differences were evident on the ungrammatical items. What these results suggest is that asking students to consciously attend to the target structure can actually impede the acquisition of implicit knowledge. This result accords with the findings of other studies of incidental instruction. N. Ellis (1993), for example, found that incidental instruction consisting of enriched input worked better than a more explicit form of instruction when the structure was a difficult one.

No group differences were evident on the grammatical or ungrammatical items in the untimed test. It might have been expected that the enhanced input condition would have helped learners improve their ability to judge the ungrammatical items of the untimed GJT if, as we have argued, this constitutes a measure of explicit knowledge. However, as we noted above, the conceptual difficulty of negative adverbs may have prevented the learners from benefiting from deliberate attention to this structure. They were simply unable to work out the rule.

To sum up, enriched input in the form of oral texts seeded with exemplars of a difficult target structure resulted in intake and also in the acquisition of implicit knowledge (as measured by the grammatical sentences of a timed GJT). However, it did not benefit explicit knowledge (as measured by an untimed GJT). Providing learners with a noticing instruction in addition to the enriched input (the enhanced input condition) conferred no advantage for either intake or acquisition, possibly because of the conceptual difficulty of the particular target structure of this study.

Conclusion

This study has shown that enriched input resulted in intake and assisted the acquisition of implicit knowledge. It has also shown that asking students to pay attention to the target structure conferred no additional advantage for either intake or acquisition. The study is supportive of the claims that have been advanced on behalf of focus-on-form instruction (Doughty & Williams, 1998). It shows that even a very unobtrusive focus-on-form strategy can be effective. However, the results of this study do not support Norris and Ortega's (2000) general finding, namely that explicit instruction is more effective than implicit instruction. This might have been because the noticing instruction provided in this study was insufficiently explicit to assist the learners.

We have attempted to look at very specific instructional options. In this respect, our study differs from many others, which have tended to investigate form-focused instruction through treatments that combine a number of options. While such studies may have ecological validity in that they reflect common pedagogical practice, they are problematic where SLA theory testing is concerned. Norris and Ortega (2000) complained that the essential features that distinguish one type of instruction from another have been inconsistently operationalized. This problem can only be overcome if researchers investigate very clearly defined instructional options. If we want to know what effect different forms of input have on L2 acquisition, we need to isolate specific instructional strategies and test for their effect on acquisition.

It is also important to attempt to distinguish the effects of instruction on implicit and explicit knowledge. As Norris and Ortega (2000) and Doughty (2003) have argued, the tests that have been typically used have been biased in favor of explicit knowledge. In this study, we have tried to obtain separate measures of implicit and explicit knowledge using a timed and untimed GJT. We recognize that GJTs in general are controversial (R. Ellis, 1991) and we acknowledge that some readers may remain skeptical of the construct validity of the tests. However, we note that we did obtain different results for the two tests (and also for the grammatical and ungrammatical sentences in the tests) and that these results are interpretable in terms of the general findings reported in Chapters 2 and 4, namely that GJTs can be used to provide relatively separate measures of implicit and explicit knowledge.

Finally, we wish to acknowledge a number of weaknesses of our study. The sample size was relatively small (the enhanced input group had only 11 learners). There was no control group, although we were able to use the nontarget items in the GJTs as a point of comparison. The total exposure time provided by the instruction was relatively limited; arguably, exposure to 36 exemplars of the target structure does not amount to an input-flood. But then it is perhaps all the more impressive that it produced a measurable effect.

Chapter 13

Implicit and Explicit Corrective Feedback and the Acquisition of L2 Grammar[1]

ROD ELLIS, SHAWN LOEWEN and ROSEMARY ERLAM

Introduction

Corrective feedback takes the form of responses to learner utterances that contain an error. The responses can consist of (a) an indication that an error has been committed, (b) provision of the correct target language form or (c) metalinguistic information about the nature of the error, or any combination of these.

There has been a growing interest in the role of corrective feedback in second language acquisition (SLA) in the last decade. A number of descriptive studies based on data collected in classrooms (e.g. Lyster & Ranta, 1997; Panova & Lyster, 2002; Sheen, 2004) and on data collected in a laboratory-type setting (e.g. Iwashita, 2003; Mackey *et al.*, 2003; Philp, 2003) have examined the types of corrective feedback received by learners and the extent to which this feedback is noticed, or uptaken, or both by the learners. Experimental studies have attempted to examine the contribution that corrective feedback makes to acquisition (e.g. Ammar & Spada, 2006; Ayoun, 2004; Han, 2002; Leeman, 2003; Lyster, 2004). This research has addressed, among other issues, the relative efficacy of implicit and explicit types of corrective feedback.

Theoretical Issues

Corrective feedback differs in terms of how implicit or explicit it is. In the case of implicit feedback, there is no overt indicator that an error has been committed, whereas in explicit feedback types there is. Implicit feedback often takes the form of recasts, defined by Long (2006: 2) as 'a reformulation of all or part of a learner's immediately preceding utterance in which one or more non-target like (lexical, grammatical etc.) items are replaced by the corresponding target language form(s), and where, throughout the exchange, the focus of the interlocutors is on meaning not language as an object'. Recasts, therefore, provide positive evidence but, as Nicholas *et al.* (2001) and Ellis and Sheen (2006) have noted, it is not clear whether they also provide negative evidence, as learners may have no conscious awareness that the recast is intended to be corrective. Explicit feedback can take two forms: (a) explicit correction, in which the response clearly indicates that what the learner said was incorrect (e.g. 'No, not goed – went') and thus affords both positive and negative evidence or (b) metalinguistic feedback, defined by Lyster and Ranta (1997: 47) as 'comments, information, or questions related to the well-formedness of the learner's utterance' – for example, 'You need past tense', which affords only negative evidence.

It can also be argued that recasts and explicit corrective strategies differ in terms of whether they cater to implicit or explicit learning. For Long (1996, 2006), recasts work for acquisition precisely because they are implicit, connecting linguistic form to meaning in discourse contexts that promote the microprocessing (i.e. noticing or rehearsing in short-term memory) required for implicit language learning. Doughty (2001), building on Long's rationale for focus-on-form, argued that recasts constitute the ideal means of achieving an 'immediately contingent focus on form' and afford a 'cognitive window' in which learners can rehearse what they have heard and access material from their interlanguage. In contrast, explicit corrective feedback strategies, such as metalinguistic feedback, are more likely to impede the natural flow of communication and to activate the kind of learning mechanisms that result in explicit rather than implicit second language (L2) knowledge. However, such a view is problematic.

First, it is not certain that all recasts are as implicit as Long (1996, 2006) and Doughty (2001) assumed. Some recasts are quite explicitly corrective. Indeed, the kind of corrective recasts that Doughty and Varela (1998) employed in their experimental study were remarkably explicit. They were preceded by a repetition of the learner's utterance with the erroneous elements highlighted by emphatic stress. If the learner did not self-correct, recasts with emphatic stress to draw attention to the reformulated elements followed. Thus, if the corrective force of the recast becomes self-evident, it is difficult to argue that it constitutes an implicit or even a relatively implicit technique. Second, recasts can only work for acquisition if learners notice the changes that have been made to their own utterances, and there are reasons to believe that they do not always do so. Lyster (1998) has shown that the levels of repair in uptake following recasts are notably lower than those following more explicit types of feedback. The findings from Lyster's research, which examined immersion classrooms in Canada, were corroborated by Sheen (2004), who found that repair occurred less frequently following recasts than following explicit correction and metalinguistic feedback in four different instructional contexts (immersion, Canadian English as a second language (ESL), New Zealand ESL and Korean English as a foreign language). Even though repair cannot be taken as a measure of learning, it is reasonable to assume that it constitutes a measure of whether learners have noticed the key linguistic forms (although noticing can occur even if there is no uptake). Further evidence of the difficulty that learners may experience in attending to the key forms comes from a study by Mackey *et al.* (2000), which demonstrated that learners often failed to perceive recasts that contained morphosyntactic reformulations as corrections. Finally, we cannot be certain that recasts promote acquisition of implicit knowledge. Indeed, it is entirely possible that recasts result in explicit knowledge, as demonstrated in Long *et al.* (1998); in this study, eight students who had learned the target structure (Spanish adverb word order) through recasts were able to explicitly and correctly formulate an explanation of the rule. Thus, there are some doubts as to how effective recasts are in promoting learning as well as to what kind of learning and knowledge they cater to.

Second, a case can also be made for the contribution of corrective strategies that are self-evidently corrective to learning. Carroll's (2001) autonomous induction theory posits that feedback can only work for acquisition if the learner recognizes the corrective intentions of the feedback. Additionally, learners must be able to locate the error; Carroll (2001: 355) noted that 'most of the indirect forms of feedback do not locate the error'. Recasts do not overtly signal that an error has been made and may or may not assist in locating the error, depending on whether the recast is full (i.e. the whole erroneous utterance is reformulated) or partial (i.e. only the erroneous part of the utterance is reformulated), as Sheen's (2006) study indicates. In contrast, explicit types of feedback not only make the corrective force clear to the learner, but also give clues as to the exact location of the error. As such, they may be more likely to induce learners to carry out the cognitive comparison between their error and the target form (Ellis, 1994), which is believed to foster acquisition (Schmidt, 1994).

Connectionist models also lend support to explicit error correction. N. Ellis (2005) distinguished between the mechanisms of conscious and unconscious learning, emphasizing the role of attention and consciousness in the former and of connectionist learning in the latter. He proposed the learning sequence in (1).

(1) external scaffolded attention → internally motivated attention → explicit learning → explicit memory → implicit learning → implicit memory, automatization and abstraction

Ellis (1994: 340) went on to suggest that 'conscious and unconscious processes are dynamically involved together in every cognitive task and in every learning episode'. Although he did not suggest that explicit corrective feedback is the ideal mechanism for achieving this continuous synergy (indeed, his discussion of feedback is restricted to recasts), it would seem that the metalinguistic time-outs from communicating afforded by explicit correction constitute a perfect context for melding the conscious and unconscious processes involved in learning. Within the context of a single interactional exchange, such a time-out creates an opportunity for learners to traverse the learning sequence sketched out in (1). Of course, no single exchange can guarantee that the targeted form will enter implicit memory, but repeated exchanges – directed at the same linguistic form – might be expected to do so. Thus, according to such a theoretical perspective, explicit corrective feedback caters not just to explicit learning and explicit memory, but also to implicit learning and implicit memory.

Previous Research on Corrective Feedback

This review will focus on studies that have compared the effects of implicit and explicit corrective feedback on L2 acquisition.[2] A number of other studies have investigated separately whether either implicit or explicit corrective feedback facilitates acquisition. Nicholas *et al.* (2001), Long (2006) and Ellis and Sheen (2006) provided reviews of the research on recasts. In general, the recast studies demonstrated that implicit feedback of this kind can have a beneficial effect on acquisition, especially when the recasts are more explicit in nature (as in Doughty & Varela, 1998). Other studies demonstrated that explicit feedback is of value. Carroll *et al.* (1992), for example, found that a group that received explicit corrective feedback directed at two complex French noun suffixes (*-age* and *-ment*) outperformed a group that received no feedback, although no generalization of learning to nouns not presented during the treatment occurred. Thus, the recast and explicit feedback studies demonstrated that both types of feedback can be effective.

Table 13.1 summarizes 11 studies that have compared implicit and explicit corrective feedback. It is not easy to come to clear conclusions about what these studies reveal due to a number of factors. First, whereas some of the studies are experimental in nature (e.g. Carroll, 2001; Carroll & Swain, 1993; Lyster, 2004; Rosa & Leow, 2004) others are not (e.g. DeKeyser, 1993; Havranek & Cesnik, 2003), as this second group of researchers investigated corrective feedback through *post hoc* analyses of normal classroom lessons. Second, the studies vary in terms of whether they involved laboratory, classroom or computer-based interaction. Third, the nature of the treatment activities performed by the learners in these studies differed considerably. In some cases, the activities involved fairly mechanical exercises (e.g. Carroll, 2001; Carroll & Swain, 1993; Nagata, 1993), in others, communicative tasks (e.g. Leeman, 2003; Muranoi, 2000; Rosa & Leow, 2004) and in others, a mixture of the two (DeKeyser, 1993). Fourth, the treatment also differed in terms of whether

Table 13.1 Studies comparing the effects of different types of corrective feedback

Study	Participants	Target structure	Design	Tests	Results
Carroll and Swain (1993)	100 Spanish adult ESL learners (low-inter-mediate)	Dative verbs	Groups: (A) direct metalinguistic feedback, (B) explicit rejection, (C) recast, (D) indirect metalinguistic feedback, (E) control Treatment: two feedback sessions, each followed by recall (i.e. production without feedback)	Recall production tasks following each feedback session	All the treatment groups performed better than the control group on both recall tasks. Group A outperformed the other groups
Nagata (1993)	32 second-year university learners of L2 Japanese	Japanese passive structures; verbal pre-dicates and particles	Groups: (A) received feedback indicating what was missing or not expected, (B) received same feedback + metalinguistic explanations Treatment: Learners performed computer-based exercises requiring them to respond to sentences produced by an imaginary partner. Sentences were computer-parsed and feedback on errors provided on the basis of group membership	Written test using same format as treatment task	Group B significantly outperformed Group A on particles but not verbal predicates. Learners expressed preference for metalinguistic explanation

Table 13.1 (*Continued*)

Study	Participants	Target structure	Design	Tests	Results
DeKeyser (1993)	25 Dutch high-school seniors learning L2 French	Variety of features, predominantly morpho-syntactic	Groups: (A) extensive explicit corrective feedback during normal class activities, (B) limited explicit corrective feedback Treatment: 10 class periods	Three oral communication tasks (interview, picture description and story-telling) Fill-in-the-blank test Tests administered twice	No statistically significant differences evident between Groups A and B. Learners with high previous achievement, high language aptitude, high extrinsic motivation and low anxiety benefited the most from error correction
Muranoi (2000)	114 first-year Japanese college students	Indefinite article to denote new information	Groups: (A) interaction enhancement (IE) by means of requests for repetition and recasts in communicative task + formal debriefing (explicit grammar explanation), (B) IE + meaning-focused debriefing, (C) control (no IE with meaning-focused debriefing)	Grammaticality Judgment Test Oral production task Written production task Two post-tests five weeks apart	Both experimental groups outperformed the control group on both post-tests. Group A outperformed Group B on post-test 1 but not on post-test 2

Table 13.1 (*Continued*)

Study	Participants	Target structure	Design	Tests	Results
Kim and Mathes (2001)	20 Korean adult ESL learners (high-beginners and intermediate)	Dative verbs	Groups: (A) received explicit metalinguistic feedback, (B) received recasts Treatment period: feedback was presented in two sessions one week apart, each followed by production with no feedback	Controlled production tasks (as in the treatment) without feedback	Differences between performance on first and second production tasks were not significant. Differences between groups for gains in production were not significant. Learners expressed preference for explicit feedback
Carroll (2001)	100 adult low-intermediate ESL learners	Forming nouns from verbs (e.g. 'help' (V) –> 'help/helping' (N)) and distinguishing thing and event nouns	Groups: as in Carroll and Swain (1993)	Elicited verb-noun conversions in a sentence format	All types of feedback helped learners to learn the items targeted by the feedback, but only explicit metalinguistic information (Group A) and indirect prompting (Group D) enabled learners to form a generalization. Recasts did not facilitate generalization

Table 13.1 (*Continued*)

Study	Participants	Target structure	Design	Tests	Results
Havranek and Cesnik (2003)	207 university students specializing in English	Variety of English phonological, lexical and grammatical features	Data on 1700 corrective feedback episodes from normal English lessons	Class-specific tests (translation, correction, reading-aloud and written and spoken completion tasks) directed at corrected items	Effectiveness of corrective feedback techniques was, in order: (1) elicited self-correction, (2) explicit rejection + recast, (3) recast alone
Leeman (2003)	74 first-year university learners of Spanish	Spanish noun-adjective agreement	Groups: (A) recast group, (B) negative evidence group (source or problem indicated but not corrected), (C) enhanced salience with no feedback, (D) control group Treatment: participants performed communicative task one-on-one with researcher	Post and delayed post picture description tasks	Only Groups A and C outperformed the control group on any post-test measure. No difference between Groups A and C
Sanz (2003)	28 first-year university learners of Spanish	Position of clitic pronouns between object and verb	Groups: (A) explicit metalinguistic feedback, (B) implicit feedback (e.g. 'Sorry, try again') Treatment: computer-delivered input processing instruction without prior explicit instruction	Interpretation tests Production tests: (a) sentence completion and (b) written video retelling	Both groups significantly increased their ability to interpret and accurately produce the target structure with no difference between the groups on any measure

Table 13.1 (*Continued*)

Study	Participants	Target structure	Design	Tests	Results
Lyster (2004)	148 (grade 5) 10–11 year olds in a French immersion program	French grammatical gender (articles + nouns)	Groups: (A) received form-focused instruction (FFI) + recasts, (B) FFI+ prompts (including explicit feedback), (C) FFI only, (D) control group	Binary choice test Text completion test (oral production tasks) Object identification test Picture description test Two post-tests: the second administered eight weeks after the first	Group B was the only group to outperform the control group on all eight measures (post-tests 1 and 2). Group A outperformed control group on five of eight measures. Group C outperformed control group on four of eight measures. Statistically significant differences were found between Groups B and C but not between Groups A and B

Table 13.1 (*Continued*)

Study	Participants	Target structure	Design	Tests	Results
Rosa and Leow (2004)[a]	100 adult university learners of L2 Spanish enrolled in advanced courses	Contrary to the fact conditional sentences in the past	Groups: (A) explicit feedback to both correct and incorrect responses involving metalinguistic explanation + opportunity to try again if incorrect, (B) implicit feedback indicating whether the answer was right or wrong, (C) control group Treatment: computer-based exposure to input-based jigsaw task characterized by task essentialness	Three multiple-choice recognition tests and three written controlled production tests Immediate and delayed post-tests	Results presented in terms of old and new items Recognition tests: a statistically significant difference evident between Groups A and B for new but not old items Production tests: a statistically significant difference was evident for the old but not the new items. Both groups outperformed the control group

[a]Rosa and Leow's (2004) study also involved other experimental conditions. These depended on whether there was a prior grammatical explanation of the target feature. The feedback conditions summarized in the table do not include any prior explanation.

it involved output processing (the vast majority of the studies) or input processing (Rosa & Leow, 2004; Sanz, 2003). Fifth, the studies vary considerably in how they operationalized implicit and explicit feedback. Given the importance of this variable, it is discussed in greater detail later in this section. Sixth, variation is evident in how learning was measured: some studies utilized metalinguistic judgments (e.g. Muranoi, 2000), selected response or constrained constructed response formats (e.g. Havranek & Cesnik, 2003; Rosa & Leow, 2004), all of which might be considered to favor the application of explicit knowledge, whereas others opted for a free constructed response format (e.g. Leeman, 2003), which is more likely to tap implicit knowledge. Finally, the studies differ in another important respect: some included an explicit explanation of the grammatical target prior to the practice activity (e.g. Lyster, 2004; Muranoi, 2000), whereas others did not (e.g. Leeman, 2003; Sanz, 2003). These differences in design reflect the different purposes of the studies, not all of which were expressly intended to compare implicit and explicit corrective feedback.

Implicit feedback in these studies has typically taken the form of recasts (Carroll, 2001; Carroll & Swain, 1993; Kim & Mathes, 2001; Leeman, 2003; Lyster, 2004). However, Muranoi (2000) employed both recasts and requests for repetition. Sanz (2003) made use of only requests for repetition ('Sorry, try again'). In Havranek and Cesnik's (2003) classroom study, which investigated naturally occurring corrective feedback, a variety of more or less implicit forms were identified, including recast, rejection + recast and recast + repetition. This bears out the claims of Nicholas *et al.* (2001) and Ellis and Sheen (2006) that recasts actually vary considerably in how implicit or explicit they are. It should be noted, therefore, that the recasts used in the different studies may not have been equivalent in their degree of implicitness versus explicitness.

Explicit feedback has also been operationalized in very different ways. A minimal form of explicit feedback consists of simply indicating that an error has been committed (e.g. Carroll & Swain's (1993) explicit rejection or Leeman's (2003) negative evidence). Rosa and Leow's (2004) implicit condition actually consisted of indicating whether the learners' answers were right or wrong and thus might have been more accurately labeled semi-explicit. Carroll (2001), Carroll and Swain (1993), Nagata (1993) and DeKeyser (1993) distinguished between a form of minimal explicit feedback, involving some specification of the nature of the error, and extensive corrective feedback, involving more detailed metalinguistic knowledge. Lyster's (2004) prompts consisted of clarification requests, repetitions (with the error highlighted suprasegmentally), metalinguistic clues and elicitation of the correct form. Prompts, therefore, include both implicit and explicit forms of feedback. The nonexperimental classroom studies (DeKeyser, 1993; Havranek & Cesnik, 2003) inevitably involved a variety of explicit forms of correction. All these studies examined explicit correction provided online immediately following learner utterances that contained errors. In contrast, Muranoi's (2000) study investigated the effects of providing an explicit grammar explanation after the treatment task had been completed.

Given the substantial differences in the purposes and designs of these studies, care needs to be taken in any attempt to generalize the findings. However, overall, the results point to an advantage for explicit over implicit corrective feedback in studies in which the treatment involved production. Carroll and Swain (1993) and Carroll (2001) reported that the group that received direct metalinguistic feedback outperformed all the other groups in the production of sentences involving dative verbs and noun formation and, also, that this type of feedback aids generalization to novel items. Muranoi (2000) found that the group that received formal debriefing (which included metalinguistic information) outperformed the group that received meaning-focused debriefing, although only on the immediate post-test. Havranek and Cesnik (2003) found that bare recasts were the least effective form of feedback in their classroom study. Lyster (2004) reported that the group that received prompts (which included metalinguistic feedback) performed better than the group that received recasts on both immediate and delayed post-tests. There is also some evidence (Nagata, 1993; Rosa & Leow, 2004) that when the comparison involves explicit feedback of both a greater or lesser type, it is the more detailed metalinguistic feedback that works better. It is also worth noting that the two studies that asked learners about what type of feedback they preferred (Kim & Mathes, 2001; Nagata, 1993) reported a clear preference for more explicit feedback.

However, not all the studies point to an advantage for explicit feedback. DeKeyser (1993) found no difference between the group that received extensive explicit feedback and the group that received limited explicit feedback. Nevertheless, his study indicated that when individual difference factors – such as the learners' proficiency and language aptitude – were taken into account, the more explicit feedback was of greater benefit to the more able learners. Kim and Mathes (2001), in a study that replicated Carroll and Swain (1993), also failed to find any statistically significant differences in the scores of the explicit and implicit groups. Explicit feedback that consists of simply indicating that a problem exists does not appear to be helpful (Leeman, 2003). In the one study that examined feedback as part of input-processing instruction (Sanz, 2003), explicit metalinguistic feedback did not confer any advantage.

It is also important to recognize that these studies provide evidence that implicit methods of feedback can assist learning. The implicit groups in Carroll and Swain (1993), Carroll (2001), Muranoi (2000), Leeman

(2003) and Lyster (2004) all scored higher than the control groups on the post-tests.

The main limitation of the research to date lies in the method of testing. As noted previously, most of the studies did not include tests that can be considered valid measures of implicit knowledge (i.e. tests that call on learners to access their linguistic knowledge rapidly online in a communicative context). The kinds of tests used (grammaticality judgment tests, sentence completion, picture prompt tests, translation tests) favored the use of explicit knowledge. It can be argued, therefore, that they were biased in favor of explicit corrective feedback. The studies that included a test likely to measure implicit knowledge did not provide clear comparisons of the effects of explicit and implicit feedback. For example, Muranoi (2000) did not examine online feedback; in this study, feedback was provided after the treatment tasks were completed. Leeman (2003), as already pointed out, did not examine explicit feedback that contained metalinguistic explanations. Lyster (2004) did not examine metalinguistic clues separately from other types of nonexplicit feedback designed to elicit the negotiation of form. In the study reported below, we made use of the types of tests designed to measure implicit and explicit L2 knowledge that have been discussed in Section 2, in an attempt to overcome the measurement problems of previous studies.

Method

Research question

The study reported in this article investigated the following research question:

Do learners learn more from implicit or explicit corrective feedback directed at their grammatical errors?

The study was designed to provide a precise comparison between implicit and explicit corrective feedback by operationalizing these constructs in terms of (a) partial recasts of those portions of learners' utterances that contained an error and (b) metalinguistic explanations in which the learner's error was repeated and followed by metalinguistic information about the target language rule but the correct target language form was not provided. The effects of the corrective feedback on learning were assessed by means of tests designed to measure learning of both implicit and explicit L2 knowledge.

Design

The present study compares the effectiveness of two types of corrective feedback. Group 1 received implicit feedback (recast group), Group 2 explicit feedback (metalinguistic group) and Group 3 (a testing control) no opportunity to practice the target structure and, thus, no feedback. The relative effectiveness of both types of feedback was assessed on an Elicited Oral Imitation Test, an Untimed Grammaticality Judgment Test (UGJT) and a Metalinguistic Knowledge Test (MKT). There were three testing times: a pre-test, an immediate post-test and a delayed post-test. The target grammatical structure was past tense -ed.

Participants

The study was conducted in a private language school in New Zealand. Three classes of students ($n = 34$) were involved. The school classified these classes as lower-intermediate, according to scores on a placement or a previous class achievement test. Information obtained from a background questionnaire showed that the majority of learners (77%) were of East Asian origin. Most of them had spent less than a year in New Zealand (the mean length of stay was just over six months). The mean age of all participants was 25 years. The learners indicated that they had been formally engaged in studying English for anywhere from eight months to 13 years with an average length of time of seven years. Around 44% of participants indicated that their studies had been mainly formal (grammar-oriented) in nature, whereas 30% had received mainly informal instruction, and the rest a mixture of both formal and informal instruction.

The teaching approach adopted by the school placed emphasis on developing communicative skills in English. Learners received between three and five hours of English language instruction a day, for which they were enrolled as part-time or full-time students. Classes were arbitrarily assigned to one of the two treatment options (Group $1 = 12$ students, Group $2 = 12$ students) or to the control group option (Group $3 = 10$ students).

Target structure

Regular past tense -ed was chosen as the target structure for two reasons. First, learners at the lower-intermediate level are likely to be familiar with and have explicit knowledge of this structure. Our purpose was not to examine whether corrective feedback assists the learning of a completely new structure, but rather whether it enables learners to gain greater control over a structure they have already partially mastered. Pre-testing demonstrated that this was, indeed, the case: on the UGJT, the learners scored a mean of 75% on past tense -ed. The second reason was that past tense -ed is known to be problematic for learners and to cause errors (e.g. Doughty & Varela, 1998); thus, it was hypothesized that although learners at this level would have explicit knowledge of this structure, they would make errors in its use, especially in a communicative context and particularly in oral production (oral production poses a problem because of Asian learners' phonological difficulties in producing consonant clusters with final [t] or [d]). Once again, pretesting demonstrated that this was, indeed, the case: on the Oral Elicited Imitation Test, which served as a measure of unplanned language use, the learners scored a mean of 30% on regular past tense -ed.

Regular past tense -ed is typically introduced in elementary and lower-intermediate textbooks, but is not among the morphemes acquired early (Dulay & Burt, 1974; Makino, 1980). It is acquired after such morphemes as articles, progressive -ing and plural -s, but before such morphemes as long plural (-es) and third person -s. The typical error made by learners is the use of the simple or present form of the verb in place of V-ed:

*Yesterday I *visit* my sister.

Hawkins (2001: 65) noted that some L2 learners 'have difficulty in establishing the regular pattern (for past tense) at all'.

Tasks

For the purposes of the study, each experimental group received the same amount of instruction – a total of one hour over two consecutive days – during which they completed two different half-hour communicative tasks. The control group continued with their normal instruction. They did not complete the tasks and did not receive any feedback on past tense -ed errors.

The tasks were operationalized according to R. Ellis' (2003) definition of tasks; that is, they included a gap, they required learners to focus primarily on meaning and to make use of their own linguistic resources, and they had a clearly defined outcome other than the display of the target feature. They constituted, what Ellis called, focused tasks; in other words, they were designed to encourage the use of particular linguistic forms and, to this end, learners were provided with certain linguistic prompts (see the description of each task).

Task 1 (day 1)

Learners were assigned to four triads. Each triad was given the same picture sequence, which narrated a short story. They were also given one of four versions of a written account of the same story. Each version differed in minor ways from the others. Learners were told that they would have only a couple of minutes to read the written account of the story and that they needed to read it carefully because they would be asked to retell it in as much detail as possible. They were not allowed to make any written notes. The stories were removed and replaced with the list of verbs that learners were told they would need in order to retell the story:

visit live walk turn kill want follow attack laugh point stay watch

The learners were given about five minutes to plan the retelling of their story. They were told that they would not be able to use any prompts other than the picture sequence and verb list. The opening words of the story were written on the board, to clearly establish a context for past tense:

'Yesterday, Joe and Bill...'

The learners were then asked to listen to each triad's collective retelling of the story. They were also told that each triad had been given a slightly different version of the same story and that they were to listen carefully to identify what was different.

Task 2 (day 2)
Learners were once again assigned to triads. Each triad was given a picture sequence depicting a day in the life of one of two characters: Gavin or Peter. Each picture sequence was different. Pictures were chosen to depict actions that would require the use of verbs with regular past tense -ed forms. Learners were given five minutes to prepare for recounting the day of either Gavin or Peter. Again, they were not allowed to take any written notes. Each triad was told to begin their account with:
'Yesterday Peter/Gavin had a day off.'
The learners in the other triads who were listening to the narrated story were provided with an empty grid and pictures that they were to place on the grid in the appropriate sequence, according to the narration. One picture card did not fit, and learners were told they would be asked to identify which card remained.

Instructional procedures

The same instructor – one of the researchers – was responsible for conducting both tasks. The learners had not met the instructor prior to the first treatment session. An observer sat in the classroom during each session to manually record on paper all instances of use of the target structure and each instance of corrective feedback. The treatment sessions were also audio-recorded.

The learners received corrective feedback while they performed the tasks. Group 1 received implicit feedback in the form of recasts, as in (2).

(2) Learner: ...they saw and they follow follow follow him
Researcher: Followed
Learner: Followed him and attacked him.

The recasts were typically declarative and of the partial type and, as such, might be considered to lie at the explicit end of the implicit-explicit

Table 13.2 Number of target forms elicited and instances of feedback

Type of feedback	Total target forms elicited[a]	Total incorrect target forms elicited	Instances of feedback
Recast			
Lesson 1	44	32	24
Lesson 2	48	30	28
Metalinguistic			
Lesson 1	52	21	17
Lesson 2	50	24	23

[a]Correct and incorrect

continuum for recasts (see Sheen, 2006). Nevertheless, because they intruded minimally into the flow of the discourse, they may not have been very salient to the learners.

The learners in Group 2 received explicit feedback in the form of metalinguistic information, as in (3).

(3) Learner: He kiss her
Researcher: Kiss – you need past tense.
Learner: He kissed

In this example, which was typical of the corrective feedback episodes in this study, the instructor first repeated the error and then supplied the metalinguistic information. It is important to note that although corrective feedback was directed at individual learners, the task was designed to ensure that the attention of the whole class was focused as much as possible on the speaker at these times.

Table 13.2 indicates the number of target forms that were elicited during each task and the total number of incorrectly produced forms. The number of instances of feedback is also given. It should be noted that the recast group received more instances of corrective feedback than the metalinguistic group.

Testing instruments and procedures

Five days prior to the start of the instructional treatments, the learners completed all the pre-tests. The immediate post-testing was completed the day after the second (and last) day of instruction, and the delayed post-testing 12 days later. During each testing session, three tests were administered in this order: UGJT, MKT, Elicited Oral Imitation Test (EIT). The EIT (see Chapter 3) was intended to provide a measure of the learners' implicit knowledge, whereas the UGJT (especially the ungrammatical sentences in this test) and the MKT were designed to provide measures of learners' explicit knowledge. The theoretical bases for the design of these tests are discussed in Chapter 2.

Elicited Oral Imitation Test

This test was designed on the same principles as the EIT described in Chapters 2 and 3. It consisted of a set of 36 belief statements. Statements were grammatically correct ($n = 18$) or incorrect ($n = 18$). Twelve statements targeted simple past tense -ed, 12 targeted comparative adjectives (a focus of another study) and 12 targeted distracter items. Examples of the past tense -ed items are given in (4).

(4) a. Everyone liked the movie Star Wars.
     b. *An American invent Microsoft Word

Statements included target items introduced during the instructional treatments (old items) and also new items. The statements containing new items were designed to test whether learners were able to generalize what they had learned to new vocabulary items. Eight of the 12 statements targeting past tense -ed presented the target structure in the context of new items.

The procedures for administering the EIT followed those described in Chapter 3. Each statement was presented orally, one at a time, on an audiotape: Test-takers were required to first indicate on an answer sheet whether they agreed with, disagreed with, or were not sure about the statement. They were then asked to repeat the statement orally in correct English. Pre-test training presented learners with both grammatical and ungrammatical statements (not involving past tense -ed) to practice with, and they were given the correct responses to these items.

Learners' responses to all items were audio-recorded. These were then analyzed to establish whether obligatory occasions for use of the target structure had been established. Errors in structures other than the target structure were not considered. Each imitated statement was allocated a score of either 1 (the grammatically correct target structure was correctly imitated or the grammatically incorrect target structure was corrected) or 0 (the target structure was avoided, the grammatically correct target structure was attempted but incorrectly imitated, or the grammatically incorrect target structure was imitated but not corrected). If a learner self-corrected, then only the initial incorrect production was scored, as it was felt that this would provide the better measure of learners' implicit knowledge. Scores were expressed as percentage correct. Three versions of the test were created for use over the three testing sessions; in each, the same statements were used but presented in a different order. Reliability (Cronbach's alpha) for the pre-test was 0.779.

Untimed Grammaticality Judgment Test

This was based on the same principles as the UGJT described in Chapters 2 and 4. However, whereas that test was computer-delivered, the test used in this study was a pen-and-paper test. It consisted of 45 sentences. Fifteen sentences targeted past tense -ed, and the remainder targeted 30 other structures. Of the 15 sentences, seven were grammatically correct and eight grammatically incorrect. Sentences were randomly scrambled in different ways to create three versions of the test. Test-takers were required (a) to indicate whether each sentence was grammatically correct or incorrect, (b) to indicate the degree of certainty of their judgment (as proposed by Sorace, 1996) by writing down a score on a scale marked from 0 to 100% in the box provided and (c) to self-report whether they used rule or feel for each sentence. Learners were given six sentences to practice on before beginning the test. Each item was presented on a new page, and test-takers were told that they were not allowed to turn back to look at any part of the test that they had already completed. For past tense -ed, seven of the 15 statements presented the target structure in the context of new vocabulary and eight in the context of vocabulary included in the instruction.

Learners' responses were scored as either correct (1 point) or incorrect (0 points). In addition to the total score, separate scores for grammatical and ungrammatical test items and also for new and old verb items were calculated. Reliability (Cronbach's alpha) for the pre-test was .63. Test-retest reliability (Pearson r) was calculated for the control group ($n = 10$) only. For the pre-test and immediate post-test, it was .65 ($p < .05$) and for the pre-test and delayed post-test, it was .74 ($p < .05$).

Metalinguistic Knowledge Test

This was based on the principles for the MKT described in Chapter 9 and followed a similar format. Learners were presented with five sentences and told that they were ungrammatical. Two of the sentences contained errors in past tense -ed. The part of the sentence containing the error in each example was underlined. Learners were asked to (a) correct the error and (b) explain what was wrong with the sentence (in English, using their own words). They were shown two practice examples. As in the previous test, each item was presented on a new page and test-takers were told that they were not allowed to turn back. Learners scored one point for correcting the error and one point for a correct explanation of the error. A percentage accuracy score was calculated.

Analysis

Descriptive statistics for the three groups on all three tests were calculated. On the EIT and the UGJT (a) total scores, (b) separate scores for grammatical and ungrammatical items and (c) separate scores for old and new items were calculated. The decision to examine grammatical and ungrammatical items separately was motivated by our previous research (see Chapter 2), which showed that they may measure different types of knowledge (i.e. ungrammatical sentences provide a stronger measure of explicit knowledge). The decision to examine old items (i.e. items that tested verbs included in the instructional treatment) versus new items (i.e. verbs not included in the instructional treatment) was motivated by the wish to examine whether the instruction resulted only in item learning or whether there was also evidence of system learning.

t-Tests showed that there were statistically significant differences among the groups on the EIT and UGJT pre-tests. To take account of this difference, ANCOVAs (with pre-test scores as the covariate) were computed to investigate to what extent group differences on the two post-tests were statistically significant.

Results

Elicited oral imitation test

The descriptive statistics for regular past tense on the imitation test (see Table 13.3) show a range in overall accuracy from 24 to 39% on the pre-test. The scores increase on both post-tests. The ungrammatical items have lower accuracy scores than the grammatical items.

Table 13.3 Elicited Oral Imitation Test results

	Pre-test		*Immediate post-test*		*Delayed post-test*	
Groups	*M*	*SD*	*M*	*SD*	*M*	*SD*
Recast						
Grammatical	.278	.278	.403	.279	.514	.180
Ungrammatical	.194	.282	.319	.240	.375	.334
Total	.236	.164	.361	.228	.444	.223
Metalinguistic						
Grammatical	.444	.192	.618	.257	.736	.194
Ungrammatical	.333	.225	.375	.267	.653	.694
Total	.389	.164	.497	.211	.694	.196
Control						
Grammatical	.307	.207	.417	.317	.400	.211
Ungrammatical	.200	.172	.217	.209	.267	.196
Total	.253	.147	.317	.188	.333	.152

The results of the ANCOVAs reveal that there is a significant difference between the groups on their pre-test scores. Once these differences are taken into account, there is no effect for group on the immediate post-test, $F(2, 34) = .961$, $p = .394$; however, there is on the delayed post-test, $F(2, 34) = 7.975$, $p < .01$. The *post hoc* contrasts for the delayed post-test showed that the metalinguistic group differed significantly from the recast and control groups. There was also a tendency towards a significant difference between the recast and control groups.

The analysis of the grammatical and ungrammatical items showed no significant group differences on the immediate post-test for either the grammatical, $F(2, 34) = .853$, $p = .436$, or ungrammatical items, $F(2, 34) = .753$, $p = .480$. However, on the delayed post-test, there were significant differences on both the grammatical, $F(2, 34) = 6.697$, $p < .01$, and ungrammatical items, $F(2, 34) = 4.769$, $p < .05$, with the metalinguistic group differing significantly from the control on both. Additionally, the metalinguistic group differed significantly from the recast group on the grammatical items, with a similar trend towards significance for metalinguistic over recasts on the ungrammatical items.

Untimed grammaticality judgment test

The descriptive statistics for regular past tense on the Grammaticality Judgment Test (see Table 13.4) show relatively high levels of accuracy on the pre-test, ranging from 69 to 78%. These accuracy scores generally increased over both post-tests.

The ANCOVAs show overall that there is no difference for group on the immediate post-test, $F(2, 34) = .714$, $p = .498$, although there is for the delayed post-test, $F(2, 34) = 4.493$, $p < .05$. The *post hoc* contrasts for the delayed post-test showed that the metalinguistic group differed significantly from the recast group, and that there was a trend towards significance for metalinguistic over the control.

The ANCOVAs did not reveal any group differences on the immediate post-test for the grammatical $F(2, 34) = 1.482$, $p = .243$, or ungrammatical items $F(2, 34) = .092$, $p = .912$. Additionally, there were no differences on the delayed post-test for the ungrammatical items, $F(2, 34) = .900$, $p = 0.417$. However, there were significant differences on the delayed post-test for the grammatical items, $F(2, 34) = 5.194$, $p < .05$, with the *post hoc* contrasts showing that the metalinguistic group differed significantly from the recast group, and also the control differed significantly from the recasts.

The Metalinguistic knowledge test

The results from the metalinguistic test (see Table 13.5) show that all three groups had high accuracy scores on the pre-test, and that these

Table 13.4 Untimed Grammaticality Judgment Test results

Groups	Pre-test		Immediate post-test		Delayed post-test	
	M	*SD*	*M*	*SD*	*M*	*SD*
Recast						
Grammatical	.714	.122	.833	.147	.784	.142
Ungrammatical	.854	.129	.844	.152	.813	.146
Total	.784	.062	.839	.071	.798	.075
Metalinguistic						
Grammatical	.738	.134	.929	.114	.941	.074
Ungrammatical	.844	.108	.833	.154	.844	.094
Total	.791	.073	.881	.115	.892	.065
Control						
Grammatical	.586	.247	.786	.181	.871	.142
Ungrammatical	.788	.145	.813	.189	.738	.190
Total	.687	.135	.799	.098	.805	.096

Table 13.5 Metalinguistic Knowledge Test results

Groups	Pre-test		Immediate post-test		Delayed post-test	
	M	*SD*	*M*	*SD*	*M*	*SD*
Recast	.958	.144	.833	.326	10.00	.000
Metalinguistic	.833	.246	.917	.194	.917	.194
Control	.850	.241	.900	.210	.850	.337

generally remained high over the two post-tests. Due to the small number of test items ($n = 2$), inferential statistics were not calculated for the metalinguistic test.

Old versus new items

Tables 13.6 and 13.7 present the descriptive statistics for test performance on past tense verbs that appeared in the treatment tasks (i.e. old items) and for past tense verbs that were not the object of feedback (i.e. new items). If the effect of the treatment was only evident on the old items, this would suggest that corrective feedback caters only

Table 13.6 Elicited Oral Imitation Test: New/old item results

Groups	Pre-test		Immediate post-test		Delayed post-test	
	M	SD	M	SD	M	SD
Recast						
New	.226	.247	.286	.220	.345	.232
Old	.250	.309	.467	.287	.583	.301
Metalinguistic						
New	.321	.203	.373	.230	.631	.223
Old	.483	.232	.657	.265	.783	.233
Control						
New	.271	.171	.271	.228	.271	.196
Old	.210	.242	.380	.239	.420	.148

Table 13.7 Untimed Grammaticality Judgment Test: New/old item results

Groups	Pre-test		Immediate post-test		Delayed post-test	
	M	SD	M	SD	M	SD
Recast						
New	.823	.113	.854	.139	.802	.125
Old	.750	.184	.821	.138	.792	.116
Metalinguistic						
New	.740	.135	.875	.131	.906	.094
Old	.857	.122	.881	.147	.869	.129
Control						
New	.613	.092	.800	.121	.750	.156
Old	.786	.226	.800	.154	.857	.117

to item learning; if the effect could be shown to extend to new items, this would constitute evidence of generalization (i.e. system learning).

The results of the ANCOVAs for the new items reveal that there were significant differences between the groups on the pre-test Elicited Oral Imitation Scores. Once these differences were taken into account, there were no differences on the immediate post-test, $F(2, 34) = .397$, $p = .676$; however, there were differences on the delayed post-test, $F(2, 34) = 8.943$,

$p < 0.01$. The *post hoc* contrasts showed that the metalinguistic group was significantly higher than both the recast and control groups. Similarly, for the old items, there was no difference on the immediate post-test, $F(2, 34) = 1.211$, $p = 0.312$, but there was on the delayed post-test, $F(2, 34) = 3.188$, $p = 0.056$, with the *post hoc* contrasts showing that metalinguistic was significantly higher than the control. Thus, the results reported for the oral imitation test as a whole apply equally to old and new items.

The results of the ANCOVAs for the Grammaticality Judgment Test reveal that there were significant differences between the groups on the pre-test scores. Once these differences were taken into account, there was no difference among the groups for the old items on either the immediate post-test, $F(2, 34) = .452$, $p = .640$, or the delayed post-test, $F(2, 34) = .817$, $p = .451$, nor for the new items on the immediate post-test, $F(2, 34) = .467$, $p = .632$. However, there was a significant difference for the new items on the delayed post-test, $F(2, 34) = 4.295$, $p < .05$, which showed the metalinguistic group to be significantly higher than the recast group, as well as a trend towards metalinguistic over the control group.

Summary

Table 13.8 summarizes the main results, focusing on the statistically significant differences in the pair-wise comparisons.

Discussion

An inspection of the pre-test EIT scores suggests that all the learners initially had only limited implicit knowledge of past tense -ed. This was especially apparent in their inability to produce the correct forms when asked to imitate and correct sentences containing errors in structure. In contrast, the Untimed Grammaticality Judgment pre-test scores were high (i.e. above 70% in the two experimental groups). It is also noticeable that scores on the ungrammatical sentences were higher than on the grammatical sentences. If the ungrammatical sentences are taken as affording a better measure of explicit knowledge than the grammatical sentences, as suggested in Chapter 2, this might explain the higher scores on the ungrammatical sentences. Also, the MKT indicated a high level of explicit knowledge of past tense -ed. Thus, the pre-test scores can be interpreted as showing that the learners generally possessed a high level of explicit knowledge of past tense -ed, but were lacking in implicit knowledge. This pattern of results mirrors the results for the regular past tense -ed reported in Table 6.3 of Chapter 6 for a much larger sample of learners – 50% for implicit knowledge and 77% for explicit knowledge.

The descriptive statistics in Table 13.3 and the results of the ANCOVAs show that the corrective feedback resulted in significant differences among the groups on the EIT for past tense -ed, but these differences

Table 13.8 Summary of statistically significant differences

Test	Pre-test	Immediate post-test	Delayed post-test
Elicited Oral Imitation Test			
Overall	Significant group differences	No significant differences	M > C (old and new items)
			M > R (new items)
			R > C (trend)
Grammatical	Significant group differences	No significant differences	M > C, R
Ungrammatical	Significant group differences	No significant differences	M > C, M > R (trend)
Untimed Grammaticality Judgment Test			
Overall	Significant group difference effects for immediate but not delayed post-test	No significant differences	M > C (trend)
			M > R (new items)
Grammatical	Significant group difference effects for immediate but not de-layed post-test	No significant differences	M, C > R
Ungrammatical	Significant group difference effects for both pret-tests	No significant differences	No significant differences

Note: M, metalinguistic group; R, recast group; C, control group

were only evident on the delayed post-test. Corrective feedback also led to gains on the UGJT. However, the gains were almost entirely due to improved performance on the grammatical sentences, which we have argued tap more into implicit knowledge.

These results suggest that corrective feedback has an effect on the learning of implicit knowledge. Indeed, overall, the feedback appears to have had a greater effect on the learners' implicit knowledge than on their explicit knowledge, although this may simply reflect the fact that the learners possessed ceiling levels of explicit knowledge at the beginning of the study. It is possible, of course, that the treatments increased learners' awareness of the grammatical targets of the oral imitation test, thus encouraging them to monitor their output using their explicit knowledge. However, we do not believe that this occurred. First, when asked at the end of the final test if they were aware of which grammatical structures the test was measuring, only one learner was able to identify past tense. Second, as Table 13.9 shows, there is no clear evidence that the experimental groups were monitoring more than the control group or more in the post-tests than in the pre-test. If the learners were attempting to use their explicit knowledge in this test, we would have expected a much higher incidence of self-correction.

Further evidence that the corrective feedback induced changes in learners' implicit knowledge can be found in the fact that the effects of the experimental treatments on the EIT scores were more evident two weeks after the instruction than one day after. This finding reflects previous research (e.g. Mackey, 1999), which has also shown that the effects of instruction become more apparent in delayed tests that tap the kind of language use likely to measure implicit knowledge. The enhanced accuracy evident in the Elicited Oral Imitation delayed post-test is indicative of the learners' successful incorporation of the target structure into their interlanguage systems.

The main purpose of the study was to investigate the relative effects of explicit and implicit corrective feedback on the acquisition of both types of knowledge. In this study, explicit corrective feedback was operationalized as metalinguistic information, and implicit corrective feedback as recasts. The results point to a distinct advantage for metalinguistic information despite the fact that the learners in the recast group received substantially more corrective feedback than those in the metalinguistic group (see Table 13.2). Nor was the advantage found for the metalinguistic group only evident in the UGJT, it was also clearly evident in the EIT. Also, metalinguistic feedback (but not recasts) was found to result in learning that generalized to verbs not included in the treatment, which suggests that system learning took place.

Table 13.9 Number of instances of participant self-correction during the Elicited Oral Imitation Test

Group	Pre-test	Immediate post-test	Delayed post-test
Metalinguistic	3	1	4
Recasts	1	7	2
Control	2	1	3

How can we explain the general superiority of explicit feedback over implicit feedback? In the earlier discussion of theoretical issues relating to corrective feedback, we noted that in connectionist models of L2 acquisition explicit corrective feedback in the context of communicative activity can facilitate the conversion of explicit knowledge into implicit knowledge.[3] Explicit feedback is more likely than implicit feedback to be perceived as overtly corrective, as the examples in (6) and (7) suggest. In both episodes, the teacher's feedback move overlaps with the learner's preceding move, but because the metalinguistic feedback is longer (six words as opposed to one), it may have been better attended to and perceived as overtly corrective. In both episodes, however, the learner successfully repairs the error following the feedback move, but again there is evidence of greater awareness that repair is needed in the metalinguistic episode. Whereas in (6) the learner simply repeats the reformulated past tense verb, in (7) the learner's 'yes' seems to overtly acknowledge that repair was required. Thus, metalinguistic feedback – in comparison to recasts – seems more likely to lead to a greater depth of awareness of the gap between what was said and the target norm, thereby facilitating the acquisition of implicit knowledge. It is also important to recognize that the metalinguistic feedback, as illustrated in (7), does not intrude unduly in the communicative flow of the activity. It constitutes a brief time-out from communicating, which allows the learner to focus explicitly but briefly on form. The effectiveness of the metalinguistic feedback, therefore, may derive in part from the high level of awareness it generates and in part from the fact that it is embedded in a communicative context.

(6) L: Yesterday two boys, Joe and Bill visit their rich uncle =
    T: = Visited
    L: Visited their rich uncle.

(7) L: Yesterday Joe and Bill ah went to ah Bill's grandmother
         and visit their grandmother =
    T: = and visit > you need past tense
    L: Visited, yes.
    Key: = signifies overlapping elements; > signifies rising
    intonation; L, Learner; T, Teacher.

The superiority of the metalinguistic feedback only reached statistical significance in the delayed Elicited Oral Imitation and Untimed Grammaticality Judgment post-tests. However, gains from pre-test to the immediate post-test were also evident. Thus, the general pattern of the results was: pre-test scores < immediate post-test scores < delayed post-test scores. That is, the benefits of the metalinguistic feedback became more evident as time passed. This finding supports the claims advanced in Chapter 1 that explicit L2 knowledge can enhance the processes involved in the development of implicit knowledge (e.g. noticing and cognitive comparison). That is, the awareness generated by metalinguistic feedback promotes the kind of synergy between explicit and implicit knowledge that is hypothesized to underlie L2 learning.

The relatively weak effect found for either type of feedback on the ungrammatical sentences in the UGJT reflects the fact that the learners possessed the explicit knowledge required for judging such sentences from the beginning, which was clearly evident from their high pre-test scores on the ungrammatical sentences on the UGJT and near perfect scores on the MKT.

One final comment is in order. All the learners in this study demonstrated partial implicit knowledge of past tense -ed, as demonstrated by their performance on the oral imitation pre-test. It is possible that for corrective feedback of any kind to have an effect on learning, the structures must be at least partially established in the learners' interlanguages. Further research is needed to establish whether corrective feedback is effective in enabling learners to acquire completely new grammatical structures.

Conclusion

This study demonstrates that explicit feedback in the form of metalinguistic information is, overall, more effective than implicit feedback (in the form of recasts) and contributes to system as well as item learning. Table 13.10 summarizes the actions that learners are hypothesized to carry out in order to process feedback for acquisition (based on Carroll's (2001) account of corrective feedback), and the extent to which the two types of feedback engage these processes. It illustrates how both implicit and explicit types of feedback may facilitate these actions and also demonstrates why explicit feedback may do so more effectively than implicit feedback. In particular, explicit feedback seems more likely to promote the cognitive comparison that aids learning.

As in all classroom studies, there are inevitable limitations. First, the sample size for this study was small. Also, we were forced to use intact groups with the result that the groups were not equivalent at the commencement of the study, thus obligating the use of analyses of covariance. Second, because our main aim was to compare the relative effectiveness of the two types of corrective feedback, we only included a testing group as a control group (i.e. we did not have a control group that completed the communicative tasks without any corrective feedback). Third, the length of the treatments was very short (approximately one hour). It is possible that with a longer treatment, recasts would have

Table 13.10 The facilitative potential of implicit and explicit feedback compared

General action	Specific step	Implicit feedback (recasts)	Explicit feedback (metalinguistic information)
Detecting the error	The learner's attention must switch from meaning to form; this can only occur if the corrective intention is recognized, which happens only if the feedback is perceived as irrelevant to the ongoing discourse The learner must be able to locate the error	Partial recasts are more likely to induce a switch in attention from meaning to form than full recasts; however, the corrective force of partial recasts is not self-evident, as repetitions serve other functions in discourse Recasts make the location of the error clear	Metalinguistic information is clearly irrelevant to the ongoing discourse, which makes a switch from meaning to form likely and the corrective intention of the feedback clear Repeating the error and then giving a metalinguistic clue make the location of the error clear
Correcting the error	The learner must be able to distinguish the phonological dissimilarity between his or her erroneous form and the target form in the feedback The learner must be able to decide whether pronunciation, morphology, syntax or semantics is causing the problem. The learner may make use of explicit knowledge to decide	Recasts make it possible for the learner to compare two phonological forms (the erroneous form and the target form), but the learner has to attend to the difference Recasts provide no clues as to the nature of the error; that is, the learner is left to infer whether the error is one of pronunciation or morphology	The process of comparing the erroneous and target phonological form is enhanced because the teacher repeated the incorrect form before supplying metalinguistic information The nature of the error is made clear. A connection is made between the implicit use of a specific form (the error) and an explicit representation of the target form required

Note: Recasts refer to partial recasts of the kind used in this study proved more effective. Fourth, the structure we chose for study was a structure that the learners had already begun to acquire. In one respect, this can be considered a strength, as it enabled us to examine which type of corrective feedback works best for structures already partially acquired. But, in another respect, it constitutes a weakness in that we are unable to say whether corrective feedback (and what type of corrective feedback) is effective in establishing new knowledge.

Notes

1. An earlier version of this chapter appeared in 2006 in *Studies in Second Language Acquisition* 28, 339–68.
2. Other studies have examined the relationship between implicit/explicit feedback and learner uptake (e.g. Oliver & Mackey, 2003), but these are not included in this review, which focuses exclusively on the effects of feedback on L2 acquisition as measured in post-tests. The extent to which uptake constitutes a measure of acquisition is controversial, with many researchers, including us, preferring to view it as evidence of noticing.
3. A reviewer of a draft version of the paper on which this chapter is based pointed out that the results could be explained in terms of the learners having automatized their declarative knowledge of past tense -ed as a result of the treatment. This interpretation draws on the distinction between declarative and procedural knowledge, which informs skill-building theories of the kind advocated by DeKeyser (1998). However, we have chosen to frame the paper in terms of the implicit/explicit distinction, noting with Eysenck (2001: 213) that recent changes in the definitions of both pairs of terms have brought them closer together, making it 'increasingly difficult to decide on the extent to which different theories actually make significantly different predictions'.

Part 5
Conclusion

In the chapter in this final part of the book, we will examine the aims of the Marsden Project and attempt an evaluation of the extent to which we feel we have been successful in achieving these aims. We will also consider a number of limitations of the research we conducted.

It is also appropriate in a final chapter to consider future research. We believe that future research should continue to explore different ways of measuring implicit and explicit grammatical knowledge and also seek ways of assessing the two type of knowledge in other areas of language – phonology, lexis and pragmatics. In addition, future research should continue to examine theoretical and educational issues in terms of the implicit/explicit distinction.

The implicit/explicit learning distinction is important for developing understanding of second language acquisition (SLA), improving language pedagogy and devising language tests. Central to work in these three areas is the development of sound methods for assessing the products of the two kinds of learning.

Chapter 14
Retrospect and Prospect

ROD ELLIS

Introduction

The research reported in this book was premised on two principal assumptions. The first was that the distinction between implicit and explicit knowledge is fundamental to understanding the nature of second language (L2) acquisition and to developing a theory to explain how it takes place. The second was that this distinction is also of potential relevance to language testing. One of the aims of the Marsden Project, which brought together researchers with expertise in both second language acquisition (SLA) research and language testing was to identify synergies between these two fields of applied linguistics.

The case for making a clear distinction between implicit and explicit knowledge was made in Chapter 1. The psycholinguistic basis for the distinction rests on the now well-attested fact that speakers of a language may be able to use a linguistic feature accurately and fluently without any awareness of what the feature consists of and vice-versa, notably in the case of many classroom learners of an L2, who may be able to verbalize about a feature without being able to use it in communicative language use. There is also a clear neurobiological basis for the distinction. Whereas implicit knowledge involves widely divergent and diffuse neural structures, including neuro-circuits in the basal ganglia, explicit knowledge is localized in more specific areas of the brain, such as sections of the medial-temporal lobe, with the hippocampus playing a major role in its formation. The neural sites that house these two types of linguistic knowledge are not specific to language – they cater, respectively, to declarative knowledge and to motor activity in general. Also, although the two types of knowledge can be distinguished psycholinguistically and neurobiologically, controversy exists as to whether they are to be viewed as distinct and dichotomous or intertwined and continuous (see Dienes & Perner, 1999). Irrespective of what position is taken on this debate, there is general acknowledgement that different types of language use draw differentially on the two types of knowledge, with, for example, fluent, communicative language use favoring implicit knowledge, and careful language use, as in text editing, calling on explicit knowledge. Anderson *et al.* (1997), drawing on the ACT-R model of learning, stress that performance of any skill involves a complex mixture of knowledge types, including the use of analogy and simple retrieval of examples, declarative (explicit) knowledge and procedural (implicit) knowledge.[1] Thus, while the distinction between implicit/explicit knowledge (and more broadly implicit/explicit memory) is now well-established, it is also clear that both are variably involved in the use of language in different contexts.

Implicit knowledge is considered primary. Any theory of L2 acquisition needs to account for how implicit knowledge is acquired. Irrespective of whether the theory is a theory of linguistic competence (as in theories based on Universal Grammar – see White, 2003), an emergentist theory of the kind espoused by N. Ellis (1998) or sociocultural theory (Lantolf & Thorne, 2006), the theory must account for how learners develop the knowledge needed to perform spontaneously but accurately in fluent, communicative language speech – implicit knowledge. Language teacher educators, irrespective of the particular instructional approach they espouse, acknowledge that the main goal of language instruction must be to develop L2 learners' implicit knowledge. Thus, SLA theorists and teacher educators are in agreement that without a foundation of implicit knowledge, oral and much written communication will be restricted and effortful. In contrast, differences abound concerning the role played by explicit knowledge. As we saw in Chapter 1, different interface positions exist, with some theorists arguing that explicit knowledge plays no role in the acquisition of implicit knowledge, others that it constitutes an initial stage for developing implicit knowledge, and yet others that it helps to fine-tune the processes responsible for the development of implicit knowledge. These theoretical disputations cannot be solved unless it is possible to identify what kind of knowledge learners are using and acquiring in the process of L2 development.

The significance of the distinction between implicit and explicit knowledge is less prominent in the field of language testing. As noted in Chapter 7, current models of language testing have tended to emphasize 'performance' rather than 'knowledge' on the grounds that assessment tasks that reflect real-life target tasks will afford more valid and more useful measures of learners' language proficiency. It is not clear what contribution a theory of implicit/explicit L2 knowledge can make to such models. However, there are alternative approaches to language assessment that draw on psycholinguistic models of language use and these do draw on the implicit/explicit distinction. Lantolf (2008: 1–2), for example, in arguing for a closer nexus between language teaching and language testing, proposes that 'both implicit and explicit knowledge would not only be necessary for optimal development of language proficiency but they would interact with each other in mutually beneficial ways', and elsewhere (see Poehner & Lantolf, 2005) has shown how dynamic assessment can capture the interplay of the two types of knowledge. Language testing, then, like language learning and language teaching, can benefit from examining the implicit/explicit distinction. A theory of L2 proficiency – like a theory of L2 acquisition or instruction – must surely acknowledge the role of these two types of knowledge.

In this chapter, I will first summarize what I see as the main achievements of the Marsden Project before considering a number of limitations in the research we have reported. I will then examine some possible future developments regarding additional ways of assessing implicit/explicit knowledge and applications of the tests of the two types of knowledge.

The Achievements of the Marsden Project

The Marsden Project had three principal aims:

(1) To develop a set of tests that would provide relatively separate measures of L2 implicit and explicit knowledge of grammar.
(2) To examine the relationship between L2 implicit/explicit knowledge and L2 proficiency as measured by standardized language tests.
(3) To examine the effects of different types of form-focused instruction (FFI) on the acquisition of L2 implicit/explicit knowledge.

I will now consider to what extent these aims were achieved.

Development of tests of L2 implicit/explicit knowledge

As De Jong (2005a: 7) noted:

Testing whether learning is implicit or explicit is very difficult, because there are no clear boundaries between implicit and explicit processes and nearly all cognitive processes have both implicit and explicit aspects. This means that implicit learning should not be ruled out as soon as awareness has been established, nor should implicit learning only be assumed when there is no awareness at all of the learning process or product. The same argument holds for implicit and explicit knowledge, which can (and often do) co-exist and operate simultaneously.

This statement articulates the challenge we faced in developing a set of tests that were capable of providing relatively separate measures of implicit and explicit knowledge. Just as it is impossible to observe the actual processes of learning, so too it is impossible to examine directly how the processes of language use draw on the two types of knowledge.

The solution we adopted to this problem was to identify a set of criteria for distinguishing implicit/explicit knowledge of language and then establish operationalizations of these criteria. We settled on four criteria that we felt could be effectively operationalized:

(1)   degree of awareness;
(2)   the time available for producing a response;
(3)   the focus of attention (on meaning or on form);
(4)   the utility of metalanguage in producing a response.

Using these criteria, we developed a battery of tests of grammatical knowledge, some of which were intended to afford measures of implicit knowledge (i.e. low awareness, limited response time, a focus on meaning and little opportunity to use metalanguage) and some explicit knowledge (i.e. high awareness, ample response time, a focus on form and opportunity to use metalanguage). The tests were then administered to a small sample of native speakers and a relatively large and mixed sample of L2 learners. Various statistical analyses of the test data were then carried out with a view to establishing to what extent our predictions regarding how test-takers would perform on the tests were confirmed.

The analyses largely confirmed our predictions. Three of the tests in the battery (the Elicited Oral Imitation Test, the Oral Narrative Test and the Timed Grammaticality Judgment Test; TGJT) were shown to load on a single factor, which in accordance with their design features, we labeled 'implicit knowledge'. The other two tests (the Untimed Grammaticality Judgment Test (UGJT) and the Metalinguistic Knowledge Test (MKT)) loaded on a second factor, which we labeled 'explicit knowledge'. In the case of the UGJT, it was found that it was the ungrammatical sentences that provided the clearest measure of this type of knowledge. We also examined other possible interpretations of the test data (e.g. 'production' versus 'decision') but found that these alternative models did not fit the data as well nor did they account for as much of the variance as did the implicit versus explicit interpretation. Part 2 of this book provides an in depth examination of four of these tests, providing further evidence of their validity as tests of either implicit or explicit knowledge.

We believe that the first aim of the Marsden Project was achieved. While acknowledging the impossibility of devising distinct measures of implicit and explicit knowledge, we were able to design tests that clearly biased test-takers to draw on one or the other.

Examining the relationship between implicit/explicit knowledge and language proficiency

A proficiency test is intended to measure a learner's command of a language. Thus, the term 'proficiency' covers both the 'knowledge' a learner has of a language and his/her 'ability to use' that knowledge.

Various models of language proficiency have informed the development of tests. These can be classified in terms of whether they view proficiency in terms of a linguistic system that exists without reference to any particular situation or context or whether they view it in terms of the ability to use language in a specific context. As Baker (1989) pointed out, tests based on these two alternative views of proficiency can be either 'direct' (i.e. based on a direct sampling of the criterion performance) or 'indirect' (based on an analysis of the criterion performance with a view to testing the specific features or components that comprise it). A further important distinction in language proficiency is between 'basic inter-personal communication skills' (BICS) and 'cognitive academic language proficiency' (CALP) (Cummins, 1983).

Ideally, to investigate the relationship between implicit/explicit knowledge and language proficiency, we needed to conduct studies that examined how scores on our battery of tests correlated with scores from different tests of language proficiency – direct and indirect system-referenced tests, direct and indirect performance-based tests and tests of BICS and CALP. However, such an extensive program of research was beyond our resources. Instead, we elected to examine the relationship with two widely used standardized tests of language proficiency – the Test of English as a Foreign Language (TOEFL) and the International English Language Testing System (IELTS). Descriptions of these two tests can be found in Chapter 7. Both tests can be considered to be indirect system-referenced tests, with TOEFL heavily biased towards CALP, and IELTS somewhat more oriented towards BICS (as it contains a general rather than academically oriented listening test and a speaking component involving face-to-face interaction).

We expected to find that both implicit and explicit knowledge would be implicated in both tests. In fact, we found that this was only the case for IELTS. For the TOEFL (including the now defunct computer-based version and the pilot version of the new internet-based test) only measures of explicit knowledge correlated with test scores. This difference in results was explicable in terms of the BICS/CALP distinction, as implicit knowledge can be expected to be more clearly required for BICS while explicit knowledge will be of greater importance for CALP. However, methodological differences in the two studies that investigated the relationships between the measures of implicit/explicit knowledge and the measures of language proficiency derived from the two proficiency tests precluded reaching a firm conclusion.

In short, we do not feel that our investigation of this relationship has been very successful. A major limitation of the study investigating the TOEFL was the exclusive reliance on the TGJT as a measure of implicit knowledge. A major limitation of the second study that investigated the IELTS was the small sample size. Both limitations arose from the logistic problems of obtaining multiple measures of implicit/explicit knowledge and language proficiency from a large sample of learners with the resources at our disposal. Thus, the extent to which the implicit/explicit distinction is useful in modeling language proficiency remains to be shown.

Form-focused instruction and the acquisition of implicit/explicit knowledge

A common criticism of much of the research into the effects of FFI on L2 acquisition is the failure of researchers to establish the validity of their measure of acquisition. Indeed, the great majority of FFI studies have failed to even address the issue of the validity of their tests. A good example of this problem can be found in Processing Instruction studies (e.g. VanPatten & Cadierno, 1993; VanPatten & Oikennon, 1996). VanPatten (2002: 796) makes it clear that Processing Instruction is intended to influence the implicit knowledge system, but as De Jong (2005a) points out, it is not possible to draw any firm conclusions from the studies conducted because these have failed to provide evidence for the implicitness of the knowledge deployed in the assessment tasks used. In general, researchers have relied on tests more likely to tap explicit than implicit knowledge and rarely has any attempt been made to explore how instruction affects both types of knowledge in a systematic way (but see DeKeyser, 1995).

One of our aims in developing tests capable of providing measures of implicit and explicit L2 knowledge was to address this lacuna in FFI research. Armed with such tests, we were able to explore to what extent different types of FFI impacted on learners' knowledge. We were able to show, for example, that output-based instruction of the present-practice-produce kind, where form-meaning mapping was clearly established, resulted in gains in implicit knowledge of the target structure, and that, overall these gains were stronger than for input-based instruction (see Chapter 11). In another study, we were able to show that explicit corrective feedback involving metalinguistic clues also contributed to implicit knowledge in the long term and to a greater extent than implicit corrective feedback (see Chapter 13). These constitute important findings as they indicate that FFI is able to affect learners' linguistic competence (i.e. their implicit knowledge system) and, furthermore, that explicit types of FFI are effective (and perhaps more effective than implicit types) in assisting this development.

In these studies we used the Elicited Oral Imitation Test to provide a measure of implicit knowledge. The great advantage of this test is that it is able to target specific grammatical features while providing a measure of implicit knowledge. In this respect, this test constitutes a powerful instrument for overcoming the problem that De Jong identified. To challenge the interpretation we have put on the results of the FFI studies in Part 4 of the book, it will be necessary to demonstrate that this test does not, in fact, constitute a valid test of implicit knowledge. In accordance with the arguments presented in Chapter 3 where this test was examined in detail, we do not expect its validity to be successfully challenged.

The limitations of the FFI studies reported in Part 4 were acknowledged. Doubtlessly, they could have been improved in several ways (and some suggestions as to how follow in the next section of this chapter). However, we believe that we have been successful in demonstrating how the tests of implicit and explicit knowledge we have developed can be applied to the investigation of FFI and can enhance the validity of such studies.

Some Limitations

The Marsden Project was ambitious, seeking not only to develop tools for investigating L2 implicit and explicit knowledge, but also to demonstrate how these tools could be applied to investigating a variety of theoretical issues in SLA (such as the nature of the complexity of grammatical structures or the role that age plays in L2 acquisition) and practical matters related to language teaching (such as teachers' metalinguistic knowledge or the role of FFI). Not surprisingly, given the scope of the project, there were a number of limitations. I will begin by focusing on a theoretical problem we faced and then point out some reservations regarding the tests of implicit and explicit knowledge and the investigations of the effects of FFI.

A theoretical problem

The theoretical issue concerns the thorny question of the relationship between 'knowledge' and 'control'. Two positions are possible. The first is that 'knowledge' and 'control' constitute two separate dimensions of linguistic representation. This is the position adopted by Bialystok (1982), McLaughlin *et al.* (1983) and myself in my earlier work (see, e.g. Ellis, 1994). Such a position allows for two intersecting continua between implicit/explicit and controlled/automatic knowledge, which leads to four prototypical types of knowledge (Type A explicit/controlled; Type B explicit/automatic; Type C implicit/controlled; Type D; implicit/automatic). This position constitutes an attempt to blend the dual distinctions of declarative/procedural and implicit/explicit knowledge. The alternative position (see, e.g. N. Ellis, 2002; Hulstijn, 2002) is to view control as an integral aspect of the type of knowledge. In other words, the procedural/declarative and the implicit/explicit distinctions are seen as labels for essentially the same mental phenomena. This affords just two types of knowledge: Type A implicit/procedural and Type B explicit/declarative. In my later work, which informed the theoretical basis for the Marsden Project, I have favored this position.

There are problems with both positions. In the case of the four-knowledge-types model, it is not clear to what extent it will ever be possible to empirically differentiate automatic implicit and automatic explicit knowledge (i.e. Types B and D) or controlled implicit and controlled explicit knowledge (i.e. Types A and C). Bialystok's (1992) attempt to develop tasks that tap into the four types of knowledge identified in this model was only partially successful. The simple dichotomy model suffers from a different problem, namely the difficulty of distinguishing explicit and implicit knowledge given that many learners start the process of learning an L2 with explicit knowledge, which they subsequently proceduralize through practice. Is the end result automatic explicit knowledge or does this at some point transform into implicit knowledge? This is the fundamental question addressed by the interface hypothesis. DeKeyser (1993) pointed out that functionally there may be no difference between automatized explicit knowledge and implicit knowledge. There would appear, however, to be a growing consensus that automaticity and implicitness are related notions as are controlled processing and explicitness. Thus, while there may be some quantitative speeding up of explicit knowledge over time, this does not amount to a transformation to implicit knowledge (Hulstijn, 2002).

Our solution to the problems that the control/knowledge issue posed was to assume that (1) implicit knowledge was automatic and explicit knowledge controlled and (2) to invoke additional characteristics of the two types of knowledge (e.g. awareness and focus on meaning/form). In this way, we hoped to overcome the problem of distinguishing automatized explicit knowledge and implicit knowledge, the former being characterized by awareness and attention to form and the latter by a lack of awareness and attention to meaning. It can still be argued, however, that what is central to our tests is the extent to which they call for online or offline processing – on-line in the case of the tests of implicit knowledge and offline in the case of the tests of explicit knowledge. In other words, the tests are most clearly distinguished in terms of the extent to which they require automatic or controlled processing. To overcome this problem, we would have needed to have developed a much more extensive battery of tests, which was unfortunately beyond our budgetary means. In a later section of this chapter, however, I will suggest some of the tests that could figure in an extended battery and that might help to resolve the problem of how to distinguish explicit knowledge (in its controlled and more automatic form) and implicit knowledge.

Testing implicit and explicit knowledge

In developing the tests of implicit knowledge, we recognized the need to balance discrete-item tests with a more holistic, integrative test and to demonstrate that they were measuring the same type of knowledge. For logistic reasons, we included only one test of relatively natural language where the focus of the test-takers was clearly on communicating propositional content rather than linguistic form – the Oral Narrative Test. The problem with this test is that it afforded measures of only a limited set of the 17 grammatical structures that constituted the linguistic content of the battery of tests. This was because it proved impossible to design a communicative test that would create obligatory contexts for many of these structures. In retrospect, we might have done better to have drawn on an instrument such as the Bilingual Syntax Measure (Burt *et al.*, 1975). The BSM II, which was designed for older learners, would have suited our sample. This test consists of cartoon-like pictures designed to elicit a range of grammatical structures in what approximates to a real conversation. Including this test in the battery would have provided us with richer data and also with access to a baseline of results (the 'natural order of acquisition') from previous research using this instrument. To sum up, perhaps the most obvious weakness in our battery of tests was the lack of an integrative test of oral communication that provided data comparable to that derived from the discrete item tests in the battery.

The battery included three tests designed to measure implicit knowledge, but only two tests of explicit knowledge. This imbalance constitutes a limitation as it may have affected the factor analyses that were conducted to examine the extent of the disassociation of the measures of the two types of knowledge. There were also limitations with both of the tests of explicit knowledge.

The UGJT cannot be considered a valid test of explicit knowledge unless it can be shown that (1) the learners were judging the specific feature intended in each sentence and (2) the learners' judgments were made consciously, i.e. that they judged the grammaticality of the sentences in accordance with linguistic knowledge that they were aware of. In recognition of the importance of demonstrating consciousness, we asked test-takers to indicate whether they used 'rule' or 'feel' to make a judgment and also to indicate the level of confidence they had in their judgment, on a scale from 0 to 100%. We were able to show that the use of 'rule' correlated significantly with measures from the tests of explicit knowledge, but not with those from the tests of implicit knowledge (see Table 2.9 in Chapter 2).

To demonstrate that the learners did judge the specific grammatical feature intended in each sentence, they might have been asked to underline the part of a sentence they judged to be ungrammatical. However, we chose not to do so because we feared this would overload them. The test consisted of 68 sentences and was one of a battery they were being asked to take. Asking them to judge the correctness of each sentence, to indicate whether they used rule or feel and to score their level of certainty was felt to be as much as could be asked in the total context of the testing session. In retrospect, however, this was an omission, as we could not be confident that learners were basing their judgments on their knowledge of the 17 target structures and also, asking them to mark the parts of the sentences they deemed to be ungrammatical would have constituted an inducement for them to use their explicit knowledge – the purpose of the UGJT.

In retrospect, we also feel that the measures of rule/feel and of certainty, designed to establish whether judgments were made using conscious knowledge, lacked sensitivity. Dienes and Scott (2005) proposed a methodology for investigating whether what they called 'judgment knowledge' was conscious or unconscious. In an artificial grammar learning experiment in which they administered a grammaticality judgment test, they asked participants to report the basis of their judgments in terms of five options, four of which are relevant here:

(1) Guess (i.e. the judgment had no basis whatsoever).
(2) Intuition (i.e. the participant felt the judgment to be correct but had no idea why it was correct).
(3) Rules (i.e. the participant has based the judgment on some rule which he/she could state if asked).
(4) Memory (i.e. the judgment was based on memory for specific items experienced previously).

Dienes and Scott proposed that (1) and (2) were indicative of unconscious 'structural knowledge' (i.e. implicit knowledge) and (3) and (4) conscious structural knowledge (i.e. explicit knowledge). They also asked participants to provide a certainty rating of each judgment on a scale from 50 to 100%.[2] They suggested that if there was no correlation between confidence and accuracy of judgment, this would indicate a lack of awareness of what they knew (i.e. demonstrate unconscious structural knowledge). Implicit in this methodology is the assumption that 'unconscious structural knowledge can be inferred from unconscious judgment knowledge' (Dienes & Scott, 2005: 340). Dienes and Scott report two studies that support this methodology. A finer grained analysis of the participants' use of 'rule' and 'feel', along the lines proposed by Dienes and Scott would have enhanced our claim that the UGJT afforded a measure of explicit knowledge. We also possibly erred in asking for certainty to be expressed on a 0–100% scale, as clearly 50% applied to a dichotomous judgment (correct versus not correct) represents a zero level of certainty.

The MKT was also somewhat limited. It afforded only receptive measures of learners' knowledge of metalanguage. In retrospect, it would have been advantageous to include a test of learners' productive metalanguage. However, this lacuna was recognized in a revised version of the MKT (see Chapter 9 and the Appendix).

Investigating form-focused instruction

Limitations were also evident in the work we completed on FFI in Phase III of the Marsden Project. Limitations related to the individual studies in Part 4 of the book were examined in the chapters reporting these studies. Here I will focus on three difficulties we faced. It should be noted, however, that these difficulties are common to work on FFI in general (see, e.g. Norris and Ortega (2000) for a discussion of the methodological problems in FFI studies).

The first difficulty derives from the fact that FFI research (including our own research) seeks to inform both SLA theory (e.g. the relative roles of input and output in L2 acquisition) and language pedagogy. For the purposes of testing theory it is important to design studies that examine the effect that narrowly defined instructional options have on L2 acquisition. For the purposes of illuminating the role that FFI can play in language pedagogy it is necessary to design studies that involve combinations of instructional options in ways that reflect current best practice. Thus, what is good for investigating theory may not be useful for informing pedagogy and vice-versa.

This dilemma is evident in the FFI studies in this book. Erlam's study of the effects of input-based and output-based language practice in Chapter 10 was, in part, motivated by a wish to test the theory that underlies Processing Instruction (VanPatten, 1996), but also by a wish to examine how practice can assist classroom language learning. She elected to combine a number of options in her experimental treatments – explicit instruction, structured input and content feedback in the case of input-based instruction, and explicit instruction, controlled and free production and corrective feedback in the case of output-based instruction. Her study demonstrated that, overall, output-based instruction was more effective – a finding that is certainly useful where language pedagogy is concerned (helping to counteract what are surely overstated claims about the role of input-based instruction), but that is less helpful in developing theory as it is not possible to identify which specific aspects of the output-based instruction aided acquisition. In contrast, Ellis *et al.*'s study in Chapter 13, examined two very specific instructional strategies (recasts and metalinguistic explanation), which served to test rival theories about the role of corrective feedback in L2 acquisition, but which, arguably, contributed little to the actual practice of conducting corrective feedback in language pedagogy given the impracticality of teachers' limiting their feedback to a single type in a real classroom. The conduct of FFI studies raises thorny questions about the relationship between research and practice, which are not easily resolved and certainly have not been in this book.

The second problem concerns how acquisition is defined. In Ellis (2006), I suggested that 'acquisition' can have very different meanings – (1) the internalization of a new form, (2) increased control over a partially learned form or (3) progress along a sequence of acquisition. Studies of implicit/explicit knowledge have been primarily concerned with how instruction affects the internalization of a new form. It was for this reason that psychological studies made use of artificial grammars, as these constitute a sure way of guaranteeing that participants had no prior knowledge of the target rule. When the target is a grammatical structure in a natural language that the learners have already been learning for some time, it becomes difficult if not impossible to identify a target that is entirely 'new' (i.e. not yet part of the learners' repertoire). Yet, from a theoretical standpoint, it is important to investigate whether instruction impacts on the acquisition of a new structure. It is one thing to show that explicit instruction can assist the acquisition of implicit knowledge in the sense of enhancing control over a partially acquired feature, and another to show that it enables learners to internalize a previously unused feature. Arguably, the interface hypothesis (see Chapter 1) can only be investigated by examining whether initial explicit knowledge of a new structure can transform via instruction into new implicit knowledge.

The point of all our studies was to investigate whether instruction led to implicit knowledge and, ideally, that necessitated selecting target structures that were both new and partially acquired. We anticipated that two of the structures we investigated (third person-s and past tense -ed) would already have been partially learned; we hoped that the other two more complex structures (the use of the indefinite article to express generic reference and word order following negative adverbials) would be new structures for the majority of the learners in our sample. However, pre-testing showed that the learners typically possessed some knowledge of even the complex target structures. In short, we were not able to investigate whether FFI led to the acquisition of new structures and for this reason we were not able to investigate the interface hypothesis. This constitutes a limitation in the studies in Part 4. Identifying structures that are new but also learnable (in terms of the participants' developmental stage) is clearly going to be a challenge for any researcher.[3]

A third problem concerns the Elicited Oral Imitation Test. This served as a main measure of the acquisition of implicit knowledge in the FFI studies. However, it was evident from the control groups' performance on this test that there was a practice effect over time. All students did better when taking the test for a second time, and, in addition they may have focused more on form in the post-test contexts. Nevertheless, the studies showed that the experimental groups performed significantly better on the post-tests than the control groups, indicating that something more than just a practice effect was involved.

Despite these limitations, we believe that the FFI studies we conducted demonstrated an important methodological advance – the use of separate tests of implicit and explicit knowledge in order to investigate the precise nature of the effect of instruction. FFI research, we would argue, must pay greater attention to the construct validity of the tests used to measure acquisition and, in particular, must acknowledge the importance of distinguishing between implicit and explicit knowledge.

Future Developments

In this final section, I will discuss a number of avenues for further research. I will first consider a number of additional ways of testing implicit and explicit knowledge. I will then propose some applications of the testing battery.

Alternative assessment instruments

The implicit/explicit distinction is applicable to all areas of language – phonology, grammar, lexis and pragmatics. The challenge, then, is to design tests that are capable of providing relatively separate measures of the two types of knowledge in all these areas.

The methodology associated with the Labovian approach to investigating stylistic variability (see Labov, 1970; Tarone, 1982) offers some possibilities for developing measures of implicit and explicit knowledge of L2 phonology. Researchers in the Labovian paradigm collect data using a variety of tasks in order to sample a range of speech styles: (1) casual speech (i.e. the relaxed speech found in the street and in bars), (2) careful speech (e.g. the speech found in interviews), (3) reading, (4) word lists and (5) minimal pairs. These styles were spread along a continuum according to the amount of attention paid by the speakers to their own speech, the least attention being paid in (1) and the most in (5). Thus, for example, a task designed to elicit spontaneous speech would satisfy the four criteria for a test of implicit knowledge (i.e. low awareness, limited response time, a focus on meaning and little opportunity to use metalanguage), while a minimal pair task could satisfy the criteria for a test of explicit knowledge (i.e. high awareness, ample response time, a focus on form and, perhaps, opportunity to use metalanguage). The problem, however, as Wolfson (1976) pointed out, is that we cannot be sure that a speaker really does attend to speech more in a 'careful' than in a 'casual' style. In other words, the crucial issue is the extent to which learners are conscious of attending to their pronunciation as they perform the tasks. One possibility, therefore, might be to obtain measures of the extent to which participants monitor their pronunciation while they perform the different tasks either by examining their self-corrections or obtaining self-reports of their awareness of monitoring on completion of a task. It is doubtful whether a test of metalinguistic knowledge of phonological features of the L2 would serve much purpose, as it is likely that most learners' metalinguistic knowledge of L2 phonology is very limited. Explicit phonological knowledge is surely of the analyzed rather than the technical kind. Overall, we would expect learners' knowledge of L2 phonology to be primarily implicit.

In contrast, knowledge of vocabulary is clearly both implicit and explicit. N. Ellis (1994) claimed that the phonetic and phonological features of new words are learned implicitly as a result of frequent exposure. That is, the motor aspects of articulation of word forms develop implicitly as a result of practice. In contrast, the meanings of words are learned explicitly, requiring conscious processing at semantic and conceptual levels and attention to form-meaning connections. It is of course possible for learners to develop explicit knowledge of lexical forms – e.g. we consciously know how to pronounce or spell some words – and also some aspects of lexical meaning are implicit – e.g. the connotative meanings of words and their collocational possibilities. But clearly, knowledge of linguistic form is primarily implicit while knowledge of lexical meaning is essentially conscious and explicit. This suggests that a test of implicit L2 knowledge of vocabulary needs to assess to what extent learners have knowledge of the phonological and graphological form of words, while a test of explicit knowledge will need to determine whether learners know the meanings of words.

A number of possibilities exist for testing learners' knowledge of phonological and graphological form. Meara and Jones's (1990) Yes/No Test is promising. This is a computer-delivered test that simply asks the test-taker to indicate whether they know a series of words presented one at a time in writing. The items in the test are taken from different vocabulary frequency levels and also include a number of pseudo-words that are used as 'controls' to guard against over reporting. To assess knowledge of lexical form as opposed to meaning, the instructions would need to direct learners to indicate words that they 'recognize' rather than 'know'. If this test were administered in a timed format (as in the TGJT used in the Marsden Project) it could provide a useful measure of learners' implicit knowledge of graphological form. It might also be possible to present the words aurally to the test-taker in order to obtain a measure of implicit knowledge of their phonological form. Another possibility is Webb's (2007) receptive and productive tests of orthography. In the productive test, learners hear a list of words one at a time and simply have to write them down under a time constraint. In the receptive test, the learners hear a list of words and have to circle the correctly spelled word in a multiple-choice format.

Testing explicit knowledge of word meanings is somewhat more complicated given the impossibility of separating the meaning of a word from its form. Laufer and Nation's (1999) Vocabulary Levels' Test uses a gapped word technique to test learners' ability to complete words in sentence contexts. Webb used a translation test. Learners were given a set of words in their L1 and asked to write the equivalent L2 word. Clearly, though, such tests require that students have knowledge of the form of the L2 words. A better approach might be to administer the Yes/No Test twice – first requiring test-takers to indicate whether they *recognize* each item (in order to measure knowledge of form) and then whether they know each word (i.e. know its meaning). It might then be possible to test whether they do actually know the meanings of the words they have indicated knowing. For example, if they click 'yes' to show they know a word, a multiple-choice item testing this knowledge could appear on the computer screen.

Knowledge of pragmatic aspects of language (such as illocutionary meaning) is likely to be largely implicit. Wolfson (1989) argued that the sociolinguistic knowledge native speakers draw on in performing illocutionary acts lies beneath the threshold of consciousness. However, classroom L2 learners may also acquire explicit knowledge of speech acts given the prevalence of functional approaches to teaching language. L2 pragmatic researchers have relied on two principal assessment instruments – role-plays and discourse completion tests (DCT). Role-plays involve simulations of communicative encounters. Learners are given an imaginary situation designed to elicit use of a specific illocutionary act and are asked to perform as themselves or in imaginary roles. Such an instrument is likely to tap into learners' implicit knowledge although some degree of monitoring using explicit knowledge is also to be expected. In a DCT, learners are given a description of a situation and an instruction to either select from a range of choices about how to respond (testing receptive knowledge) or to say/write how they would respond (assessing productive knowledge). Golato (2003: 92) argues that a DCT is metapragmatic and suggests that it is 'a valid instrument not for measuring pragmatic action, but symbolic action'. As such, it constitutes a measure of learners' explicit knowledge. Roehr (2008) proposed an alternative way of measuring metapragmatic knowledge. In one section of her MKT, she required learners to describe and explain why paraphrases of three short passages were inappropriate, arguing that this task type forced learners to consider L2 features that depended on pragmatic and discursive context.

Two final points deserve a brief discussion. The first concerns the use of dual as opposed to single tasks. The former require the test-taker to perform two separate tasks (e.g. to recite numbers in a random order while making a judgment about grammatical accuracy), while the latter poses a single demand on the test-taker (e.g. to simply make a judgment). It can be argued that dual tasks are more likely to elicit procedural/implicit knowledge because it places fewer demands on control mechanisms. Learners will experience difficulty in accessing their declarative/explicit knowledge while performing two separate tasks. The Elicited Oral Imitation Test can be seen as a dual task in that learners had to decide whether they agreed/disagreed with each statement and also to imitate it. Further research is needed to ascertain whether performance on dual (as opposed to single) tasks correlates with other measures of implicit knowledge.

The second point is that it is possible that implicit and explicit knowledge need to be distinguished in terms of whether they are receptive/productive, giving four knowledge types (i.e. receptive/implicit, receptive/explicit, productive implicit and productive/explicit). As De Jong (2005a: 17) noted, 'theories should make clear statements about whether they assume that the same knowledge base – whether implicit or explicit – and the same set of processing mechanisms are drawn upon in receptive and productive tasks'. We clearly neglected to do this in developing the battery of tests for the Marsden Project. We included both productive and receptive tests of implicit knowledge but only receptive tests of explicit knowledge (but see the revised MKT in the Appendix). De Jong reviews the literature related to the receptive/productive distinction, pointing out that considerable disagreement exists, but concluding that developmentally receptive representation precedes productive representation and that thereafter there is at least some shared representation. His own study (see De Jong, 2005b) of the effects of listening training on the acquisition of a grammatical feature in an artificial language included both receptive and productive tests designed to measure implicit and explicit knowledge but, as De Jong himself acknowledged, it was not possible to determine from the results of the study what kind of knowledge (implicit or explicit) the learners had acquired.

Clearly, much work needs to be done to investigate the validity of tests of implicit and explicit L2 knowledge of the different aspects of language. Hopefully, the approach we adopted in the Marsden Project will afford a methodology for carrying out this work in the future. Tests need to be designed in accordance with a theoretical model of L2 knowledge and systematically evaluated in relation to hypotheses derived from the model.

Applications of tests of implicit and explicit knowledge

In Part 3, we examined a number of ways in which the battery of tests of implicit/explicit knowledge could be put to use. In Chapter 6, we explored how the tests shed light on the thorny problem of grammatical complexity by examining how the learning difficulty of grammatical structures varies depending on whether it is considered in terms of implicit or explicit knowledge. In Chapter 7, we examined to what extent standardized proficiency tests reflect the implicit/explicit distinction. In Chapter 8, we focused on the relationship between groups of learners who varied in both their implicit/explicit knowledge profile and exogenous and endogenous aspects of their background. We used a revised MKT to examine the metalinguistic knowledge of native and non-native groups of teacher trainees. We believe that the availability of the battery tests reported in Part 2 of the book affords a number of other potentially fruitful applications.

One such application is in research investigating the role of individual differences (ID) in language learning. To what extent do ID factors, such as language aptitude, learning style, personality and motivation, impact on the acquisition of implicit and explicit knowledge? To date, researchers have examined the impact of ID factors only in terms of general measures of learners' proficiency or achievement (e.g. using standardized proficiency tests or teacher grades). Of much greater theoretical (and possibly practical) interest, however, is the *type* of knowledge that ID factors influence. As an illustration of the importance of distinguishing type of knowledge in ID research, consider the debate that exists regarding the role of language aptitude. DeKeyser (2000) argued that language analytical ability only influences the extent to which learners develop explicit knowledge. While there is no doubt that language analytical ability on the one hand and knowledge of meta-language and the ability to describe/explain errors on the other are strongly related in at least some learners (see, e.g. Roehr's (2008) study of university-level learners of L2 German[4]), there are also reasons to believe that language analytical ability is also related to implicit knowledge, as Robinson (2005) has argued and Ranta's (2002) research demonstrates. Such controversies can only be resolved by obtaining separate measures of the two types of knowledge.

Another controversy surrounds L1 transfer. Is transfer of L1 features more apparent in implicit or in explicit knowledge? The answer to this question rests on the ability to identify the extent to which transfer is conscious or unconscious in both communication transfer (i.e. the borrowing of L1 forms to facilitate communication) and learning transfer (i.e. the incorporation of L1 forms into the learner's interlanguage system). In the case of communication transfer, learners are likely to be fully aware that they are drawing on their L1. In the case of learning transfer, different positions have been advanced. Krashen (1983) argued that transfer played very little role in 'acquisition' but could contribute to 'learning'. It would follow from such a position that learners' L2 implicit knowledge would display little or no evidence of the transfer of L1 forms whereas their explicit knowledge would. Other researchers (e.g. Möhle & Raupach, 1989), however, have argued that L2 development can involve both subconscious and conscious transfer. From this point of view, L1 forms would be apparent in both types of knowledge. Again, to resolve this controversy, separate measures of implicit and explicit knowledge are required.

Finally, the tests of implicit and explicit knowledge may help to address some of the abiding problems associated with the grading of the contents of structural syllabuses. Such syllabuses have been criticized on the grounds that they do not reflect the actual order and sequence of acquisition that learners follow (Krashen, 1982). That is, they do not accord with how implicit knowledge is gradually and dynamically acquired. In Ellis (1993), however, I argued that a structural syllabus can still be viewed as a valid basis for teaching explicit knowledge. Irrespective of whether the structural syllabus is designed to teach implicit or explicit knowledge, it will be necessary to grade items in the syllabus. While the grading of items remains a complex matter (with different criteria competing against each other), there is an obvious need to take account of learning difficulty. This will need to be established separately for implicit and explicit knowledge (as shown in Chapter 6). Tests of implicit and explicit knowledge, then, can assist course designers in deciding the order of items in a syllabus and can also help teachers establish to what extent their students have developed implicit and/or explicit knowledge of a specific target feature.

Conclusion

In his introduction to the special issue on implicit/explicit learning in *Studies in Second Language Acquisition*, Hulstijn (2005: 129) opens with this statement: 'There are good theoretical and educational reasons to place matters of implicit and explicit learning high on the agenda for SLA research'. In the Marsden Project, as reported in this book, we set out to examine a number of these theoretical and educational reasons for investigating implicit/explicit learning. But this was not the main focus of this book. Later in the same introduction, Hulstijn (2005: 137) commented 'if we continue to focus on the conceptual and speculative aspects of theory construction, neglecting measurement issues, theories of implicit and explicit L2 learning will not survive'. Indeed so. We cannot hope to address implicit/explicit learning unless we have instruments that will provide us with valid measures of the different products of such learning. It was our recognition of this fundamental point that led us to focus on 'measurement issues'. We would not claim that we have satisfactorily solved these issues, but we believe we have made a useful start and hope that in doing so we have provided a baseline for prospective research on implicitness/explicitness in SLA and, perhaps, in language testing.

Notes

1. The terms implicit/explicit and procedural/declarative derive from different theories, but as De Jong (2005: 14) points out 'declarative/procedural knowledge and explicit/implicit knowledge may not be two co-existing systems of knowledge but rather a different description of the same system'.
2. Confidence rating can be elicited in different ways – on a continuous scale as in Dienes and Scott (2005), in a binary form and by means of verbal categories (e.g. guess, somewhat confident and very confident). See Rebuschat (2008) for a discussion of confidence-ratings in judgment tests.
3. Robinson (2005) used a completely new language (Samoan) as the source of targets in his study of implicit/explicit learning with Japanese learners. The problem here is identifying which grammatical structures are reasonable candidates for acquisition at the very beginning stage of acquisition.
4. On the basis of the strong correlations Roehr found between her measures of metalinguistic knowledge and language analytic ability, she argued that 'the ability to correct, describe, and explain highlighted L2 errors, and the ability to identify the grammatical role of parts of speech in L2 sentences may in fact be components of the same complex construct' (Roehr, 2008: 193).

Appendix

This appendix includes the main instruments used in the Marsden Project:

  A. The Background Questionnaire
  B. Stimuli used in the Elicited Oral Imitation Test
  C. Text used in the Oral Narrative Test
  D. The GJT Test Items
  E. Metalinguistic Knowledge Test
  F. Revised Metalinguistic Test (Chapter 9)
  G. Sample scoring procedure for part 1 of the revised Metalinguistic Knowledge Test (Chapter 9)
  H. Sample instructional materials (Chapter 10)

A. Background Questionnaire

  1. Which country do you come from? _____
  2. What is your mother tongue (i.e. the language first acquired)? _____
     (If your answer to Question 2 is English, go to Section 6.)
  3. How old were you when you started to learn English? ____ years old
  4. How many years have you been learning English (including the years at school in New Zealand)? _____ years
  5. Altogether, how many years have you spent living in a country where English is widely spoken (including New Zealand)? ___ years
  6. What other languages have you studied?

Language	Length of time I have studied it

  7. At present, which language do you use the most every day? _____
  8. How many years have you studied English at school? _____ years
  9. What was the instruction in English that you received at school like? (Tick the best answer)
     A. Mainly formal (i.e. a lot of time was spent studying grammar)

B. Mainly informal (i.e. most of the time was spent communicating in English)

C. A mixture of informal and formal

If you are interested in participating in further research, please give us your contact detail.

Phone: _____   E-mail: _____

B. Elicited Oral Imitation Test

Stimuli used in Oral Elicited Imitation Test. The structures targeted are highlighted in the text.

1. New Zealand is **greener** and **more beautiful** than other countries.
2. New Zealanders **want to keep** their country clean and green.
3. Children play rugby **well** and soccer **badly** in New Zealand.
4. People should report the police stolen money.
5. Everyone **loves** comic books and **read** them.
6. The film that **everyone likes** is Star Wars.
7. People **can win** a lot of money in a casino.
8. Spending 10 hours in an aeroplane isn't much fun, **is it**?
9. People should report a car accident to the police.
10. People have been using computers **since** many years.
11. The software **that Bill Gates invented it** changed the world.
12. A good teacher **makes** lessons interesting and **cares** about students.
13. It is not a good idea for **teachers** to punish **students.**
14. Not everyone **can to** learn a second language.
15. To speak English well you must study **for** many months.
16. It is **more harder** to learn Japanese than to learn English.
17. Princess Diana **loved** Prince Charles but **divorced** him.
18. If Prince Charles had loved Princess Diana **she will be** happier.
19. Princess **Diana's death** shocked the whole world.
20. The number of Africans with AIDS **was increased** last year.
21. The Americans were first to land on the moon, **isn't it**?
22. If Russia had got to the moon first, America **would have been worried**.
23. Everyone wants to know what is President Bush like.
24. When man **invented** the motor car, life **change** for everyone.
25. Last year the population of the world **increased** a lot.
26. Young people visit **often** clubs and drink **a lot.**
27. Young women like **cigarettes** and fast **car**.
28. Parents have **a responsibility** to care for their children.
29. People worry about their **parent health** and their **children's future**.
30. Every child needs **good father**.
31. It is a silly question to ask **'Do a woman need to marry?'**

32. People in love usually **want getting** married as soon as possible.

33. A wife always wants to know **what** her **husband is doing**.

34. It is difficult to ask **'Do you really love me?'**

C. Text used in Oral Narrative Test

Every morning Mr Lee gets up at 6:30 am, walks to the dairy in Ponsonby Road and buys a newspaper. He has toast and tea for breakfast and reads the newspaper. Then, if he feels like it, he goes to work. But often he stays at home and sits in the sun. On these days Mrs Lee complains. But he always smiles and says, 'I want to take life easy. I want to enjoy myself'.

Yesterday Mr Lee's life changed for ever. Mrs Lee's life changed too. This is what happened.

Mr Lee found a wallet. It contained 55 dollars, some credit cards and two lottery tickets. Mr Lee checked the lottery ticket's numbers in the newspaper. He couldn't believe it. He had the winning ticket. It was worth 6 million dollars.

Mr Lee didn't know what to do. After all it wasn't really his ticket. 'Do I keep the money for myself? or 'Do I give the ticket back to the wallet's owner? he asked Mrs Lee.

After a while he knew what to do. He took the bus to the address of the wallet's owner. He knocked on the door. An old woman opened the door.

'Do you know a Mr Martin?' asked Mr Lee.

'Just a minute. He is my daughter's husband', said the old woman.

Mr Martin came to the door. Mr Lee showed him the ticket and the newspaper.

'This is your ticket,' said Mr Lee, 'I want you to have it back'.

Mr Martin couldn't believe that he had won $6 million dollars.

'I want to thank you for being so honest', he said. 'I want to give you a reward. Do you think that a million dollars is enough?'

Mr Lee accepted the million dollars. His life changed. He no longer needed to work. In fact he and Mrs Lee lived happily ever after.

D. The Grammaticality Judgment Test Items (for both timed and untimed versions)

Item
1. I haven't seen him for a long time.
2. I think that he is nicer and more intelligent than all the other students.
3. The teacher explained the problem to the students.

APPENDIX (*Continued*)
Item
4. *Liao says he wants buying a car next week.
5. *Martin completed his assignment and print it out.
6. *We will leave tomorrow, isn't it?
7. He plays soccer very well.
8. *Did Keiko completed her homework?
9. *I must to brush my teeth now.
10. *If he had been richer, she will marry him.
11. *He has been living in New Zealand since three years.
12. Pam wanted to know what I had told John.
13. *They had the very good time at the party.
14. *Between 1990 and 2000 the population of New Zealand was increased.
15. *Liao is still living in his rich uncle house.
16. *Martin sold a few old coins and stamp to a shop.
17. *I have been studying English since a long time.
18. *I can to speak French very well.
19. *Joseph miss an interesting party last weekend.
20. Keiko eats a lot of sushi.
21. Bill wanted to know where I had been.
22. Did Cathy cook dinner last night?
23. Rosemary reported the crime to the police.
24. Mary is taller than her sisters.
25. *Hiroshi live with his friend Koji.
26. Keum wants to buy a computer this weekend.
27. *She writes very well English.

APPENDIX (*Continued*)

Item
28. If she had worked hard, she would have passed the exam.
29. *Tom wanted to know whether was I going.
30. *I saw very funny movie last night.
31. *The teacher explained John the answer.
32. I must finish my homework tonight.
33. *Keum went to the school to speak to her children teacher.
34. Keiko has been studying in Auckland for three years.
35. *This building is more bigger than your house.
36. That book isn't very interesting, is it?
37. Her English vocabulary increased a lot last year.
38. Hiroshi received a letter from his father yesterday.
39. Does Keum live in Auckland?
40. Liao left some pens and pencils at school.
41. *If he hadn't come to New Zealand, he will stay in Japan.
42. *My car is more faster and more powerful than your car.
43. Joseph flew to Washington to meet the President's advisor.
44. *Joseph wants finding a new job next month.
45. Liao works very hard but earns very little.
46. Japan is a very interesting country.
47. I can cook Chinese food very well.
48. They enjoyed the party very much.
49. *The boys went to bed late last night, is it?
50. *She wanted to know why had he studied German.
51. *He reported his father the bad news.
52. Keiko spoke to the professor's secretary.

APPENDIX (*Continued*)
Item
53. Liao stayed at home all day and finished the book.
54. Hiroshi found some keys on the ground.
55. They did not come at the right time.
56. If he had bought a ticket, he might have won the prize.
57. Martin says he wants to get married next year.
58. *An accident was happened on the motorway.
59. *Keum lives in Hamilton but work in Auckland.
60. *She likes always watching television.
61. *Did Martin visited his father yesterday?
62. Something bad happened last weekend.
63. *Keum bought two present for her children.
64. She is working very hard, isn't she?
65. *The bird that my brother caught it has died.
66. *The boat that my father bought it has sunk.
67. The book that Mary wrote won the prize.
68. The car that Bill has rented is a Toyota.

*Ungrammatical

E. Metalinguistic Knowledge Test

(Part 1)

In this part of the test there are 17 sentences. All of them are ungrammatical. The part of the sentence containing the error is underlined. For each sentence choose which statement best explains the error. Circle a, b, c or d to indicate your choice.

Example Sentence One

Keiko said, 'I have lost <u>mine ring</u>'.

    a. Replace the word 'mine' with 'my'.
    b. Mine cannot be used as a possessive word.

c. Should be 'her ring' because Keiko is the subject.

d. Before a noun use the possessive adjective, not the pronoun.

Example Sentence Two

He saw a elephant.

a. The word 'elephant' refers to the normal verb.

b. We must use 'elephant' instead of 'a elephant'.

c. You should use 'an' not 'a' because elephant starts with a vowel sound.

d. The wrong form of the indefinite article has been used.

Now start.

1. **You must to wash your hands before eating.**

a. 'Must to' is the wrong form of the imperative.

b. Change to 'must have to wash' to express obligation.

c. Modal verbs should never be followed by a preposition.

d. After 'must' use the base form of the verb not the infinitive.

2. **Hiroshi wants visiting the United States this year.**

a. 'Visiting' should be written in the base form.

b. The verb following 'want' must be an infinitive.

c. We cannot have two verbs together in a sentence.

d. It should be 'visit' because the event is in the future.

3. **Martin work in a car factory.**

a. Work is a noun so it cannot have the subject 'Martin'.

b. We must use the present simple tense after a pronoun.

c. We need 's' after the verb to indicate third person plural.

d. In the third person singular the present tense verb takes 's'.

4. **If Jane had asked me, I would give her some money.**

a. 'would' is conditional so it should appear in the 'if' clause not the main clause.

b. The first clause tells us that this is an impossible condition, so use the subjunctive.

c. We must use 'would have given' to indicate that the event has already happened.

d. When 'if' clause is in the past perfect tense, main clause verb is in the past conditional.

5. **Learning a language is more easier when you are young.**

a. 'More' is an adjective so we must use 'easily' not 'easier'.

b. The comparative ending of a two-syllable adjective is 'er'.

c. The 'er' ending indicates comparison, so 'more' is not needed.

d. You cannot have two adjectives together in the same sentence.

6. Keiko grew <u>some rose</u> in her garden.

a. The noun is countable, so after 'some' use the plural form.

b. The wrong adjective has been used before 'rose'.

c. A noun must always have 'a' or 'the' before it.

d. Use 'a few' not 'some' with countable nouns.

7. His school grades <u>were improved</u> last year.

a. The verb 'improve' can never be used in the passive form.

b. We should insert 'by him' after the verb to indicate the agent.

c. Use 'improved' as the sentence refers to a specific event last year.

d. 'Improve' should take the active form even though the subject is not the agent.

8. Martin lost <u>his friend book</u>.

a. We need possessive 's' to show that the friend owns the book.

b. You cannot have two nouns next to one another in a sentence.

c. The verb refers to a personal object, so must have an apostrophe.

d. Insert 'of' before book to show that it belongs to the friend.

9. Keum <u>happen</u> to meet an old friend yesterday.

a. It took place yesterday, so use a past tense verb ending.

b. Third person singular verbs always have an 's' ending.

c. We don't use a preposition after the verb 'happen'.

d. 'Happen' never follows the subject of a sentence.

10. Because he was late, he called <u>taxi</u>.

a. Insert 'a' before taxi because it is not a specific one.

b. Use 'some taxis' because taxi cannot be singular.

c. We must always use 'the' before countable nouns.

d. Use the indefinite article because the taxi is unique.

11. They were interested in <u>what was I doing</u>.

a. In embedded questions the word order is the same as that in statements.

b. Change the word order, because 'what' is always followed by a pronoun.

c. The subject should always come in front of the verb after question words.

d. The clause 'What was I doing' should be followed by a question mark.

12. Does Liao <u>has</u> a Chinese wife?

a. With questions, always use the auxiliary 'have'.

b. We must use the base form after 'do/does'.

c. Use 'have' not 'has' because 'does' is in the past tense.

d. The word order changes when we use the question form.

13. Jenny likes very much her new job.

a. Adverbial phrases should occur after nouns not verbs.

b. An adverb should not come between a verb and its object.

c. The phrase 'very much' always occurs at the end of a sentence.

d. The adverbial phrase must always precede the verb.

14. They have already finished, isn't it?

a. We cannot use 'it' because the main verb 'finish' does not have an object.

b. 'have' should be used instead of 'is' in all question tags referring to past time.

c. The tag question should be positive because the main verb is in the affirmative.

d. The form of the question tag must relate to the subject and verb in the main clause.

15. He has been saving money since 10 years.

a. The wrong conjunction has been used in the time clause.

b. We cannot use 'since' because the exact date is specified.

c. Use 'for' following any verb in the past perfect continuous tense.

d. Use 'for' not 'since' for a noun phrase referring to a period of time.

16. I explained my friend the rules of the game.

a. The indirect object must never precede the direct object of a verb.

b. 'Explain' (unlike the verbs 'tell' and 'give') can only have one object.

c. After 'explain' we must insert a preposition before the indirect object.

d. The preposition 'to' is always used for the dative form of a noun or pronoun.

17. The cake that you baked it tastes very nice.

a. Omit 'that' when the relative pronoun is subject of the clause.

b. We should use 'which' instead of 'that' when referring to things.

c. Omit 'it' in the relative clause because it refers to same thing as 'that'.

d. Omit 'that' when using 'it' in the relative clause to avoid having two pronouns.

(Part 2) *Adapted from Alderson* et al. *(1997)*

1. Read the passage below. Find ONE example in the passage for each of the grammatical features listed in the table. Write the examples in the table in the spaces provided. The first one is done for you. Note: it may be possible to choose the same example to illustrate more than one grammatical feature.

The materials are delivered to the factory by a supplier, who usually has no technical knowledge, but who happens to have the right contacts. We would normally expect the materials to arrive within three days, but this time it has taken longer.

Grammatical feature	*Example*
definite article	the
verb	
noun	
preposition	
passive verb	
conditional verb	
adjective	
adverb	
countable noun	
indefinite article	
relative pronoun	
auxiliary verb	
modal verb	
past participle	
conjunction	
finite verb	
infinitive verb	
agent	
comparative form	
pronoun	

2. In the following sentences, underline the item requested in brackets:
    1. Poor little Joe stood out in the snow. (SUBJECT)
    2. Joe had nowhere to stay. (INFINITIVE)

3. The policeman chased Joe down the street. (DIRECT OBJECT)
4. The woman gave him some money. (INDIRECT OBJECT)

F. Revised Metalinguistic Knowledge Test Part 1 (Chapter 9)

In this part, there are 17 sentences. They are <u>all</u> ungrammatical. The part of the sentence containing the error is underlined. For each sentence, if you know a rule that explains why the sentence is ungrammatical, write it in English in the space provided. If you do not know a rule, leave it blank and go on to the next sentence.

Here are some examples.

Example One: I have lost mine ring.

_____

_____

_____

_____

Example Two: He saw <u>a elephant</u>.

_____

_____

_____

_____

Now start the test.

1. I <u>must have to</u> wash my hands.

_____

_____

_____

_____

2. Hiroshi <u>wants visiting</u> the United States this year.

_____

_____

_____

3. If Jane had asked me, I <u>would give</u> her some money.

4. Learning a language is <u>more easier</u> when you are young.

5. Keiko grew <u>some rose</u> in her garden.

6. His school grades <u>were improved</u> last year.

7. Martin lost <u>his friend book</u>.

8. Keum <u>happen</u> to meet an old friend yesterday.

_____

_____

9. Because he was late, he called <u>taxi</u>.

_____

_____

_____

_____

10. They were interested in <u>what was I doing</u>.

_____

_____

_____

_____

11. Does Liao <u>has</u> a Chinese wife?

_____

_____

_____

_____

12. Jenny likes very much her new job.

_____

_____

_____

_____

13. They have already finished, <u>isn't it?</u>

_____

_____

_____

_____

14. He has been saving money <u>since 10 years.</u>

_____

_____

_____

_____

15. The cake <u>that you baked it</u> tastes very nice.

_____

_____

_____

_____

G. Sample scoring procedure for part 1 of the revised Metalinguistic Knowledge Test

Q.1. I <u>must have to</u> wash my hands.

Rule: (1 mark)	must and have to both express same meaning/ obligation – you don't need both
OR	must and have to are both modal verbs/or a semimodal and a modal – you don't need both
Metalang: (1 mark)	modal/semimodal/auxiliary

Q.2. Hiroshi <u>wants visiting</u> the United States this year.

Rule: (1 mark)	after certain types of verb you must use to-form (infinitive)/you can't use gerund
Metalang: (1 mark)	infinitive/gerund

Q.3. If Jane had asked me, I <u>would give</u> her money.

Rule: (1 mark)	answer must contain some reference to the relationship (syntactic interdependency) between the two parts of the sentence
Metalang: (1 mark)	past perfect/conditional/present perfect

H. Sample instructional materials (Chapter 10)

<u>Output activity</u>

Students, in pairs, role-play talking to an alien.
Each student receives one of two cards:

Activity 4

Card 1.

You will meet an alien from planet Zlog.
The alien will ask you, 'What's a human?'
Explain clearly 3 characteristics of a human.
Find out 3 things about a zlog.

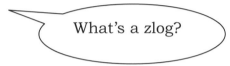

What's a zlog?

Card 2

You are an alien from planet Zlog.
Find out 3 things about a human.
The human you meet will ask you, 'What's a zlog?'
Explain clearly 3 characteristics of a zlog.

Input activity

Activity 7

Getting around

In this activity the article 'a' is used with two meanings. You have to
sort out which meaning it has – whether it is general or ONE particular
thing. Tick the 'General' or 'Particular' box.

	General	*Particular*
1. I bought a new bicycle.	☐	☐
2. I bought a bus ticket with my last dollar.	☐	☐
3. A helicopter can land just about anywhere.	☐	☐
4. A car costs a lot of money to run.	☐	☐
5. A parachute is the fastest way of getting out of a plane.	☐	☐

APPENDIX (*Continued*)

	General	Particular
6. A helicopter flies over my house every morning.	☐	☐
7. A ferry leaves every hour.	☐	☐
8. A bus ticket costs very little.	☐	☐
9. A huge liner has just docked in Auckland harbour.	☐	☐
10. A large liner can carry over a thousand passengers.	☐	☐
11. I took a ferry to Devonport.	☐	☐
12. A bicycle is a cheap means of transport.	☐	☐
13. Whenever I go in a plane I take a parachute.	☐	☐
14. A car crashed into my house yesterday.	☐	☐

References

Adams, R. and Koo, S-T. (1993) *Quest: The Interactive Test Analysis System*. Quest: Australian Council for Educational Research.

Akakura, M. (2009) The effectiveness of teaching grammar on implicit and explicit language knowledge. Unpublished PhD thesis, The University of Auckland.

Alanen, R. (1995) Input enhancement and rule presentation in second language acquisition. In R. Schmidt (ed.) *Attention and Awareness in Foreign Language Learning* (pp. 259–302). Honolulu, HI: University of Hawai'i.

Alderson, J.C. (1993) The relationship between grammar and reading in an English for academic purposes test battery. In D. Douglas and C. Chapelle (eds) *A New Decade of Language Testing Research: Selected Papers from the 1990 Language Testing Research Colloquium: Dedicated in Memory of Michael Canale* (pp. 203–219). Alexandria, VA: Teachers of English to Speakers of Other Languages.

Alderson, J.C., Clapham, C. and Steel, D. (1997) Metalinguistic knowledge, language aptitude and language proficiency. *Language Teaching Research* 1, 93–121.

Allen, L.Q. (2000) Form-meaning connections and the French causative: An experiment in processing instruction. *Studies in Second Language Acquisition* 22, 69–84.

Allwright, R. (1984) Why don't learners learn what teachers teach? In D. Singleton and D. Little (eds) *Language Learning in Formal and Informal Contexts* (pp. 3–18). Dublin: IRAAL.

Allwright, R. (1984a) The importance of interaction in classroom language learning. *Applied Linguistics* 5, 156–171.

Ammar, A. and Spada, N. (2006) One size fits all?: Recasts, prompts, and L2 learning. *Studies in Second Language Acquisition* 28, 543–574.

Anderson, J. and Lebiere, C. (1998) *The Atomic Components of Thought*. Mahwah, NJ: Erlbaum.

Anderson, J.C., Matessa, M. and Lebiere, C. (1997) ACT-R: A theory of higher level cognition and its relation to visual attention. *Human-Computer Interaction* 12, 439–462.

Andersen, R. (1984) The one to one principle of interlanguage construction. *Language Learning* 34, 77–95.

Andrews, S.J. (1994) The grammatical knowledge/awareness of native-speaker EFL teachers – what the trainers say? In M. Bygate, A. Tonkyn and E. Williams (eds) *Grammar and the Language Teacher* (pp. 69–89). Hemel Hempstead: Prentice Hall.

Andrews, S.J. (1999) Why do L2 teachers need to 'know about language'?: Teacher metalinguistic awareness and input for learning. *Language and Education* 13 (3), 161–177.

Andrews, S.J. (2003) Teacher language awareness and the professional knowledge base of the L2 teacher. *Language Awareness* 12, 81–95.

Andrews, S.J. (2005) Professional standards in TEFL – a challenge for Asia. *Journal of Asia TEFL* 2 (1), 1–22.

Arbuckle, J. (2004) *AMOS 5.0.* Chicago, IL: Small Waters Corporation.

Ayoun, D. (2004) The effectiveness of written recasts in the second language acquisition of a spectual distinctions in French: A follow-up study. *The Modern Language Journal* 88(1), 31–55.

Bachman, L. (1990) *Fundamental Considerations in Language Testing.* Oxford: Oxford University Press.

Bachman, L. and Palmer, A. (1996) *Language Testing in Practice: Designing and Developing Useful Language Tests.* Oxford: Oxford University Press.

Baddeley, A.D. (1999) *Essentials of Human Memory.* Hove: Psychology Press.

Baddeley, A., Gathercole, S. and Papagno, C. (1998) The phonological loop as a language learning device. *Psychological Review* 105, 158–173.

Baker, D. (1989) *Language Testing: A Critical Survey and Practical Guide.* London: Edward Arnold.

Bard, E.G., Robertson, D. and Sorace, A. (1996) Magnitude estimation of linguistic acceptability. *Language* 72, 32–68.

Bartke, S., Rosler, F., Streb, J. and Wiese, R. (2005) An ERP-study of German "regular" and "irregular" morphology. *Journal of Neurolinguistics* 18, 29–55.

Batstone, R. (2002) Contexts of engagement: A discourse perspective on "intake" and "pushed output". *System* 30, 1–14.

Benati, A. (2001) A comparative study of the effects of processing instruction and output-based instruction on the acquisition of the Italian future tense. *Language Teaching Research* 5, 95–127.

Berry, D.A. (2001) Mechanisms of modal and nonmodal phonation. *Journal of Phonetics* 29 (4), 431–450.

Bialystok, E. (1978) A theoretical model of second language learning. *Language Learning* 28, 69–84.

Bialystok, E. (1979) Explicit and implicit judgments of L2 grammaticality. *Language Learning* 29, 81–103.

Bialystok, E. (1981) The role of linguistic knowledge in second language use. *Studies in Second Language Acquisition* 4, 31–45.

Bialystok, E. (1982) On the relationship between knowing and using forms. *Applied Linguistics* 3, 181–206.

Bialystok, E. (1990) *Communicative Strategies.* Oxford: Blackwell.

Bialystok, E. (1991) *Language Processing in Bilingual Children.* Cambridge: Cambridge University Press.

Bialystok, E. (1994) Analysis and control in the development of second language proficiency. *Studies in Second Language Acquisition* 16, 157–168.

Bialystok, E. (1994a) Representation and ways of knowing: Three issues in second language acquisition. In N. Ellis (ed.) *Implicit and Explicit Learning of Languages* (pp. 549–569). London: Academic Press.

Bialystok, E. and Ryan, E.B. (1985) A metacognitive framework for the development of first and second language skills. In D.L. Forrest-Pressley, G.E. Mackinnon and T.G Wallter (eds) *Metacognition, Cognition and Human Performance: Vol 1: Theoretical Perspectives* (pp. 207–252). San Diego, CA: Academic Press.

Bigelow, M. and Tarone, E. (2004) The role of literacy level in SLA: Doesn't *who* we study determine *what* we know? *TESOL Quarterly* 38 (4), 689–700.

Birdsong, D. (1989) *Metalinguistic Performance and Interlinguistic Competence.* New York: Springer.

Birdsong, D. (1992) Ultimate attainment in second language acquisition. *Language* 68, 706–755.

Birdsong, D. (2004) Second language acquisition and ultimate attainment In A. Davies and C. Elder (ed.) *The Handbook of Applied Linguistics* (pp. 82–105). Oxford: Blackwell Publishing.

Birdsong, D. (2006) Age and second language acquisition and processing: A selective overview. In M. Gullberg and P. Indefrey (eds) *The Cognitive Neuroscience of Second Language Acquisition* (pp. 9–49). Malden, MA: Blackwell.

Blackwell, A., Bates, E. and Fisher, D. (1996) The time course of grammaticality judgement. *Language and Cognitive Processes* 11, 337–406.

Bley-Vroman, R. and Chaudron, C. (1994) Elicited imitation as a measure of second-language competence. In E. Tarone, S. Gass and A. Cohen (eds) *Research Methodology in Second-language Acquisition* (pp. 245–261). Mahwah, NJ: Lawrence Erlbaum.

Bley-Vroman, R. and Joo, H.R. (2001) The acquisition and interpretation of English locative constructions by native speakers of Korean. *Studies in Second Language Acquisition* 23 (2), 207–219.

Bolitho, R. (1988) Language awareness on teacher training courses. In T. Duff (ed.) *Explorations in Teacher Training: Problems and Issues* (pp. 72–84). Harlow: Longman.

Bossers, B. (1992) *Reading in Two Languages: A Study of Reading Comprehension in Dutch as a Second Language and in Turkish as a First Language.* Rotterdam, The Netherlands: Drukkerij Van Driel.

Breen, M. (1989) The evaluation cycle for language learning tasks. In R.K. Johnson (ed.) *The Second Language Curriculum* (pp. 187–206). Cambridge: Cambridge University Press.

Brisbois, J.E. (1995) Connections between first- and second-language reading. *Journal of Reading Behaviour* 27, 565–84.

Brown, R. 1973. *A First Language.* Cambridge, MA: Harvard University Press.

Brumfit, C., Mitchell, R. and Hooper, J. (1996) 'Grammar', 'Language' and 'Classroom Practice'. In M. Hughes (ed.) *Teaching and Learning in Changing Times* (pp. 70–87). Oxford: Blackwell.

Burt, M., Dulay, H. and Hernandez, E. (1975) *Bilingual Syntax Measure II Handbook.* New York: Harcourt Brace Jovanovich.

Burt, M. and Kiparsky, C. (1972) *The Gooficon: A Repair Manual for English.* Rowley, MA: Newbury House.

Butler, Y. (2002) Second language learner' theories on the use of English articles: An analysis of the metalinguistic knowledge used by Japanese students in acquiring the English article system. *Studies in Second Language Acquisition* 24, 451–480.

Byrne, B.M. (2001) *Structural Equation Modeling with AMOS: Basic Concepts, Applications, and Programming.* Mahwah, NJ: Lawrence Erlbaum.

Cadierno, T. (1995) Formal instruction from a processing perspective: An investigation into the Spanish past tense. *The Modern Language Journal* 79, 179–193.

Campbell, D.T. and Fiske, D.W. (1959) Convergent and discriminant validation by the multitrait-multimethod matrix. *Psychological Bulletin* 56, 81–105.

Canale, M. (1983) From communicative competence to language pedagogy. In J. Richards and R. Schmidt (eds) *Language and Communication* (pp. 2–27). London: Longman.

Canale, M. and Swain, M. (1980) Theoretical bases of communicative approaches to second language teaching and testing. *Applied Linguistics* 1, 1–47.

Carroll, J.B. (1962) The prediction of success in intensive foreign language training. In R. Glaser (ed.) *Training Research and Education* (pp. 87–136). Pittsburgh: University of Pittsburgh Press.

Carroll, S. (2001) *Input and Evidence: The Raw Material of Second Language Acquisition*. Amsterdam: John Benjamins.

Carroll, S. Roberge, Y. and Swain, M. (1992) The role of feedback in adult second language acquisition: Error correction and morphological generalizations. *Applied Psycholinguistics* 13, 173–198.

Carroll, S. and Swain, M. (1993) Explicit and implicit negative feedback: An empirical study of the learning of linguistic generalizations. *Studies in Second Language Acquisition* 15, 357–366.

Celce-Murcia, M. and Larsen-Freeman, D. (1999) *The Grammar Book* (2nd edn). Boston: Heinle & Heinle.

Chaudron, C. (1983) Research on metalinguistic judgments: A review of theory, method and results. *Language Learning* 33 (3), 343–377.

Chaudron, C. (1985) Intake: On models and methods for discovering learners' processing of input. *Studies in Second Language Acquisition* 7, 1–14.

Chaudron, C. and Russell, G. (1990) The status of elicited imitation as a measure of second language competence. Paper presented at the Ninth World Congress of Applied Linguistics, Thessaloniki, Greece.

Cheng, A. (1995) Grammar instruction and input processing: The acquisition of Spanish ser and estar. Unpublished PhD thesis, University of Illinois, Urbana-Champaign.

Clapham, C. (2001) The assessment of metalinguistic knowledge. In C. Elder, A. Brown, E. Grove, K. Hill, N. Iwashita, T. Lumley, T. McNamara and K. O'Loughlin (eds) *Experimenting with Uncertainty: Essays in Honour of Alan Davies* (pp. 33–43). Cambridge: Cambridge University Press.

Clapham, C. and Alderson, C. (1997) Constructing and trialling the IELTS Test – Research Report 3. The British Council/University of Cambridge Local Examination Syndicate/IDP Education Australia.

Cohen, J. (1988) *Statistical Power Analysis for the Behavioral Sciences* (2nd edn). Hillsdale, NJ: Lawrence Erlbaum.

Collentine, J. (1998) Processing instruction and the subjunctive. *Hispania* 81, 576–587.

Coniam, D. and Falvey, P. (2002) Selecting models and setting standards for teachers of English in Hong Kong. *Journal of Asian Pacific Communication* 12 (1), 13–38.

Connell, P. and Myles-Zitzer, C. (1982) An analysis of elicited imitation as a language evaluation procedure. *Journal of Speech and Hearing Disorders* 47, 390–396.

Coughlan, P. and Duff, P.A. (1994) Same task, different activities: Analysis of a SLA task from an activity theory perspective. In J. Lantolf and G. Appel (eds) *Vygotskian Approaches to Second Language Research* (pp. 173–194). Norwood, NJ: Ablex.

Council of Europe (1996) The Common European Framework. On WWW at http://www.coe.int/t/dg4/linguistic/Source/Framework_EN.pdf.

Crowell, S. (2004) The neurobiology of declarative memory. In J. Schumann *et al.* (eds) *The Neurobiology of Learning: Perspectives from Second Language Acquisition*, (pp. 75–109). Mahwah, NJ: Lawrence Erlbaum.

Cummins, J. (1983) Language proficiency and academic achievement. In J. Oller (ed.) *Issues in Language Testing Research*, (pp. 108–130). Rowley, MA: Newbury House.

Czizér, K. and Dörnyei, Z. (2005) Language learners' motivational profiles and their motivated learning behaviour. *Language Learning* 55 (4), 613–659.

Davies, A. (2008) *Assessing Academic English: Testing English Proficiency, 1950–1989: The IELTS Solution*. Cambridge: Cambridge University Press.

Davies, A. and Elder, C. (2004) Validity and validation in language testing. In E. Hinkel (ed.) *Handbook of Research in Second Language Teaching and Learning* (pp. 795–815). Mahwah, NJ, Lawrence Erlbaum.

Davies, W.D. and Kaplan, T. (1998) Native speaker vs. L2 learner grammaticality judgments. *Applied Linguistics* 19 (2), 183–203.

De Graaf, R. (1997) *Differential Effects of Explicit Instruction on Second Language Acquisition*. Netherlands: Holland Institute of Generative Linguistics.

De Jong, N. (2005a) Learning second language grammar by listening. Unpublished PhD thesis, Netherlands Graduate School of Linguistics.

De Jong, N. (2005b) Can second language grammar be learner through listening? An experimental study. *Studies in Second Language Acquisition* 27, 205–234.

Dekeyser, R.M. (1993) The effect of error correction on L2 grammar knowledge and oral proficiency. *The Modern Language Journal* 77(4), 501–514.

DeKeyser, R. (1995) Learning second language grammar rules: An experiment with a miniature linguistic system. *Studies in Second Language Acquisition* 17, 379–410.

DeKeyser, R. (1998) Beyond focus on form: Cognitive perspectives on learning and practicing second language grammar. In C. Doughty and J. Williams (eds) *Focus on Form in Second Language Acquisition* (pp. 42–63). Cambridge: Cambridge University Press.

DeKeyser, R. (2000) The robustness of critical period effects in second language acquisition. *Studies in Second Language Acquisition* 22 (4), 499–533.

DeKeyser, R. (2003) Implicit and explicit learning. In C. Doughty and M. Long (eds.) *Handbook of Second Language Acquisition* (pp. 313–349). Malden, MA: Blackwell.

DeKeyser, R. (2005) What makes learning second language grammar difficult? A review of issues. *Language Learning* 55 (1), 1–25.

DeKeyser, R. (2007) Introduction: Situating the concept of practice. In R. DeKeyser (ed.) *Practice in a Second Language: Perspectives from Applied Linguistics and Cognitive Psychology* (pp. 1–18). New York: Cambridge University Press.

DeKeyser, R., Salaberry, R., Robinson, P. and Harrington, M. (2002) What gets processed in processing instruction? A commentary on Bill VanPatten's 'Update'. *Language Learning* 52, 805–823.

DeKeyser, R. and Sokalski, K. (1996) The differential role of comprehension and production practice. *Language Learning* 46, 613–642.

Derwing, T.M. and Munro, M.J. (2005) Pragmatic perspectives on the preparation of teachers of English as a Second Language: Putting the NS/NNS debate in context. In E. Llurda (ed.) *Non-native Language Teachers* (pp. 179–191). New York: Springer.

Dienes, Z. and Perner, J. (1999) A theory of implicit and explicit knowledge. *Behavioral and Brain Sciences* 22, 735–808.

Dienes, Z. and Scott, R. (2005) Measuring unconscious knowledge: Distinguishing structural knowledge and judgment knowledge. *Psychological Research* 69, 338–351.

Donaldson, M. (1978) *Children's Minds*. London: Fontana.

Dornyei, Z. (2005) *The Psychology of the Language Learner*. Mahwah, NJ: Lawrence Erlbaum.

Doughty, C. (1991) Second language instruction does make a difference: Evidence from an empirical study on SL relativization. *Studies in Second Language Acquisition* 13, 431–469.

Doughty, C. (2001) Cognitive underpinnings of focus on form. In P. Robinson (ed.) *Cognition and Second Language Instruction* (pp. 200–257). Cambridge: Cambridge University Press.

Doughty, C. and Varela, E. (1998) Communicative focus on form. In C. Doughty and J. Williams (eds) *Focus on Form in Class Second Langusge Acquisition* (pp. 114–138). Cambridge: Cambridge University Press.

Doughty, C. (2003) Instructed SLA: Constraints, compensation and enhancement. In C. Doughty and M. Long (eds) *The Handbook of Second Language Acquisition* (pp. 256–310). Malden, MA: Blackwell.

Doughty, C. and Williams, J. (1998a) Issues and terminology. In C. Doughty and J. Williams (eds) *Focus on Form in Classroom Second Language Acquisition* (pp. 1–11). New York: Cambridge University Press.

Doughty, C. and Williams, J. (1998) Pedagogical choices in focus on form. In C. Doughty and J. Williams (eds). *Focus on Form in Classroom Second Language Acquisition* (pp. 197–261). Cambridge: Cambridge University Press.

Douglas, D. (2001) Performance consistency in second language acquisition and language testing: A conceptual gap. *Second Language Research* 17, 442–456.

Duff, P. and Polio, C.G. (1990) How much foreign language is there in the foreign language classroom? *The Modern Language Journal* 74 (2), 154–166.

Dulay, H. and Burt, M. (1973) Should we teach children syntax? *Language Learning* 23, 245–258.

Elder, C. (1994) Performance testing as benchmark for foreign language teacher education. *Babel Journal Federation of Modern Language Teachers Associations* 29(2), 9–19.

Elder, C. (ed.) (2000) Defining standards and monitoring progress in languages other than English. *Australian Review of Applied Linguistics* S Number 18, ANU, Canberra.

Elder, C. (2001) Assessing the language proficiency of teachers: Are there any border controls? *Language Testing* 18, 149–170.

Elder, C., Erlam, R. and Philp, J. (2007) Explicit language knowledge and focus on form: Options and obstacles for TESOL teacher trainees. In S. Fotos and N. Hossein (eds) *Form-focussed Instruction in Teacher Education: Studies in Honour of Rod Ellis* (pp. 225–241). Oxford: Oxford University Press.

Elder, C., Iwashita, N. and McNamara, T. (2002) Estimating the difficulty of oral proficiency tasks: What does the test-taker have to offer? *Language Testing* 19 (4), 347–368.

Elder, C. and Manwaring, D. (2004) The relationship between metalinguistic knowledge and learning outcomes among undergraduate students of Chinese'. *Language Awareness* 13, 145–162.

Elder, C., McNamara, T. and Congdon, P. (2003) Rasch techniques for detecting bias in performance assessments: An example comparing the performance of native and non-native speakers on a test of academic English. *Journal of Applied Measurement* 4 (2), 181–219.

Elder, C., Warren, J., Hajek, J., Manwaring, D. and Davies, A. (1999) Metalinguistic knowledge: How important is it in studying a language at university? *Australian Review of Applied Linguistics* 22, 81–95.

Ellis, N. (1993) Rules and instances in foreign language learning: Interactions of explicit and implicit knowledge. *European Journal of Cognitive Psychology* 5, 289–319.

Ellis, N. (1994) Introduction: Implicit and explicit language learning – an overview. In N. Ellis (ed.) *Implicit and Explicit Learning of Languages,* (pp. 1–31). San Diego, CA: Academic Press.

Ellis, N. (ed.) (1994a) *Implicit and Explicit Learning of Languages.* London: Academic Press.

Ellis, N. (1994b) Vocabulary acquisition: The implicit ins and outs of explicit cognitive mediation. In N. Ellis (ed.) *Implicit and Explicit Learning of Languages* (pp. 211–282). London: Academic Press.

Ellis, N. (1996) Sequencing in SLA: Phonological memory, chunking and points of order. *Studies in Second Language Acquisition* 18, 91–126.

Ellis, N. (1998) Emergentism, connectionism, and language learning. *Language Learning* 48, 631–664.

Ellis, N. (1999) Cognitive approaches to SLA. *Annual Review of Applied Linguistics* 19, 22–42.

Ellis, N. (2001) Memory for language. In P. Robinson (ed.) *Cognition and Second Language Instruction* (pp. 33–68). Cambridge: Cambridge University Press.

Ellis, N. (2002) Frequency effects in language processing: A review with implications for theories of implicit and explicit language acquisition. *Studies in Second Language Acquisition* 24, 143–188.

Ellis, N. (2004) The processes of second language acquisition. In B. VanPatten *et al.* (eds) *Form-meaning Connections in Second Language Acquisition* (pp. 49–76). London: Academic.

Ellis, N. (2005) At the interface: Dynamic interactions of explicit and implicit knowledge. *Studies in Second Language Acquisition* 27, 305–352.

Ellis, N. (2006) Selective attention and transfer phenomena in L2 acquisition: Contingency, cue competition, salience, interference, overshadowing, blocking, and perceptual learning. *Applied Linguistics* 27, 164–194.

Ellis, N. (2008) Implicit and explicit knowledge about language. In J. Cenoz and N. Hornberger (eds) *Encyclopaedia of Language and Education* (pp. 119–131). New York: Springer.

Ellis, N. and Schmidt, R. (1997) Morphology and longer distance dependencies: Laboratory research illumination the A in SLA. *Studies in Second Language Acquisition* 19, 145–172.

Ellis, R. (1984) *Classroom Second Language Development.* Oxford: Pergamon.

Ellis, R. (1991) Grammaticality judgements and learner variability. In R. Burmeister and P. Rounds (eds) *Variability in Second Language Acquisition: Proceedings of the Tenth Meeting of the Second Language Research Forum Volume 1,* (pp. 25–60). Eugene, OR: University of Oregon.

Ellis, R. (1991) Grammaticality judgments and second language acquisition. *Studies in Second Language Acquisition* 13 (2), 161–186.

Ellis, R. (1993) Second language acquisition and the structural syllabus. *TESOL Quarterly* 27, 91–113.

Ellis, R. (1994) A theory of instructed second language acquisition. In N. Ellis (ed.) *Implicit and Explicit Learning of Languages* (pp. 79–114). San Diego, CA: Academic Press.

Ellis, R. (1994) *The Study of Second Language Acquisition.* Oxford: Oxford University Press.

Ellis, R. (1995) Interpretation tasks for grammar teaching. *TESOL Quarterly* 29 (1), 87–105.

Ellis, R. (1997) *Second Language Acquisition.* Oxford: Oxford University Press.

Ellis, R. (1998) Discourse control and the acquisition-rich classroom: Learners and language learning. In W. Reynandya and G. Jacobs (eds) *Learners and Language Learning* (pp. 145–171). Singapore, SEAMEO RELC.

Ellis, R. (1998a) *SLA Research and Language Teaching*. Oxford: Oxford University Press.

Ellis, R. (1999) Input-based approaches to teaching grammar: A review of classroom-oriented research. *Annual Review of Applied Linguistics* 19, 64–80.

Ellis, R. (2001) Investigating form-focused instruction. In R. Ellis (ed.) *Form-focused Instruction and Second Language Learning*, (pp. 1–46). Malden, MA: Blackwell.

Ellis, R. (2002) Does form-focused instruction affect the acquisition of implicit knowledge? A review of the research. *Studies in Second Language Acquisition* 24, 223–236.

Ellis, R. (2004) The definition and measurement of explicit knowledge. *Language Learning* 54, 227–275.

Ellis, R. (2005) Measuring implicit and explicit knowledge of a second language: A psychometric study. *Studies in Second Language Acquisition* 27 (2), 141–172.

Ellis, R. (2005a) Instructed language learning and task-based teaching. In E. Hinkel (ed.) *Handbook of Research in Second Language Teaching and Learning* (pp. 713–728). Mahwah, NJ: Lawrence Erlbaum.

Ellis, R. (2006) Modelling learning difficulty and second language proficiency: The differential contributions of implicit and explicit knowledge. *Applied Linguistics* 27, 431–463.

Ellis, R. (2006a) Researching the effects of form-focused instruction on L2 acquisition. In K. Bardovi-Harlig and Z. Dörnyei (eds) *Themes in SLA Research AILA 19* (pp. 18–41). Amsterdam: John Benjamins.

Ellis, R. (2008) *The Study of Second Language Acquisition* (2nd edn). Oxford: Oxford University Press.

Ellis, R. and Loewen, S. (2007) Confirming the operational definitions of explicit and implicit knowledge in Ellis (2005). *Studies in Second Language Acquisition* 29, 119–126.

Ellis, R. and Sheen, Y. (2006) Reexamining the role of recasts in second language aquisition. *Studies in Second Language Acquisition* 28, 575–600.

Ellis, R., Loewen, S. and Erlam, R. (2006) Implicit and explicit corrective feedback and the acquisition of L2 grammar. *Studies in Second Language Acquisition* 28, 339–68.

Ericsson, K. and Simon, H. (1993) *Protocol Analysis: Verbal Reports as Data* (2nd edn). Boston, MA: MIT Press.

Erlam, R. (2003) Evaluating the relative effectiveness of structured-input and output-based instruction in foreign language learning. *Studies in Second Language Acquisition* 25, 559–582.

Erlam, R. (2006) Elicited imitation as a measure of L2 implicit knowledge: An empirical validation study. *Applied Linguistics* 27 (3), 464–491.

Eysenck, M. (2001) *Principles of Cognitive Psychology* (2nd edn). Hove: Psychology Press.

Farley, A. (2001) Processing instruction and meaning-based output instruction: A comparative study. *Spanish Applied Linguistics* 5, 57–94.

Farley, A. (2004) The relative effects of processing instruction and meaning-based output instruction. In B. VanPatten (ed.) *Processing Instruction: Theory, Research and Commentary* (pp. 143–168). Mahwah, NJ: Lawrence Erlbaum.

Felix, S. (1985) More evidence on competing cognitive systems. *Second Language Research* 1, 47–72.

Field, A. (2005) *Discovering Statistics Using SPSS* (2nd edn). Thousand Oaks, CA: Sage Publications.

Flege, J.E. and Liu, S. (2001) The effect of experience on adults' acquisition of a second language. *Studies in Second Language Acquisition* 23 (4), 527–552.

Flege, J.E., Yeni-Komshian, G.H. and Liu, S. (1999) Age constraints on second language acquisition. *Journal of Memory and Language* 41, 78–104.

Fotos, S. and Ellis, R. (1991) Communicating about grammar: A task-based approach. *TESOL Quarterly* 25, 605–628.

Fotos, S. and Nassaji, H. (2007) *Form-focused Instruction and Teacher Education: Studies in Honour of Rod Ellis.* Oxford: Oxford University Press.

Fraser, C., Bellugi, U. and Brown, R. (1963) Control of grammar imitation, comprehension, and production. *Journal of Verbal Learning and Verbal Behaviour* 2, 121–35. Reprinted in C.A. Ferguson and D.I. Slobin (1973) *Studies of Child Language Development* (pp. 465–85). New York: Holt, Rinehart and Winston.

Fujiki, M. and Brinton, B. (1980) Sampling reliability in elicited imitation. *Journal of Speech and Hearing Disorders* 48 (1), 85–89.

Gallimore, R. and Tharp, R. (1981) The interpretation of elicited imitation in a standardized context. *Language Learning* 31, 369–392.

Gass, S. (1983) The development of L2 intutions. *TESQ Quaterly* 17(2), 273–291.

Gass, S. (1994) The reliability of second-language grammaticality judgments. In E. Tarone, S. Gass and A. Cohen (eds) *Research Methodology in Second Language Acquisition* (pp. 302–322). Hillsdale, NJ: Lawrence Erlbaum.

Gass, S. (1997) *Input, Interaction, and the Second Language Learner.* Mahwah, NJ: Lawrence Erlbaum.

Gass, S. and Mackey, A. (2002) Frequency effects and second language acquisition: A complex picture? *Studies in Second Language Acquisition* 24, 249–260.

Gass, S. and Mackey, A. (2005) *Second Language Research: Methodology and Design.* Mahwah, NJ: Lawrence Erlbaum.

Gass, S., Svetics, I. and Lemelin, S. (2003) Differential effects of attention. *Language Learning* 53, 497–545.

Gathercole, S. and Baddeley, A. (1993) *Working Memory and Language.* Hove, UK: Lawrence Erlbaum.

Genesee, F. (1987) *Learning Through Two Languages: Studies of Immersion and Bilingual Education.* Cambridge, MA: Newbury House.

Gernsbacher M. and Kaschak, M. (2003) Neuroimaging studies of language production and comprehension. *Annual Review of Psychology* 54, 91–114.

Golato, A. (2003) Studying compliment responses: A comparison of DCTs and recordings of naturally occurring talk. *Applied Linguistics* 24, 90–121.

Goldschneider, J. and DeKeyser, R. (2000) Explaining the "Natural Order of L2 Morpheme Acquisition" in English: A meta-analysis of multiple determinants. *Language Learning* 51, 1–50.

Goss, N, Ying-Hua, Z. and Lantolf, J. (1994) Two heads may be better than one: Mental activity in second language grammaticality judgements. In E. Tarone, S. Gass and A. Cohen (eds) *Research Methodology in Second Language Research* (pp. 263–286). Hillsdale, NJ: Lawrence Erlbaum.

Gower, R. and Walters, S. (1983) *Teaching Practice Handbook.* Oxford: Macmillan ELT.

Green, P. and Hecht, K. (1992) Implicit and explicit grammar: An empirical study. *Applied Linguistics* 13, 168–184.

Gregg, K. (2003) The state of emergentism in second language acquisition. *Second Language Research* 19, 95–128.

Hamayan, E., Saegert, J. and Laraudee, P. (1977) Elicited imitation in second language learners. *Language and Speech* 20, 86–97.

Hameyer, K. (1980) Testing oral proficiency via elicited imitation. *Revue de Phonetique Appliquée* 53, 11–24.

Hammerly, H. (1982) *Synthesis in Language Teaching: An Introduction.* Blaine, WA: Second Language Publications.

Han, Y. (2000) Grammaticality judgment tests: How reliable and valid are they? *Applied Language Learning* 11 (1), 177–204.

Han, Y. and Ellis, R. (1998) Implicit knowledge, explicit knowledge and general language proficiency. *Language Teaching Research* 2, 1–23.

Harley, B. (1989) Functional grammar in French immersion: A classroom experiment. *Applied Linguistics* 19, 331–359.

Harley, B. (1994) Appealing to consciousness in the L2 classroom. In J. Hulstijn and R. Schmidt (eds) *Consciousness in Second language Learning* (pp. 57–68). AILA Review 11.

Harley, B., Allen, P., Cummins, J. and Swain, M. (1990) *The Development of Second Language Proficiency.* Cambridge: Cambridge University Press.

Harrington, M. (2004) Commentary: Input processing as a theory of processing input. In B. VanPatten (ed.) *Processing Instruction: Theory, Research and Commentary* (pp. 79–93). Mahwah, NJ: Lawrence Erlbaum.

Hatch, E. and Farhady, H. (1982) *Research Design and Statistics for Applied Linguistics.* Rowley, MA: Newbury House.

Havranek, G. (2002) When is corrective feedback most likely to succeed?' *International Journal of Educational Research* 37, 255–270.

Hazeltine, E. and Ivry, R. (2003) Neural structures that support implicit sequence learning. In L. Jimenez (ed.) *Attention and Implicit Learning* (pp. 71–108). Philadelphia, PA: John Benjamins.

Hedgcock, J. (1993) Well-formed vs. ill-formed strings in L2 metalingual tasks: Specifying features of grammaticality judgements. *Second Language Research* 9, 1–21.

Helms-Park, R. (2001) Evidence of lexical transfer in learner syntax: The acquisition of English causatives by speakers of Hindi-Urdu and Vietnamese. *Studies in Second Language Acquisition* 23 (1), 71–102.

Housen, A. and Pierrard, M. (2006) Investigating instructed second language acquisition. In A. Housen and M. Pierrard (eds) *Investigations in Instructed Second Language Acquisition,* (pp. 12–27). Berlin: Mouton de Gruyter.

Hu, G. (2002) Psychological constraints on the utility of metalinguistic knowledge in second language production. *Studies in Second Language Acquisition* 24, 347–386.

Hulstijn, J. (1989) Implicit and incidental second language learning: Experiments in the processing of natural and partly artificial input. In H. Dechert and M. Raupach (eds). *Interlingual Processes* (pp. 49–73). Tubingen: Gunter Narr.

Hulstijn, J. (2002) Towards a unified account of the representation, processing and acquisition of second language knowledge. *Second Language Research* 18, 193–223.

Hulstijn, J. (2003) Incidental and intentional learning. In C. Doughty and M. Long (eds) *The Handbook of Second Language Acquisition* (pp. 349–381). Oxford: Blackwell.

Hulstijn. J. (2005) Theoretical and empirical issues in the study of implicit and explicit second language learning: Introduction. *Studies in Second Language Acquisition* 27, 129–140.

Hulstijn, J. and De Graaf, R. (1994) Under what conditions does explicit knowledge of a second language facilitate the acquisition of implicit knowledge? A research proposal. In J. Hulstijn and R. Schmidt (eds) *Consciousness in Second Language Learning* (pp. 97–112). AILA Review 11.

Hulstijn, J. and Hulstijn, W. (1984) Grammatical errors as a function of processing constraints and explicit knowledge. *Language Learning* 34, 23–43.

Hyltenstam, K. and Abrahamsson, N. (2003) Maturational constraints in SLA. In C.J. Doughty and M.H. Long (eds) *The Handbook of Second Language Acquisition* (pp. 539–587). Malden, MA: Blackwell.

IELTS (2005) International English Language Testing System. On WWW at http://www.ielts.org/mediacentre/latestieltsdevelopments/1649_IELTShbk_2005.pdf.

Inagaki, S. (2001) Motion verbs with goal PPs in the L2 acquisition of English and Japanese. *Studies in Second Language Acquisition* 23 (2), 153–170.

Ioup, G. (2005) Age in second language development. In E. Hinkel (ed.) *Handbook of Research in Second Language Teaching and Learning* (pp. 419–436). Mahwah, NJ: Lawrence Erlbaum.

Isemonger, I. (2007) Operational definitions of explicit and implicit knowledge: Response to Ellis (2005) and some recommendations for future research in this area. *Studies in Second Language Acquisition* 29, 101–118.

Iwashita, N., Elder, C. and McNamara, T. (2001) Can we predict task difficulty in an oral proficiency test? Exploring the potential of an information-processing approach to task design. *Language Learning* 51, 401–436.

Izumi, S. (2002) Output, input enhancement and the noticing hypothesis. *Studies in Second Language Acquisition* 24, 541–577.

Izumi, S. (2003) Comprehension and production processes in second language learning: In search of the psycholinguistic rationale of the output hypothesis. *Applied Linguistics* 24, 168–196.

Izumi, S. and Bigelow, M. (2000) Does output promote noticing and second language acquisition? *TESOL Quarterly* 34 (2), 239–278.

Izumi, S., Bigelow, M., Fujiwara, M. and Fearnow, S. (1999) Testing the output hypothesis: Effects of output on noticing and second language acquisition. *Studies in Second Language Acquisition* 21 (3), 421–452.

James, C. and Garrett, P. (1992) *Language Awareness in the Classroom*. London: Longman.

Jia, G. and Aaronson, D. (2003) A longitudinal study of Chinese children and adolescents learning English in the United States. *Applied Psycholinguistics* 24, 131–161.

Jimenez, L. (ed.) (2003) *Attention and Implicit Learning*. Amsterdam: John Benjamins.

Johnston, B. and Goettsch, K. (2000) In search of the knowledge base of language teaching: Explanations by experienced teachers. *Canadian Modern Language Review* 56, 437–468.

Johnson, J. and Newport, E. (1989) Critical period effects in second language learning: The influence of maturational state on the acquisition of English as a second language. *Cognitive Psychology* 21, 60–99.

Johnson, J. and Newport, E. (1991) Critical period effects on universal properties of language: The status of subjacency in the acquisition of a second language. *Cognition* 39, 215–258.

Jourdenais, R., Ota, M., Stauffer, S., Boyson, B. and Doughty, C. (1995) Does textual enhancement promote noticing? A think-aloud protocol analysis. In

R. Schmidt (ed.) *Attention and Awareness in Foreign Language Learning* (pp. 183–216). Honolulu, HI: University of Hawai'i Press.

Juffs, A. (2001) Psycholinguistically oriented second language research. *Annual Review of Applied Linguistics* 21, 207–222.

Kachigan, S. (1991) *Multivariate Statistical Analysis: A Conceptual Introduction.* New York: Radius Press.

Kachru, B. (1985) Standards, codification and sociolinguistic realism: The English language in the outer circle. In R. Quirk and H. Widdowson (eds) *English in the World. Teaching and Learning the Language and Literatures* (pp. 11–30). Cambridge: Cambridge University Press.

Kelch, K. (1985) Modified input as an aid to comprehension. *Studies in Second Language Acquisition* 7, 81–90.

Kemp, C. (2001) Metalinguistic awareness in multilinguals: Implicit and explicit grammatical awareness and its relationship with language experience and language attainment. Unpublished PhD thesis, University of Edinburgh.

Kim, S-H. and Elder, C. (2005) Language choices and pedagogic functions in the foreign-language classroom: A cross-linguistic function analysis of teacher-talk. *Language Teaching Research* 9 (4), 1–26.

Kim, S-H. and Elder, C. (2008) Target language use in foreign language classrooms: Practices and perceptions of two native speaker teachers in New Zealand. *Language Culture and Curriculum* 21 (2), 167–185.

Kline, P. (1999) *The Handbook of Psychological Testing* (2nd edn). London: Routledge.

Kojic-Sabo, I. and Lightbown, P. (1999) Students' approaches to vocabulary learning and their relationship to success. *Modern Language Journal* 83, 176–192.

Krashen, S. (1977) Some issues relating to the Monitor Model. In H. Brown, C. Yorio and R. Crymes (eds) *On TESOL'77*. Washington, DC: TESOL.

Krashen, S. (1981) *Second Language Acquisition and Second Language Learning*. Oxford: Pergamon.

Krashen, S. (1982) *Principles and Practice in Second Language Acquisition*. Oxford: Pergamon.

Krashen, S. (1983) Newmark's ignorance hypothesis and current second language acquisition theory. In S. Gass and L. Selinker (eds) *Language Transfer in Language Learning* (pp. 135–153). Rowley, MA: Newbury House.

Krashen, S. (1989) We acquire vocabulary and spelling by reading: Additional evidence for the input hypothesis. *Modern Language Journal* 74, 440–464.

Kumaravadivelu, B. (1994) Intake factors and intake processes in adult language learning. *Applied Language Learning* 5, 33–71.

Lantolf, J. (2000) Second language learning as a mediated process. *Language Teaching* 33, 79–96.

Lantolf, J. (2008) Interview for Asian EFL Journal. Asian EFL Journal – The EFL professional's written forum. On WWW at http://www.asian-efl-journal.com/interviews.

Lantolf, J. and Johnson, K. (2007) Extending Firth and Wagner's (1997) ontological perspective to L2 classroom praxis and teacher education. *Modern Language Journal* 91, 877–892.

Lantolf, J. and Thorne, S. (2006) *Sociocultural Theory and the Genesis of Second Language Development*. Oxford: Oxford University Press.

Lardiere, D. (1998) The case of tense in the 'fossilized' steady state. *Second Language Research* 14, 1–26.

Larsen-Freeman, D. (1978) An ESL index of development. *TESOL Quarterly* 12, 439–48.

Larsen-Freeman, D. (2003) *Teaching Language: From Grammar to Grammaring.* Boston, MA: Heinle.

Laufer, B. and Nation, P. (1999) A vocabulary size test of controlled productive ability. *Language Testing* 16, 33–51.

Lee, N. (2004) The neurobiology of procedural memory. In J. Schumann *et al.* (eds) *The Neurobiology of Learning: Perspectives from Second Language Acquisition,* (pp. 43–73). Mahwah, NJ: Lawrence Erlbaum.

Leeman, J., Arteagoitia, I., Fridman, D. and Doughty, C. (1995) Integrating attention to form incontent-based Spanish instruction. In R. Schmidt (ed.) *Attention and Awareness in Foreign Language Learning* (pp. 217–258). Honolulu, HI: University of Hawai'i.

Leow, R. (1997) Attention, awareness, and foreign language behavior. *Language Learning* 47, 467–505.

Leow, R. (2000) A study of the role of awareness in foreign language behavior: Aware vs. unaware learners. *Studies in Second Language Acquisition* 22, 557–584.

Leow, R.P. (1993) To simplify or not to simplify. *Studies in Second Language Acquisition* 15, 333–355.

Leow, R.P. (1995) Modality and intake in second language acquisition. *Studies in Second Language Acquisition* 17, 79–89.

Leow, R.P. (1998b) Toward operationalizing the process of attention in second language acquisition: Evidence for Tomlin and Villa's (1994) fine-grained analysis of attention. *Applied Psycholinguistics* 19, 133–159.

Levelt, W. (1989) *Speaking: From Intention to Articulation.* Cambridge, MA: Newbury House.

Lightbown, P. and Spada, N. (1990) Focus on form and corrective feedback in communicative language teaching: Effects on second language learning. *Studies in Second Language Acquisition* 12, 429–448.

Lightbown, P. and Spada, N. (1994) An innovative program for primary ESL in Quebec. *TESOL Quarterly* 28, 563–579.

Liu, J. (2005) Chinese graduate teaching assistants teaching freshman composition to native English speaking students. In E. Llurda (ed.) *Non-native Language Teachers* (pp. 154–177). New York: Springer.

Llurda, E. (2005) Non-native TESOL students as seen by practicum supervisors. In E. Llurda (ed.) *Non-native Language Teachers* (pp. 131–154). New York: Springer.

Loewen, S. and Philp, J. (2006) Recasts in the adult L2 classroom: Characteristics, explicitness and effectiveness. *Modern Language Journal* 90 (4), 536–556.

Long, M. (1996) The role of the linguistic environment in second language acquisition. In W.R. Ritchie and T.J. Bhatia (eds) *Handbook of Second Language Acquisition* (pp. 413–468). San Diego, CA: Academic Press.

Long, M. (2000) Focus on form in task-based language teaching. In R.D. Lambert (ed.) *Language Policy and Pedagogy* (pp. 179–192). Philadelphia, PA: John Benjamins.

Long, M. and Robinson, P. (1998) Focus on form: Theory, research and practice. In C. Doughty and J. Williams (eds) *Focus on Form in Classroom Second Language Acquisition* (pp. 15–41). Cambridge: Cambridge University Press.

Losey, J. (1986) The relationship between elicited imitation and spontaneous language and between elicited imitation and auditory memory span. Unpublished PhD thesis, University of Oklahoma.

Lyster, R. and Ranta, L. (1997) Corrective feedback and learner uptake: Negotiation of form in communicative classrooms. *Studies in Second Language Acquisition* 19, 37–66.

Mackey, A. and Gass, S. (2005) *Second Language Research: Methodology and Design*. Mahwah, NJ: Lawrence Erlbaum.

Macrory, G. and Stone, V. (2000) Pupil progress in the acquisition of the perfect tense in French: The relationship between knowledge and use. *Language Teaching Research* 4, 55–82.

Mandell, P. (1999) On the reliability of grammaticality judgment tests in second language acquisition research. *Second Language Research* 15 (1), 73–99.

Markman, B., Spilka, I. and Tucker, G. (1975) The use of elicited imitation in search of an interim French grammar. *Language Learning* 75, 31–41.

Masny, D. (1987) The role of language and cognition in second language metalinguistic awareness. In J.P. Lantolf and A. Labarca (eds) *Research in Second Language Learning: Focus on the Classroom* (pp. 59–73). Norwood, NJ: Ablex.

McDade, H., Simpson, M. and Lamb, D. (1982) The use of elicited imitation as a measure of expressive grammar: A question of validity. *Journal of Speech and Hearing Disorders* 47, 19–24.

McDonald, J. (2000) Grammaticality judgments in a second language: Influences of age of acquisition and native language. *Applied Psycholinguistics* 21, 395–423.

McLaughlin, B. (1978) The Monitor Model: Some methodological considerations. *Language Learning* 28, 309–332.

McLaughlin, B. (1987) *Theories of Second Language Learning*. London: Edward Arnold.

McNamara, T.F. (1996) *Measuring Second Language Performance*. London: Longman.

Meara, P. and Jones, G. (1990) *Eurocentres Vocabulary Size Test, Version E1.1/K10*. Zurich: Eurocentres Learning Service.

Mitchell, R. (1988) *Communicative Language Teaching in Practice*. London: CILT.

Mitchell, R. (2000) Anniversary article. Applied linguistics and evidence-based classroom practice: The case of foreign language grammar pedagogy. *Applied Linguistics* 21 (3), 281–303.

Mohle, D. and Raupach, M. (1989) Language transfer and procedural knowledge. In H. Dechert and M. Raupach (eds) *Interlingual Processes*. Tübingen: Gunter Narr.

Montrul, S. (2005) On knowledge and development of unaccusativity in Spanish L2. *Linguistics* 43 (6), 1153–1190.

Morgan-Short, K. and Bowden, H.W. (2006) Processing instruction and meaningful output-based instruction. *Studies in Second Language Acquisition* 28, 31–65.

Munnich, E., Flynn, S. and Martohardjono, G. (1994) Elicited imitation and grammaticality judgment tasks: What they measure and how they relate to each other. In E. Tarone, S. Gass and A. Cohen (eds) *Research Methodology in Second-language Acquisition* (pp. 227–245). Mahwah: NJ.

Muranoi, H. (2007) Output practice in the L2 classroom. In R. DeKeyser (ed.) *Practice in a Second Language: Perspectives from Applied Linguistics and Cognitive Psychology* (pp. 51–84). New York: Cambridge University Press.

Murphy, G. and Shapiro, A. (1994) Forgetting verbatim information in discourse. *Memory and Cognition* 22, 85–94.

Nabei, T. and Swain, M. (2002) Learner awareness of recasts in classroom interaction: A case study of an adult EFL student's second language learning. *Language Awareness* 11 (1), 43–63.

Nassaji, H. and Fotos, S. (2004) Current developments in research on the teaching of grammar. *Annual Review of Applied Linguistics* 24, 126–145.

Nation, I.S.P. (1990) *Teaching and Learning Vocabulary*. New York: Newbury House.

Nemtchinova, E. (2005) Host teachers' evaluations of nonnative-English speaking teacher trainees – a perspective from the classroom. *TESOL Quarterly* 39 (2), 235–263.

Norris, J. and Ortega, L. (2000) Effectiveness of L2 instruction: A research synthesis and quantitative meta-analysis. *Language Learning* 50 (3), 417–528.

Oller, J. (1979) *Language Tests at School*. London: Longman.

Paradis, M. (1994) Neurolinguistic aspects of implicit and explicit memory: Implications for bilingualism and second language acquisition. In N. Ellis (ed.) *Implicit and Explicit Language Learning* (pp. 393–419). London: Academic Press.

Paradis, M. (2004) *A Neurolinguistic Theory of Bilingualism*. Amsterdam: John Benjamins.

Parrott, M. (2000) *Grammar for English Language Teachers*. Cambridge: Cambridge University Press.

Patkowski, M. (1980) The sensitive period for the acquisition of syntax in a second language. *Language Learning* 30, 449–472.

Patkowski, M. (1990) Age and accent in a second language: A reply to James Emil Flege. *Applied Linguistics* 11, 73–89.

Peterson, R. and McIntyre, C. (1973) The influence of semantic 'relatedness' on linguistic integration and retention. *American Journal of Psychology* 86, 697–706.

Pienemann, M. (1989) Is language teachable? Psycholinguistic experiments and hypotheses. *Applied Linguistics* 10, 52–79.

Pienemann, M. (1998) *Language Processing and Second-language Development: Processability Theory*. Amsterdam: John Benjamins.

Pienemann, M. (2005) An introduction to processability theory. In M. Pienemann (ed.) *Cross-linguistic Aspects of Processability Theory* (pp. 1–60). Amsterdam: John Benjamins.

Polio, C.G. and Duff, P.A. (1994) Teachers' language use in university foreign language classrooms: A qualitative analysis of English and target language alternation. *Modern Language Journal* 78 (3), 313–326.

Potter, M. and Lombardi, L. (1990) Regeneration in the short term recall of sentences. *Journal of Memory and Language* 29, 633–654.

Purpura, J. (2004) *Assessing Grammar*. Cambridge: Cambridge University Press.

Radwan, A.A. (2005) The effectiveness of explicit attention to form in language learning. *System* 33, 69–87.

Ranta, L. (2002) The role of learners' language analytic ability in the communicative classroom. In P. Robinson (ed.) *Individual Differences in Instructed Language Learning* (pp. 159–180). Amsterdam: John Benjamins.

Read, J. (2008) Identifying academic language needs through diagnostic assessment. *Journal of English for Academic Purposes*. (In press)

Rea-Dickins, P. (2001) Fossilization or evolution: The case of grammar testing. In C. Elder, A. Brown, E. Grove, K. Hill, N. Iwashita, T. Lumley, T. McNamara and K. O'Loughlin (eds) *Experimenting with Uncertainty: Essays in Honour of Alan Davies* (pp. 251–263). Cambridge: Cambridge University Press.

Reber, A. (1976) Implicit learning of synthetic learners: The role of instructional set. *Journal of Experimental Psychology, Human Learning and Memory* 2, 88–94.

Reber, A. (1993) *Implicit Learning and Tacit Knowledge: An Essay on the Cognitive Unconscious*. Oxford: Oxford University Press.

Reber, A., Walkenfeld, F. and Hernstadt, R. (1991) Implicit and explicit learning: Individual differences and IQ. *Journal of Experimental Psychology: Learning Memory and Cognition* 11, 888–896.

Rebuschat, P. (2008) Implicit learning of natural language syntax. Unpublished PhD thesis, University of Cambridge.

Renou, J.M. (2000) Learner accuracy and learner performance: The quest for a link. *Foreign Language Annals* 33 (2), 168–180.

Renou, J. (2001) An examination of the relationship between metalinguistic awareness and second language proficiency of adult learners of French. *Language Awareness* 4 (10), 248–267.

Robinson, P. (1996) Learning simple and complex rules under implicit, incidental rule-search conditions, and instructed conditions. *Studies in Second Language Acquisition* 18, 27–67.

Robinson, P. (1997) Generalizability and automaticity of second language learning under implicit, incidental, enhanced and instructed conditions. *Studies in Second Language Acquisition* 19, 223–247.

Robinson, P. (2005) Cognitive abilities, chunk strength, and frequency effects in implicit artificial grammar and incidental L2 learning: Replications of Reber, Wakenfeld, and Hernstadt (1991) and Knowlton and Squire (1996) and their relevance to SLA. *Studies in Second Language Studies* 27, 235–268.

Robinson, P. (2005a) Aptitude and second language acquisition. *Annual Review of Applied Linguistics* 25, 46–73.

Roehr, K. (2006) Metalinguistic knowledge in L2 task performance: A verbal protocol analysis. *Language Awareness* 15 (3), 180–198.

Roehr, K. (2008) Metalinguistic knowledge and language ability in university-level L2 Learners. *Applied Linguistics* 29 (2), 173–199.

Rosa, E. and O'Neill, D. (1999) Explicitness, intake, and the issue of awareness: Another piece to the puzzle. *Studies in Second Language Acquisition* 21, 511–553.

Rumelhart, D., McLelland, J. and the PDP Research Group (eds) (1986) *Parallel Distributed Processing: Explorations in the Microstructure of Cognition Volume 1: Foundations.* Cambridge, MA: MIT Press.

Sachs, J. (1967) Recognition memory for syntactic and semantic aspects of connected discourse. *Perception and Psychophysics* 2, 437–442.

Salaberry, M.R. (1997) The role of input and output practice in second language acquisition. *The Canadian Modern Language Review* 53, 422–451.

Schmidt, R. (1990) The role of consciousness in second language learning. *Applied Linguistics* 11, 129–158.

Schmidt, R. (1994) Deconstructing consciousness in search of useful definitions for applied linguistics. *AILA Review* 11, 11–26.

Schmidt, R. (1994a) Implicit learning and the cognitive unconscious: Of artificial grammar and SLA. In N. Ellis (ed.) *Implicit and Explicit Learning of Languages* (pp. 165–209). London: Academic Press.

Schmidt, R. (2001) Attention. In P. Robinson (ed.) *Cognition and Second Language Instruction.* Cambridge: Cambridge University Press.

Schmidt, R. and Frota, S. (1986) Developing basic conversational ability in a second language: A case-study of an adult learner. In R. Day (ed.) *Talking to Learn: Conversation in Second Language Acquisition* (pp. 237–326). Rowley, MA: Newbury House.

Schwartz, B. (1993) On explicit and negative data effecting and affecting competence and linguistic behavior. *Studies in Second Language Acquisition* 15, 147–163.

Scott, M. (1994) Auditory memory and perception in younger and older adult second language learners. *Studies in Second Language Acquisition* 16, 262–281.

Scovel, T. (1988) *A Time to Speak: A Psycholinguistic Inquiry into the Critical Period for Human Speech*. Rowley, MA: Newbury House.

Seliger, H.W. (1979) On the nature and function of rules in language teaching. *TESOL Quarterly* 13 (3), 359–369.

Selinker, L. (1972) Interlanguage. *International Review of Applied Linguistics* 10, 209–231.

Shanks, D. (2003) Attention and awareness in "implicit" sequence learning. In L. Jimenez (ed.) *Attention and Implicit Learning* (pp. 11–42). Philadelphia, PA: John Benjamins.

Sharwood Smith, M. (1981) Consciousness-raising and the second language learner. *Applied Linguistics* 2, 159–169.

Sharwood Smith, M. (1991) Speaking to many minds: On the relevance of different types of language information for the L2 learner. *Second Language Research* 7, 118–132.

Sharwood-Smith, M. (1993) Input enhancement and instructed second language acquisition. *Studies in Second Language Acquisition* 15, 65–85.

Shiotsu T. and Weir C. (2007) The relative significance of syntactic knowledge and vocabulary breadth in the prediction of reading comprehension test performance. *Language Testing* 24 (1), 98–128.

Shook, D.J. (1994) FL/L2 reading, grammatical information, and the input-to-intake phenomenon. *Applied Language Learning* 5, 57–93.

Skehan, P. (1998) *A Cognitive Approach to Language Learning*. Oxford: Oxford University Press.

Skehan, P. (2001) Tasks and language performance assessment. In M. Bygate *et al.* (eds.) *Researching Pedagogic Tasks, Second Language Learning, Teaching and Testing* (pp. 167–185). Harlow: Longman.

Slobin, D. and Welsh, C. (1968) Elicited imitation as a research tool in developmental psycholinguistics. *Working Paper* 10. Reprinted in C.A Ferguson and D.I. Slobin (1973) *Studies of Child Language Development* (pp. 485–497). New York: Holt, Rinehart and Winston.

Sorace, A. (1985) Metalinguistic knowledge and language use in acquisition-poor environments. *Applied Linguistics* 6, 239–254.

Sorace, A. (1996) The use of acceptability judgments in second language acquisition research. In W. Ritchie and T. Bhatia (eds) *Handbook of Second Language Acquisition* (pp. 375–409). San Diego, CA: Academic Press.

Sorace, A. and Robertson, D. (2001) Measuring development and ultimate attainment in non-native grammars. In C. Elder *et al.* (eds) *Experimenting with Uncertainty* (pp. 264–274). Cambridge, MA: Cambridge University Press.

Sorace, A. and Shomura, Y. (2001) Lexical constraints on the acquisition of split intransitivity. *Studies in Second Language Acquisition* 23 (2), 247–278.

Spada, N. (1997) Form-focussed instruction and second language acquisition: A review of classroom and laboratory research. *Language Teaching* 30, 73–87.

Speciale, G., Ellis, N. and Bywater, T. (2004) Phonological sequence learning and short-term capacity determine second language vocabulary acquisition. *Applied Linguistics* 25, 293–321.

Stauble, A. (1984) A comparison of the Spanish-English and Japanese-English interlanguage continuum. In R. Andersen (ed.) *Second Language: A Cross-linguistic Perspective* (pp. 323–353). Rowley, MA: Newbury House.

Swain, M. (1985) Communicative competence: Some roles of comprehensible input and comprehensible output in its development. In S. Gass and C. Madden (eds) *Input in Second Language Acquisition* (pp. 235–253). Cambridge, MA: Newbury House.

Swain, M. (1988) Manipulating and complementing content teaching to maximize second language learning. *TESL Canada Journal* 6, 68–83.

Swain, M. and Lapkin, S. (1995) Problems in output and the cognitive processes they generate: A steptowards second language learning. *Applied Linguistics* 16, 371–391.

Tarone, E. (1982) Systematicity and attention in interlanguage. *Language Learning* 32, 69–82.

Tarone, E. (1988) *Variation in Interlanguage*. London: Edward Arnold.

Tokowicz, N. and MacWhinney, B. (2005) Implicit and explicit measures of sensitivity to violations in second language grammar: An even-related potential investigation. *Studies in Second Language Acquisition* 27, 173–204.

Tomlin, R. and Villa, V. (1994) Attention in cognitive science and second language acquisition. *Studies in Second Language Acquisition* 16, 183–203.

Toth, P. (2006) Processing instruction and a role for output in second language acquisition. *Language Learning* 56, 319–385.

Trahey, M. (1996) Positive evidence in second language acquisition: Some long-term effects. *Second Language Research* 12, 111–139.

Trahey, M. and White, L. (1993) Positive evidence and preemption in the second language classroom. *Studies in Second Language Acquisition* 15, 181–204.

Ullman, M. (2001) The declarative/procedural model of lexicon and grammar. *Journal of Psycholinguistic Research* 30, 37–69.

University of Cambridge Local Examinations Syndicate (1988) *IELTS, International English Language Testing System*. Cambridge: University of Cambridge.

Upshur, J. (1976) Discussion of 'A program for language testing research'. In H.D. Brown (ed.) Papers in Second Language Learning: Proceedings of the Sixth Annual Conference on Applied Linguistics at the University of Michigan. *Language Learning, Special Issue* 4, 167–174.

VanPatten, B. (1989) Can learners attend to form and content while processing input? *Hispania* 72, 409–417.

VanPatten, B. (1990) Attending to form and content in the input. *Studies in Second Language Acquisition* 12, 287–301.

VanPatten, B. (1996) *Input Processing and Grammar Instruction in Second Language Acquisition*. Norwood, NJ: Ablex.

VanPatten, B. (2004) Input and output in establishing form-meaning connections. In B. VanPatten *et al.* (eds) *Form-meaning Connections in Second Language Acquisition* (pp. 29–48). Mahwah, NJ: Lawrence Erlbaum.

VanPatten, B. (2004) *Processing Instruction: Theory, Research, and Commentary.* Mahwah, NJ: Lawrence Erlbaum.

VanPatten, B. and Cadierno, T. (1993) Explicit instruction and input processing. *Studies in Second Language Acquisition* 15, 225–243.

VanPatten, B. and Sanz, C. (1995) From input to output: Processing instruction and communicative tasks. In F. Eckman, D. Highland, P. Lee, J. Mileham and R. Rutkowski Weber (eds) *Second Language Acquisition Theory and Pedagogy* (pp. 169–185). Mahwah, NJ: Lawrence Erlbaum.

VanPatten, B. and Wong, W. (2004) Processing instruction and the French causative: Another replication. In B. VanPatten (ed.) *Processing Instruction: Theory, Research and Commentary* (pp. 97–119). Mahwah, NJ: Lawrence Erlbaum.

Vinther, T. (2002) Elicited imitation: A brief overview. *International Journal of Applied Linguistics* 12, 54–73.

Wallach, D. and Lebiere, C. (2003) Implicit and explicit learning in a unified architecture of cognition. In L. Jimenez (ed.) *Attention and Implicit Learning* (pp. 215–252). Philadelphia, PA: John Benjamins.

Webb, S. (2007) Learning word pairs and glossed sentences: The effects of a single context on vocabulary knowledge. *Language Teaching Research* 11 (1), 63–81.

Weber-Fox, C.M. and Neville, H.J. (1996) Maturational constraints on functional specializations for language processing: ERP and behavioral evidence in bilingual speakers. *Journal of Cognitive Neuroscience* 8(3), 231–256.

Westney, P. (1992) Rules and pedagogical grammar. In T. Odlin (ed.) *Perspectives on Pedagogical Grammar* (pp. 72–96). Cambridge: Cambridge University Press.

White, J. (1998) Getting learners' attention: A typographical input enhancement study. In C. Doughty and J. Williams (eds) *Focus on Form in Classroom Second Language Acquisition* (pp. 85–113). New York: Cambridge University Press.

White, L. (2003a) *Second Language Acquisition and Universal Grammar*. Cambridge: Cambridge University Press.

Williams, J. (1999) Memory, attention and inductive learning. *Studies in Second Language Acquisition* 21, 1–48.

Williams, J. (2005) Learning with awareness. *Studies in Second Language Acquisition* 27, 269–304.

Williams, J. and Lovatt, P. (2003) Phonological memory and rule learning. *Language Learning* 53, 67–121.

Wolfson, N. (1989a) *Perspectives: Sociolinguistics and TESOL*. Rowley, MA: Newbury House.

Wong, W. (2001) Modality and attention to meaning and form in the input. *Studies in Second Language Acquisition* 23, 345–368.

Wright, T. (1991) Language awareness in teacher education programmes for nonnative speakers. In C. James and P. Garrett (eds) *Language Awareness in the Classroom* (pp. 62–77). Harlow: Longman.

Wright, T. (2002) Doing language awareness: Issues for language study in language teacher education. In H. Trappes-Lomax and G. Ferguson (eds) *Language in Language Teacher Education* (pp. 113–130). Amsterdam: John Benjamins.

Wright, T. and Bolitho, R. (1997) Towards awareness of English as a professional language. *Language Awareness* 6 (2&3), 162–170.

Young, R. (1996) Form-function relations in articles in English interlanguage. In R. Bayley and D. Preston (eds) *Second Language Acquisition and Linguistic Variation* (pp. 135–175). Amsterdam: John Benjamins.

Zobl, H. (1995) Converging evidence for the 'acquisition-learning' distinction. *Applied Linguistics* 16, 35–56.

Index